*This book is dedicated to the possibilities
of all children, including our own—
Alicia and Carl Grant and Lily Gomez Sasse.*

Preface

Now, more than at any other time in our nation's history, teachers on campuses and in elementary and middle school classrooms are inquiring about how to make our teaching responsive to the student diversity transforming our classrooms and campuses. Seeking responses to this question has led many universities and schools to invite us and many of our chapter authors to discuss and work toward solutions to this challenge. *Making Schooling Multicultural: Campus and Classroom* has grown out of our collective efforts to develop a comprehensive response for our university and elementary and middle school colleagues and their students.

About the Text

As we have worked with elementary, middle school, and university students, and our university and school colleagues, there is one important theoretical and practical question we are asked time and again. Which approach or definition of multicultural education should we (universities and K-12 schools) use to prepare our students for life *today* and in the *21st century*?

"Education that is multicultural and social reconstructionist" with its focus on all aspects of education—curriculum, instructional pedagogy, staff, personal awareness, advocacy, etc.— has become the choice for educators who are developing a vision and constructing/reforming their programs for today's and tomorrow's schools. *Making Schooling Multicultural: Campus and Classroom* was written from this perspective.

The book contains four sections. An **introductory section** comprises two chapters—the first offers readers a theoretical orientation to the volume and a summary of the individual chapters, and the second contains an historical overview of multiculturalism in the United States. Chapters in the **second section** focus on general issues of pedagogy—how to create teaching and learning environments that are multicultural and social reconstructionist.

A **third section** contains chapters that engage readers in considering how individual academic disciplines—mathematics, science, art, etc.—can be taught in ways that invite all students to learn. In this section of the book, chapter authors explain how to infuse into each academic discipline the theory and practices of education that are both multicultural and social reconstructionist. Authors provide examples of teachers' struggles to transform their teaching for equity and social justice.

The **fourth section** is aimed at helping prospective teachers and teacher educators on campuses and in elementary and middle school classrooms to make the teacher education experience one that embraces multicultural and social reconstructionist goals and practices. Throughout the volume, authors describe and discuss the personal tensions that proponents of multicultural teaching often experience.

There is no simple answer or recipe for infusing education that is multicultural and social reconstructionist into elementary and middle school education, teacher education programs, and/or class assignments. We know this from personal experience and our extensive reviews of the education literature. We do believe, however, that *Making Schooling Multicultural: Campus and Classroom* charts an excellent course for preparing teacher educators, their students, classroom teachers, and their students for educating the diversity of people they find in their lives today and those they will encounter in the 21st century.

Acknowledgments

Making Schooling Multicultural: Campus and Classroom was developed from the efforts of many colleagues, students, and friends. We are indebted to them for their patience and understanding as we toiled to make a vision of how multicultural and social reconstructionist education can be a reality. We especially thank the chapter authors who embraced the opportunity to discuss their academic disciplines from this point of view. We learned a great deal from them.

We also thank Prentice Hall and Merrill Publishing Company and its staff members—particularly our editor, Debbie Stollenwerk—for their support and patience. Deadlines were changed numerous times, but Debbie was always encouraging and full of good humor. We also extend our appreciation to Amy Hutler, whose typing and wit were always on target.

We thank our students, whose questions and quests for learning pushed us to take on this project. We also thank the reviewers of this book for their insightful analyses during the review process: Janet Goldenstein Ahler, University of North Dakota; Jo Alexander, Auburn University, Montgomery; Minerva L. Caples, Central Washington University; Wanda S. Fox, Purdue University; Barbara Gerner de Garcia, Gallaudet University; Barbara L. Jackson, Fordham University; P. Rudy Mattai, State University College at Buffalo; and Elizabeth Quintero, University of Minnesota, Duluth.

Finally, we have to thank each other because we each broadened our understanding of collegiality and friendship through our work on this project.

Carl A. Grant
Mary Louise Gomez

Contents

Chapter 6   Reconstructing Bilingual Education from a Multicultural Perspective   111

Chapter 7   Multicultural Concerns and Classroom Management   133

Part 3
The Subject Matters   161

Chapter 8   Telling and Critiquing Stories of Our Teaching— for Literacy   163

Chapter 9 Mathematizing and the Democracy: The Need for an Education that is Multicultural and Social Reconstructionist   185

Chapter 10 Learning Science as a Transformative Experience   203

Chapter 11 Teaching Social Studies for Decision-Making and Action   221

Chapter 14 Curriculum and Instruction in Primary School Physical Education: A Critique and Visionary Perspective for Reform in Teacher Education   289

Chapter 15 Integrating Diversity and Multiculturalism in Health Education   311

The journey of a thousand miles begins with a single step.

Lao-Tse

The acceptance of women as authority figures or as role models is an important step in female education.... It is this process of identification, respect, and then self-respect that promotes growth.

Judy Chicago, Through the Flower; My Struggle as a Woman Artist, 1975

You see things as they are; and you ask "Why?". But I dream things that never were and I ask "Why not?".

George Bernard Shaw

I touch the future. I teach.

Christa McAuliffe

Even if I knew that tomorrow the world would go to pieces, I would still plant my apple tree.

Martin Luther

Part 1

◆ ◆ ◆ ◆

An Introduction to Multicultural Teaching

Chapter 1

◆ ◆ ◆ ◆

Journeying Toward Multicultural and Social Reconstructionist Teaching and Teacher Education

Carl A. Grant

and

Mary Louise Gomez

University of Wisconsin-Madison

Introduction

In Barry Lopez's fable *Crow and Weasel* (1990), two young men travel farther north than any of their people have ever gone. During their journey, which is spiritual and self-reflective as well as physically challenging, they encounter many varied experiences. At one point, they come upon a weary fellow traveler, Mouse, who is resting by the roadside and exchange the following remarks.

> "We come in peace," said Weasel.
>
> "Good" said Mouse. "I'm a peaceful man."
>
> "We are traveling north through these woods," said Crow.
>
> "I am going to the west. I am on a vision quest."
>
> "We are trying to go farther north than our people have ever gone before," offered Weasel, getting down from his mare. "Already we have come farther than anyone, but we are still going on."
>
> "I am traveling a long way myself," said Mouse. "Among my people, west is the direction we fear most, so that is the direction we travel when we go on a vision quest."
>
> "We have that custom among our people as well," said Crow, who had also dismounted. "Only with us, we do not travel far."
>
> "We travel very far," said Mouse. "We travel to some high place and fast and wait for a dream that will give our lives a good direction."
>
> "We have that same custom," said Weasel.
>
> The three of them remained silent for a while.
>
> "It's very difficult to lead a good life," said Crow finally. "What you have set out to do," he said, turning to Mouse, "is hard. But our older people tell us that without a dream you do not know what to do with your life. So it is a good thing, I think, what you do, what your people believe."
>
> "Yes. To be a good hunter," said Mouse, "is to be a good family man, to be truthful instead of clever with people, to live in a community where there is much wisdom—that is what all of us want."
>
> "Ah," said Crow. "But it takes your life to learn to do these things."
>
> "Hah!" said Mouse, and they all laughed.
>
> They camped the night together. (pp. 19–21)

Like Crow and Weasel, we are travelers. Our journey, like theirs, is both self-reflective and corporeal. We, too, are seekers after dreams. Today, when teachers must negotiate the terrain of teaching in increasingly complex contexts, it seems timely to invite you to come with us—and our friends and colleagues who have contributed to this book—in pursuit of dreams.

We ask you to join us in seeking how to teach and learn across the disciplinary areas in ways that are equitable and just for all people. While the pathways for our travels are not always smooth or easy, we are propelled by social, economic, and moral imperatives. In this chapter, we outline the concerns that motivate our work and clarify what a multicultural social reconstructionist perspective on teaching and teacher education entails.

In part, our work is fueled by a sense of urgency concerning the social and economic distress in which many U.S. children live. As Haveman and Wolfe have recently written: "The debate over educational reform—school choice, magnet schools, busing—starts from a common judgment that neither schools nor families are serving children well" (1994, p.3).

Haveman and Wolfe document a bleak picture of many U.S. children's family lives today:

- One-quarter of children in the United States are born to an unwed mother.
- Fewer than 75 percent of children live with two parents.
- Parental child care time has been reduced from 30 hours of contact per week in 1965 to 17 hours per week in the late 1980s.
- 30 percent of all children experience divorce, up from 19 percent 30 years ago.
- 20 percent of all children live in poverty—up from 15 percent in 1973—and 40 percent of children of color live in poverty. (p. 3)

Not only are children's lives challenged by the decreasing support offered them at home, but they are failed often at school as well. Recently, countless educational reports have reminded us that as more children of color, low-income children, students with other than English language backgrounds and students with special learning needs come to U.S. schools, rates of dropping out, violence and truancy increase and achievement (as measured by grades and standardized test scores) falls. We and our colleagues do not consider students' disillusionment with schooling and their academic failures to be the fault of them and their families alone. Rather, we see universities and schools—along with other representatives of U.S. economic and social institutions—acting with families and children to reproduce these unjust conditions.

Haveman and Wolfe (1994) argue that children's life success is determined by three primary factors: a social or government investment in their lives, a parental investment, and the choices each child makes over time. While at first glance, and without explication, this model can appear somewhat linear and deterministic (as Haveman and Wolfe also posit), it highlights for us the significant role that social institutions—like schools—play in children's lives, and the importance of good schools and teachers.

We developed this book with the schooling of all U.S. children in mind, because we recognize this crucial role that good teachers play in everyone's life success. We are especially concerned, however, with providing children who are the most socially and economically distressed with the knowledge, skills, and dispositions to make choices for their future and that provide them with a safe haven for their bodies and spirits. Because, as teachers, we are so critical to all children's opportunities, we ask you to consider why today we require, more than ever, personal and professional self-reflection and a teacher education that is multicultural and social reconstructionist.

Statistics concerning who teachers are and who children are in our schools may not surprise or concern you at first glance. However, in the next paragraphs, we make the case that differences in the race, social class, language background and sexual orientation of U.S. teachers should concern us all—not because people who are different from one another should be apart, but because the differences among us often lead to unjust, inequitable treatment of those we see as "Others."[1] Who are teachers and what are their perspectives on people who are not like them?

Gomez (1994) has written that there are great differences in the race, socioeconomic group, and language background of U.S. teachers and students and that these, along with differences in sexual orientation of teachers and students, often lead to diminished expectations and different educational experiences for children who are unlike their teachers—children who are already more likely to live with one parent in poverty. Gomez writes:

> In 1990, for example, when the kindergarten through grade 12 population of the nation was 40 percent children of color, nearly 90 percent of teachers were White (National Center for Education Statistics, 1992). The race of those teaching and those taught will continue to differ in the future as numbers of school-age children of color increase and numbers of teachers of color decrease in the U.S.A. (Hodgkinson, 1991). There are also increasing social class differences between students and their teachers. In 1989, for example, 15 percent of White children, 44 percent of African American children and 36 percent of Latino children lived in poverty and these numbers continue to rise (Children's Defense Fund, 1991, p. 24). Nearly half of all children living in poverty in the U.S.A. live in central cities (Children's Defense Fund, 1991, p. 2). In contrast, most U.S. teachers come from lower middle-class and middle-class homes and have grown up in rural and suburban areas of the nation (Zimpher, 1989). There are also increasing gaps in language background between U.S. teachers and students. There were 2 million limited English proficiency students enrolled in grades K–12 in the U.S.A. in 1990; this is a 36 percent increase from 1986 (Olsen, 1992), yet most U.S. teachers continue to be monolingual in English (Zimpher). (1989, p. 320)

On the surface, these differences only say that, as teachers, we differ from our students. Unfortunately, these differences lead to negative perspectives,[2] or biased beliefs and classroom actions toward some children. In analyses of several large-scale studies concerning teachers' attitudes toward "Others," their willingness to live near and be part of communities with "Others," to teach "Others," and to expect that "Others" can learn, Gomez found the following:

Those new teachers working in inner cities, small towns, and rural areas were more likely to cite influences outside of school as challenging students' ability to learn than were their counterparts teaching in suburbia. Teachers working with students of color and students from low-income families were also more likely to point to outside-of-school influences as detrimental to students' learning and achievement. Taken together, these responses from novice teachers indicate that early in their careers, many teachers locate problems of learning and achievement not as outcomes of teachers' beliefs about and behaviors towards children in school, but as consequences of children's outside-of-school lives—beyond the purview of teachers, schools and schooling. (p. 321)

We believe that classroom and campus experiences in teacher education that support or maintain such beliefs about children must be changed, or the already bleak future of many of our nation's children becomes unimaginable. Changes in teacher education experiences offered to new teachers become imperative as four factors assure us that, for some time in the future, we will continue to educate prospective teachers resembling those in our current cohort to teach increasingly diverse populations of children.

These are (1) the predictions of demographers regarding the characteristics of and numbers of different incoming student populations (see Hodgkinson, 1985, 1991, for discussion of contemporary population trends), (2) the continuing availability of higher-status, higher-paying positions in professions outside of teaching for people of color, (3) current efforts to "professionalize" teaching (e.g., the National Board of Professional Teaching Standards, various state department mandates for selection, credentialing and licensure) that often result in rejecting or sifting out people unlike those already credentialed, and (4) the pervasive racism, sexism, and homophobia marking life in the United States (Gomez, 1994).

Required changes in teachers' beliefs and attitudes toward "Others" are clearly difficult to make—even when a teacher is highly motivated to do so—and, as Paley (1991) vividly portrays in *White Teacher,* are nearly impossible to do alone. In her book, Paley examines how she thought and acted when she first taught African American children in her kindergarten classroom at the University of Chicago Laboratory School. She ruefully acknowledges how she alternately practiced a color-blind and then color-centric focus in her teaching as she struggled toward teaching that invites all children's learning. It was only through discussion with African American and White colleagues in her campus school, through talking with children in her classroom and their families, and through reading and self-reflection that Paley could initiate changes in her theories and practices.

Paley tells us that her story, "like anyone's story, is a morality tale" (p. xv). We believe the tales told in the chapters to follow are also morality tales; that is, teaching and teacher education that is multicultural and social reconstructionist are aimed deliberately at changing the ways that teachers and schools as institutions work.

A Multicultural and Social Reconstructionist Framework for Teaching

Several interpretations can be assigned to multicultural education. These interpretations are usually related to how issues of race, class, gender, disability, and sexual orientation are dealt with in school policies and practices. Banks (1994), for example, posits four approaches to integrating cultural content into curriculum. These approaches to multicultural curriculum reform are (1) the contribution approach, in which content presented about ethnic and cultural groups is linked, for the most part, to holidays and celebrations; (2) the additive approach, in which the cultural and ethnic concepts, content, and themes included in the curriculum do not modify the basic goals structure of the classroom activity and characteristics; (3) the transformation approach, in which the structure of the curriculum is changed to provide students the opportunity to examine concepts, problems, events, and issues from the perspective of different ethnic and cultural groups; and (4) the social action approach, in which students investigate social issues and problems and take civic action to further learn about concepts and events that they have studied.

Sleeter and Grant (1993) assigned five interpretations or approaches to multicultural education that include curriculum reform and address race, class, gender, disability and sexual orientation in societal goals, school goals, instruction, and other classroom and schoolwide concerns. These approaches are the following:

- Teaching the Exceptional and Culturally Different
- Human Relations
- Single-Group Studies
- Multicultural Education
- Education That Is Multicultural and Social Reconstructionist

Teaching the Exceptional and Culturally Different

This approach fits students into the existing social structure and culture. By building bridges between the students' backgrounds and the schools, teachers teach a dominant traditional academic curriculum. Instruction builds on students' learning styles and is adapted to their existing skills. This approach accommodates students who are exceptional or culturally different through the use of teaching strategies or culturally relevant materials that otherwise might be used in a "pull-out" program for students with "special needs." While this approach may help students remain in their regular classroom and enable them to participate in its ongoing daily life, the problem of cultural discontinuity remains that of the individual student.

Human Relations

This approach to multicultural education attempts to assimilate individual students into the dominant discourse and practices of the classroom. The focus is on the fostering of positive affective relationships among students of diverse backgrounds and personal characteristics in the school so that each student has a strong self-concept and can work in harmony with the group. The Human Relations approach undergirds a curriculum that includes lessons about stereotyping and individual differences. It encourages instruction that includes collaborative and cooperative learning among students.

Teacher education grounded in a Human Relations approach prepares teachers to honor the diverse backgrounds of the students whom they will teach and to promote good will among all students. Actual conflicts between individuals and groups can be glossed over in support of an "I'm okay, you're okay" ideology.

Single-Group Studies

This approach promotes social structural equality for and the immediate recognition of an identified group. Commonly implemented in the form of ethnic studies and labor studies, this approach assumes that because of past curriculum biases, knowledge about particular oppressed groups should be taught separately from conventional classroom knowledge in either separate units or separate courses.

The Single-Group Studies approach seeks to raise consciousness levels about an identified group by teaching both its members and others about the history, culture, and contributions of the group, as well as how that group has been oppressed by or worked with the dominant group in society.

Multicultural Education

This approach to education promotes social equality and cultural pluralism. Curriculum is organized around the contributions and perspectives of different cultural groups. It pays close attention to gender equity. For example, teachers drawing on a multicultural approach learn how gender-biased socialization and oppression are located in their own teaching practices and they learn to alter these as well as become aware of how males and females from different ethnic backgrounds are socialized.

Teachers build on students' learning styles, adapt instruction to the existing skills of students in the class, and involve students in thinking through and analyzing the life situations of different people. This approach encourages both the maintenance of students' native languages and multilingual acquisition for all students. Further, proponents of multicultural education advocate the staffing of schools with a diverse population.

Education That is Multicultural and Social Reconstructionist

We believe this approach is the responsible interpretation to use as the theoretical framework for *Making Schooling Multicultural: Campus and Classroom,* because it extends the previous approaches and supports education for everyone. It promotes social and structural equality and cultural pluralism. It provides a climate in which students can work toward structural equality, accept lifestyles different from their own, and understand the importance of equal opportunity for all people. The curriculum is organized around social issues involving race, class, gender, disability, and sexual orientation. It also involves the history and lives of many United States peoples and uses the lives of students in the classroom as the starting point for analyzing oppression, teaching critical thinking skills, and developing social action and empowerment skills.

From this viewpoint, instruction involves students' active and democratic decision-making. It builds on students' learning styles, adapts to students' skills and encourages student cooperation and collaboration. Education That is Multicultural and Social Reconstructionist affirms the active involvement of parents, families, and other community members in children's learning and the evaluation of their progress in school and outside of school.

We advocate this approach for several reasons. It provides teachers with an ideology of what "ought to be." It is a set of beliefs that advocates changes in the prevailing social structure and order—changes that promote cultural pluralism and structural equality. Education That is Multicultural and Social Reconstructionist provides teachers with the theory and (guide to) practice to help them shape their educational philosophies and develop teaching strategies for successfully teaching all students.

This approach contributes to an awareness and understanding of the changing student demographics in many classrooms across the nation. It validates and supports the need for second-language instruction and the importance of non-English language students to maintain their native language as well as learn a new one. It prepares teachers to make both their formal and informal curriculum developmentally appropriate and culturally authentic. It shows teachers how to integrate multicultural education into different academic disciplines, it creates an awareness of how student evaluation and assessment is interpretive and contextual, and it includes parent participation.

Education That Is Multicultural and Social Reconstructionist prepares teachers to understand that successful and student-appropriate classroom discipline and management is based on a teacher's knowledge of self, a teacher's knowledge of students and their homes and communities, and a teacher's willingness to involve parents as partners in their children's learning.

Finally, this approach helps teachers prepare students to examine and conceive of ways to challenge the problems and issues that impede self-empowerment. It prepares students to take charge of their lives, work collectively with others, and speak out to bring about social change.

Making Schooling Multicultural in Every Discipline

In the chapters that follow, our colleagues offer their perspectives on achieving a multicultural, social reconstructionist approach to teaching and learning in their disciplines. In Chapter 2, Peter Stearns reminds us that multiculturalism has a long history in U.S. educational traditions. He traces how U.S. schools, like their counterparts in other parts of the world, have been designed for the assimilation and acculturation of citizens aimed at "a single ultimate Americanness." Stearns also shows how recent political and demographic shifts in our nation and in the world—as well as changes in how thinkers in various disciplines are reconstructing their fields—have created a more welcoming climate for multiculturalism. Yet he cautions that much of what people apparently sympathetic to multiculturalizing schools say can also be read as new cloaks for homogenizing school curricula.

In Chapter 3, Geneva Gay discusses curriculum development, instruction, and assessment with a chapter focusing on definitions and components of curriculum. She draws attention to how the formal and informal curricula of schools operate simultaneously in classrooms, and how teachers pursuing multicultural practices must be aware of and work toward altering both of these. She highlights how multicultural curriculum reform is most effective when it is target-specific, developmentally appropriate, and culturally authentic.

Carla Cooper Shaw's work on instructional pluralism in Chapter 4 complements Gay's chapter on curriculum through discussion of how students' varied approaches to learning are outcomes of their individual characteristics and of their membership in cultural groups. Shaw lays out the debate on the merit of recognizing and teaching to accommodate varied student learning styles. She helps readers understand, through multiple examples, how building on what students bring to the classroom as their preferred ways of learning and their "cultural habits of thought" can enhance learning.

In Chapter 5, Mary Catherine Ellwein and M. Elizabeth Graue present a strong case to teachers for rejecting positivistic and fragmented ways of knowing how and what students are learning. They argue for the recognition that assessment of students' learning is an interpretive act, and they call for exploration of evaluative tools that consider individual, social, and contextual dimensions of learners and learning.

Ellwein and Graue begin with a description and critique of the development of testing in the United States. They point out that most teachers have not received education or formal training in assessment, and that teachers who do receive such training find it often fails to meet their specific classroom needs. Ellwein and Graue offer realistic vignettes that contrast traditional and technical means of understanding children's learning with new efforts to comprehend how and what children are learning in collaboration with their families.

In Chapter 6, Toni Griego-Jones highlights how, from the time that diverse American Indian cultures dominated this land and hundreds of American Indian languages were spoken, what is now known as the United States has always been a multilingual, multicultured land. In the chapter "Reconstructing Bilingual Education from a Multicultural Perspective," Griego-Jones traces how people from various language groups have attempted to maintain their cultural identities while living in the United States through schooling in their native tongues.

Griego-Jones points out that it is not possible to simply characterize how bilingual education is conducted in this country, as it is carried out in varied ways. Bilingual education programs differ with regard to the amount of time and effort expended on the maintenance of a student's native language versus that devoted to the learning of additional languages. She envisions a future in which all children in the United States learn another language and appreciate the heritage and traditions of other peoples. As she puts it, bilingual education could then be an enhancement to all children's lives rather than a remedy for some.

In Chapter 7, on classroom management, Mary Lou Fuller explores various models of teachers managing classrooms and argues that teachers must understand students' behavior as an outcome of both their personal motivation and as a consequence of their cultural group membership. To illustrate her discussion, Fuller depicts how one prospective teacher struggled to understand the behavior and effectively teach students from varied ethnic groups. Readers see the complex dimensions of managing a classroom of students with diverse backgrounds through one novice teacher's experiences.

Mary Louise Gomez's chapter on teaching for literacy—Chapter 8—launches a series of chapters in which authors discuss how students can understand and construct knowledge in various disciplinary fields via a multicultural, social reconstructionist approach. Through stories of her own teaching experiences and those of prospective teachers with whom she has worked, Gomez shows how reading, writing, and other communication skills can be taught in culturally relevant and inviting ways. She demonstrates critical reflection through a form of narrative inquiry that asks participants to tell stories about their own teaching and to critique their own actions as well as those of others in supportive cohort communities of peers.

In Chapter 9, focusing on teaching mathematics from a multicultural and social reconstructionist perspective, William F. Tate IV argues that the values of the mathematizer or the person doing mathematics play a large role in how a situation is quantified and understood. Concomitantly, he argues that the ways mathematics has been framed as an activity—one that fosters the economic, social, and cultural advancement of a society and that is best suited for an elite group practicing a deductive system of logic—have played a large role in how mathematics is presented in schools and how mathematics has served as a gateway to higher education and high status jobs. Tate argues for teaching mathematics from a centric perspective, one that locates students within the context of their own cultural references so they can create their own mathematical knowledge and critique that made by others.

In Chapter 10, "Learning Science as a Transformative Experience," Jean Lythcott and James Stewart take their readers on an exploration of science materials as they show us how elementary and middle school children can learn about solids, liquids, and gases. The authors embark on a lively discussion about what it means for teachers and children to construct—within a diverse classroom community—conceptual understandings about the world. Lythcott and Stewart point out, however, that multicultural and social reconstructionist science education is about more than conceptual and intellectual understandings; it is also about enabling learners to transform themselves and their world as they come to know and understand it.

James Banks, in Chapter 11, "Teaching Social Studies for Decision-Making," describes four major periods in the development of social studies education in the United States and lays out the goals of social studies education in a pluralistic and democratic society that result in a decision-making/social action model of curriculum. Further, he demonstrates how the model comes to life in a junior high school social studies classroom. Banks shows how, in a decision-making focused social studies curriculum, students can learn the following: to identify the sources of their values, to determine how their values are compatible or conflictive with one another, to identify and choose among alternative values, and to justify their values and the actions based on them in light of societal values such as social justice, equity, and dignity for all people.

In Chapter 12, "The Social Reconstruction of Art Education: Teaching Visual Culture," Kerry Freedman challenges the purposes that Western art teaching has served. Rather than instill the aesthetic values of an elite few into all, Freedman argues for art education that presents all visual cultures as socially constructed, meaningful, and changing. Rather than focus on the individual as a "self-expressive maker of art" who is therapeutically treated via art production, Freedman argues that art can be at the center of a curriculum on culture, because understanding the dimensions of visual culture, including artifacts, ceremonies, and costumes, is fundamental to understanding human existence. She suggests that teachers of art can provide the foundation for students to produce and critique art and explodes seven common myths that reflect current debates about multiculturalism in education.

In Chapter 13, which focuses on a social reconstructionist approach to music education, Julia Eklund Koza first shows readers how, since the late 1960s, music educators in the United States have been developing a multicultural agenda. Next, she suggests how changes in schooling at large, in the music education paradigm, and in the curriculum and instruction of music education can facilitate a multicultural social reconstructionist agenda. She grounds her arguments regarding what a social reconstructionist music education might look like in four principles she views as "departures" from "business as usual" in music teaching and learning. These are the following: (1) music is a worthwhile and basic matter for inclusion in the elementary and middle school curriculum, (2) any teacher is capable of creating an environment in which children can learn music, (3) classroom teachers as well as music specialists are responsible for helping students learn music, and (4) the compartmentalization of music as a "special" subject area is artificial and marginalizing. Koza argues for and describes how one can develop music education that is diverse, inclusive, and respectful of all people.

Jepkorir Rose Chepyator-Thomson creates a new vision for physical education in Chapter 14 that embraces the interests and activities of many peoples. She places contemporary physical education curricula and instruction in a historical context, arguing that, from its inception in U.S. schools, physical education has been Euro-centered. Chepyator-Thomson outlines four paradigms that have dominated physical education practices in this country to date: a physical fitness model, developmentally based physical education, movement education, and humanistic physical education.

She follows this discussion with a multicultural and social reconstructionist perspective on physical education that, in addition to inviting students' participation in the games and sports of diverse peoples, fosters analyses of how sports have developed—who has been encouraged and who has benefitted from playing them—and helps students find ways to be fit and powerful in active play.

Veronica Acosta-Deprez argues in Chapter 15 that health education can be effective only when teachers take into account the cultural beliefs and values that students hold regarding what constitutes health and how one maintains it. She explores seven principles of planning and teaching a health curriculum. These principles involve the following: (1) teachers' acquisition of knowledge regarding the health practices of varied peoples, and (2) teachers' rethinking of the role of health educator from one of information provider to a partnership of problem solving with students, their families and community members. Acosta-Deprez emphasizes the importance of looking first to students—their interests and needs—in planning and teaching for health.

In Chapter 16, "Multiculturalism and Educational Theater," Mark Riherd and Nancy Swortzell describe two movements in educational theater, drama-in-education and theater-in-education. Both are predicated on the belief that people's behavior and the social institutions that we create can be changed. Riherd and Swortzell show how educational theater teams around the world have responded to oppression through the making of theater experiences for and with audiences of young people. They offer principles on which educational theater aimed at social change is predicated and give a detailed example of a theater experience grounded on these postulates.

In Chapter 17, "Television and Film in the Classroom: The Presence and Absence of People of Color," Ann DeVaney focuses attention on how the available images surrounding people help us construct portraits of ourselves and the possibilities that lie before us. In particular, DeVaney shows us how the representations of people on television and in films create and sustain representations of people of color that are narrow and limited, stereotypical, and oppressive. She offers readers a structural method for critically reading media images and gives examples from familiar contemporary television programs and films to illustrate how teacher-viewers can employ this method themselves and with their students.

In Chapter 18, "Field Experiences: Planting Seeds and Pulling Weeds," Marilynn Boyle-Baise and Christine Sleeter draw attention to the knowledge and experiences—the perspectives or "web of beliefs"—that everyone brings to teacher education. The authors show how one's perspectives serve as filters or interpretive lenses through which teachers view students and families and their role as educators.

Boyle-Baise and Sleeter note that field experiences generally serve as transitional experiences in which prospective teachers move from roles as students to classroom leadership that often imitates their cooperating teacher role models. But they argue that field experiences also can be opportunities for reflection and rethinking of one's perspectives. The authors offer examples of how prospective teachers can take responsibility for examining and altering their perspectives on people different from themselves through field experiences.

In Chapter 19, Maureen Gillette closes the text with "It's Got to Be in the Plan: Reflective Teaching and Multicultural Education in the Student Teaching Semester." Gillette focuses on what is generally the capstone of teacher preparation—the student teaching semester—and contrasts the work of two student teachers whose goals are to become multicultural and social reconstructionist teachers. Gillette's chapter is a fitting conclusion to this book as she explores how two sets of cooperating teachers and student teachers work together with a supervisor colleague to examine the encouragements and constraints of implementing a multicultural and social reconstructionist pedagogy across the curriculum.

Finally

As you finish reading, we hope that you, like Crow and Weasel, will continue to be self-reflective in your preparation for teaching and in your classroom practices. We hope that, like them, your journey has offered you new ways of thinking and acting. As Weasel says to Crow after they have finished their trip, "Our journey, seeing different ways of life, has made me wonder about many things."

He adds the following:

> One day perhaps my son will return and the people will listen to what they have to say. And then their children. It will go on like that, and that way our people will look into the heart of wisdom.
>
> Crow pondered his friend's words. His eyes followed an Appaloosa mare on the hill below them. "The wonder and the strangeness," he said, "the terror of the world will never be over." He turned and regarded Weasel. "Imagine our daughters," he said. "Traveling." (pp. 78–79)

We imagine you traveling as well.

Notes

1. Grumet (1988) uses the phrase *Other people's children* to heighten our sense of responsibility to teaching all children in the ways that we would teach our own. Delpit (1988) uses the same phrase to challenge teachers to acknowledge how their participation in the "culture of power" constrains their understanding and teaching of diverse children.

2. Tabachnick, Zeichner, Densmore, & Hudak (1988) point out that the notion of perspective has its theoretical roots in the work of Mead (1938) and his concept of the "act." Contemporary uses of the term *perspective* to discuss teachers' beliefs about their work and the classroom actions that give meaning to these beliefs date to the Becker, Geer, Hughes, & Strauss (1961) study of medical students' socialization. Becker et al. define *perspective* as "a coordinated set of ideas or actions a person uses in dealing with some problemetic situation; a person's ordinary way of thinking about an act or situation" (p. 34).

References

Banks, J. A. (1994). *An introduction to multicultural education*. Boston: Allyn and Bacon.

Becker, H., Geer, B., Hughes, E., Strauss, A. (1961). *Boys in white*. Chicago: University of Chicago Press.

Delpit, L. (1988). The silenced dialogue: Power and pedagogy in educating other people's children. *Harvard Educational Review, 58,* 280–289.

Gomez, M. L. (1994). Teacher education reform and prospective teachers' perspectives on teaching "other peoples'" children. *Teaching and Teacher Education, 10,*(3), 319–334.

Grumet, M. R. (1988). *Bitter milk: Women and teaching*. Amherst, MA: University of Massachusetts Press.

Haveman, R., and Wolfe, B. (1994, Winter). America's children: Status, prospects, policy. *The LaFollette Policy Report, 6,*(1), 3–5.

Hodgkinson, H. L. (1985). *All one system: Demographics of education—Kindergarten through graduate school*. Washington, DC: Institute for Educational Leadership.

Hodgkinson, H. L. (1991, April 10). Remarks made on a video teleconference. *Who's missing from the classroom? The need for minority teachers*. Washington, DC: American Association of Colleges for Teacher Education and the ERIC Clearinghouse on Teacher Education.

Lopez, B. (1990). *Crow and Weasel*. New York: HarperCollins Perennial.

Mead, G. H. (1938). *The philosophy of the act*. Chicago: University of Chicago Press.

Paley, V. (1989). *White teacher*. Cambridge: Harvard University Press.

Sleeter, C. E., & Grant, C. A. (1993). *Making choices for multicultural education: Five approaches to race, class, and gender* (2nd ed.). Englewood Cliffs, NJ: Merrill/Prentice Hall.

Tabachnick, B. R., Zeichner, K. M., Densmore, K., & Hudak, G. (1983). *The development of teacher perspectives*. Paper presented at the annual meeting of the American Educational Research Association, Montreal.

Chapter 2

◆ ◆ ◆ ◆

Multiculturalism and the American Educational Tradition

Peter N. Stearns

Carnegie Mellon University

Introduction

The current goals of multicultural education bear a positive relationship to many features of the American educational tradition, as it has developed for more than a century-and-a-half. The decentralized quality of American education, though modified in recent decades by increased planning at state levels, contributes to a certain amount of cultural flexibility. Nothing in the American tradition compares to the classic centralist model of French schooling, which deliberately set out to crush regional distinctiveness as the public system confirmed its hold in the later 19th century. No American education official has ever rivaled the boasts of the French minister in the 1880s who would look at his watch and claim to know what was happening in every classroom across the nation—and no serious official ever wanted this degree of homogenization (Weber, 1976).

The American system has long been committed to an ethic of social mobility, which has also opened educational access to people of many different backgrounds; here, too, the national tradition has been more flexible than that of many other nations where more deeply rooted social hierarchies tempered mobility messages. In seeking to use education to reflect the validity of differing norms (for example, in religion) and to help people of varied cultural backgrounds achieve their goals, the American schooling tradition may prove congenial to the new appeals for more explicit attention to diverse identities. The nation's educational history provides positive background for some aspects of multiculturalism (Cremin, 1970, 1980, 1988).

This is not the whole story, however. American education has long been seen by the bulk of its leadership as a source and enforcer of vital values, essential to creating a degree of national consensus amid a varied population. Schooling, in other words, has from its inception worked to change habits on the part of groups regarded as foreign or inferior. Education formed a key center of efforts to convert traditional workers into modern, efficient producers imbued with appropriate middle-class zeal and to mold new arrivals into "good Americans." The tradition of using education to shape children and youths according to a powerful if not always fully defined set of values is at least as profoundly rooted as the tradition of tolerance and flexibility. Here, multiculturalism as currently conceived must do battle with established habits, and its advocates must be aware of the powerful momentum toward insistence on conformity.

American educational traditions, in sum, embody deep-seated tensions that must be understood and sorted out if a realistic multicultural approach is to emerge. The traditions, not surprisingly, mirror and help explain current debate about multicultural issues, with both partisans and opponents pointing to different features of our educational past. Partisans of multiculturalism, for example, correctly emphasize the longstanding association of schooling and curricula with democracy and religious tolerance, because Americans have taken pride in the openness of their educational system and its ability to group students of varied backgrounds. Opponents, however, also correctly point to the longstanding link between schooling and the shaping of citizen consensus of definitions of Americanness and how the United States fits into the cultural panoply of the larger world (Ravitch & Schlesinger, 1990; Himmelfarb, 1987). To these opponents, multiculturalism is a dangerous, divisive innovation. Their arguments can be understood only if current political disputes are seen in the perspective of more durable features of our educational past.

Nothing more clearly reflects the double-edged quality of American education, confronting varied cultural strains within society at large, than the hallowed image of the melting pot, taught to generations of school children through the first three quarters of the 20th century. On the one hand, the melting pot image was welcoming. It not only recognized but also celebrated the unprecedented racial and ethnic diversity of the United States after 1900. Folded into the image was pride in the American tradition of religious freedom and separation of church and state, which had infused public education (after initial decades of sectarian domination) by the middle of the 19th century. Schools imposed no single denomination. Despite disproportionate Protestant influence, they came to include many Catholic and Jewish students, and by the middle of the 20th century (despite common insistence on some Christian symbolism) the schools made this ecumenicalism a positive virtue. Religion aside, the melting pot imagery treated the variety of peoples of the nation (particularly, of course, the ethnic immigrants) as a source of strength. A distinctive national character resulted from the combination of diverse peoples and their own special qualities.

Yet the pot was supposed to fuse its mixed ingredients, which is where the consensus strand re-entered strongly. The melting pot ideal was carefully couched to emphasize a single ultimate Americanness, an evolutionary product to be sure, enhanced by the (often unspecified) qualities contributed by immigrant cultures. Ongoing diversity was not the point. To be sure, the melting pot was compatible with after-school excursions into specific religious programs or the occasional folk festival, seen as compatible with "real" Americanness, but on essentials a single set of values predominated: There was one proper set of fundamental political beliefs (by the 1920s socialism and then communism need not apply); there was one valid set of economic values, with emphasis on hard work, productivity and commitment to a capitalist order. The verb "Americanize," coined at about the same time as the melting pot idea began to enter classroom currency, expressed this authoritative aspect of the educational culture explicitly. The melting pot was viable because its components had been Americanized, and the very school system that held up the melting pot symbol played a vigorous and self-conscious role in the Americanization process. As current proponents of multiculturalism recognize, the traditional celebration of diversity was predicated on a firm understanding that, in the habits that counted, diversity would quickly yield to a single American standard.

The lessons of the melting pot apply to the implications of American educational history more generally. There are traditions to cherish, curricular themes that can be embellished in providing a framework for multiculturalism. Yet many educational emphases are also hostile to significant diversity and, exacerbating the tension, a certain amount of myth-making may mask the strong homogenizing impulse.

The Burdens of Schooling's History

The framework for American public education began before diversity issues loomed large—though, in fact, as revisionist educational historians have emphasized, they were present in some forms from the outset. Katz (1968, 1987) and others have noted how the schools that began to spread in the northern states from the 1830s complacently built curricula on middle-class and disproportionately urban values, held to be valid standards for a growing working class, new immigrants, and the rural majority. Local school board control modified the impositions somewhat, particularly for agricultural districts. Sincere beliefs in the openness of the American system concealed the impositions to some extent. The fact remained that educational authorities pushed not only a single set of basic skills but also a single set of republican virtues, highlighted by embellished stories of national heroes such as Washington. Students either were sufficiently similar to accept this common fund or should be made similar by accepting it.

The distinctiveness of the American political system, at this educational incubation point, reduced explicit awareness of the homogenizing impulse. The early establishment of political democracy (for White males) and, in most northern states, of extensive public school systems and attendance requirements obviously linked mass education to political empowerment and to social mobility. By the 1830s many Americans were being taught that, whatever their backgrounds, education provided them a means of participating in intelligent citizenship and gaining opportunities for advancement. The American educational system did not have the elitist bias of most of the systems being established (usually more gradually) in Europe in the 19th century. The state did not set up special kinds of secondary schools, like the German *gymnasiums*, that would be open only to a tested, select few. As a university system emerged, it was relatively heterogeneous, again avoiding the rigid tracking that described European systems. A related sign of openness was the relatively early American commitment to substantial co-education, despite debates and misgivings that extended from 1850 into the early 20th century (Tyack & Hansot, 1990). Women were not systematically shunted into separate school tracks, and while their curricula emphasized certain subjects appropriate for domestic life—like the ubiquitous home economics of the 1900s—they also shared many substantive classes with their male counterparts. The rise of the American high school, as a unique institution designed for relatively broad access, at precisely the time that other industrial countries (including Japan by the 1880s) were firming up a highly tracked and discriminatory secondary educational system, symbolized and furthered the unusual equation of American education with wide access to students of diverse backgrounds (Perlmann, 1988). Small wonder that educational leaders had little sense that they were imposing cultural standards, in contrast to their more frankly authoritarian counterparts in 19th century Europe.

There were serious qualifications to the love affair between educational tradition and American democracy, however, well before 1900. Until the 20th century a minority of high school students were working class; economic differentiation posed a formidable barrier to opportunity. University access, though not constrained by a single, state-run hierarchy, was even more limited. On another front: the domination of most public school systems by Protestants repelled many immigrants, who fled to the growing parochial school network. Nineteenth-century Americans tolerated a certain amount of diversity in education—including local pockets of foreign-language schools, like the German systems in rural Wisconsin—but their tolerance mainly involved parallel institutions, not widely acknowledged diversity under a single school roof.

The public school system, as it spread in the northern states, had a reasonably well-defined, if somewhat implicit, value system. It was open-ended in welcoming students from reasonably diverse backgrounds, but it expected to homogenize them in crucial ways. Members of the working class, rural and urban, were taught middle-class standards about punctuality, avoidance of political excess, and cleanliness and hygiene. Dress codes carried the message, as did lessons in civics. Immigrants, like the Irish who flooded in from the 1840s onward, were to learn similar habits—which, along with religious differences, helps explain considerable interest in alternative school systems and a tendency to pull students out of schooling at a relatively early age. Diversity in background was fine, in principle and to an impressive degree in fact; diversity in outcomes or in educational process was not sought. Rather, schools operated as institutions of social control, where socially dubious segments of the population could be taught appropriate standards. From this process, in turn, talented students could rise in an education-linked mobility pattern that depended on the combination of openness and assimilation to middle-class values.

The tensions embodied in this educational tradition boiled over after 1900, when for a time widespread access no longer seemed compatible with instilling a single set of values. At the lowest educational levels in the north, to be sure, older traditions largely prevailed. Students were mixed in the primary schools (except where residential segregation constrained the process—and 20th century suburban flight played a growing role in constraining real classroom diversity) and taught a growing array of lessons about political propriety, diligence at work, and personal grooming. The growing cultural diversity of the overall student population, however, as a result of new waves of immigration plus growing (if limited) incorporation of African-American students during the Great Migration from the South threatened to overwhelm the system as defined by the dominant White, Protestant middle class, particularly at the high school level. The opportunity for opening to a wider cultural array within individual classrooms was not seriously considered, except for women's education, which steadily advanced. Rather, new forms of institutional separation were introduced to keep distinct cultural groupings apart—except for those talented and adaptable individuals that might break through.

Separation took two forms. In southern states, which were just establishing full public school systems and attendance requirements after 1900, segregation kept Whites and Blacks apart. African-American education had advanced considerably during Reconstruction, through efforts by freedpeople themselves (Wiener, 1978). It was not systematically focused on a distinctive African-American culture. Nor of course was pervasive school segregation designed to avoid multiculturalism explicitly. The result of separation, however, limited any need to confront diversity issues in the South.

Northern cities had experimented with racially segregated schools, at least de facto. The onslaught of immigrants from southern and eastern Europe, held to be inferior to Yankee and old-immigrant stock, led to slightly more subtle efforts to keep various groups apart. Batteries of aptitude tests were developed as the basis of tracking into different high school programs (Chapman, 1988). Academically talented students aimed in one direction, while various technical sequences received the students who tested less well. It was assumed that groups like Italian-Americans, Slavs, Hispanics, and, soon, the growing flood of African-American migrants from the South would largely test into the non-academic tracks, and like many prophecies this one proved largely self-fulfilling. The new testing mania assumed, of course, that one set of standards accurately identified student quality. Diversity was shunned, recognized only through the existence of separate programs with largely separate career results. Not coincidentally, this same early 20th-century transition saw the reduction of the autonomy of local school boards within major cities, as more standardized controls and curricula were spread through the big urban systems.

Test-based tracking, despite the racist thinking that underlay it, was based as much on the impulse to homogenize as on that to exclude. Students who could demonstrate their talent could be admitted to the top standardized programs. Those programs would lead them to the most prestigious urban high schools and soon, despite more outright discrimination, to the "best" universities. Many children of Jewish immigrants thus made it into places like Boston Latin or Philadelphia's Central High School. A significant number of talented African-Americans and others also made it in the terms of the system—like Margaret Lawrence, the first African-American woman psychiatrist, whose academic success took her from the South to the classical Wadleigh High School in New York and ultimately to Cornell (Labaree, 1988; Lightfoot, 1988). The point was not only that the cards were stacked against most minority aspirants, but also that they were expected to internalize the standard cultural baggage of the White Protestant majority. Their talent for assimilation, not their diversity, was rewarded; their ethnic or racial background was officially ignored, not highlighted. As Nathan Glazer recently put it, referring to the period when Jewish and Italian-American students dominated New York City's public schools, students were told that the European-American forefathers of the American republic were their forefathers, not that they had a distinct or valued identity or history (Glazer, 1991). The message that being American was a single experience, launched in the primary grades, was maintained in the tracked system that confronted the reality of increased diversity in the early decades of this century.

With time, of course, the effect of early 20th century school reforms was modified. Students from a wider variety of backgrounds managed to pass into the academic mainstream. Cessation of massive immigration between 1923 and the 1960s eased fears of diversity somewhat and permitted the development of such comforting notions as the melting pot (modified, of course, by growing residential separations). In the 1950s and 1960s, the Civil Rights movement, zeroing in on educational targets, produced legislation that further limited school segregation and other forms of separation.

It is important to recognize that the educational reforms of the early 20th century, though undeniably racist in assumption, were dealing with important educational issues. Defining and maintaining academic standards in a mass educational environment can prompt concern even aside from racism. When high schools became normal and not exceptional experiences, by 1910 or 1920, they had to consider more bureaucratic methods of sorting students. Balancing local and systemwide curricular responsibilities in growing urban school systems involved complex issues after 1900, as is the case today. Furthermore, outside the South the solutions adopted did not totally block out any cultural grouping, while as we have seen the historical treatment of immigrants produced some curricular support for at least limited recognition of the value of diversity. American education retained some fruitful tension between the implications of its openness and the use of schooling for standardized acculturation.

It remains true that the American educational tradition, from its founding to its first clear multicultural crisis around 1900, opted largely for a single cultural standard, to which minority groups were expected to bow. The standard did not embrace all beliefs; religious diversity, most obviously, was still tolerated and to some degree honored. Yet growing emphasis on political conformity (amid the "Red scare" of the 1920s), increasingly detailed rules about sex and hygiene (amid germ theories and residual Victorianism), and pervasive assumption about proper economic discipline drove the single standard home. Agreement on the key values to be conveyed, and institutional mechanisms to keep apart students seen as too diverse, kept potential multicultural issues largely at bay for decades.

Only in the aftermath of Civil Rights legislation and amid sweeping changes in student demography resulting from differential racial birthrates and the massive renewal of immigration—this time from Latin America and Asia, with heritages still more distinctive than those brought by the immigrants of the turn of the century—has the educational tradition and the reforms introduced to support it been challenged anew. The contemporary debate about multiculturalism looms, historically, as the second great challenge to dominant educational assumptions created in the 19th century and asserted victoriously against initial challenge between 1900 and 1920.

Americanization Through Curriculum

The same tensions that produced institutional changes in response to growing diversity in the population, without totally closing access to varied groups (save in the South), inevitably shaped characteristic curricula. Pervasive curriculum themes drove home the standard messages authorities wanted students to learn; all subject areas reflected a concern for emphasizing a single basic standard, a unitary truth. Gradual movements toward greater curricular standardization—in citywide school districts, as part of college preparation with the formation of College Board guidelines early in the 20th century, and more recently with the powerful trend toward statewide curricular mandates—worked in the same direction from one school to the next (Valentine, 1987). At the same time openness to diversity was not entirely cast aside, as programs in literature and some aspects of history showed some sensitivity to varied interests and contexts.

Courses in science reflected dominant cultural beliefs in a single set of valid methods and findings, and as science was worked increasingly into the curriculum, by the later 19th century, this helped set the general tone for education. Religious explanations for natural phenomena were entertained concurrently for a time, but faded in the face of scientific claims, particularly after the dramatic Scopes trial of the 1920s. Scientific truth was singular, and science remains the most difficult area to adapt to multicultural goals.

Through most of the 20th century, programs in music and literature were particularly revealing of the avoidance of diversity issues. Literature taught great works in the European and American tradition, as defined by scholarly arbiters of taste. Art and music appreciation involved exposure to great works in the same traditions. Civilized taste, in other words, focused on appreciation for a single set of works: Shakespeare—as his work was removed from boisterous popular appreciation and sterilized in classrooms by the later 19th century (Levine, 1988), leading 19th-century novelists, and a few more recent figures. Music was Bach and Beethoven, art the wonders of Greece and Rome and the Italian Renaissance. Literary and artistic productions from other parts of the world, by other groups within European and American society, or in forms other than standard genres, need not apply (Bloom, 1987).

Reading programs enforced another kind of value-setting, even before students were old enough to receive the great canon. Reading materials featured standard (or idealized-standard) middle-class settings, logical to most of the authors involved and essential (seemingly) in creating agreed-upon cultural values. People lived in individual houses with chimneys; they were usually blonde; they were clean and family size was small. Readers began to form these images with materials presented in the first grade, and they were rarely subjected to additional nuance as their student careers continued.

The consistent strand in the humanities curriculum, beginning with pablum reading and moving on to high school literature courses, was the belief in a clear and singular cultural standard. Students should be taught, through early reading, that there was one civilized way to live—the houses and the smiling mothers—and they should progressively learn that there was also one civilized definition of humanistic culture. A result, for many students—not only recently, but in the early 20th century as well—was a massive disparity between life as lived, culture as experienced in popular media, and what was learned about proper standards. To an extent, this was precisely the intention of the curriculum planners, for reading and art materials were designed to help children, culturally inferior by dint of age, and groups judged culturally inferior because of their racial or ethnic origins, gain access to the knowledge propriety and good taste required. Diversity was not specifically shunned; it was simply not seriously considered. Underlying assumptions even had a certain optimistic quality, since it was believed that movement toward more civilized standards was possible; the inferior were not forever condemned.

One final facet of humanities curricula reflected national concern with standard-setting. Foreign languages received short shrift, as subjects to be introduced early or seriously. Language concern centered on teaching "standard" English and displacing immigrant languages and dialects. This focus, and the desire to instill familiarity with American literature staples as part of building a national cultural consciousness, permitted, and perhaps caused, a striking national neglect of foreign language teaching.

Treatments in history or, as became increasingly common after the 1930s, social studies programs in some respects simply replicated the assumptions of the arts and literature courses. Social studies advocates long emphasized an even more explicit assimilationist message than more traditional advocates of standard classical or American history courses (Armento, 1986). New work in civics, while diluting the historical diet, was designed to show how American institutions worked and what proper American citizenship entailed, on a definite assimilationist model. There were, additionally, some specific twists in this general social studies-history-social sciences area that warrant particular attention in revealing deeply held assumptions about what the United States was and how it fit into the world, that not only ignored much diversity but in some ways explicitly combatted it.

As in literature courses, topic selection leaned heavily on elite or elite-led developments. The evolution of constitutional structure, major wars, major presidencies, and reform movements such as Progressivism headed the list in American history, with occasional excursions into cultural topics such as transcendentalism or pragmatism. By the 20th century some attention to immigration leavened the mix, but there was no consistent attention to popular behaviors; for a considerable time even slavery was largely passed over. America was shaped primarily by the thoughts and actions of formal leaders, like the framers of the Constitution or presidents like Lincoln. The values and institutions they shaped in turn formed the centerpiece requirements of civics. Here was the historical and social studies equivalent to the Great Books diet of high school literature.

Beyond this, certain theoretical assumptions, rarely trotted out for explicit debate, enhanced the monochromatic portrait of the past. American history was given a central place in the social studies curriculum, with remaining attention (if any) devoted largely to West European societies (particularly Britain) seen as progenitors of American values. To the allocation of attention was added an implicit belief in American exceptionalism: The United States, as it formed from the 17th through the 19th centuries, proved to be a unique society, which could be understood in terms of American context alone (brief bows to West European antecedents notwithstanding) and which could be credited with an array of distinctive and mainly beneficent achievements. Religious freedom, political democracy wedded with unusual political stability (the Civil War aside), belief in individual initiative, unusual equality of opportunity joined with exceptional upward mobility—these were some of the themes that followed from the American exceptionalist framework. At times, international claims might be added: Americans acted unselfishly in their diplomacy, compared with the grasping European imperialists; Americans did not start wars, though of course they won them.

American exceptionalism encouraged students, and many of their teachers, to ignore patterns in the rest of the world as irrelevant to their own lives and lamentably inferior. It encouraged them to claim more distinctiveness in their society—concerning social mobility rates, for example—than real comparison would have warranted (Kaelble, 1986). It encouraged them to overcome any lingering sense of cultural inferiority to Western Europe by pointing to the nation's political superiority, business dynamism, freedom from greedy international entanglements. It encouraged neglect of some of the complexities of American history itself (Stearns, 1988; Stearns, in press).

Reliance on rags-to-riches mobility themes might explain a lack of explicit treatment of lower-class groups, which after all would ultimately rise to become part of the great, homogeneous national middle class. American political stability brought rather unconsidered praise for the two-party system and distaste for political ideology. The same history might be interpreted in terms of an unwillingness to confront difficult political issues and a tendency to force dissent into nonpolitical behaviors such as violent protest and crime.

In sum: The curricular assumptions in the major fields of study, focused on conveying a fairly uniform set of values and standards and an inordinately simple definition of the national past, shaped in the late 19th century with the waning of classicism, have persisted in most respects to the present day. Some may be judged entirely justifiable. But justifiable or not, the United States has certainly not been unique in using its public education system to push political loyalty and to attack cultural variance. In some respects the basic tradition is a bit less inward-looking than average; at the least, British as well as American literature receives some attention, and, in many schools, the Western experience is introduced, not simply American history alone.

Nevertheless, the most obvious result of a long and durable curricular pattern, bent on instilling standard definitions of cultural and personal and political goals, offers a massive challenge to serious multicultural education. As most of the essays in this volume suggest, no subject area can be easily converted from present practice to genuine multiculturalism. Undoing current routines is vital, because these routines are built on curricular goals that either ignored diversity or consciously combatted it.

Recent Change and Illusion

To be sure, the curricular tradition has not been immune to change, even apart from recent developments such as the California curriculum reform. Political currents set in motion by the Civil Rights and feminist movements have produced modifications. The science tradition remains largely immune, given beliefs in its ability to generate demonstrable and unitary truths. Literature courses, on the other hand, added works by African-American authors, and more basic readers included more stories and illustrations based on inner cities and the experiences of racial and ethnic minorities. Social studies courses, correspondingly, generated new lessons on the African-American experience. History texts introduced at least supplemental sections on women and other groups. More and more high schools shifted from Western civilization to world history courses, including items such as the great African kingdoms of Ghana, Mali, and Songhay.

Changes of this sort during the past two decades point in some promising directions. They have not, however, as yet overcome the homogenization tradition. At best they have modified, at worst merely cosmeticized. The content of many world history courses turns out to be Western civilization barely altered. Additions to American history are often inserts that do not seriously alter the standard political and cultural emphases. Certain other trends, indeed, move in contrary directions: While attention to minority groupings has gone up, so have standardized, statewide testing programs, which tend to highlight familiar factual fare along of course with presumably "basic" skills (Resnick, 1980).

Even apparently sympathetic educators reflect a distressing, if unsurprising, ability to adopt multicultural labels while maintaining a homogenization thrust—and this aside from the vociferous outright opponents of multiculturalism. Thus Ravitch (1990), long a perceptive commentator on social studies curricula and more recently a sometime critic of multiculturalism in favor of the need for a national consensus, offers a revealing aside. Noting specifically that the old melting pot idea, suggesting erasure of group differences, has yielded to the idea of variety as a national strength, she proclaims: "Cultural pluralism is a national resource rather than a problem to be solved." She quickly adds: "The unique feature of the United States is that its common culture has been formed by the interaction of its subsidiary cultures" (Ravitch, 1990, p. 339). The words are new, the understanding and curricular implications less clearly so. A common culture remains front and center, overshadowing subsidiary elements; how this differs from the melting pot is not apparent. Further, the hallowed belief in American uniqueness is triumphantly reasserted, with no felt need to demonstrate through comparative analysis. A curriculum derived from this kind of thinking would surely allow a bit more place for the idea that various groups in American society brought distinctive and valid cultural contributions, and this would be an adjustment for the better. It would not, however, serve as basis for a real multicultural examination of the presentation of American history or of the larger world context into which American history should fit. Again, the potency of the assimilationist tradition, bent on instilling a mainstream, assertively distinctive American standard, stands out. Reform statements easily turn into mere tinkering formulas when confronted with the tradition's force.

Against this force, built into a host of curricular routines cherished by many able teachers—the comforting litany of major presidencies, the awesome power of Shakespeare, the message of a distinctive American commitment to social mobility—serious reformulation faces many obstacles. Many educational authorities, sincerely attracted to some multicultural goals, will find conversion impossibly traumatic—and many, of course, will persuasively argue that big chunks of the tradition remain objectively valid.

The Force for Multiculturalism

There is, however, a recent historical ingredient to insert. The context for American education has obviously changed, raising challenges for the assimilationist tradition arguably greater than at any time in the more distant past. This is an obvious statement at one level: Why else would multiculturalism be so vigorously on the agenda? Yet a brief historical assessment is useful, in pointing to the several strands that combine to suggest change—rather than the one or two most commonly emphasized.

Student demographics have shifted dramatically and will continue to shift. Differential birth rates and the most impressive tide of immigration in our history—and from largely non-European parts of the world—produce a more diverse student body than ever.

The effects of desegregation and other Civil Rights measures put this huge change in student body composition into a distinctive political context as well. More self-conscious feminism adds another political ingredient working in the same direction. These developments do not automatically assure a fundamental reevaluation of assimilationist curricula. Many opponents of multiculturalism emphasize the need for a single canon, in literature and history, precisely because of new degrees of student diversity. They, too, reflect change:

The canon they point to is far more rigid than is traditional in American curricula, particularly in literature. Nevertheless, the case for multiculturalism commonly begins with the new student body, sometimes adding human relations criteria related to goals of tolerance and personal adjustment. Too often, indeed, the case ends with these factors, and many convinced multiculturalists surely believe that student diversity and adjustment needs amply justify the reevaluation of assimilationist traditions in the K–12 curricula.

Two other important changes, however, add to the force of the argument and give additional direction to the multiculturalist thrust. The first, related admittedly to the new student body, involves the changing position of the United States in the world. Europe remains a vital reference point for American culture and diplomatic and economic activity, but it has long lost its monopoly on attention and effect. Latin America has been of vital concern for more than 150 years, and the Middle East, other parts of Asia, and Africa now figure in strongly (McNeill, 1988). The international context for life in the United States has become truly global, even apart from its new immigration patterns, and this impels curricular development sensitive to issues of cultural diversity even vaster than represented within the nation itself.

Finally, key disciplines from which curricula are logically drawn have shifted dramatically during the past 25 years, for the most part in directions relevant to multiculturalism. The study of literature at the scholarly level no longer simply involves a standard summary of great works. It opens these works to new kinds of assessment, in terms of wider cultural context, implicit assumptions about such issues as gender roles, and audience interaction. The same scholarship also turns to other works—novels by less-prominent authors, other media—as attention moves to understanding culture, not insisting on a single aesthetic standard (Kennedy, 1991). Historical scholarship has shifted at least as fundamentally, particularly through the growing dominance of research in social history (Gardner & Adams, 1983). Social historians argue that societies and social change must be grasped in terms of the interactions of various groups, elites with ordinary folk, women with men, regional, racial and ethnic groups with more centralizing forces. The past is not simply constructed by the doings and ideas of great men. Social values cannot be understood simply through the ideas of the most creative thinkers; indeed, their ideas are shaped, revised, supplemented, sometimes rejected outright by various cultural groups in the wider society. Political structures involve not only formal constitutions, but also power relationships at work, in the family, even in leisure pursuits; and they involve recurrent protest and violence. The past expands, and the nature of change has been fundamentally reconceived.

Major shifts in scholarship, particularly in social studies and humanities fields, provide vital support and some guidance for multicultural educational change, in combination with the other conditioning factors. Too often, pressure for multicultural reform seems purely political, and sometimes to be sure the political interests deriving from a changing student body do have a life of their own. Thus Nathan Glazer, largely supporting the multicultural implications of the recent New York report on diversity, emphasizes political impulses primarily (Glazer, 1991). Yet the new scholarship must be recognized in allowing educational reform to combine multiculturalism with a better understanding of how cultures operate, how societies function. Deciding what groups to serve through multiculturalism is not the only reorientation required; reconceiving key disciplines, in light of some extraordinarily fruitful innovations, figures in as well.

Three strands of change, then, mutually interrelated, serve as the basis for reassessing longstanding assumptions and routines in American education. Student needs and related political interests do not stand alone. Broader international developments and a real recasting of scholarship in the humanities and social sciences provide powerful support for many multicultural arguments and further basis for directing these arguments into practical curricula. Multiculturalism in this context means finding ways to address varied groups in the student population, but also raising levels of global understanding and building teaching programs, even in the early grades, in explicit relationship to exciting changes in scholarship. Arguments in behalf of multiculturalism broaden correspondingly.

Conclusion

American education has an impressive history. Despite varied problems, the achievements of American education, including the ability to reflect a genuine commitment to beliefs in considerable democracy of opportunity, are substantial by any comparative standard. On balance, however, its historical role has emphasized provision of chances for people from diverse backgrounds to learn some common "American" values, largely middle-class, and to use their education to advance in the larger society on these terms. Even for the nonmobile, it has helped teach a common fund of beliefs about what the nation stands for and about the values that define appropriate political, economic and in some respects even personal behavior.

The educational system indeed contributes greatly to one of the striking features of the American historical record: the ability, despite unprecedented ethnic and racial diversity, to avoid permanent political groupings and conflicts based on race and ethnicity alone. Curricular traditions have been shaped to fill these functions, though not without some ambivalence. They have been open enough to allow new claimants some space: Thus African Americans have long had a few representatives in American history textbooks, carefully selected to highlight individuals who largely accepted the American system and achieved success within it.

Choices of American literary works were not so rigid as to preclude some ranges of authors, and this could give at least token voice to groups seeking greater recognition and identity. Nevertheless, the insistence on a distinctive and definable national value system, mastery of which was held to be part of appropriate assimilation into the national society, clearly predominated, particularly in the history and civics courses that most directly purported to teach what the American system was all about.

The emphases and tensions of the American educational tradition raise a host of fascinating historical and policy questions. How fully did the focus on assimilation dampen group identities and complicate the process of functioning in the United States? What emphases should be largely ignored, in favor of more diverse values, and at what cost? How essential was the assimilationist approach, and the curricula that translated it, in maintaining political stability and in encouraging some individuals to achieve "American" success more rapidly than they could have done without school guidance? Will a shift toward real multiculturalism destroy schooling's role in maintaining American unity and political capacity, as some critics seriously claim?

The American educational tradition helps explain the persistence of these kinds of questions in the current policy context. The successes and the limitations of the tradition play directly into current debate. Opponents of multiculturalism, most obviously, while arguably incorrect in their goals, accurately reflect important ingredients of our educational past; this helps explain their fervor and their strength. They exaggerate certain elements—claiming for example a more uniform canon in literature than ever really prevailed in the past, while downplaying prior diversities; but they are correct in pointing to the assimilationist bent of the educational tradition.

Correspondingly, teachers who work in a more multicultural environment must be aware not only that many powerful educational authorities disagree with them—that's obvious enough—but also that elements of their own curricular experiences as students need to be rethought. This enhances the task of taking hard looks at the principles that should guide the presentation of American and more general history or at selections and interpretations of literature. Multiculturalism does not attack all the basic principles of American education, but it certainly challenges some deep-seated impulses. It builds however on a number of far-reaching changes not only in the schools but in underlying scholarship that must themselves be appreciated to mount effective alternatives. A grasp of the factors history thrusts into current debates helps improve an understanding of the choices to be made and the disputes to be faced. The same history does not make the choices simple or the results secure.

References

Armento, B. (1986). Research on teaching social studies. In M. C. Wittrock (Ed.), *Handbook of research on teaching* (pp. 131–173). Englewood Cliffs, NJ: Merrill/Prentice Hall.

Bloom, A. (1987). *The closing of the American mind: How higher education has failed democracy and impoverished the souls of today's students.* New York: Simon & Schuster.

Chapman, P. D. (1988). *Schools as sorters: Lewis M. Terman, applied psychology, and the intelligence testing movement, 1890–1930.* New York: New York University Press.

Cremin, L. A. (1970). *American education: The colonial experience, 1607–1783.* New York: Harper and Row.

Cremin, L. A. (1980). *American education: The national experience, 1783–1876.* New York: Harper and Row.

Cremin, L. A. (1988). *American education: The metropolitan experience, 1876–1980.* New York: Harper and Row.

Gardner, J. B., & Adams, G. R. (Eds.). (1983). *Ordinary people and everyday life: Perspectives on the new social history.* Nashville, TN: American Association for State and Local History.

Glazer, N. (1991, September 2). In defense of multiculturalism. *New Republic, 205,* 15–22.

Himmelfarb, G. (1987). *The new history and the old: Critical essays and reappraisals.* Cambridge, MA: Belknap Press.

Kaelble, H. (1986). *Social mobility in the nineteenth and twentieth centuries.* New York: St. Martin.

Katz, M. B. (1968). *The irony of early school reform: Educational innovation in mid-nineteenth century Massachusetts.* Cambridge, MA: Harvard University Press.

Katz, M. B. (1987). *Reconstructing American education.* Cambridge, MA: Harvard University Press.

Kennedy, A. (1991). Memory and values: Disengaging cultural legacies, *77,* (3), 34–39.

Labaree, D. F. (1988). *The making of an American high school: The credentials market and the Central High School of Philadelphia, 1938–1939.* New Haven, CT: Yale University Press.

Levine, L. (1988). *High brow, low brow: The emergence of cultural hierarchy in America.* Cambridge, MA: Harvard University Press.

Lightfoot, S. L. (1988). *Balm in Gilead: Journey of a healer.* Reading, MA: Addison-Wesley.

McNeill, W. (1988). Pursuit of power: Criteria of global relevance. In B. Gifford (Ed.), *What shall we teach: History in the schools* (pp. 129–137). Englewood Cliffs, NJ: Merrill/Prentice Hall.

Perlmann, J. (1988). *Ethnic differences: Schooling and social structure among the Irish, Italians, Jews and Blacks in an American city, 1880–1935.* Cambridge: Cambridge University Press.

Ravitch, D., & Schlesinger, A., Jr. (1990, October). Statement of the committee of scholars in defense of history. *Perspectives, 26,* (15).

Ravitch, D. (1990, Summer). Multiculturalism: E pluribus plures. *American Scholars, 59,* 339–347.

Resnick, D. P. (1980). Educational policy and the applied historian: Testing, competency and standards. *Journal of Social History, 14,* 539–559.

Stearns, P. N. (1988). Social history in the American history course: Whats, whys and hows. In B. Gifford (Ed.), *What shall we teach: History in the schools* (pp. 138–161). Englewood Cliffs, NJ: Merrill/Prentice Hall.

Stearns, P. N. (in press). *Meaning over memory: Recasting the teaching of culture and history*. Chapel Hill, NC: University of North Carolina Press.

Tyack, D., & Hansot, E. (1990). *Learning together: A history of coeducation in American schools*. New Haven, CT: Yale University Press.

Valentine, J. A. (1987). *The college board and the school curriculum: A history of the college board's influence on the substance and standards of American education, 1900–1980*. New York: College Entrance Examination Board.

Weber, E. (1976). *Peasants into Frenchmen: The modernization of rural France, 1870–1914*. Stanford, CA: Stanford University Press.

Wiener, J. M. (1978). *Social origins of the new South: Alabama, 1860–1885*. Baton Rouge, LA: Louisiana State University Press.

◆ ◆ ◆ ◆

Teach the young people how to think, not what to think.

Sidney Sugarman

Those of us who stand outside the circle of this society's definition of acceptable women; those of us who have been forged in the crucibles of difference; those of us who are poor, who are lesbians, who are black, who are older, know that *survival is not an academic skill.* It is learning how to stand alone unpopular and sometimes reviled, and how to make common cause with those other identified as outside the structures, in order to define and seek a world in which we can all flourish. It is learning how to take our differences and make them strengths. *For the master's tools will never dismantle the master's house.*

Audre Lorde

Had she paints, or clay, or knew the discipline of dance, or strings; had she anything to engage her tremendous curiosity and her gift for metaphor, she might have exchanged the restlessness and preoccupation with whim for any activity that provided her with all she yearned for. And like any artist with no art form, she became dangerous.

Toni Morrison

I learned to make my mind large, as the universe is large, so that there is room for paradoxes.

Maxine Hong Kingston, The Woman Warrior *(New York: Vintage, 1977), p. 35*

Part 2

◆ ◆ ◆ ◆

Curriculum, Instruction, and Assessment

Chapter 3

◆ ◆ ◆ ◆

A Multicultural School Curriculum

Geneva Gay

University of Washington

Introduction

Curriculum can be confusing and intimidating. This is due in part to inadequate conceptual understanding of its basic features, the different ways it is defined, and its various shapes and forms. However, curriculum plays a fundamental role in the design and implementation of educational processes at all levels of schooling. It is the anchor of instruction and evaluation, and the embodiment of educational ideals, goals, purposes, visions, and missions.

Effective multicultural education reform requires that the various types of school curricula be dealt with directly and forthrightly. Some ideas for this reform are developed in greater detail in this chapter. Specific issues discussed are curriculum definitions, different types of curricula, some guidelines for multiculturalizing the curriculum, and strategies for reforming two types of curricula to incorporate cultural pluralism.

Curriculum Definition

Curriculum is usually defined in five ways: as a product, content, program, intended learning outcomes, and the experiences of learners (Beane, Toepfer, Conrad, & Alessi, 1986; Cushner, McClelland, & Safford, 1992; Zais, 1976). Curriculum as *product* translates into documents, such as subjects offered, course syllabi, lists of objectives and content to be mastered, and titles of textbooks. Curriculum as *content* means the specific information or data to be taught in a course or subject. Thus, one teaching an Introduction to Literature course might describe the curriculum as poetry, prose, drama, and the essay, short story and novel.

When thought of as a *program*, curriculum usually refers to the courses of study offered or the subjects taught by educational institutions. For example, a magnet school specializing in the fine arts might have a curriculum each for dance, music, and theater. Or a middle school curriculum might be described as math, science, social studies, English, physical education, and exploratory units.

Curriculum as *intended learning outcomes* deals with the specific knowledge, skills, attitudes and behaviors students are supposed to learn. They, too, are typically identified in some kind of written documents. Some examples are school or district level student learning objectives (SLOs), lists of state minimum competencies, individualized educational plans (IEPs) for students in special education, and scope and sequence charts.

Curriculum as *experiences of learners* is different from the other four concepts in that it reports what actually happens to students whereas the others only indicate what should happen. It includes planned and unplanned experiences, because students learn from the formal instructional encounters sanctioned by the school as well as from the structural arrangements and social environments in which materials are presented and teaching-learning interactions occur (Cushner, McClelland, & Safford, 1992; Zais, 1976). Students can experience a curriculum of cultural hegemony, racial prejudice, and social class bias without these being deliberately taught. They can be transmitted by allowing rules, regulations, and materials used in instruction to stem from Eurocentric, middle-class cultural frames of reference.

Another curriculum concept is a *plan* or *blueprint* for instruction. Taba (1962) calls it "a plan for learning" (p. 11); Glatthorn (1987) says it is "the plans for guiding learning in schools . . ." (p. 3); and Saylor, Alexander, and Lewis (1981) describe it as a "plan for providing sets of learning opportunities for persons to be educated" (p. 8). The definition Armstrong (1989) offers is consistent with these views, but is more precise and encompassing. He sees curriculum as "a master plan for selecting content and organizing learning experiences for the purpose of changing and developing learners' behaviors and insights" (p. 4). The emerging notions of Afrocentricity, whole language instruction, and transitional bilingual education programs are examples of master plans for instruction.

In this chapter, the concept of curriculum as a plan for guiding instruction is used. Some attention also is given to the processes involved in making decisions about the components of this plan, and how these can and should be modified to be more inclusive of ethnic, cultural, and social pluralism.

Curriculum Components

Scholars agree that curriculum as a plan for instruction should include five common elements, regardless of its magnitude or level of operation. These are what is to be taught, why, how, with what, and how its effectiveness will be determined. They are called goals and objectives, rationale, content, activities, and evaluation, respectively. Together they constitute the "anatomy of the curriculum" (Zais, 1976). The interrelationship of these components is shown in Figure 3.1. Frequently, resources, timelines, and tables of specification are added to these.

Curriculum components and the designs they produce may be simple or elaborate, depending on whether the intent is to create a plan of instruction for a single lesson, a unit of study, a course, a series of courses, or an entire program for a given school or district. The components of the curriculum, and their configuration, offer different challenges and possibilities for multicultural education reform.

Knowing some of the key traits of each of the constituent parts of a curriculum is necessary to make them more multicultural. A *rationale* is a general statement of why curriculum designers believe certain knowledge and skills should be taught in particular ways. It embodies values and assumptions about "the role of the individual in society, the societal role of education, the nature and purposes of society and human beings, the relation of the future to the present, the question of what knowledge is most useful, and the purpose for which it should be useful" (Posner & Rudnitsky, 1986, p. 42).

The rationale is one of the most difficult parts of the curriculum to devise, and it is often ignored or merely implied. Yet, it is a critical one because it establishes the parameters for all the other components. The rationale justifies the learnings students are to acquire and the teaching methods and procedures; it guides and directs decisions about goals, objectives, contents, activities, evaluation, and resources; it sets the emphasis and tone for the teaching and learning processes; and it is a benchmark for determining internal consistency about the other components (Posner & Rudnitsky, 1986).

Goals and objectives are expected learning outcomes, expressed as knowledge, attitudes, values, and skills. An example of a goal statement might be to "understand and appreciate the contributions of different ethnic and cultural groups to the culture of the United States." Related objectives would specify the groups and areas of contribution, such as "Compare the gifts of Asian and African Americans to medicine in the United States," or "Name the foods common in the U.S. diet that were introduced by American Indians, Hispanics, and Africans."

The *content* component of the curriculum is the database or information source for teaching the goals and objectives. It includes knowledge (facts, observations, explanations, principles, definitions, relationships), skills

FIGURE 3.1   Curriculum development process.   This diagram shows that a rationale establishes the parameters and directions for all other curriculum components, and all of the other components influence and reflect each other.

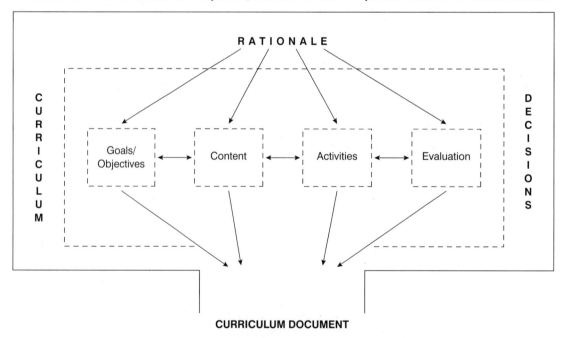

CURRICULUM DOCUMENT

(numerical calculations, map-making, persuasive debating, original research), processes (thinking, analyzing, deciding, communicating), and values (beliefs about right/wrong, good/bad, just/unjust, beautiful/ugly). Curriculum content may be in the form of books, reports, films, videotapes, recordings, newspapers, magazines, personal observations, real and vicarious experiences, and interviews.

Learning activities identify what students will do with the content as they practice the skills embedded in the goals and objectives. These may include analyzing films, taking field trips, conducting surveys, doing library research, writing critical essays, engaging in peer coaching, simulating experiences, or participating in role plays. To a large extent, the nature of the activity is shaped by the kind of content to be taught. To illustrate, students might be asked to look at films in the "Eye on the Prize" or "Profiles in Courage" series to compile information about different women and people of color who have made significant contributions to science, technology, politics, music, art, and literature. Other activities might have students interviewing people from different race, socioeconomic, age, and gender groups to see how they feel about the significance of ethnic contributions to U.S. development. A third activity might involve students in finding out how ethnic contributions, nationally and internationally, affect their lives from day to day.

The *evaluation* component of the curriculum deals with performance assessment. It identifies the methods, techniques, and procedures that will be used to determine how well students have achieved the intended learning outcomes, or objectives. These may include pencil-and-paper tests, analysis of individual and group projects, portfolios, behavioral observations, inventories, student journals, and oral and written reports (Beane, Toepfer, Conrad, & Alessi, 1986). Thus a point-counterpoint team debate on how and why X groups have made more significant contributions to the development of the United States than Y groups can be as effective in assessing learning as giving a pencil-and-paper test on ethnic gifts or having students write reports on individual contributors.

Types of Curricula

School curricula are often identified as *formal* or *informal*. The formal curriculum is expressly stated in school documents such as textbooks, guides, scope and sequence charts, policy mandates, and other legally sanctioned plans for instruction, and officially taught in the classroom. It is intentional because it is composed of learning experiences that the school system plans deliberately (Glatthorn, 1987). Glatthorn refers to this form as the *written curriculum*.

He refines the category further to include three other manifestations: the recommended, supported, and tested curricula. The *recommended* curriculum comes from requirements of federal and state policy makers, and proposals of individual scholars, professional associations, and reform commissions. Examples of this type are Public Law 94–142, which requires IEPs and "least restrictive environments" in educating students with disabilities; the America 2000 strategy and National Education Goals adopted by President Bush and the state governors in April 1991 (U.S. Department of Education); the Paideia Proposal offered by Adler (1982); and the recommendations of the American Association for the Advancements of Science (1989) in *Science for All Americans.*

The *supported* curriculum is reflected in and shaped by the resources allocated to its development and implementation, including funds, time, personnel, facilities, and materials. Two of the best illustrations of this type of curriculum are the textbooks adopted for use in the classroom and the subjects and skills that are given priority in the hiring and assignment of teachers. The *tested* curriculum is the learnings assessed by district and state competency tests and norm-referenced standardized tests, such as the Iowa Test of Basic Skills (ITBS), the California Achievement Test (CAT), and the various National Assessment of Educational Progress (NAEP) tests.

Several terms exist for the *informal* curriculum. Among these are the hidden, subtle, covert, invisible, lived, and experiential curriculum (Beane, Toepfer, Conrad, & Alessi, 1986; Glatthorn, 1987; Goodlad, 1979; Snyder, 1971; Zais, 1976). Because many of its intents and content are coded in and conveyed through a network of school symbols, it also can be called the *symbolic curriculum.* While the formal curriculum is official and focuses on what is taught overtly and directly, the symbolic one is more covert and indirect. It has defacto legitimacy and is grounded in customary practices, rituals, routines, and codes of behavior.

Some of the major benchmarks of the symbolic curriculum are the assignment of students to different instructional programs; attitudes and values attached to various subjects and skills; school systems of rewards and punishments, sanctions, and incentives; and the celebrations and ceremonies routinely practiced in elementary, middle, and high schools. In traditional schools, the symbolic curriculum transmits values that emphasize individualism, competition, conquest, control, division of labor, and fragmentation (Giroux & Penna, 1981). Although these are consistent with the capitalistic cultural ethos of mainstream U.S. society, they are contradictory to the values of many groups of color, females, and children of poverty. They also are incompatible with the goals and visions of multicultural education that emphasize common destiny, interdependence, and reciprocity among diverse groups.

Significance of the Symbolic Curriculum

The hidden, informal, or symbolic curriculum is especially evident in the type of schoolwork students from different social and economic backgrounds receive and how this access operates as tacit preparation for adult roles as laborers, managers, leaders, and policy makers in the world of work. Curriculum offerings, teaching practices, and instructional materials are not necessarily the same across socioeconomic and ethnic groups of students and the schools they attend. Middle-class, European-American students tend to be treated more favorably in all aspects of curriculum and instruction than lower socioeconomic group students and children of color. These discrepancies cause inequities in access to knowledge capital, personal competence, power and authority relationships, and leadership skills acquired in school that are subsequently reproduced in society (Anyon, 1981).

The customary ways of "doing schooling," the social, emotional, and valuative contexts and procedural rules that surround the formal curriculum, transmit certain powerful, pervasive, and persistent messages to students about which attitudes, values, behaviors, and personas are likely to be rewarded. Jackson (1990) summarizes some of the most significant messages in *Life in Classrooms*. Among them are learning how to (1) exist in crowds but operate in social solitude, (2) function in what are basically and persistently evaluative settings, (3) understand the clear distinctions between powerless students and powerful teachers, (4) be patient and passive, (5) recognize that violations of institutional expectations are more consequential than academic attainment, (6) develop work ethics and habits of conformity, compliance, obedience, and docility, and (7) that access to the system of praise, encouragement, recognition, and reward is differentiated by socioeconomic, racial, ethnic, and gender group identity.

The symbolic curriculum and its messages have different forms and are transmitted through various media. These include the structures, relationships, etiquette, expectations, and ambience that exist in schools; the institutional rules and regulations that govern the social behaviors of students and teachers; the organizational mechanisms used to manage students within the educational program; the social values taught by example; the types of knowledge and learning experiences accessible to different groups of students; the procedures used to make the school acceptable to the larger society; and system of symbols and rituals instituted to embody the image and essence of the school.

Students must learn to master both the formal and the symbolic curricula to succeed in school. This requires at least two systems of skills, because those that contribute to intellectual achievement may not necessarily facilitate successful social adaptation to institutional norms. Furthermore, what is taught through the symbolic and formal curricula is often dichotomous, with the lessons learned from the former frequently being much more powerful, lasting, and transferable to life beyond school than those of the latter (Anyon, 1981; Beane, Toepfer, Conrad, & Alessi, 1986; Giroux & Penna, 1981). In addition, both types of curricula must be actively engaged in teaching all students knowledge of and respect for cultural diversity, skills for living in a pluralistic world, and commitment to constructing a more morally just and egalitarian society. All aspects of all kinds of curricula have tremendous ramifications for orchestrating multicultural curriculum reform relative to priorities, content, techniques, and focus. However, specific strategies need to be tailored differently for formal and symbolic curricula.

Guiding Principles for Curriculum Reform

Efforts to multiculturalize the curriculum should be contextually specific, developmentally appropriate, and culturally authentic. *Contextualizing* curriculum reform involves awareness that certain techniques are better for some subjects, units of instruction, grade levels, student populations, and school environments than others. For example, because education in the elementary school tends to concentrate on reading and math skills development and evoke the "learning activities" component of the plan, multicultural education reform in formal elementary curriculum should be similarly focused. In the arena of symbolic curriculum, elementary schools typically do a lot with school and classroom decorations. These are fertile avenues for incorporating cultural pluralism. By comparison, high school teaching emphasizes mastery of subject matter, thereby giving priority to the "content" component of the planning process. Evidence of their symbolic curricula appears as various types of celebrations, recognition assemblies, and social dances.

The predominant middle school focus is less definitive, even though ideally it includes a combination of subject matter and skills, thus highlighting both the content and activities components of official plans for instruction. The symbolic representations of the hidden curriculum are more similar to those of high school, as can be seen in school songs, insignia, rituals, clubs, and activity programs. Multicultural education curriculum reform in middle and high schools also should parallel these emphases. This approach may not be ideal but it is a realistic starting point. Educators are more amenable to change when some of it can be accomplished within their existing points of reference than when totally new frameworks, information, and operational styles must be accommodated simultaneously.

Achieving *developmentally appropriate* reform simply means matching techniques and efforts to the competency levels of the reformers and the intended consumers of the reform, or the curriculum designers, teachers, and students. The details of specific strategies will differ according to the levels of expertise about and ideological commitment to multiculturalism among those who are creating the reform.

This idea is embedded in suggestions of Banks (1989), Gay (1983), and Sleeter and Grant (1988) that approaches to dealing with cultural pluralism in instructional programs increase in complexity as those providing the leadership become more informed and sophisticated. This progression has tended to move (1) from studying single ethnic groups to multiple ethnic groups to multiple cultural groups; (2) from supplementary multicultural information, lessons, and units added to existing curricula to integrating multiculturalism into all dimensions of curriculum and instruction; and (3) from teaching the contributions of diverse groups to transforming all aspects of schooling to reflect cultural pluralism and developing skills for the ultimate reconstruction of American society.

This developmental character of multicultural education reform recognizes that individuals just beginning the task are not capable of accomplishing the same changes as those who have been working in the field for a long time. While studies of contributions and profiles of separate ethnic groups may be appropriate for novices, they are not so for experts. It would be more developmentally reasonable to expect educators experienced in multiculturalism to design strategies for infusion across the entire spectrum of schooling, curriculum transformation, and social reconstruction. Yet, both novices and experts should be held accountable for the highest quality of multicultural curriculum reform within their respective developmental levels.

Another important dimension of developmental appropriateness is the readiness level of the students and the climate of the school for which the curriculum is designed. The essentials of multicultural education must be translated into instructional delivery systems suitable for students and schools in different psychosocial states based on such factors as age, attitudes, previous experiences, existing knowledge levels, and the diversity mixes among school and classroom populations. Dealing with racism is a fundamental component of multicultural education. Although combatting racism is a complex and volatile issue, it is nonetheless imperative that skills for this purpose be taught to all students, beginning in kindergarten. The challenge for curriculum designers is how to do this in meaningful and appropriate ways for students in early elementary, intermediate, middle, and high school grades; for students of color and European-American students; for students in single- and multiracial school settings; for students in social studies and language arts as well as math and science; for school environments experiencing racial tensions and those that are harmonious.

Cultural authenticity in curriculum reform requires that the information included in instructional plans about diverse ethnic, racial, social, and gender groups is accurate and significant, and covers a wide range of experiences and perspectives. This means curriculum designers must bring to their task a clear understanding of the elements of different groups' heritages, lifestyles, sociopolitical experiences, and cultures that factor most directly into defining the various components of the curriculum.

Of particular relevance are cultural values and contributions, communication styles, learning styles, inter-relational patterns, levels of ethnic identity development and affiliation, and how ethnic attitudes and cultural values are encoded in and transmitted through expressive human behaviors. Knowledge of these components of culture helps curriculum designers avoid common pitfalls in dealing with diversity in schools, such as focusing on a few individuals who have achieved exceptional feats or fame, exotic rituals and ceremonies, and historical experiences to the exclusion of contemporary issues. It is also necessary to incorporate appropriate elements of cultural pluralism into all parts of formal plans for instruction (that is, goals, objectives, rationale, content, learning activities, and evaluation), and into the climates and contexts that constitute the school culture, or symbolic curriculum.

Strategies for Multiculturalizing the Curriculum

Examining the implications of every element of formal and symbolic school curricula for multicultural reform is beyond the scope of this chapter. Suffice it to say that all are susceptible, and should be affected by reform. The focus here is on those parts of the curricula that make up much of what goes on routinely and habitually in schools and classrooms, and are most fundamental in shaping the quality of learning experiences provided to students. Because they require different techniques, multiculturalizing the formal and symbolic curricula are discussed separately.

The Formal Curriculum

Various proposals have been offered for revising the official school curriculum to include ethnically, culturally, and socially pluralistic content, experiences, and perspectives. These have ranged from adding facts to existing frameworks, to introducing new courses, to replacing entire programs of study. What has been lacking in these recommendations are operational explanations for how to mesh these proposals with other curriculum mandates. For example, how does one systematically integrate ethnic contributions into the teaching of basic skills, higher-order thinking skills, and standard subjects like algebra, science, geography, family living, and industrial arts?

Curriculum designers, teachers, administrative leaders, and anyone else in the school who influences learning can accomplish this by answering four key questions within the parameters of different subjects and skills routinely taught in elementary and secondary schools. These are:

1. What do you want students to learn about ethnic and cultural pluralism?
2. Why are these learnings particularly desirable for diverse students, the various subjects and skills taught, and a culturally pluralistic society?
3. How will these learnings be facilitated and accomplished within culturally pluralistic contexts?
4. How will culturally pluralistic frameworks, techniques, and procedures be used to determine if or when the desired learnings have been accomplished?

These questions respectively address the goals/objectives, rationale, content and activities, and evaluation components of plans for instruction.

Some hypothetical situations may help illustrate how answering these questions can help educators successfully multiculturalize the formal school curriculum. Three examples are presented here:

Middle School Curriculum Reform   Suppose that middle school math teachers want their students to "apply computational skills in understanding ethnic and gender disparities in employment." This is their *goal* statement. Related objectives might include learning how to read ethnic employment statistics, working cooperatively to complete learning tasks, and becoming aware of different types of ethnic and gender discrimination in local businesses and industries. The teachers then explain that this is desirable because (1) mathematical skills are learned more thoroughly when they are connected to meaningful life experiences of students; (2) students live in a society inundated with devastating examples and effects of inequities in educational and economic opportunities by race, gender, socioeconomic, and ethnic group; and (3) learning how to apply math skills in analyzing social problems increases students' social consciousness, equips them with tools to make better decisions about social issues, and cultivates a sensitivity to the need for social change. These are parts of their *rationale*.

The teachers decide the desired learnings will be facilitated by teaching students how to use state and federal labor charts on ethnic and gender employment statistics, how to conduct surveys of local businesses to determine patterns of employment by race and gender, and how to calculate percentages, ratios, and comparison distribution charts of the types of jobs performed by different ethnic and gender groups in various businesses. These suggestions constitute the *content and activities* portions of their curriculum.

The students' understanding and mastery will be assessed by the accuracy with which they are able to plot their numerical calculations of employment distributions on a variety of charts and graphs, and extrapolate and explain the different ethnic, racial, and gender employment trends embedded in them. Thus, translating information from one form to another and interpreting it accurately replace the traditional pencil-and-paper tests used so often for *evaluation*.

Language Arts Curriculum Reform   The eighth-grade language arts teachers use a somewhat different approach to answering the key questions. In revising the literature segment, they decide to leave the general objective of having students "learn how social and political points of view are expressed through different literary forms and techniques" intact. Previously, they had used various political essays and debates as the *content* for this objective, and students spent most of their *learning activities* examining their structural elements. The teachers had justified these emphases on the basis that students needed to know the technical components of various literary genres.

They decide to create culturally pluralistic *contexts* in which the objectives are taught and learned. They modify the content to reflect their hypothesis that literary forms and techniques of social and political commentary vary by ethnic, gender and cultural groups, and by time of occurrence. The emphasis on examining different examples of commentary shifts from structure and form to substance, aesthetics, and effect. A variety of examples by ethnic and cultural groups are used to demonstrate these differences in techniques. The selections include the "sermon" for African Americans, the "debate" for European Americans, the "song" for Hispanics, "body adornment" for the youth counterculture, "protest" politics for American Indians, and "literary criticism" for women. Learning outcomes are evaluated by having students explain how the literary techniques they learned about in their case studies analyses are translated into other expressive forms, such as poetry, paintings, symbolic dress, and dramatic performance.

K–1 Curriculum Reform   The K–1 teachers choose "learning activities" and "classroom climate" for their reform efforts. They decide to culturally diversify all the experiences provided to help their students master the basic, routine skills of reading, writing, arithmetic, and social and physical development. They want to create a classroom environment that radiates pride in cultural diversity. Their list of specific reform strategies includes the following:

- Design and use multiethnic alphabets in which each letter stands for different groups, their cultures, and contributions. For example, "A" is for Asian and African Americans.
- Consistently use culturally diverse items, images, and artifacts in classroom decorations.
- Use ethnic games and folk dances to practice gross motor coordination, for recreation, and for physical education skills development.
- Always use culturally diverse books of myths, facts, fiction, and folklore to teach basic reading skills.
- Practice spelling skills with words from different ethnic and cultural traditions.
- Have culturally diverse individuals regularly facilitate story time, through personal or mediated appearances.
- Change the focus of routine seasonal activities (such as pilgrims and turkeys for Thanksgiving, jack-o-lanterns for Halloween, and snowflake cutouts for winter) to reflect ethnically diverse experiences, practices, and celebrations.
- Institute a cross-ethnic "Adopt a Grandparent Program" in which students from one ethnic group choose grandparents from a different group.
- Create a "media center" with time allotted regularly to present students with positive visual images of culturally diverse individuals and experiences.
- Have students practice writing skills using ethnic and culturally diverse issues and themes.
- Institute a ritual of celebration of diversity in which students conduct a monthly "ceremony of praise" for specific features of cultural diver-

sity, such as remembering historical people, giving thanks for how diversity enriches their daily lives, and recognizing how their peers are honoring diversity.

These three scenarios give a quick glimpse of a single segment of an entire revised curriculum. They represent how different concentrations for change can be translated into specific curriculum components. They also demonstrate the points made earlier that (1) each of the standard five components of the formal curriculum is amenable to multicultural reform; however, it is not always necessary to change all of them to be effective, and (2) changes made in the curriculum should be appropriate for the human, grade, and subject or skill contexts for which they are intended.

The Symbolic Curriculum

As is true with the formal curriculum, efforts to change the informal or symbolic curriculum to reflect more sensitivity to cultural diversity need to be target-specific. This can be best achieved by identifying its different components, and then designing change strategies specific to them.

Because the messages of the informal curriculum are embodied in and transmitted through symbols and rituals, the curriculum can be multiculturalized by revising, expanding, and even replacing them. Demonstrating how to do this for all school symbols is a mammoth task, which far exceeds the boundaries of this chapter. Therefore, only four types are developed here to illustrate the process. These are the arrangement of physical space, work habits and rituals, recognitions and awards, and institutional affiliation. Other dimensions of the symbolic curriculum which should be included in the total range of reform are rules regulating the movement of students throughout the school; protocols that surround teaching-learning interactions regarding permission to participate, paying attention, and appropriate performance and presentation styles; interactions among students during instruction and on learning tasks; and how behavior is sanctioned and rewarded.

Rules, rituals, and ceremonies are the primary conduits of the symbolic curriculum. They are to it what goals, objectives, content, and activities are to the formal curriculum. Invariably, the values and beliefs taught through these symbols are those of the Eurocentric, middle-class society. Among them are such prized American values as individuality, competition, rationality, linearity, objectivity, productivity, control, and conquest.

The arrangement of traditional school environments discourages familiarity, collaboration, group effort, and personal enjoyment in learning. The austerity of the color schemes and the relative lack of decorations in classrooms (especially in middle and secondary schools) create antiseptic environments that appear cold and uncaring. They imply formality and social distance in interpersonal interactions, attaching a certain somberness, even severity, to the learning process. Some students from culturally different groups, such as Hispanics, African Americans, American Indians, and Appalachians, find these environments distractive to learning. They prefer warmer settings that are more friendly, informal, social, communal, interactive, and animated. To accommodate these preferences, schools and classrooms can do the following:

- Change the color schemes to warmer and brighter pastel color, instead of the conventional institutional gray, beige, or green.
- Replace the standard 6-by-6-block seating arrangement with circles and small clusters of chairs.
- Close the "existential distance" between students and teachers by having teachers become more like friends and partners with students, rather than distant, authoritative directors of learning.
- Use cooperative learning as the standard structure of instruction instead of the current model of large-group, direct teaching, and competitive individualistic learning.
- Make the physical space of the school and classroom a reflection of and testimony to the value that accepts cultural diversity as a regular and prized feature of everyday life by always having visual images of diversity on display.
- Make the classroom into a participatory laboratory of learning in which students are habitually engaged in active inquiry, discovery, and application of learning instead of the current model of passive absorption of facts.

Homework and the conditions under which it is assigned are symbolic approximations of the American capitalistic work ethic—individual effort and the survival of the fittest. Homework tends to reinforce achievement distinctions between students. Those who are already doing well are more likely to do homework than those who are not. Also, many students do not have the resources to successfully complete their homework at home. Unquestionably, practice is necessary for learning for most students. But it does not necessarily have to be relegated to "homework." This component of the symbolic curriculum can be reformed by changing school schedules and mindsets to allow time and assistance during the school day for students to work together in study teams and do their "practice work." This revision has the added benefit of promoting cooperative learning and making time, space, materials, supervision, and expertise readily available to students who need them.

Awards and recognition ceremonies in school serve similar purposes for students as those in society do for adults. The implicit objective of choosing homecoming kings, queens and courts, conducting honor society initiations, granting varsity letters for athletic accomplishments, and giving perfect attendance and citizenship awards is to publicly praise and celebrate individuals who personify the institution's values and norms in exceptional ways. These rituals create folk heroes and heroines who serve as models for other students to emulate. They can be multiculturalized in two major ways.

First, the criteria used to select candidates for consideration in existing areas of recognition should be broadened to be more culturally pluralistic. For example, committees judging beauty kings and queens can include traits specific to different ethnic groups. Thus, an African American female selected to be a beauty queen would have classic African American features instead of looking like a Black imitation of European-American images. Other modifications in these standards might include not considering any slate of candidates for special recognition unless it is racially and ethnically diverse, and applying affirmative action standards to the selection of members to organizations such as the student government and extra-curricular activities.

A second way awards rituals can be multiculturalized is by creating new categories for recognition and celebration that symbolize the school's commitment to cultural pluralism. A new citizenship award might be granted to a student who models desirable ways to respect cultural diversity, such as being leaders in eliminating racial and gender biases in schools. Achievement awards could be given on the basis of exceptional mastery of significant learnings related to understanding, appreciating, and promoting cultural pluralism. These could be cultivated and acknowledged through "odyssey of the mind," academic olympiad, and scholarship bowl competitions that test students' knowledge of different ethnic groups' cultures, histories, and heritages. Service awards could be designed for students who do something noteworthy in communities and groups that are culturally different from theirs. And, in general, greater emphasis should be placed on *group achievements,* because this format is the preference of some ethnic groups in the United States.

The efforts of schools to develop institutional allegiance among students is analogous to what the larger society does to evoke feelings of corporate affinity and national loyalty. Many of these are embodied as school songs, mottos, mascots, and insignia. They parallel, in purpose and function, the national anthem, the flag, the red, white and blue colors, and the Pledge of Allegiance. The problem with these is that they may conjure up images and emotions that are either irrelevant or undesirable to some students from different ethnic, racial, social, and national origin backgrounds. Two cases in point are the reactions of some African Americans to schools whose spirit song is *Dixie,* and the responses of some American Indians to schools that use "Braves," "Indians," and "Chiefs" as mascots.

These symbols of institutional allegiance and affiliation should be revised to avoid stirring up negative historical experiences, eliminate stereotypical racial images, and include more culturally diverse perspectives and experiences. In many instances, this will mean abandoning old symbols and creating new ones which embody new value commitments to pluralism. These should include inspirational mottos, emblems, jackets and T-shirts, songs and pledges. The school's commitment to cultural pluralism as transmitted through its symbolic images will be unmistakable, and students from many diverse cultural backgrounds will wear them equally proudly because their perspectives are an integral part of the symbols.

The rituals and symbols adopted by the Carson Montessori Elementary School in Cincinnati, Ohio, to daily praise the worth of each student and demonstrate the need for students to work together illustrate how school symbols can be used to teach powerful lessons about diversity. For the 1991–92 academic year, the school adopted "RESPECT" as its guiding motto, with the added slogan, "Together We Can Make It Happen." Each letter in the motto was expanded to represent an element of respect: **R**esponsibility; **E**nvironment; **S**elf-discipline; **P**ride; **E**ffort; **C**onfidence; and **T**ruth. A song was composed, assemblies were conducted, bulletin board displays in the halls and classrooms were created, and formal lessons were taught regularly on what each letter of RESPECT represents, as well as the entire concept. Students of all ages took leadership roles in conducting these activities by planning the programs, writing and reading pertinent essays, and sharing personal experiences before the student body. Students also learned a pledge written by the principal.

▼ I Am a Special Human Being

I am a special human being

There is no one like me.

I have unique ideas that make me proud of me.

No one can challenge my originality only

Because it signifies who I am supposed to be.

Others may have questions about what makes me exceptional,

The only answer that I may give is that the Creator only

Made one of me.

And since the mold is broken I must feed

My mind to become the best that I can be!

The students at Carson sing their RESPECT song and recite their school pledge with the same regularity in classes and assemblies that they sing the national anthem and recite the Pledge of Allegiance. They also wear T-shirts, display pennants, and use folders and book covers emblazoned with their motto and pledge. A strong feeling of institutional identity, pride, and communal bonding radiates throughout this school, which is racially and culturally diverse. Even the youngest students recite their motto and pledge with vigor and conviction. This school is successfully creating visible symbols that represent its value commitment to diversity. It is institutionalizing a set of rituals for students to regularly practice this value at the same time they are learning about cultural pluralism in their academic subjects. Thus, the formal and symbolic curricula are complementary extensions of each other. This is a model well worth emulating as a way to teach multicultural education through informal or symbolic curricula.

Conclusion

Most advocates of multicultural education agree that its successful implementation in schools requires systemic and intentional change. Within the context of curriculum, or plans for instruction, this means recognizing that there are two major types of curricula operating in schools simultaneously. The formal curriculum is the officially stated plan of what students are expected to learn in various subjects or skill areas, and the tools and techniques that will be used to facilitate this learning. The symbolic curriculum is less explicit and conscious. It exists in the environment, the ecology, and the ethos of the climates we create for learning. It comprises the values that underlie the codes of behavior, social etiquette, and work ethics that students are expected to practice as they go about the process of living and learning in schools. These lessons are embodied in and transmitted through sets of rules, rituals, symbols, ceremonies, celebrations, and sanctions. Both the formal and symbolic curricula must be revised to be more culturally pluralistic, because both now tend to disproportionately reflect the experiences, perspectives, cultures, and contributions of the mainstream, Eurocentric middle class.

Efforts toward multicultural curriculum reform are more effective when they are target-specific, contextualized, developmentally appropriate, and culturally authentic. These guidelines require that curriculum designers identify the specific dimension of learning or curriculum component to be revised and ensure that the intended reform is in sync with the subject being taught, the principles of multiculturalism, and the developmental levels of students and teachers. The guidelines also require that the information included about culturally different groups is accurate, significant, and representative of a wide range of perspectives and experiences within and among them.

The ultimate challenge and purpose of multicultural curriculum reform is to demonstrate how mastery of subject matter, academic skills, and cultural pluralism can be natural complements of each other, and all can be accomplished simultaneously without doing injustice to any. This must be the goal of curriculum design if it is to play a central role in preparing students to be fully functioning and socially responsible citizens in a society and world that are increasingly ethnically, socially, racially, and culturally pluralistic.

References

Adler, M. J. (1982). *The Paideia proposal: An educational manifesto.* Englewood Cliffs, NJ: Merrill/Prentice Hall.

American Association for the Advancement of Science. (1989). *Science for all Americans.* Washington, DC: Author.

Anyon, J. (1981). Social class and the hidden curriculum at work. In H. A. Giroux, A. N. Penna, & W. F. Pinar (Eds.), *Curriculum & instruction: Alternatives in education* (pp. 317–341). Berkeley, CA: McCutchan.

Armstrong, D. C. (1989). *Developing and documenting the curriculum.* Boston: Allyn and Bacon.

Banks, J. A. (1989). Integrating the curriculum with ethnic content: Approaches and guidelines. In J. A. Banks & C. A. McGee Banks (Eds.), *Multicultural education: Issues and perspectives* (pp. 189–207). Boston: Allyn and Bacon.

Beane, J. A., Toepfer, C. F., Jr., Conrad, F., & Alessi, S. J., Jr. (1986). *Curriculum planning and development.* Boston: Allyn and Bacon.

Cushner, K., McClelland, A., & Safford, P. (1992). *Human diversity in education: An integrative approach.* New York: McGraw-Hill.

Gay, G. (1983). Multiethnic education: Historical developments and future prospects. *Phi Delta Kappan, 64,* 560–563.

Giroux, H. A., & Penna, A. N. (1981). Social education in the classroom: The dynamics of the hidden curriculum. In H. A. Giroux, A. N. Penna & W. F. Pinar (Eds.), *Curriculum & instruction: Alternatives in education* (pp. 209–230). Berkeley, CA: McCutchan.

Glatthorn, A. A. (1987). *Curriculum leadership.* Glenview, IL: Scott, Foresman.

Goodlad, J. I. (1979). *Curriculum inquiry: The study of curriculum practice.* New York: McGraw-Hill.

Jackson, P. W. (1990). *Life in classrooms.* (Reissued). New York: Teachers College, Columbia University.

Posner, G. J., & Rudnitsky, A. N. (1986). *Curriculum design: A guide to curriculum development for teachers.* New York: Longman.

Saylor, J. G., Alexander, W. M., & Lewis, A. J. (1981). *Curriculum planning.* (4th ed.). New York: Holt, Rinehart and Winston.

Sleeter, C. E., & Grant, C. A. (1988). *Making choices for multicultural education: Five approaches to race, class, and gender.* Englewood Cliffs, NJ: Merrill/Prentice Hall.

Snyder, B. R. (1971). *The hidden curriculum.* New York: Alfred A. Knopf.

Taba, H. (1962). *Curriculum development: Theory and practice.* New York: Harcourt Brace and World.

U.S. Department of Education. (1991). *America 2000: An education strategy.* Washington, DC: Author.

Zais, R. S. (1976). *Curriculum principles and foundations.* New York: Thomas Y. Crowell.

Chapter 4

◆ ◆ ◆ ◆

Instructional Pluralism: A Means to Realizing the Dream of Multicultural, Social Reconstructionist Education

Carla Cooper Shaw

Northern Illinois University

An air of anticipation pervades the school auditorium as parents, brothers and sisters, teachers, and administrators await the parting of the stage's curtain. The audience soon will witness fifth graders dramatizing original plays and reading stories they have written about American Indians. Members of the audience will be invited onstage to join a fireside tale-telling session. Student scholars will point to charts while they deliver minilectures on shifts in American Indian populations and solutions to environmental crises from an American Indian perspective. When the curtain has fallen and both students and teacher have taken their bows, audience members will exit through the lobby, where they will see American Indian-style artwork on display.

This evening's entertainment is the culmination of an interdisciplinary unit focusing on a variety of American Indian cultures, as well as on the collective American Indian experience. The whole language approach begins with the teacher reading aloud children's literature about American Indians. Students then read silently and out loud, individually and in groups. They have written original folktales, as well as stories from the points of view of American Indian characters envisioned with the help of guided imagery.

Students brainstorm conflicts that might arise between American Indians from various tribes. Using what they have learned about their systems of governance, students role play tribal councils as they resolve these conflicts.

In cooperative groups, students construct concept maps for the cultures of several American Indian tribes. Later, the class works together to merge the maps into one large web representing aspects of culture shared by these tribes. Eventually, students use this web to compare American Indian cultures with their own and to European American culture.

Students locate the territories of various American Indian tribes on the map and research the plant and animal life, topography, and climate of these regions. They take field trips to the countryside, where they practice the observational skills in which American Indians from traditional cultures excel.

Drawing on the literature they have read, students explore views of nature common to various tribes, developing concept maps or other visual representations of the American Indian's relationship with nature. They discuss how today's environment might be different if European settlers had never come to the New World and how American Indians might solve current environmental problems.

Students write and solve mathematics word problems relevant to American Indian day-to-day life, as well as problems using demographic figures related to the population of American Indians now and in the past. They devise bar graphs and pie charts, which the teacher uses to reinforce fractions. Students draw conclusions about changes in American Indian populations over time, hypothesize reasons for shifts, and make projections.

Interspersed throughout the unit are art experiences in which students use natural materials that American Indians from traditional cultures use today.

This unit exemplifies what Sleeter and Grant (1993) call Multicultural Education. It promotes equal opportunity to learn for all students, cultural pluralism, and respect for those who differ from the mainstream, and it has the potential to become Education that is Multicultural and Social Reconstructionist. Further, this unit takes a transformational approach to the integration of ethnic content into the curriculum. When implemented with similar units focusing on a variety of cultural groups, it enables students "to view concepts, issues, events, and themes from the perspectives of diverse cultural groups" (Banks & Banks, 1993) and to channel their insights into social action. This unit is praiseworthy not only for its emphasis on cultural pluralism, but also for its incorporation of *instructional* pluralism. That is, the unit displays a sensitivity to diverse learning styles and translates this sensitivity into diverse and meaningful learning experiences.

Learning style refers to the characteristics students bring to situations that influence how they learn. There are several possible dimensions to learning style. For example, students may have perceptual preferences. Auditory learners learn best when they hear instructional material, visual learners prefer material to be presented in a visual format, and tactile-kinesthetic learners learn most effectively with hands-on experiences.

Another dimension of learning style is conceptual level. Students with high conceptual levels need a minimum amount of structure in their learning experiences, while students with low conceptual levels require highly structured activities. Another dimension concerns social preferences—whether students learn best by working individually, in pairs, in small groups, or as a whole class.

No matter which dimensions the educator emphasizes, there are four central aspects of style. First, everyone has a learning style. Second, while one's learning style is amenable to change, it is relatively consistent over time. Third, no particular learning style is innately superior to another; rather, certain styles may be more or less effective in given situations. Finally, style is pervasive in that it reveals itself not only in the formal environment of school, but also in the wider context of life, from social situations to job tasks. As such, learning style serves the astute observer as a window to the personality of the individual.

Hilliard (1989) defines style as the following:

> Consistency in the behavior of a person or a group that tends to be habitual—the manifestation of a predisposition to approach things in a characteristic way. (p. 67)

While Hilliard's definition captures the essence of other conceptions of individual learning styles, it also attributes style to groups. Much as individuals have preferred ways of knowing, so do cultures. Individual learning style is to the personality of a person as cultural learning style is to the personality of a culture.

Hilliard identifies key aspects of style as it relates to culture. Culture, as opposed to nature, is an invention of humankind and thus, cultural styles are learned, not innate. They also can be unlearned—or at least, changed. Consequently, people can learn to use more than one style, or "code switch." Hilliard says "style tends to be rooted at a deep structural level and so may be manifest in a highly generalized way" (p. 67). How, then, do these roots develop, and what are their behavioral outgrowths?

The roots of learning style may lie in how children are raised and how their families function. Cohen (1969) makes a compelling case for the origin of two opposite "conceptual styles," relational and analytic, that emerge from deeply engrained socialization practices. Cohen argues that relational learners come from shared-function families in which *family* is defined to include relatives, friends, and neighbors. Group functions are shared among all members, and status roles change easily, with no one person being in power for an extended length of time. The following passage from a short story by Hunter (1973), *You Rap, I'll Reap,* illustrates a shared-function group. The narrator is Gloria, an African American teen-ager, speaking of life in her housing project.

> Take last week when old Mrs. Dawkins across the hall was late getting her check. I borrowed ten dollars toward her rent from Mrs. Stevens, the lady I work for after school. Mrs. Dawkins got the rest from Lola, the new girl my age down the hall who has a baby, and from Po Boy, the numbers writer, and Madame James, the card reader, and Pork Chop, who runs the newsstand on the corner. Then her check finally came, so on Sunday she cooked a big dinner, ham and fried chicken and yams and cornbread and greens, and invited everybody in the building who'd helped her make her rent. . . .
>
> Course, Mrs. Dawkins couldn't pay us back right away, not after buying all that food. We didn't ask her to. How could we, when she'd been so nice to us? We don't exactly keep books on each other in the projects, but it all works out somehow. Mrs. Dawkins, now, she does favors for everybody. At the party she offered to keep Lola's baby anytime she couldn't pay a sitter. And she lets *me* stay over her place anytime I want.
>
> I stayed with Mrs. Dawkins two whole months one time. My Aunt Lou and her daughters had come up from down South and had no place to go. I didn't mind giving them my room. . . . Over Mrs. Dawkins' I can do anything I want, study and read in peace and quiet or stay up all night and watch TV. (pp. 89–90)

The shared-function group in this passage operates as an extended family. Members consist of family, neighbors, and friends, who share their money and time freely with one another. Child care is no one person's exclusive responsibility, just as no one is the boss all the time. Whatever happens to one person influences everyone. "One for all and all for one" defines the pragmatic approach to life of the shared-function group and its relational members.

For relational learners at the extreme end of the continuum, learning is an intensely affective, social experience. They learn material with a human and social theme more easily, and their writing is peppered with personal references ("you," "we") to their audiences. Relational learners tend to be field dependent; they focus on the whole picture, rather than on individual parts, and the context of learning is important to them. In many instances, the affective and social preferences of relational learners help them survive in the real world, where cooperation and sensitivity to context are important. However, the relational style is at odds with the style of most schools, which tends to be analytic.[1]

Analytic learners, in contrast to relational learners, often come from families in which group functions are specialized, formally defined, and assigned to status roles. These roles, along with relationships within the family, seldom change and often are hierarchically organized. That is, authority figures remain constant over time. The formally organized group is exemplified by the prototypical, 1950s nuclear family of *Leave It to Beaver* in which Ward brings home the bacon, June cooks it, Wally tells Beaver how to eat it, and Beaver sticks it in his ear. Analytic learners tend to come from White, middle-class homes. Males, in particular, from this background are often analytic learners.

For analytic students at the far end of the continuum, learning is neither particularly affective nor social. They do not require emotional or social themes in the material they learn, and their writing often is impersonal, with the writer being referred to in the third person. Analytic learners tend to be field independent; they are able to focus on parts of the whole picture, and context is not especially important for them. They are confident about control over their environments, as they are about their intellectual problem-solving abilities. This confidence translates into an ambitious approach to learning. Alex Keaton of television's *Family Ties* caricatures the extreme analytic learner when he says, "I'm going to read these books and find out what my feelings are. And memorize them." However dissonant the analytic style may be with regard to many demands of life outside school, where cooperation and consideration of context are required, the analytic style is consonant with the style of most schools, which emphasizes individual competition.[2]

Another origin of cultural learning style may lie in the adaptation of cultures to their environments. For example, many African Americans appear to be acutely sensitive to spoken language—in terms of intonation, rhythm, inflection, connotations of words, and verbal variation. They also appear to be sensitive to nonverbal cues, or body language (Pewewardy & Huber, 1990; Shade, 1982). Such sensitivity may have developed in part out of a need to detect both overt and subtle cues—to survive—in a hostile, racist world.

Correspondingly, American Indians in traditional societies display well-honed spatial abilities and are especially observant and perceptive of the natural world (Diessner & Walker, 1986; Marashio, 1982). It is likely that such skills grew out of the need to navigate and survive in nature.

The Debate

Whatever its origins, cultural learning style, like individual learning style, predisposes people to respond in characteristic ways to certain learning situations. Learning style, then, is resonant with implications for instruction. One goal of multicultural education is to improve the achievement of all students. An obvious and logical means to fulfilling this goal would appear to be matching cultural learning styles with teaching styles. For example, because American Indians tend to excel in the spatial domain, Diessner and Walker (1986) suggest that visual formats might be used to teach material to American Indian students. In addition, many Mexican American children tend to be less competitively oriented and more cooperatively disposed than their European-American counterparts (Kagan & Madsen, 1971). It would seem logical, then, to employ cooperative learning as a dominant instructional method for them.

Advocates of matching learning style with instructional style say empirical evidence supports their argument. They believe that learning style is resistant to change, and when instruction accommodates learning style, students score significantly higher on measures of attitudes and achievement than when instruction proceeds as "business as usual" (e.g., Dunn, Beaudry, & Klavas, 1989).

Critics oppose matching students' learning styles and teachers' instructional styles. They find scant evidence to support matching, which they say might even be detrimental in some cases. Further, they believe learning styles are malleable, not static. Critics of matching argue that children can "code switch"; that they are able to adapt to the demands of a variety of learning tasks and out-of-school situations.

Questions of feasibility also arise when matching is considered. The task of deciding which dimensions to emphasize can prove overwhelming. For example, given the dimensions discussed previously, should the teacher concentrate on perceptual preferences, on conceptual level, or on social preferences—or perhaps some combination?[3]

Even after one has identified the dimensions to emphasize, practical and ethical considerations arise. When exposed to *cultural* learning styles, well meaning, prospective and experienced teachers alike often respond with exasperation: "Must I plan a different activity for each ethnic group in my class? What about the girls?" The planning of such instruction clearly demands more time than most teachers have. Newcomers to cultural learning styles continue their complaint: "And doesn't all this differentiation smack of stereotyping?"

Some educators would say yes, and indeed, there are those in the academic community who dispute the existence of learning styles specific to particular groups. They contend that uniform style does not hold within families, much less whole cultures. For these critics, learning style is strictly an individual matter, not a group matter, and variation is the rule (e.g., Dunn, Beaudry, & Klavas, 1989).

The Solution

If matching is not advisable, how are multiculturally minded teachers to use their knowledge about learning styles? And what if they do not hold with the notion of cultural learning styles? They can use their sensitivity to diverse learning styles, whether individual or cultural, to make instruction more varied. The multiculturally minded teacher, as Hilliard (1989) puts it, can make instruction "better for all," for the "traditional approaches have tended to be rigid and uncreative. They are far from exhausting the wonderful possibilities of teaching and learning" (p. 68). This is a statement with which numerous educational reformers have concurred.

The solution to the problem of rigid, uncreative teaching does not lie in strict matching. Rather, it lies in building on learning styles, as four of the five approaches to multicultural education described by Sleeter and Grant (1993) advocate, and in drawing on cultural "habits of thought":

> *Every* culture brings habits of thought . . . which have built into them vehicles that promote learning and inquiry. Accordingly, children of *any* culture can and should have curriculum and instructional practices that draw from that culture. (Jones & Fennimore, 1990, p. 16)

Building and drawing involve using one's awareness of diverse learning styles to suggest diverse learning experiences. They involve instructional pluralism, or variability. Highly effective teachers know that more than one instructional path can lead to achievement of the same objective. In other words, there is more than one way to skin a cat—as the rest of this chapter shall make clear.

Instructional pluralism consists of a variety of possible learning experiences, which grow out of the interplay between cultural learning styles and goals of Education That Is Multicultural and Social Reconstructionist.

The goals listed below represent a synthesis of the goals enumerated by Sleeter and Grant (1993) for Multicultural Education and Education That Is Multicultural and Social Reconstructionist. Listed under goals 3 and 4 are prerequisite classroom goals.

1. Promote equal opportunity to learn; improve achievement of all students, especially those from victimized groups.
2. Promote cultural pluralism.
3. Promote respect for those who differ.

   a. Help students develop positive attitudes toward people who differ from them; encourage the reduction of prejudice.

   b. Develop perspective-taking skills.

   c. Aid the development of empathy.
4. Prepare citizens to work actively toward social structural equality.

   a. Develop attitudes and skills necessary for personal and group empowerment.

      b. Facilitate the growth of a propensity for social action.

      c. Develop critical thinking skills.

Following are discussions of instruction based on the interaction of learning style characteristics and goals of Education That Is Multicultural and Social Reconstructionist. The discussions illustrate how teachers can plan instruction with their educational goals as well as students' learning styles in mind. The following examples include general approaches, such as interdisciplinary teaching; broad methods, such as cooperative learning; specific methods, such as guided imagery; and particular strategies, such as using the concrete as a vehicle to the abstract.

Cooperative Learning

Recommended by Sleeter and Grant (1993) as a key instructional practice of Education That is Multicultural and Reconstructionist, cooperative learning is in tune with the affective orientation and social, cooperative preferences of students from shared-function families. Such applicability is especially apparent among American Indian students. As members both of extended families and of a culture that values harmony with self, others, and nature, American Indian children are already advanced in the social skills of getting along with others, taking turns, and sharing—and so, are predisposed to benefit from cooperative learning (Soldier, 1989).

Of 68 studies reviewed by Slavin (1990), 49 showed positive effects in terms of academic achievement for the groups involved in cooperative learning. In five studies investigating cooperative learning's effectiveness, Black students and students with learning and physical disabilities outperformed both their control counterparts and White, high-achieving, and nondisabled treatment students. The studies were conducted at elementary and middle school levels.

Cooperative learning also has been shown to improve ethnic relations. Students in grades 2–8 in schools with non-White populations ranging from 13 percent to 61 percent (who were involved in cooperative learning for 10–12 weeks) gained more in interracial friendships than did control students. As one of these studies found, gains persisted into the following year when treatment students indicated that about 38 percent of their friendship choices were from outside their race compared with 10 percent for the control students.

In another study, more cross-racial interaction during free time was observed among students in cooperative classes than among those in individualized classes. Other researchers found that cooperative learning with teams composed of White, Black, and Hispanic students resulted in fewer teacher reports of interethnic conflict.[4]

The potential uses of cooperative learning are many. Kagan (1989–90) outlines 14 structures, each with its own academic and social functions. Among the most promising for multicultural education are activities called Jigsaw, Team World Webbing, the Three-Step Interview, and Numbered Heads Together.

After being assigned a topic for Jigsaw, students in "home" groups number off and then convene with students having the same numbers. In numbered groups, students learn about an aspect of the topic, either from teacher-supplied materials or by conducting research. Once back in their home groups, students teach their expert knowledge to their team members. For example, in science, when studying fish, numbered groups might study the characteristics of various classes of fish and collect examples of these. In social studies, numbered groups might study different aspects of a particular country, such as demographics, religion, natural resources, and commerce. As an interdisciplinary variation on this activity, the teacher might direct numbered groups to investigate a particular culture's approaches to science and mathematics and contributions to art and music.

This activity would attain interdisciplinary status by segueing into Team Word Webbing. In this activity, students create schemas, or concept maps, showing different aspects of a topic and their relationships to one another. In the previous example, numbered groups would devise schemata for science, math, art, and music, and then home groups would attempt to connect the four maps into one large schema representing the culture as a whole.

Team Word Webbing might operate on a less grand scale as well with topics as concrete as "animals" or as abstract as "prejudice." In numbered groups, students might develop individual schemata and then synthesize them into one in their home groups, or they might all work together from the outset. Teachers might use Team Word Webbing at the beginning of a unit to ascertain what students already know about a topic, then build on it. They also might use the webbing to conclude a unit by reinforcing students' knowledge of a topic's components and how they fit together. More on schema construction as an instructional response will follow.

Three-Step Interview provides a structure for sharing personal information related to stimulus material, such as hypotheses and responses to stories, poems, and provocative newspaper articles. Within groups, students interview each other in pairs and then share with the group information gleaned from the interviews. The teacher might enhance the potential for instructional pluralism by encouraging students with different learning styles to interview each other.

The Numbered Heads Together framework provides a cooperative structure for recitation, which usually is driven by competition among students. After learning material, either in groups or as a whole class, students number off within teams. The teacher asks a question and instructs teams to put their heads together to come up with an answer. The teacher then calls a number and students with that number may raise their hands. A student is chosen and if the response is incorrect, the teacher calls on a student from another group whose hand was raised.

In addition to surrounding the often dull practice of drill with a gamelike, motivating atmosphere, Numbered Heads Together provides for competition within a context of cooperation. To the extent that both competition and cooperation are necessary for success in school and in life, this combination of learning styles should benefit both relational/field dependent and analytic/field independent learners.

Using the Concrete as a Vehicle to the Abstract

Using the concrete as a vehicle to the abstract in the classroom helps relational learners, who tend to think concretely. The teacher first finds something with which students are familiar, then links this to new, potentially difficult, abstract material, referring back to the familiar when necessary. Teachers can use the concrete ("your family") as an example of an abstract concept ("interdependence"). Or a concrete analogy may be used to explain abstract material, as in Gen. Schwarzkopf's comparing the Gulf War military strategy to strategy used in football. Similarly, the teacher of science or health might explain the body's use of nutrients by referring to an automobile's use of fuel.

In the film *Stand and Deliver,* Jaime Escalante uses the concrete as a vehicle to the abstract to dramatic effect. Explaining the concept of negative numbers, he exhorts Angel, who, like most of his classmates, is Latino and lives near the ocean, to think of the space left on the beach from scooping out sand as analogous to negative numbers. By filling in the space, the beach becomes level again, which is like zero. Escalante further explains that zero is a concept first conceived by their ancestors, the Mayans.

The rest of the lesson is noteworthy for Escalante's rapid-fire variability. After his interaction with Angel, he leads the class in a spirited chanting of "A negative times a negative equals a positive." Satisfied that they have memorized the rule, he abruptly asks, "Why?" In the space of a few minutes, Escalante takes his students from a concrete analogy to an abstract notion to concrete memorization and back to the abstract.

Relevance

Relevance involves relating material to be learned to something from students' lives, something in which they are interested. Literature is replete with opportunities for injecting relevance. For example, as an introduction to *Romeo and Juliet,* the teacher of students living in neighborhoods where gangs are prevalent might ask students to relate the gang life in their area to that in the films *West Side Story* or *Grease.* With such an emphasis on relevance to their lives, students would be more motivated to tackle *Romeo and Juliet.*

As a preamble to reading *The Secret Garden,* the teacher might ask students if they have their own special places where they can escape to be alone and daydream. "What is it like?" "If you could have any kind of special place, what would it be?" The teacher then might entice students to read by informing them that the book they are preparing to read is about a girl and her special place.

Sometimes tapping the relevance of a subject involves grasping the "teachable moment." For example, as soon as a tornado warning has been lifted, the teacher might take advantage of students' curiosity by teaching about tornadoes then and there, or at least taking time to discuss their observations and feelings. In science class, the teacher might seize the burning out of a fluorescent tube as an opportunity to teach about electricity.

There are numerous instructional opportunities for making math and science relevant to students' lives and cultures. For instance, *Applied Mathematics* (Center for Occupational Research and Development, 1988), a series of workbooks and videotapes used in rural Illinois, presents students with problems from the farmer's world. In St. Paul, Minnesota, Henke (1992), a math teacher of multicultural classes, reinforces math skills by drawing on students' cultural heritages. For example, after reading about Benjamin Banneker, an African American who was one of two surveyors of Washington, D.C., in the late 1700s, students use their protractors to draw property lots according to specifications. In another instance, students learn of the original purposes of the Great Wall of China and how it was constructed and then compute the area of a cross section of the wall.

In science, students at Wound School in South Dakota learn that American Indians used ingredients now found in more than 200 modern medicines and that the origin of the science of ecology lies in American Indian cultures. After studying Black astronauts, students at Malcom X Academy in Chicago delve into African American ancestry by discussing the means by which slave ships were powered and the physiological effects of lying chained in the bottom of slave ships for extended periods of time (Ross-Flanigan, 1992).

Of particular relevance to multicultural education is the use of statistics regarding the changing population and poverty demographics of the United States. Students might solve problems using figures from *Statistical Abstracts* related to the current and projected ethnic and socioeconomic composition of the country, as well as constructing bar graphs and pie charts and writing their own word problems.

Simulations

Simulations often incorporate perspective-taking and empathy exercises, cooperative learning, and using the concrete as a vehicle to the abstract, and they draw on virtually all cultural learning style characteristics. Simulations take complex situations and systems from the real world, such as cross-cultural communication and urban planning, in which students make realistic, well-informed decisions, often in collaboration with others. As such, the simulation epitomizes the hands-on learning experience with all its motivational appeal. Simulations may take the form of role playing or board games or a combination; they also may be computerized.

Simulations often, but not always, involve group decision making. In one particularly innovative simulation, *Sound Foundations,* students with learning disabilities develop math skills as they act as managers of rock bands over the course of the year. There are daily quizzes, and each band must achieve 10 "milestones," including Formation, Equipment Purchase, Recording Contract, and Concert Publicity. Of the students involved in the first year of *Sound Foundations,* 92 percent of the group passed the New York Regents Competency Exam, compared with 20 percent of a similarly composed group the previous year with traditional instruction (Gerver & Sgroi, 1983).

Many commercially packaged simulations are on the market, but with a little imagination, a creative teacher can customize simulation experiences to the curriculum. For example, students learning computer programming might simulate the functioning of a computer as they role play parts of the computer. As the Central Processing Unit follows on foot each line of a program written on butcher paper and placed on the floor, he or she does the following: directs Output to write the appropriate output on the chalkboard, indicates to the User when it is time for input, instructs Memory to write values for variables on index cards and place them in the correct memory boxes. In addition to reinforcing programming skills, this simulation draws on tactile-kinesthetic learning styles.

In studying the nature and effects of prejudice, students might engage in a short version of the well-known simulation, *Brown Eyes-Blue Eyes,* in which students are divided into two groups according to eye color or some other physical characteristic. The first day, one group is discriminated against by being ignored, subjected to inferior treatment, and having its privileges arbitrarily suspended. The next day, the roles are reversed. During the ensuing debriefing session, which is of crucial importance given the intensely emotional nature of the simulation, students discuss the injustice of discrimination, how they felt as both victims and victimizers, and steps they might take in their own lives and in society to minimize discrimination.

Literature provides ample opportunity for students to identify with the lives of characters through simulation experiences. For example, after reading *Island of the Blue Dolphins,* a novel in which children live on an island, students from the Texas School for the Deaf took a field trip to an area lake. Working in cooperative groups, students explored the area and used the survival skills they had read about to locate a site for a shelter, collect samples of materials to use in building the shelter, and devise means for getting water and food. Students presented their plans to the teachers in charge, who evaluated them according to criteria that teachers and students had agreed upon beforehand.

Guided Imagery

As a teaching tool, guided imagery derives from theories relating the role of the subconscious to learning and creative thinking. By tapping visual and right hemispheric dimensions of thinking, guided imagery exercises help students focus in imaginative ways on upcoming tasks. Following is an example of such an exercise.

In a soothing voice, a teacher tells the students to get comfortable, close their eyes, become aware of the rhythm of their breathing, and relax their bodies from their toes to their facial muscles. She then invites students to visualize themselves waking up to a morning 20 years in the future. She asks them to imagine how they will look and how they will feel as they read the headlines on their Compu-view news screen. She tells them they are members of a special presidential task force that will decide who will travel on the Space Ship Save to a space station, gleaming silver and silent in the far reaches of space, to form a new society. She asks students to envision the society they will create and the kinds of people they will select to be the pioneers. The teacher instructs students to gradually and slowly return to this time and this place, but to remember their thoughts and their feelings on that day in the future.

On mentally returning to the classroom, students envision a future society, creating travelers on the Space Ship Save and pioneers of the new world and justifying their decisions in light of the ideal, multicultural societies they imagine. It is likely that these students will engage in more lively discussions and come up with more original and elaborate ideas than students who are asked simply to describe future societies.

There are two types of guided imagery of interest to the classroom teacher, cognitive and affective. Two examples of guided cognitive imagery follow.

- The teacher of reading and social studies takes his students on mental journeys into the past or the future and to distant places. He includes many sensory details to help students remember factual information and obtain a feel for the times and places in which reading selections and periods of history are set.

- As an introduction to the circulatory system, the teacher "shrinks" students to microscopic proportions. Students travel in a tiny submarine through veins and arteries and in and out of the heart, as the teacher describes what the travelers see, hear and feel.

In contrast to cognitive imagery, which focuses on fairly specific aspects of academic performance, guided affective imagery seeks to influence more general attitudes and behaviors.

- Galyean (1983) describes a study in which students, who ranked in the lowest 25th percentile in reading ability and were involved in gang activities, meditated for five minutes at the beginning of each Spanish class for four months. They visualized themselves being bathed in warm light on top of a beautiful mountain and saw themselves doing everything well. Results indicated a substantial decrease in disruptive behavior and an increase in Spanish language skills.

- Before reading *The Secret Garden,* students might take mental journeys to their secret places, visualizing their hideaways in elaborate detail and summoning their feelings while there. In addition to using this guided imagery to relate *The Secret Garden* to students' own imaginative experience, the teacher might take students on return trips to their secret places anytime they seem to be under stress, much as the Spanish class students found respite by visualizing themselves on mountaintops.

Perspective-Taking/Empathy Exercises

Perspective-taking and empathy exercises help develop in students a crucial trait of the multicultural sensibility—flexibility of perspective. Children low in prejudice show sensitivity and openness to other points of view and are able to think critically. Research suggests that activities and materials with a strong affective component that invite children to enter vicariously into the lives of people of different ethnic groups help develop this flexibility of perspective (Byrnes, 1988). Once students begin to feel empathy, they are well on their way toward respecting diverse points of view, thereby becoming less prejudiced and self-centered in their organization of experience.

Literature, especially multicultural children's literature, films, and creative writing all provide potent possibilities for emotional identification with characters of diverse cultural groups. Potential for the growth of empathy and flexibility of perspective is embedded in several instructional responses, such as simulations and guided imagery. Cooperative learning, by its very nature, depends on the contributions of members who are heterogeneously grouped. More particularly, cooperative learning structures that promote sharing of personal responses, such as the Three-Step Interview, are especially conducive to the growth of respect for other points of views. Using the Jigsaw structure, the teacher might instruct students in the home groups to assume different perspectives on a particular issue or event, such as American Indians' fishing rights in Wisconsin. In their numbered groups, students flesh out their positions for presentation in their home groups, where they attempt to reconcile their diverse points of view.

Similarly, debates might serve as opportunities for perspective-taking. Not only should students develop their positions on issues, they also should argue positions that diverge from their own. Debates can take place in virtually all subject areas—from such issues as capital punishment and affirmative action in social studies to genetic engineering and national health plans in science.

If students are to attain true flexibility of perspective—which is a habit of mind, rather than an occasional performance of mental acrobatics—perspective and empathy exercises should be woven throughout the curriculum. In social studies, the teacher routinely might ask students to consider the points of view of various players in history. For example, in studying the Westward Expansion (or the Invasion from the East), students might write journals from the perspectives not only of male settlers and White cowboys, but also of Black cowboys, women both in towns and on farms and ranches, male, female, and juvenile American Indians and Mexicans.

Perspective-taking exercises need not always be used in reference to cultural groups or individual people. In math, the teacher might encourage students to assume different physical points of view by asking, "How would a sphere look if you were inside it?" In science, in lieu of the guided imagery exercise described previously, the teacher simply might ask students to imagine how blood vessels would look from the points of view of passengers in a tiny submarine traveling through the circulatory system. Or the teacher might instruct students to take the roles of electrons, protons, and neutrons and describe and act out the activity inside an atom. In addition to reinforcing the skill of perspective-taking, these brief exercises in math and science draw on tactile-kinesthetic learning styles.

Schema Construction

Everyone has schemata, or internal representations of knowledge. One way students and teachers can externalize schemata is through concept maps, which are visual, nonlinear depictions of the aspects of a topic and their relationships to one another.

Teachers can use completed concept maps to visually present complex, interrelated, and potentially difficult material. When used in this way, schemata enhance student understanding. However, the true value of schemata as teaching tools in the classroom lies in students actively constructing them and in building on what they already know.

The uses of schemata are limited only by the imagination of the teacher and students. To introduce students to schema construction, the teacher might select a current event or other topic familiar to students and model the process. Students are then asked to brainstorm aspects of the topic and then decide on the most important ones. On the chalkboard, the teacher visually arranges these aspects, encouraging students to discuss, debate, and justify their placement of important aspects and the means of showing relationships among them.

Once familiar with the process, students are ready to construct schemata. Following are several suggestions.

- As homework, students might construct schemata to show understanding of reading assignments.

- Before teacher presentations and other relatively passive activities aimed at the acquisition of information, the teacher might provide students with skeletal schemata as advance organizers, with only the most general and inclusive aspects filled in. As the teacher presentation progresses, students add more specific features.

- To analyze current events, students might construct schemata showing cause-and-effect relationships. These connections might extend beyond the past and present into predictions about future, related events. Using schema construction in this way enables students to arrive at an understanding of the global consequences of seemingly localized events, such as the effect of South African apartheid on world business. Students might use the understanding gleaned from these schemata to deliberate solutions to the problems posed by current events and to communicate their insights to people in power.

- To stimulate analogical thinking, the teacher might derive partial analogies from already constructed schemata for students to complete and encourage students to devise their own analogies. Examples from a hierarchical schema showing classes of animals include: *dog : mammal :: crocodile : reptile* and *member : group :: human : mammal*.

- As discussed previously for cooperative learning, students might use the structure of Team Word Webbing to construct group schemata.

- Instead of constructing schemata on paper, students might develop *physical* concept maps. After writing aspects of a topic on cards to which magnetic tape has been attached, students might construct schemata by arranging and rearranging the cards on a magnetized surface, such as a chalkboard or a filing cabinet. Using another variation, students themselves, with the appropriate labels attached, might represent aspects of a topic by physically arranging themselves in relationship to one another, using yarn to show the connections.

Many of the cognitive benefits accruing to students from schema construction, or concept mapping, depend on particular classroom applications. However, there are two pervasive advantages. One is the transformation of unwieldy masses of information into connected sets of knowledge. The other advantage is the "aha!" perception of relationships, which might not be as apparent in less visual representations. Students with relational learning styles may be especially inclined to grasp such relationships through the use of schemata.

Other cognitive advantages in using schema construction include the following:

- Drawing on visual and nonlinear styles of learning and encouraging their development.
- Building on tactile-kinesthetic preferences in the case of physical schemata.
- Building on the facility of field dependent learners at perceiving whole entities and constructing meaning within contexts.
- Facilitating the organization of knowledge, which leads to improved retention, accessibility and retrievability of information for problem solving.
- Prompting students to analyze their organization of knowledge and so, to think about their own thinking. By thinking metacognitively, students become more capable critical thinkers in all subject areas.

The multicultural teacher, too, stands to benefit from schema construction. It is probable that students from diverse cultural and socioeconomic groups possess qualitatively different internal schemata (Reynolds, Taylor, Steffensen, Shirey, & Anderson, 1982). By encouraging students to externalize these representations before instruction, the teacher can accumulate a wealth of information about her students' backgrounds. This information can be especially useful if the teacher's culture differs from that of her students. Thoughtful interpretation of these data can provide the teacher with direction in planning instruction.

In a similar vein, the teacher can use these early schemata to gain insight into students' initial conceptions of material to be covered. When detecting faulty connections, the teacher can parlay his insights into diagnostic tools. However, the teacher should exercise caution in labeling such connections as erroneous, for they may reflect cultural practices and world views different from his. Hence, students may draw on their internal stores of information to make inferences that don't match the teacher's, but are still "correct" in terms of their own cultural backgrounds (Smith, 1982).

Interdisciplinary Teaching

Interdisciplinary learning and teaching represent the full flowering of instructional pluralism, especially for relational learners. The term *relational* implies an ability to readily perceive connections between and among dissimilar bodies of knowledge. But this is not necessarily the case. Relational learners could more aptly be called "holistic" learners, for they tend to focus on global characteristics rather than parts, and they have self-centered orientations to topics. On tests of sorting ability, relational learners usually are able to come up with only one means of classifying items (Cohen, 1969). Without instructional intervention, their initial perceptions are likely to become lasting and resistant to transfer to other areas.

Interdisciplinary teaching is a viable approach to improving the chances for transfer from one academic task to another, from subject to subject, and from school to outside life. In constructing many connections among subjects, students are more likely to touch upon topics of relevance to them.

Possibilities for interdisciplinary learning are contained in several of the instructional responses suggested in this chapter. Schema construction and certain cooperative learning structures, such as the Jigsaw and Team Word Webbing activities, can help students make connections between disciplines. Further, using concrete analogies to make abstract concepts more easily understood facilitates the perception of relationships between dissimilar subject areas.

A teacher or team of teachers might incorporate these instructional responses into full-blown interdisciplinary units. Examples of such incorporation include the following:

- Four subject areas converge to provide students with a multifaceted understanding of stars. In social studies, students learn of various cultures' beliefs about the heavenly bodies, while they read related myths and legends and write their own in language arts. In science, students construct sun dials, study the life of a star, and discuss how this life cycle might be represented in myths they have read and written. Finally, students learn the mathematics of rudimentary astronomy (adapted from Baker, Cross, Mills, & Rogers, 1991).

- Students master the scientific method through the combination of science and language arts. They read detective fiction, write endings to incomplete mysteries, compose original stories, play board games such as *Clue* and *221B Baker Street* and computerized games such as those in the *Carmen Sandiego* series, and participate in detective simulations. In tandem with these activities, students conduct scientific experiments designed to highlight the scientific method. Throughout the unit, students are encouraged to note similarities in the thinking of detectives and scientists.

The first unit focuses primarily on the relationships among the content of different subjects, while the second focuses on process. Ideally, interdisciplinary units emphasize both, as in the unit described at the beginning of this chapter. This unit, centering on individual American Indian cultures and American Indian culture as a whole, represents the intersection of two areas—*content* of social studies and *processes* of social studies, reading and writing, science, math, and art—with the skill of perspective-taking woven throughout. A collection of this and similar units focusing on a variety of cultural groups might attain the status of Education That Is Multicultural and Social Reconstructionist by encouraging students to apply their new understandings to functioning in multicultural communities.

The Place of Instructional Pluralism in Elementary and Middle School Programs

If during the discussion of instructional responses, readers have heard some new ideas, thought about the corollaries of some responses (e.g., individualized instruction for cooperative learning, outlines for schemata), and best of all, generated ideas of their own—then they have gotten the chapter's message, and they possess a frame of mind crucial to the multicultural teacher.

This chapter's message is instructional pluralism—or sensitivity to multiple learning styles and consequent variability of instruction. The teacher's personal style of delivery should be varied and animated, but instructional pluralism also must encompass classroom activities and the entire curriculum.

The willingness to embrace variability entails a certain frame of mind—which is heuristic, rather than prescriptive in nature—on the part of teachers. Multicultural teachers are creative people who consider the interaction of their students' learning styles and needs, their teaching styles, the demands of the subject matter, and the goals of Education That Is Multicultural and Social Reconstructionist when planning instruction. They also are cognizant of their own learning styles and use their awareness to avoid one-dimensional instruction and favoritism toward students of the same style. Multicultural teachers do not feel compelled to ignore differences to avoid stereotyping; they see not only unity in diversity, but also diversity in unity.

Multicultural teachers think schematically—with one idea generating another, which generates yet another. They also think in a more linear, logical fashion in organizing instruction so as to achieve tangible outcomes. They possess expertise in instructional implementation, which includes selecting and planning both traditional and alternative learning experiences, dealing with logistics, stepping in and out of various teaching roles, evaluating student learning, and effecting good classroom management.

Implementation of instructional pluralism in its entirety should pose no problems in elementary, self-contained classrooms. Interdisciplinary teaching, however, may prove to be more involved in middle schools, necessitating more flexibility than is customary in scheduling instructional blocks of time and teachers' planning periods. When flexibility is not possible, teachers of diverse subjects need to confer with one another, for they can still point out connections or help their students discover them.

Instructional pluralism is feasible in the nation's classrooms. It does not require massive restructuring of the current system. Rather, it requires a willingness to embrace variability, together with a frame of mind that is creative and logical, by turns.

Proponents of special education for the gifted believe that talented youth should receive instruction that is different from the regular fare. It should be more varied, and it should require higher levels of thinking and more active student involvement. No doubt these educators are right, but all students, gifted or not, need varied instruction. A change in the definition and practice of "regular" instruction is imperative if all learners are to succeed.

By setting instructional pluralism into motion, we not only come closer to "exhausting the wonderful possibilities of teaching and learning" (Hilliard, 1989) but we also build and draw on various learning styles and provide *all* students with an equal opportunity to learn. In educating our students to be adept in diverse ways of knowing, we prepare them to code switch—to function multiculturally, as situations require, in a pluralistic society they will help to construct. Cultural pluralism demands instructional pluralism.

Notes

1. For discussions of relational style, see Cohen (1969); Anderson (1988a); Cooper (1980).

2. For discussions of analytic style, see Cohen (1969); Anderson (1988a); Cooper (1980).

3. For critiques of matching learning styles and teaching styles, see Doyle and Rutherford (1984); Hilliard (1989); Hyman and Rosoff (1984); Davidman (1981).

4. For research on the effects of cooperative learning at improving ethnic relations, see Johnson and Johnson (1981); Slavin (1977); Slavin (1979); and Weigel, Wiser, and Cook (1975).

References

Anderson, J. A. (1988a). Cognitive styles and multicultural populations. *Journal of Teacher Education, 39*(1), 2–9.

Anderson, J. A. (1988b). *Enhancing the academic productivity of minority students by increasing the multicultural competency of teachers.* Paper presented at the annual meeting of the Association of Teacher Educators, San Diego, CA.

Baker, J., Cross, J., Mills, O. F., & Rogers, M. (1991). *An interdisciplinary study of the stars.* Presentation conducted for CISE 533, Northern Illinois University, DeKalb, IL.

Banks, J. A., & Banks, C. A. M. (1993). *Multicultural education: Issues and perspectives* (2nd ed.). Boston: Allyn and Bacon.

Boykin, A. W. (1979). Psychological/behavioral verve: Some theoretical explorations and empirical manifestations. In A. W. Boykin, A. J. Franklin, & J. F. Yates (Eds.),

Research directions of Black psychologists (pp. 351–367). New York: Russell Sage Foundation.

Byrnes, D. A. (1988). Children and prejudice. *Social Education, 52,* 267–271.

Center for Occupational Research and Development. (1988). *Applied mathematics, Unit 15: Using formulas to solve problems.* Waco, TX: Author.

Cohen, R. A. (1969). Conceptual styles, culture conflict, and nonverbal tests of intelligence. *American Anthropologist, 71,* 828–856.

Cooper, G. C. (1980). Everyone does not think alike. *English Journal, 69*(4), 45–50.

Davidman, L. (1981). Learning style: The myth, the panacea, the wisdom. *Phi Delta Kappan, 62,* 641–645.

Diessner, R., & Walker, J. L. (1986). A cognitive view of the Yakima Indian student. *Journal of American Indian Education, 25*(2), 39–43.

Doyle, W., & Rutherford, B. (1984). Classroom research on matching learning and teaching styles. *Theory Into Practice, 23,* 20–25.

Dunn, R., Beaudry, J. S., & Klavas, A. (1989). Survey of research on learning styles. *Educational Leadership, 46*(6), 50–58.

Galyean, B. (1983). Guided imagery in the classroom. *Educational Leadership, 40*(6), 54–58.

Gerver, R., & Sgroi, R. (1983). Sound foundations: Math motivation through rock 'n' roll. *Curriculum Review, 22,* 65–68.

Gitter, A. G., Black, H., & Mostofsy, D. (1972). Race and sex in the perception of emotion. *Journal of Social Issues, 28,* 63–78.

Henke, M. E. (1992). We all count. Paper presented at the annual meeting of the National Association of Multicultural Education, Orlando.

Hilliard, A. S. III (1976). *Alternatives to IQ testing: An approach to the identification of gifted minority children.* Sacramento, CA: California State Department of Education.

Hilliard, A. S. III (1989). Teachers and cultural styles in a pluralistic society. *NEA Today, 7*(6), 65–69.

Hunter, K. (1973). *Guests in the promised land.* New York: Charles Scribner's Sons.

Hyman, R., & Rosoff, B. (1974). Matching learning and teaching styles: The jug and what's in it. *Theory Into Practice, 23,* 35–43.

Johnson, D. W., & Johnson, R. T. (1981). Effects of cooperative and individualistic learning experiences on interethnic interaction. *Journal of Educational Psychology, 73,* 444–449.

Jones, B. F., & Fennimore, T. F. (1990). *Restructuring to promote learning in America's schools. The new definition of learning: The first step for school reform. Guidebook.* Alexandria, VA: Public Broadcasting System; Elmhurst, IL: North Central Regional Educational Laboratory.

Kagan, S. (1989–90). The structural approach to cooperative learning. *Educational Leadership, 47*(4), 12–15.

Kagan, S., & Madsen, M. C. (1971). Cooperation and competition of Mexican, Mexican American, and Anglo American children of two ages under four instruction sets. *Developmental Psychology, 5,* 32–39.

Marashio, P. (1982). Enlighten my mind . . . : Examining the learning process through Native Americans' ways. *Journal of American Indian Education, 21*(2), 2–10.

Matthews, B. (1977). Voices of Africa in the Diaspora. *New Directions, 4,* 16–19.

Perney, V. H. (1976). Effects of race and sex on field dependence-independence in children. *Perceptual and Motor Skills, 42,* 975–980.

Pewewardy, C., & Huber, T. (1990). *Maximizing learning for all students: A review of literature on learning modalities, cognitive styles and approaches to meeting the needs of diverse learners.* Paper presented at the annual meeting of the Association of Teacher Educators, Las Vegas.

Ramirez, M. III, & Price-Williams, D. R. (1974). Cognitive styles of children of three ethnic groups in the United States. *Journal of Cross-Cultural Psychology, 5,* 212–219.

Ramirez, M. III & Price-Williams, D. R. (1976). Achievement motivation in children of three ethnic groups in the United States. *Journal of Cross-Cultural Psychology, 7,* 49–60.

Reynolds, R. E., Taylor, M. A., Steffensen, M. S., Shirey, L. I., & Anderson, R. C. (1982). Cultural schemata and reading comprehension. *Reading Research Quarterly, 17,* 353–366.

Ross-Flanigan, N. (1992, March 15). Educators mix science, cultural themes. *Chicago Tribune,* sec. 5, p. 3.

Shade, B. J. (1982). Afro-American cognitive style: A variable in school success? *Review of Educational Research, 52,* 219–244.

Slavin, R. E. (1977). *Student team learning techniques: Narrowing the achievement gap between the races* (Report No. 228). Baltimore: Johns Hopkins University, Center for Social Organization of Schools.

Slavin, R. E. (1979). Effects of biracial learning teams on cross-racial friendships. *Journal of Educational Psychology, 71,* 381–387.

Slavin, R. E. (1990). *Cooperative learning: Theory, research, and practice.* Englewood Cliffs, NJ: Prentice Hall.

Sleeter, C. E., & Grant, C. A. (1993). *Making choices for multicultural education: Five approaches to race, class, and gender* (2nd ed.). Englewood Cliffs, NJ: Merrill/Prentice Hall.

Smith, M. R. (1982). Science for the Native oriented classroom. *Journal of American Indian Education, 21*(3), 13–17.

Soldier, L. L. (1989). Cooperative learning and the Native American student. *Phi Delta Kappan, 71,* 161–163.

Weigel, R. H., Wiser, P. L., & Cook, S. W. (1975). Impact of cooperative learning experiences on cross-ethnic relations and attitudes. *Journal of Social Issues, 31*(1), 219–245.

White, J. (1970). Guidelines for Black psychologists. *The Black Scholar, 1*(5), 52–57.

Young, V. H. (1974). A Black American socialization pattern. *American Ethnologist, 1,* 405–413.

Chapter 5

◆ ◆ ◆ ◆

Assessment as a
Way of Knowing Children

Mary Catherine Ellwein

University of Virginia

M. Elizabeth Graue

University of Wisconsin-Madison

Introduction

> You will have 15 minutes to complete this portion of the test. Use a No. 2 pencil to answer each question by filling in the bubble next to your choice. Keep your eyes on the page and stay in your seat. Raise your hand if you have a question. Do not get up. When you come to the word *stop*, put your pencil down, close your test booklet, and cover your answer sheet.

Sound familiar? You probably have been asked to follow such directions, and you may someday be asked to give them to your students. But for what purpose? And with what consequences? Experience tells us that tests are used to measure what students know about a particular subject. By figuring the number of correct answers, we determine what and how well a student has achieved. This information is then used to assign a grade, flunk a student, or refer someone for special help. We believe this practice is simplistic and too shallow to meet the challenges of diversity and change. This chapter is designed to encourage you to question the assumptions behind conventional teach-learn-test models and ask new and harder questions about how we know students.

Unlike the stereotypical view, the act of teaching is more than merely delivering information to generic students. To be most effective, teachers must also gather data about their students so they know what and how to teach. Traditionally, this has been one purpose of testing. In this chapter, we propose a more inclusive approach to information gathering. We suggest a move beyond the use of static measures (e.g., tests) to an integrated and dynamic activity that can be thought of as a way to know children. Conceiving of assessment as a learning activity can help teachers make the necessary instructional changes that facilitate learning and transformation in all students. Assessment becomes an integral part of classroom life, inseparable from day-to-day teaching and learning.

A multicultural and social reconstructionist approach to assessment attempts to redefine the historical, social and cultural contexts in which children are defined in schools. Traditional psychometric perspectives take assessment as a rational and scientific process based on identifiable characteristics. But new visions of assessment perceive assessment as a social and political act that is essentially interpretive. At its core is motivation to engage all participants in the act of knowing children so that teaching serves all learners.

This chapter is about making the transition from a technological and fragmented way of knowing students to one that is interpretive and contextual. Before making that shift, however, it is important to understand the circumstances that make the transition necessary in the first place. First, we explore the historical and social contexts that led to the traditional place of testing in schools and teacher education.

Historical View of Testing in the United States

The reasons given for testing, the forms it has taken, and the consequences attached to tests have changed over time as the political winds that shape schools have shifted. Since the turn of the century, three historical themes have structured testing practice and focus in the schools: efficiency, equity, and excellence (Linn, 1986). We explore these three themes briefly to highlight how public attention to schools shapes the testing enterprise.

Efficiency

A population explosion in the early 20th century and enactment of child labor laws prompted a crisis for public schools: More children were enrolling earlier and staying longer (Linn, 1986; Wiggins, 1989). Educators sought efficient ways to meet the needs of an increasingly diverse student population. The tracking system developed, with students placed in college preparation, general, or vocational tracks on the basis of test results (Oakes, 1985). Motivated to group students of like ability, educators viewed tests as a more "fair" and scientific way to manage this sorting process than relying on privileges of birth (i.e., favoring children from families of higher social status). The psychology of individual differences took root and the resulting testing technology enabled schools to group students with like abilities through the use of intelligence tests (Resnick, 1982).

Equity

In response to calls in the 1960s for more equitable distribution of educational resources and experiences, the federal government provided millions of dollars on special programs and materials for the "disadvantaged" (Haney & Madaus, 1989). Among these programs were Head Start, Follow Through, Title I, and special education placements such as those for learning disabilities. Testing was used for two purposes. The first was to determine who was eligible for these programs; poor performance on a test was typically a ticket into programs with more resources than might be found in the regular classroom. Second, tests were used to measure effectiveness of the programs—continued funding was contingent on proof that children who had participated in an education program had gained ground educationally.

The purpose of testing was still to help sort children by ability as defined by the test, but the focus shifted to ensuring that those with less got more when they came to school. This focus inadvertently advantaged schools: Identifying more children as having special needs meant more money for school programs. When a close look was taken at exactly who ended up in these special programs, a disturbing profile emerged: Children of color and of the working class were much more likely to be placed in remedial and special education programs. Allegations of bias spread, and critics charged that instead of determining ability, the tests were measuring how much access children had to the mainstream White culture, with its particular language, behaviors, and skills. Tests were seen as confirming the racist orientations that formed the foundations of inequality in the first place (Williams, Mosby, & Hinson, 1976).

In addition, educators began to question the process of identifying, labeling and placing children in settings away from their agemates (Heller, Holtzman, & Messick, 1982). The identification process was found to be highly variable and despite promises, many students did not receive the kind of quality education they would have in their regular program. Experts began to argue that unless a special placement had some proven benefit for students, children should remain in the regular classroom program. The use of standardized tests to determine the ability of minority students in particular became less popular, with court challenges reinforcing the doubt (Linn, 1986). Eventually, most in the measurement community agreed that testing minority children was problematic and any claims for benefits of placement in special programs must be weighed against the potential damage of labels that stigmatize and placements that do not provide appropriate challenge (Shepard, 1989).

Excellence

In the 1980s a spate of reports on education led to calls for more testing. Beginning with *A Nation at Risk* (1983), these reports asserted that the quality of American schools had deteriorated; the evidence given was lower test performance than our international neighbors. Focusing on the economic effect of being perceived as second best, authors of these reports called for reform. Likening schools to businesses, focus was turned on the quality of the "product" and measurement of these educational outcomes became of great concern.

Tests became levers for educational reform, with scores used as evidence that the schools were doing their job. Districts and states developed promotional gates tests to check whether students had learned the material and accumulated the skills taught at a particular grade level (Ellwein & Glass, 1989). Kindergartners were tested to determine if they were ready for school (Gnezda & Bolig, 1988) and high school students in many states were tested to see if they were ready to graduate. In Texas, teachers were tested for basic literacy skills (Shepard & Kreitzer, 1987). The focus of this testing was the effectiveness of the educational system; a measure of whether the public was getting its money's worth.

The Social Context of Testing and Its Influence on Classroom Life

It is interesting to examine the effects that these two most recent testing eras have had on instructional materials and practices to gain a sense of how we have arrived at our current testing activities. In this section we will compare the focus of the equity and excellence periods, the motivations that drove actions during these times and how instruction related to testing.

Equity

With a focus on pulling children out of the regular classroom for special instructional programs, educators depended on tests to identify and sort. The guiding idea was that students with special needs would be more effectively taught in homogeneous groups. The testing industry grew by leaps and bounds as tests were developed to guide and justify placement decisions.

One problem with this approach was that the tests reflected values that unduly narrowed the view on what things were worth learning. Children were compared on these limited dimensions and difference, as portrayed in skills and achievement, was often interpreted as deficit. Trusting the authority of test scores and their own ideas of the "average" student, classroom teachers steered children into these special programs. As we noted earlier, most participants turned out to be children of color or from working class homes and many practices intended to "compensate" only kept children at a disadvantage by providing watered-down instruction premised on low expectations.

Concerns about normative and potentially biased comparisons fed the interest in criterion-referenced testing, which focused on descriptions of students' performance relative to some task and not other students. Teachers were trained to develop behavioral objectives for all classroom tasks in measurable forms (Baker & Stites, 1991). As a result, teachers' work came to resemble that of a technician running a machine according to clearly specified directions. Concerns about bias receded into the background because many believed that the learning process, as defined by the criterion-referenced tests, was more explicit, concrete, and fair.

Excellence

The reform movement's focus on testing as a prod for progress had pervasive effects on daily practice in many classrooms. Because test results had high stakes, instruction was shaped to avoid the consequences attached to poor performance. Wanting students to do well, teachers focused on the content of the local test, interpreting test content as what should be taught. Because they were not prominent test components, science, writing, social studies, solving complex problems, computer education, and long-term, creative projects were increasingly excluded from the curriculum (Rottenberg & Smith, 1990).

Not only was the content of the curriculum narrowed by the testing movement, but the form of teaching changed as well (Shepard, 1991). Looking toward an upcoming test, teachers frequently made their teaching more test-like. Constructivist, manipulative-based approaches were abandoned for fill-in-the-blank, find-the-right-answer worksheets that mimicked the test. Schools developed programs to teach "test wiseness" and began to purchase workbooks that practiced certain test formats (Smith, 1991).

The drill mode of instruction was differentially applied to students: Excellence was only expected of some. Low-achieving students were presented with low-level drill activities so that they would get the basics, while high-achieving students, because they were seen as able to perform on the test, were provided with more complex and interesting activities (Darling-Hammond, 1991; Garcia & Pearson, 1991). Darling-Hammond made this chilling conclusion about the misuse of basic skills tests on students in the lower track classes: "In short, they are denied the opportunity to develop the capacities they will need in the future, in large part because our tests are so firmly pointed at educational goals of the past" (p. 222).

In the flurry of attention to test performance, there was, in fact, an increase in scores. But did that rise really indicate better achievement? Were students learning more? Not necessarily. Teaching to the test, lax test security, blatant cheating, and testing only those students likely to score high (e.g., excluding special education or bilingual students) have all been suggested as competing explanations for increased test scores (Koretz, 1988; Linn, Graue, & Sanders, 1990). Charges of fraud directed at both testing companies and schools flew fast and furiously. Faith in the tests as a tool of reform and a measure of student learning diminished until new promises for improved testing technology and practices were made.

Testing and Teachers

Clearly, testing that developed during both the equity and excellence periods has had a significant effect on curriculum, instruction, and students' schooling experiences. In the following section, we investigate the extent to which testing principles influence teacher preparation and eventual practice.

Teacher Preparation

Given its influence, one might reasonably expect that prospective teachers have been educated about testing theory and technology. Historically, that has not been the case and even today, less than 50 percent of accredited programs require a course in tests and measurement (Schafer & Lissitz, 1987). Few state departments of education, the agencies responsible for certifying teachers, require teachers to take a measurement course or demonstrate competence in measurement-related concepts (O'Sullivan & Chalnick, 1991). Moreover, teacher educators report little to no pressure from public schools to provide such training (Lissitz, Schafer, & Wright, 1986).

Few teachers have taken a course in tests and measurement at either the undergraduate or graduate levels (Gullickson & Ellwein, 1985; Wise, Lukin, & Roos, 1991). A traditional tests and measurement course usually discusses the technical aspects of paper-and-pencil test construction such as writing objectives and items, scoring, and statistical analysis. Other typical units would address the standards by which tests and measures are judged (e.g., reliability and validity); the selection and use of standardized tests; and the evaluation of students and programs (Sax, 1980). Although social, legal and ethical implications of testing might be addressed, the technical aspects usually take precedence in an introductory course.

While these and other topics are part of the measurement knowledge base, they do not address all that practicing teachers deem important or relevant to their own practice. Teachers say they want to know more about assessing students with non-test methods. With few exceptions, however, textbooks provide minimal information or help in that regard and measurement professors do little to fill the void (Gullickson, 1986; Stiggins & Bridgeford, 1985).

As a result, a small number of teachers begin their careers with some knowledge about testing, but most enter their classrooms without a repertoire for assessing their students. With few ideas as to why, when, and how to assess their students, practicing teachers draw on their own experiences as students, they look to their colleagues, they experiment, and they use tests provided by textbook publishers (Wise, Lukin, & Roos, 1991; Stiggins & Bridgeford, 1985). Practicing teachers do not ask for courses or inservice training in tests and measurement; surveys indicate that teachers do not see them as pertinent or effective ways of dealing with their assessment concerns (Gullickson, 1984; Stiggins & Bridgeford, 1985).

Teacher Practice

The prominent role of testing in schools and its relative absence in teacher education set the stage for a range of problematic situations for teachers. On the one hand, more teachers have been asked to implement or help develop tests imposed by policymakers. On the other hand, teachers have been left to their own devices to figure out how to assess their students. In the following paragraphs, we describe these two circumstances and show how they characterize the traditional and asymmetric relationship between measurement and teaching in the schools.

Traditionally, the lives of teachers and testing specialists rarely intersect. Testing specialists are usually hired to coordinate the selection and administration of standardized tests and, increasingly, they develop tests to satisfy policymakers' mandates. Teachers are often involved, but usually in ways that are prescribed or highly structured. For example, teachers are expected to administer standardized tests according to a central schedule and specific procedures. Although testing specialists can be a resource for teachers during this time, they generally are responsible for ensuring that tests are administered properly. Throughout the standardized testing process, teachers have little choice in the testing process. They collect information over which they have little control and which they have little opportunity or reason to use.

In other instances, extracurricular effort may be required of some teachers. In some settings, teachers have been told that if students did not meet minimum standards on a new set of tests, they would be flunked (Ellwein & Glass, 1989). Under the direction of testing specialists, committees of teachers produced objectives, items, and the minimum score to pass each test. Ironically, teachers produced a test that was intended to limit their own professional decision-making. When finished with their task, these teachers returned to their classrooms with more technical knowledge, but knowledge that had no obvious links to their own classroom assessment practices and needs.

Stories like this attest to the fact that the production of reform-oriented tests depends, in part, on the labor of teachers. Some work willingly and enthusiastically while others may act out of a sense of obligation or a fear of leaving the work to others. Whatever their reasons, teachers have contributed time and effort to the development of tests mandated by policymakers and structured by testing experts.

In sharp contrast, few policymakers or testing experts have invested in teachers' classroom assessment practices and needs. These practices affect the day-to-day lives of both students and teachers and the cumulative effects of these practices may be a greater influence on students' experiences than intermittent testing events. Indeed, some claim that teachers spend 20 percent to 30 percent of their classroom time assessing students (Stiggins, 1988). Nevertheless, relatively few people have asked teachers how they assess and why. Fewer have taken the time to observe and document teachers' practices. And even fewer have asked teachers what they want or need and what can be done to help.

In the last 10 years, however, classroom assessment has gained more attention. Following is a brief discussion of available research on teachers' assessment practices.

Regardless of grade level, most teachers use non-test methods including oral questioning, class discussion, student papers, and performance assessment (Gullickson, 1985; Stiggins & Bridgeford, 1985). Although some studies have shown that elementary teachers use a more diverse set of assessment strategies than teachers in upper grades (Gullickson, 1985), both lower and upper grade teachers say that they rely more on tests to (1) diagnose student weaknesses, (2) group students for instruction, (3) grade, (4) report to parents, and (5) evaluate instruction (Stiggins & Bridgeford, 1985). More primary grade teachers use published tests, many of which accompany textbooks, while upper elementary and middle-school teachers usually construct their own tests. The only time tests are not favored is when primary grade teachers use spontaneous performance assessments to diagnose students.

To summarize, teachers seldom receive training and assistance in the mechanics of classroom assessment. When they do take traditional courses in tests and measurement, teachers find that the content is largely irrelevant to their needs. They consequently enter their classrooms with either no knowledge or highly specialized knowledge that eventually is displaced by trial-and-error and convenience. Instead of emerging from a wide array of methods and conditions, information about students is filtered through standardized and other published tests as well as teachers' own prepared measures. Instead of providing teachers with relevant assistance to expand and improve their practices, policymakers and administrators simply make more demands on them, such as asking them to assist in the development or implementation of external tests.

A Testing Critique

There is an unsettling irony about how external tests and classroom assessments have been valued and used. Tremendous resources are directed to standardized testing activities that are decontextualized from or inappropriate for students' learning experiences. In contrast, few resources are provided to improve practices that have a direct and regular effect on individual students and their schooling.

Because of their scientific organization and techniques, external tests appear to be a meaningful and coherent system to track student learning. Classroom assessments, however, are seen as disorganized and haphazard measurements of student skill, taken at convenient intervals during the school year. Little faith is put in classroom assessment and teachers' capacities to know their students. We suggest that more weight should be given to classroom assessment. If done effectively, it has the potential to be more congruent with the learning goals and instructional practices of the classroom.

Teachers need to be able to think about and practice in ways that facilitate better learning and teaching. Externally imposed tests have not necessarily helped in this regard and have often been shown to counter efforts to work for diversity and change. We suggest that their form and function should not serve as a template for instructional and learning activity in the classroom. One way to understand why is to look at testing situated in an instructional context. In the next section, we describe a common activity—discussion of student progress in a parent-teacher conference—that is unduly limited by an over-reliance on a testing model.

▼ Reading comprehension: 2.6

Nichole Gardner sits outside Mrs. Hamilton's classroom paging through the most recent public relations brochure for the Adams School District. One of the key points is the recent rise in achievement test scores—a goal that school officials tout proudly. As she checks her watch, the door opens. Nichole takes a deep breath, wondering why these conferences make her so nervous.

"Ms. Gardner?" Mrs. Hamilton says with a smile as she stands at the table at the front of the room. "I'm so glad you could come in. Would you like to have a seat?" The room is bright, with colorful bulletin boards and materials everywhere. Ms. Gardner sits down at a table that has neat stacks of folders at one end and a space clear in the middle and books at the other. Settling herself in the third-grade size chair, the teacher and parent engage in a little small talk. As they chat, Mrs. Hamilton pulls a thin folder out of the pile at her left and places it on the table.

"I'd like to show you some of the information we have about where Damien is right now. What I thought we would do is to look over the results of the testing we did earlier in the fall that tell us how he is doing relative to lots of other third graders. Damien has had some good growth so far. My main concern is that he seems to struggle in reading. He is in the reading group that has been working on many of the entry-level third-grade skills in the past few weeks. You can see his skill level from his test scores—you'd expect a child in the beginning of third grade to have a grade level score of about 3.0—Grade 3, no months. [She pulls out the test printout and points to the reading section.] Damien falls below grade level in his reading skills: reading vocabulary: 2.5; reading comprehension: 2.6. He still is working at a skill level a little below what we'd like to see for a third grader. His difficulty in reading carries over into the other academic areas because they depend so much on using those reading skills. His math scores are closer in areas that don't require working with words: arithmetic computation: 3.0; arithmetic concepts: 2.9; arithmetic applications: 2.8."

Mrs. Hamilton continues to describe the test results, comparing Damien's achievements with that "average" third grader. His mother tries to make sense of what her son can and can not do from the test results and begins to wonder what she could do at home to help.

"So overall, the test shows he's working at or a little below grade level in reading, math, and language arts. That can help us understand how he does in the classroom, I think. Damien is a good worker—he gets right in on any activity, but struggles a little because he has to work so hard. Here's his report card . . ." [She pulls out the single sheet that details the academic subject areas and work habits.] "Language arts—mechanics: B–; writing: B–; speaking: B." Damien's mother listens as the grades are read off and tries to imagine her son sitting at his desk for the length of the school day. He has so much energy at home that the image is hard to pull together. She wishes that she could see more of his work—most of it seems to disappear into that black hole between home and school.

"You know, I have thought about having him tested for learning disabilities, to try to get a handle on why he struggles so. But his difficulty seems to be at about the same level across all subjects so he wouldn't qualify. I have a few goals for him that I think you could reinforce at home. Overall, I'd like to get him to the point where he is more comfortable reading. To do that I think we have to have him reading more. If we set a goal for him to read one book a week. . . ."

Ms. Gardner thinks, "It's funny—Damien does read quite a bit at home. He grabs the newspaper every morning and can give minute details about his favorite sports teams. He reads to his little sister—those easy baby books, but he really enjoys that."

"So if you don't have any questions," Mrs. Hamilton says, "I'll ask you to sign his progress report and let you get on your way. You've probably had a long day, haven't you?"

What does Ms. Gardner know now that she didn't know before? She came to the conference hoping to understand her son's school life a little better. Her interaction with Mrs. Hamilton was pleasant and prompted Ms. Gardner to think of ways that she could help Damien at home. But several opportunities were missed in this meeting. Mrs. Hamilton's comments were strongly shaped by the measurement information she used to think about Damien.

She relied heavily on standardized test scores and report card grades to describe Damien and his progress. But the test scores reflected only how Damien performed on a set of tasks taken by a representative group of third graders. It told nothing about his school tasks or how he performed them. There is little sense of the curriculum, and a limited view of Damien as a student. Unfortunately, the discussion focuses on deficit—where Damien falls behind in various subject areas. A competent and enthusiastic child is portrayed as behind in his skills. The rich knowledge that his mother possesses is not solicited and neither is she helped to understand the information that the teacher has about Damien.

Overall, the picture is cloudy and fragmented and gives little prescription for action. Using this kind of information obscures Mrs. Hamilton's vision of possibility for Damien—it seems that all she can see are problems. Damien becomes a composite of discrete skills that need to be improved. For Ms. Gardner, there appears to be a discrepancy between Damien at home and Damien at school. Wanting to help him succeed, she wishes she knew more about what happens in the classroom. The information given is so far removed from what he does in school, however, that she is left with more questions than answers. What could be done to improve the situation? Are these the things that we want to see happen in a multicultural and social reconstructionist setting?

Our reply, as you may suspect, is no. We hold a quite different vision for assessment in schools. Before moving on to new models, we summarize nine elements that have drawn criticism from a growing number of educators across disciplines and academic philosophies. Table 5.1 outlines the elements of our testing critique and summarizes our vision for assessment.

Intent, Focus, and Comparisons

The traditional intent of most large-scale and classroom testing in schools has been to form conclusions about individual students' aptitude and achievement. The information generated from tests reveals a static, almost fossilized glimpse of what students did at the time they were tested. Coupled with a tendency to focus on weaknesses, those who interpret tests have been inclined to draw conclusions about students' limitations rather than their potential. Because tests are like a snapshot of a group of individuals at any given time, interpreters have tended to make normative comparisons among students.

TABLE 5.1   Features of Assessment and Testing Perspectives

Features	Assessment	Testing
intent	generating questions about the learning process	forming conclusions about achievement
focus	student strengths and instructional limitations	student weaknesses and program evaluation
type of comparisons	within individuals	across individuals and groups
type of task	holistic and contextualized	fragmented and decon-textualized
relationship to instruction	formative and recursive	summative and episodic
role of professional judgment	discretionary	constrained
students' roles	participatory	passive and reactive
parents' roles	collaborative	recipient
role of values	explicit and monitored	tacit and assumed consensus

Type of Task

Traditional standardized tests are not "authentic" measures of educational achievement, largely because of the fragmented and decontextualized nature of the tasks (McLean, 1990). Whole activities such as reading are broken down into constituent skills that are presumed to "add up" to good reading comprehension. In addition, many of the questions designed to tap this array of skills have been divorced from contexts that are meaningful to students.

Tests look this way largely because of the implicit theories that testing specialists hold to be true about learning (Shepard, 1991). Many testing specialists believe that learning involves the "sequential mastery of constituent skills" (p. 9), which should be explicitly tested at each learning step. Although these beliefs have strongly influenced the nature of testing tasks, they have been shown to be mostly obsolete by research in cognitive psychology and the various subject matters.

Despite their capacity to limit curriculum and drive instruction, externally imposed tests cannot be a regular and meaningful part of the teaching-learning process. Tests are administered infrequently and months-long delays in receiving test results subvert attempts to use them to adapt instruction to meet learners' needs. Even if results were communicated more quickly, they are not sensitive or concrete enough to guide day-to-day learning activities. Although discrepancies in test scores can indicate where students are having problems in general, the scores themselves are too intangible to help teachers or students do what they need to do.

Traditional standardized tests have structured the roles of teachers, students, and parents in particularly disturbing ways. Teachers' professional judgment has been both informed and constrained by traditional tests. As we have discussed, pressure to make a good showing on standardized tests has prompted many teachers to adapt content and form to more closely match a multiple-choice format.

Students also find their roles constrained by traditional testing. Their cooperation is vital, but they have no power to shape their own testing experiences. Moreover, parents are not usually given a part in the testing system; their role has been defined as that of consumers and recipients of testing information.

A final point warrants elaboration. In traditional testing circles, values are not readily discussed. Much of the work invested in test development and use has been premised on the belief that the instruments reflect commonly held values that students should know and teachers should teach. Some people go so far as to say that the tests themselves are value-free.

Asserting that testing is a neutral technique for gathering information implies that methods can somehow be disentangled from human agency and values. This in itself is a value statement that provokes considerable disagreement. Rather than claiming that tests are value-free, we suggest that tests have been based on implicit values about power and privilege as well as the nature of knowledge, learning, and instruction.

When educators and others in power fail to question such values or beliefs, they accept the dominant view of students, teachers, schools, and society. As a result, they unwittingly limit the options of others in nondominant groups such as people of color and those who are poor, female, or disabled. These practices can be seen as hegemonic and attempts to counter them will not be well received because those in power steadfastly believe that their practices are both reasonable and just (Erickson, 1987).

Multicultural and social reconstructionist education, by definition, supports efforts aimed at identifying and reversing hegemonic practices. Erickson (1987) suggests how this can and should be accomplished:

> Particular individuals can scrutinize the options enjoined by the conventional wisdom of practice. They can decide which aspects of that conventional wisdom to adopt and which to reject, creating learning environments that not only do not stigmatize minority students, but stimulate them to achieve. (p. 353)

To this point, we have focused on acquainting you with conventional testing practice and its critique. Rather than blindly accepting or rashly rejecting all forms of testing, we hope you can use this as a guide for following Erickson's advice to act critically and consciously. The guide is, of course, incomplete without a list of alternatives to conventional practice. The rest of this chapter is devoted to a discussion of multicultural and social reconstructionist assessment. We explain how its dimensions form a basis for practicing in ways that enable rather than limit children and their families. Specifically, we recommend actions that can provide meaningful alternatives to conventional testing practice—alternatives that stimulate learning for children, families, and teachers.

Creating a Vision for Classroom Assessment

Knowledge about subject matter and pedagogy is necessary to facilitate learning, but teachers must also know their students. What do students know? What can they do? What are their interests? How do they learn best? Answers to these questions will change across subject matter, time, contexts, and of course, individuals; therefore teachers need to pose them often and regularly to be responsive to students' individual and collective needs.

This sort of responsiveness depends on your ability to integrate your role as a learner with your developing identity as a teacher. Assessment becomes a vehicle for your own education as well as that of your students. Before elaborating on this point, however, we return briefly to the nine features of assessment and testing to describe how assessment should be distinct from traditional testing practices.

Relationship to Instruction

The purpose of assessment is twofold: (1) to generate questions or hypotheses about the learning process, and (2) to gather evidence to address these questions. Instead of relying on intermittent tests to form conclusions about what individual students know, you will be watching students regularly in response to your own questions about where they are and where they need to go next. The evidence you gather will document the learning process and shape it as you adapt your instruction. It will also serve as a springboard for generating new questions.

Assessment is based on knowledge and assumptions about the learning process that are quite different from those that have driven traditional testing practices (Shepard, 1991). Learning is not a process of absorption as much as it is one of construction. Any learner actively constructs knowledge in part by applying current knowledge and understandings (Resnick, 1989). This knowledge is situational and subject to change; that is, we do not learn rules and principles in isolation from the contexts in which they are used. The contexts themselves define what can and should be learned.

Because learning depends in part on prior knowledge and skills, assessments need to focus on students' strengths. By asking what children can do, teachers are in a better position to modify their instruction or arrange opportunities that allow children to cultivate their talents or use them to develop new ones.

Weaknesses will inevitably be noted, but they are best used to generate more questions about the student and the contexts in which they work. Such questions should not be geared only to asking why the student is "not achieving." They should first be treated as clues to our own lack of understanding. Indeed, "when children of a different culture do not seem to make sense, it is probably our fault for not knowing how to recognize it" (McDermott & Goldman, 1983).

Whereas traditional practices compare individuals at a given point in time, assessment should be used to document changes over time of individual students within their contexts. Group assessments are also appropriate when you want to understand how a group has changed over time or how group members work together toward a goal. In this way, while any one piece of assessment information is temporary, they can be strung together to provide a picture of an individual that is more comprehensive than a set of abstract scores collected each spring.

Assessments should be taken frequently and regularly enough to guide instruction as well as document learning. Consequently, teachers need a repertoire of methods at their disposal. Some methods allow them to capitalize on spontaneous or naturally occurring events in the classroom. Others may be the result of planned activities designed for a particular purpose. Whether the method or situation is natural or contrived, good assessment tasks include whole activities or some reasonable components that are meaningful to students.

Professional Judgment

Professional judgment is a critical aspect of assessment. Teachers need to exercise a variety of ways to know their students. Tacit or "gut" knowledge can be developed and used in conjunction with more formal ways of knowing (e.g. observing, testing). But freedom to draw on a range of resources has serious responsibilities. For example, if you need to decide which two students will work with a remedial reading teacher, you cannot rely only on your gut instincts as to who is in most need or who will benefit most. A teacher must be able to gather corroborating evidence and to interpret it wisely; that is, consider the conditions under which it was gathered as well as the implications for acting on it. Because so much depends on professional judgment, teachers must have strong connections with their peers who facilitate mindful discussion, examination, and questioning of practice.

The Role of Students

Like teachers, students have the opportunity to play much more active roles in classroom assessment. Children at all grade levels can and should be encouraged to generate and collect information about their learning activities. Independent and collective participation in assessment activities enables children to understand their efforts and experiences in a way that is not possible with traditional testing practices.

With changes in the roles of both teachers and students, their relationships can evolve and mature. Traditionally, the unequal distribution of power between students and teachers has often led to adversarial relationships, especially in testing situations (Johnston, 1987). Teachers and students can work together in ways that recast the role of the teacher as an advocate for the students rather than a keeper of the right answers. By shifting the focus to the individual in context, it will not be necessary or desirable to divorce individual students from their natural interactions with their peers and their teachers.

The Role of Parents

Parents, like students, can become active partners in classroom assessment. Teachers and students can generate concrete information that provides complex but accessible and meaningful pictures for parents. With this information, parents will be better able to understand how their children's activity in school compares with what they see at home. Parents' knowledge of their children can and should be welcomed by teachers. By learning about a family or students' reading habits and interests, for example, the teacher will be in a better position to assess the extent to which classroom learning opportunities are either building on or undermining students' strengths.

The Role of Values

Values cannot be ignored in assessment; teachers must identify and monitor the ways their values influence what and how they assess. For every choice to assess a particular concept or action, teachers choose to ignore something else. Teachers should consciously reflect on the values that frame their actions and interpretations so they can begin to understand the filters they use to make judgments about students. Reflection on your own values is coupled with the values of students, parents, schools, and community. By actively reflecting on these contextual forces, participants in schooling can better identify those that dominate, structure and limit learning opportunities.

By regarding assessment as a learning opportunity, we can shift from a reliance on tests and technology to a conscious and deliberate activity that includes all forms of information and understanding. Assessment must occur at multiple levels; that is, teachers must learn about students individually and collectively as well as the contexts in which they teach and students learn. We evaluate students and their responses to our teaching, we also assess our own responsiveness to students. It is this reflexivity, when practiced with sensitivity and informed judgment, that stimulates learning and transformation in students and teachers alike.

Enacting a Vision for Assessment

Let us peek into Claire Morrow's third-grade classroom to see how she integrates assessment into the "readers' workshop." We chose this example to show how assessment is conducted in the service of learning; note how Ms. Morrow adopts the role of a learner as well as a teacher as she asks questions and generates information about Marcus in the context of his reading *Top Secret*.

▼ Me first today?!

The first few bars from George Winston's *Autumn* gently remind Ms. Morrow's third-graders to retrieve their book tubs and find a niche for private reading time. Rachel, Towanda, Juan, Marcus and Chi Li—Wednesday's children—flock behind the bookshelves in the conference corner as Ms. Morrow makes her way toward them. Towanda and Chi Li claim the spot under the table today, leaving the others room to spread out along the table. While children shuffle through their books and reading journals, Ms. Morrow settles into the empty seat next to Marcus.

"Me first today?!" His plaintive tone is a thin mask for his pride and eagerness. "I'm almost done—chapter nine!"

"Good for you! Just let me remind the others of what they need to do. Towanda and Chi Li, Juan and Rachel, remember to write your weekly letter sometime today—either during private or buddy reading time. I like how you have been describing your books and what happens in them—lots of colorful words—so keep up the good work! Remember to think and write about your reactions to the book, too."

Perched on the edge of his seat, Marcus squirms and sighs expectantly, barely containing his impatience to start his conference. Ms. Morrow invites him to bring her up to date on his current book while she retrieves a conference form out of his reading folder. She listens intently to his description, noting on the conference form "Emphasizes characters, plot, & his own reaction to book." As Marcus finishes, Ms. Morrow follows up with, "Did the main character change during the story?" Marcus thinks for a moment before nodding. "How?" And for the next four or five minutes their conference continues until Marcus asks, "Let me read you this one part—it's my favorite so far." While he searches for page and paragraph, Ms. Morrow jots down snippets from their conference on the form:

Date	Book	Comprehension & strategies
11/30	*Top Secret*	—he asked for Chris' recommendation —said I couldn't remember much about bk— he said, "Read the back cover!" —previewed bk together —ENTHUSIASTIC!
12/6	*Top Secret* Chap 9	—excited to tell me about book —emphasizes charac/plot/own reaction —knew how character had changed —couldn't tell how change affected plot —wanted to read aloud fav. part

"Marcus, because parent conferences are next week, I'd like to do one more running record. OK?"

Eyes glued to the page, he nods eagerly as she pulls out a grid form composed of 100 empty cells (10 rows by 10 columns). For every word Marcus calls correctly, Ms. Morrow checks one cell. In the first sentence, he says "pond" for "pound" and she quickly pencils in "pound/pond" in the corresponding cell, making similar notes with other miscalls. Some go by unnoticed by Marcus, while he corrects others after reading to the end of the sentence. Once he's read 100 words, she stops marking but continues to listen intently until he comes to a natural stopping point. Beaming, Marcus looks up from the page and Ms. Morrow nods, "I can tell that you really like that part of the story! You read with lots of expression—way more than you did with *Chocolate Fever!*"

"Yeah, that book was too BORRRRRING! And HARD!"

"You know what else, Marcus?"

"Huh?"

"You were a strategic reader! I noticed how you used a new strategy to figure out words you didn't know."

"Yeah?"

"Um hmmm, instead of rereading the entire sentence once you got to an unknown word, you read to the end of the sentence before going back."

"Oh yeah! That helps me figure out what the word might be. Yihua—you know, my 5th grade buddy—did that yesterday."

Before bringing the 12-minute conference to a close, Ms. Morrow asks about the setting, mood, and style of the passage, something they did not discuss at the onset.

"What will you read once you've finished *Top Secret?*"

"Is there anything more by the author?"

"I think so . . . why don't you check on it during library time today? Get back to me if you have any problems, OK?"

"OK. I'm ready to read some more—do you want me to get Towanda?"

"Sure. Thanks, Marcus."

Marcus slips under the table to summon Towanda, ready to snag her place under the table. While Towanda approaches, Ms. Morrow adds a few more notes to Marcus' conference form under the column for comprehension/strategies.

She completes three more conferences before the timer's buzzer splits the silence of the hour-long sustained, silent reading time. Some of Wednesday's children remain at the center to finish their letters or conferences while the individual readers take out their reading logs and record their book titles and comments before snaring a partner for buddy reading time. Before starting her conference with Chi Li, Ms. Morrow pauses and speaks over the low roar, "Remember to continue your interviews with each other—conferences are next week!"

Clearly, assessment was an integral part of instruction and learning during Ms. Morrow's readers' workshop. Ms. Morrow put her careful listening and observational skills to use by recording what Marcus said and did. In the excerpt, we can see how she attended to his interests and strengths as well as her own responses and actions. Ms. Morrow situated her comments about his comprehension and skills in the context of the book Marcus was reading. Marcus was free to influence the conference and she capitalized on his request to read to her by taking a "running record" of his fluency. The conference notes and running record form will be stored in his folder, giving both Marcus and Ms. Morrow access to a growing database of his reading activities over the school year. Taken together, they could construct a dynamic picture of his reading development linked to real world tasks. Finally, students' daily reading logs, their weekly letters, and their quarterly buddy interviews all served as concrete evidence for students' activities as well as how they make sense of them.

Before we discuss the whats and the hows of assessment, we draw your attention to a fundamental theme illustrated in this vignette: Teachers' assessment activities must complement their instructional philosophies and practices. Although we have discussed constructivist assumptions about learning, we have not explicitly addressed pedagogy and subject matter. Because many of the chapters in the book are devoted to this set of topics, we shall briefly outline a pedagogical orientation that is congruent with the specific assessment principles discussed in this chapter and the general tenets of education that is multicultural and social reconstructionist.

In keeping with constructivist learning principles, a learner-centered orientation requires teachers to see themselves as facilitators instead of experts who deliver knowledge. Their role is to encourage the active construction of knowledge by arranging appropriate learning opportunities that build on students' current knowledge and strengths. Teachers provide assistance and support to help students reach higher ground. Such strategies, including "reciprocal teaching," are congruent with learner-centered orientations in that teachers and students alike have a shared responsibility for thinking and acting (Brown & Palincsar, 1989). This type of teaching requires a classroom organization that provides multiple opportunities to gather information. Assessment occurs in many contexts, in a variety of formats and with multiple components. In addition, arranging these opportunities requires knowledge of how students communicate their understandings. Communication is primarily a cultural activity, therefore knowledge of student interaction patterns is vital to understanding learning.

Assessment Dimensions

As we noted earlier, testing practices have focused on the "project" of learning, such as the number of correct answers on a mathematics test. Although appropriate in some instances, the focus on achievement is too narrow and often leads to inappropriate conclusions about what students cannot or will not be able to do. Responsive assessments, in contrast, must seek multidimensional and grounded interpretations of students' performance and knowledge. To that end, we suggest that assessment be directed to three general and interrelated dimensions: individual, social, and contextual.

Individual Assessment   Constructivist learning principles suggest that any assessment includes attention to three related qualities. First, attention should be paid to the actual learning process. By assessing the strategies students use in tasks or activities, and the meanings they have for their actions, teachers are better able to appreciate students' perspectives as well as adapt instruction to bring about desired ends. Second, teachers need to consider what students know about their own learning (Glaser, Lesgold, & Lajoie, 1987). This kind of knowledge includes (1) knowing when or what one knows or does not know, (2) predicting the correctness or outcomes of actions, (3) planning ahead and allotting time effectively, and (4) checking and monitoring the results of actions.

Finally, you will want to understand how students' interests and backgrounds shape their attitudes toward school subjects and activities. Their interests, attitudes, motivations, and experiences are more than cognitive; they are emotional, social, cultural, historical, and political. By looking at schooling (e.g., goals, expectations, doubts, fears, resistance) through your students' eyes, you will be in a better position to adapt your expectations and actions to facilitate learning.

Social Assessment   Traditionally, tests have been designed to measure individual student knowledge. But assessment should not rely only on static evidence generated in isolation. It should incorporate interactions among students as well as between teacher and student. This type of information is more authentic in that it is closer to the rhythm of classroom activity. If cooperative learning is a curricular goal, one set of important dimensions includes the assessment of group processes such as planning and group problem solving (McLean, 1990).

A second factor of social assessment is the extent to which students benefit from assistance. Rather than focusing only on what a student can do alone, teachers should assess what the student can do with help from the teacher or a peer. Based on a concept known as the "zone of proximal development," dynamic assessment is premised on the idea that if we look carefully at what students can do with assistance, we can create a glimpse of their developmental future (Vygotsky, 1978). Assessment of assisted performance provides students with a vision of learning potential and the opportunity to gain motivation, momentum, and direction for learning.

Contextual Assessment   Finally, responsive assessment must take into account the resources available to learners such as the materials used, the specific activities, and the people involved. In other words, you will want to examine the conditions of the learning context. For example, in addition to knowing the strategies they use and the meanings they hold for a task, you will want to understand the demands imposed by the materials (e.g., the topic and difficulty level of the text). The materials and the activities are not the only contextual dimensions to assess. What you say and do, as well as how, will affect what a student does or what you see. Performance is task-dependent, and to understand fully how a student learns, you have to understand the activity in which students are engaged.

Assessment Strategies

Classroom assessment, as we have described it, depends on a teacher's ability to use a variety of strategies. The choice of strategies will be influenced by factors that include (1) the subject matter, (2) the levels and dimensions of assessment, (3) who is generating the information, and (4) whether the situation is contrived or naturally occurring.

To think about these ideas, it will help to liken the roles of teachers to that of field anthropologists. As part of their efforts to know and understand a culture, anthropologists rely on three basic strategies: observations, interviews, and the collection of artifacts. In the same way, teachers must watch, listen, and gather evidence to learn about their students and their cultures, both those they bring with them and that which is created in the classroom.

Observation   Perhaps the most accessible but undervalued strategy, observation allows the teacher to look at both the learning process and product. For example, the preceding vignette illustrated how Ms. Morrow used informal observation skills while Marcus read aloud. Her keen perceptions helped her recognize that Marcus was using a new strategy for figuring out unknown words. By noting its appearance and use, Ms. Morrow could see if Marcus' comprehension was enhanced or inhibited by the strategy. She also used a more formal observation—the running record. By systematically recording the number and types of miscalls in a reading passage that was meaningful to Marcus, Ms. Morrow was able to document his oral fluency. The miscalls could be analyzed to determine if Marcus needed specific help.

In both instances, Ms. Morrow was looking at her student's performance embedded in a regularly occurring instructional activity—the reading conference. Contrived activities allow teachers to observe other types of performance, also. For example, a first-grade teacher may want to assess students' knowledge of basic math combinations. Instead of handing out a math worksheet filled with addition facts to all children at the same time, the teacher can assess individual children at pivotal points in the learning. During math time, individual children meet with the teacher to play the "hand game" for a particular number. For example, together they count out seven small objects held by the teacher. Transferring some to a closed hand and revealing the rest of the set, the student is asked to give the appropriate combination. When three objects are shown, the student would respond, "Three plus four is seven." The teacher works through all the combinations of seven several times until satisfied that the student can quickly and correctly identify them. This provides rich information on student problem-solving and knowledge of quantity.

Observations during group activities enable teachers to watch how students interact and work together. They can look for patterns in participation, explanation giving, interpretations, and resolutions as well as noting the roles students do or do not play in providing support or creating conflict (Brown & Palincsar, 1989).

Observations need not be as in-depth as implied by the preceding examples. Teachers may "take a pulse" or snapshot of classroom activity to document such things as students' engagement with tasks, their use of materials, and with whom students choose to work. For example, by keeping a running log of students' language activities (planning, drafting, revising, editing, publishing, reading, conferencing, or choosing a book), teachers can determine what areas students might be avoiding or overemphasizing.

As illustrated in the vignette, teachers keep track of their observations by writing notes. Some teachers prefer to keep separate files for each child and subject. Others prefer to develop forms that help them organize their information, and still others may be comfortable with less structure. One simple way of keeping track is to maintain a log or journal. Teachers can observe and record spontaneous, anecdotal events throughout the day along with more formal or systematic activities. Naturally, the level of detail will vary with the available time and situation, but a regular journal will be a rich source of information on student learning. As computers become a common part of classrooms, word-processed journal entries will allow teachers to sort and print out information to share with students, their parents, and future teachers. They might even choose to videotape students engaged in their activities to have a more permanent record.

Interviews   Another everyday activity that serves well as an assessment strategy is the interview—a special case of a conversation between two or more people. Like observations, interviews may be spontaneous or planned and can be used at both the individual and group levels. Although teacher-student interviews are common, students can learn how to interview one another. Whatever the format, interviews enable the participants to learn more about the other's perspective.

Clearly, interviews are natural ways to elicit information from students and parents about student interests, attitudes, values, and experiences, but they can also be used to assess their strategies, knowledge, and interests. Conversations that prompt students to explain their procedures or rationales for their actions help the teacher understand how they approach a task and what misunderstandings—whether those of the student or teacher—might be limiting success. Students' explanations may also help the teacher see that different interpretations of an activity are possible and valuable in and of themselves—that there may be more than one "correct" route or process.

Interviews can be used to monitor students' problem-solving and strategic understandings (Glaser, Lesgold, & Lajoie, 1987). Several generic questions may be posed during or after an activity that can shed light on students' understanding of the tasks and their actions:

1. How would you do this?
2. Why would you do this?
3. What does it tell you?

4. What do you think the problem is?

5. What do you plan to do next?

As we noted earlier, such direct questions may be culturally inappropriate for some children; lack of participation should not be taken to mean the students do not understand the task. A teacher must be creative and sensitive in devising alternate ways to assess these understandings. The key is asking the right question or arranging the right opportunity for children to share their knowledge. Integrating these into activities and modeling them so that students can take on the task may be one such way. Keeping track of interview information may be done by recording directly onto an interview form or in the above-mentioned journal. Taping interviews provides information on fluency and interaction style that is not readily available in other formats.

Artifacts   Simply put, artifacts are samples of student work. Portfolios of students' work are increasingly being used to chronicle their development in areas such as math or language. In the following paragraphs, we describe what artifacts might be included in a portfolio as well as how teachers and students might use it.

Like that of an artist, a student's portfolio is an expanding file that holds materials representing the depth and breadth of their growing expertise. One type of artifact to include in the portfolio is the work that students naturally produce as a result of their regular learning activities. For example, pieces of student writing at planning, drafting, revising, editing, and publishing stages would permit a look at how students (1) develop and express their ideas, (2) use relevant skills in context (e.g. punctuation), and (3) understand the purposes of the different stages. Such artifacts, if produced in activities that authentically represent the real world task, give contextual and specific insight into what students know and can do.

Any systematic record of what students have done in the classroom constitutes a second type of artifact. For example, the reading logs that students kept in Ms. Morrow's classroom would be logical and meaningful documents to include in their portfolios, because they display the number and types of books that each person read over time. Such logs can be easily maintained for any subject beginning in first grade. By incorporating them into the daily learning routines, students begin to assume ownership of their activities and they create a lasting record that reminds them and others of their accomplishments.

A third type of artifact serves both assessment and learning: the reflective journal (Cambourne & Turbill, 1990). By setting aside 10–15 minutes a day, teachers can provide students with the opportunity to think about what they have done and learned in a particular subject area. Whether their reflections are incorporated into the journal or into a written literacy event, or recorded on tape, they should be shown how and encouraged to consider what they accomplished, understood, and struggled with as they engaged in a learning activity.

Making Sense of Assessment Information

The array of information in the form of written notes, logs, student performance, reflective journals, work samples, and interviews does not lend itself to simple analysis. Teachers cannot distill the information into a "percent correct" or grade level equivalent. Such information is brimming with the intricacies of the learning process and the analysis must honor and preserve that complexity.

The teacher-as-anthropologist metaphor can be extended from the collected information to how teachers make sense of it (Cambourne & Turbill, 1990). First, teachers need to inspect and read their "data" to note recurring categories and patterns. In some instances, they might develop checklists that reflect goals and values about the learning process—but checklists can be misused when assessment information is decontextualized from the learning activity. Rather than spend time developing summary tools, we suggest teachers consider the evidence as pieces they can use to build a mosaic about students' learning. By inspecting the pieces and making connections among them, they can begin to understand how students' individually and collectively are faring in their classroom.

This process requires individual as well as collective deliberation. Critical reflection and meaning-making depend on the teacher's ability to share ideas and concerns with students, their families, and other colleagues. By asking supportive colleagues to play the role of devil's advocate, for example, teachers can uncover potential blind spots and elicit alternative hypotheses for the things they have observed. By discussing their insights and questions, both teacher and students can reach a more conscious understanding of what is and is not occurring in the classroom.

This vision for classroom assessment has limitations, which we will discuss shortly. Before doing so, however, we show how this vision can inform and reshape the parent-teacher conference illustrated earlier. Rather than discuss how this conference is different, we will leave it to you to pick up the important aspects of communication in which Damien is an expert about his own learning. As you imagine the scene, extend it into a three-way conference following this interaction in which Damien, his mother, and his teacher share information and build a vision for schooling.

▼ "It lets you look back and see how you've improved."

Pulling the thick manilla folder out of the drawer, Damien beams as he hands it to his mom. "You won't believe all the stuff in there. It's really cool." They sit at a table outside Mrs. Hamilton's classroom and Damien pulls out his checklist of topics to cover with his mom. At the same time, Ms. Gardner takes a list from her purse that Damien's teacher sent home as a way to help parents see some of the important things in their children's portfolios. On the list is the following:

Notice

Type of writing appearing in the collection

Changes in writing over time

Use of writing in different contexts (language arts, math, science)

Ask questions about what your child has learned and how that shows up in the collection

"So what's in here?" Damien's mother asks as she reaches for the bulging folder. "Is this the reason I don't get to see your work coming home? You really aren't dumping it on the way home so I won't see it?"

"I told you Mama, we keep it at school so we can see all the stuff we do during the year. It lets us look back and see how we've improved. It helps us feel proud of what we're doing."

He opens the folder and pages from back to front. "Like, I look to see how much better my handwriting is now. At the beginning of the year I did an autobiography—you know, I wrote about me. Now I know how to do paragraphs and words—it's not nearly as bad. See, I didn't even know where to put periods!" He is speaking rapidly now, pointing to one of the papers in the front of the folder.

"There's all kinds of stuff in here," Damien continues. "I have both my rough drafts and my dummy copies. Dummy copies are where you go through and check your rough draft and make sure that everything is what you want. It's before the final thing. We also have these pink slips— they tell why we want to put things in our portfolio. Why we like what we did. I'm interested in writing about cats. So that's what I'm working on a lot." Damien is pointing to various pages in the folder as he talks.

"You did all of this yourself?" his mother asks.

"When I need help with my writing other kids will help me," Damien says. "I put my name on the board and then I can ask them questions. We have these groups in class—we read and we get help one day a week all together. And we have our spelling cards—words we got wrong. Not just the ones we got wrong but the ones we got right too. See how many more I get right now?"

Mrs. Gardner smiles and shakes her head, "You have been working hard. I'm really proud of you." She has never seen Damien so excited about school—and it seems to be showing in his work. And he knows so much about what he is learning—he can look at his progress just by going through the things he has done in the past few months.

"So tell me," she asks, "you could see how you know where to put periods in your work. What else have you learned?"

"This picture of me and my science project. Having this in here helps me look back and remember what I did. It was a lot of work but I learned a lot about cats—you know, what they eat, where they live, what they need. I can draw way better than at the beginning of the year. See?"

The door opens and Sylvie and her dad leave the classroom talking. Noticing Damien and his mother, Sylvie pretends to speak into a microphone, "Up next, Damien Gardner!" Gathering up his materials, Damien pokes his mom, "C'mon—now you get to hear about me from somebody else."

Limitations of Assessment

These suggested assessment practices have limitations and cautions that should be discussed. Change of this type does not occur within a vacuum, and to be effective, it will be necessary to rethink other conventional forms of schooling and instructional practice. Four issues must be dealt with to make these ideas viable: beliefs, knowledge, time, and power.

Matching Instructional and Assessment Beliefs

Teachers' instructional practices are rooted in their beliefs about how children learn and how it is best to teach them (Clark, 1988). Assessment practices are no less connected to these beliefs, and researchers are beginning to look at how that relationship plays out in practice. Examining the implementation of portfolio assessment in one district, Lamme & Hysmith (1991) found a relationship between portfolio implementation and the degree to which teachers practice whole language principles. Teachers who took a skills-oriented approach to teaching and learning were less enthusiastic about using portfolios to assess their students; it did not fit their instructional philosophy and they saw it as an add-on to their work. On the other hand, teachers who espoused principles congruent with whole language or math instruction took issue with test-based models of assessment and supported the non-test perspectives and strategies described in this chapter (Cambourne & Turbill, 1990; Ellwein, 1992).

The key to making these alternative assessment strategies work is perceiving assessment and instruction as recursive and the process of learning as dynamic and contextualized. Teachers with other instructional beliefs will find these strategies frustrating, disorganized and intimidating. Teachers need to understand their own instructional practices, and a sense of their beliefs about learning is a beginning step in implementing these strategies.

Acquiring and Developing Assessment Knowledge

As we stressed earlier in the chapter, teacher training typically does not include much information and practice in models of gathering information about students. While there is strong support for alternative assessment models from a variety of audiences, the methods are still new and underdeveloped. For preservice teachers, we would advocate a move away from the view that assessment is a separate entity, with delivery of information in a single course. All methods classes should have an assessment component spanning both the testing models and more holistic assessment strategies. In that way, instructional and assessment practice is integrated under the umbrella of subject matter content. For many practicing teachers, these methods will be just as new and will require both inservice and consultant services to help them implement assessment as we have described it (Gomez, Graue, & Bloch, 1991). To avoid reinventing the wheel, schools must support teachers so they can work together to develop and share strategies to track their students' work.

Time

The seemingly informal nature of the model we suggest should not lull teachers into thinking it can be implemented easily and quickly. In fact, most teachers who have tried it would probably tell you it can be exhausting, confusing, and overwhelming. It requires a vision of learning and assessment that is broader than required for the traditional testing model. Teachers need to be creative in arranging situations that allow them to learn the things that they need to know about their students. Portfolio use has been described as a labor-intensive process that took untold hours after school to plan activities, review student products, and integrate instruction and assessment ideas (Gomez, Graue & Bloch, 1991).

Assessment does not lend itself well to large group instruction and requires intense interaction in small groups. Teachers need to be good observers of events in their classrooms and that means taking the time to observe. Ms. Benson, the teacher described by Gomez et al. (1991), found it difficult to justify sitting and watching—everything she knew about being a teacher said that she should be teaching, not sitting. Thinking about assessment as part of instruction makes this easier to accept, but still requires a major shift in conception of what teachers do when they are with their students.

Beyond observation, taking time to talk with students about ongoing projects and help them evaluate their own learning requires reallocation of in-class time from classic instructional activity. In addition to rethinking how time is spent in the classroom with students, planning time is pivotal (Gomez et al., 1991). Release time for individuals and groups of teachers, provided consistently, will be needed to plan assessment. In addition, teachers need time to review collections of student work so that they can develop an ongoing picture of student progress. Collaborative evaluation, with teachers working together to understand student growth, provides another rich opportunity in this kind of assessment practice, but one that requires an environment that fosters cooperation among staff members and a commitment to the value of the activity. Space and time for such interaction is not frequently found in today's elementary and middle schools.

Power

One of the problems inherent in old conceptions of testing is that it does not invest much power in local educational settings for negotiation of the form or consequences of testing. For the most part, teachers, parents, and students were passive agents expected to react to the demands of outside authorities. By their very nature, the forms of assessment suggested in this chapter distribute power in different ways than we are accustomed to in schools. They require individuals to take on different roles, to take new kinds of responsibility, and to have different relationships as they negotiate and construct assessment practice.

The most obvious change will occur for teachers, who will have the central role in making these assessments work. Reclaiming the authority and the responsibility for assessment, teachers will need to construct a system of assessment in their classroom, connecting subject matter areas, devising standards, and developing communication strategies for students, parents, administrators, and other audiences. This is a great increase in professional responsibility, requiring more knowledge of subject matter, as well as greater awareness of the ways that culture and language influence learning (Garcia & Pearson, 1991). Building a contextualized view of how learning occurs, teachers can create culturally appropriate assessment activities for all children, rather than rely on tasks developed for White, middle-class children. Probably the most important aspect of this new responsibility will be that a teacher reflects about practice and values the role of the learner as part of instructional activity.

Students will also assume a new role, becoming collaborators with their teachers in building a composite of their learning over time. Given responsibility to develop a case that portrays their development, students can delve into the process of being a student as well as an evaluator of their progress. A new relationship emerges for teachers and students, requiring much more active communication about the student's work and aspirations and the teacher's expectations and standards. This will not occur spontaneously with implementation of portfolio, performance, or authentic assessments.

These relationships and responsibilities must be cultivated over time in each setting, informed by cultural information gathered by teachers. Strategies to include students in decision-making will be as diverse as the students in a classroom and should be responsive to a variety of needs. An interesting question in this kind of assessment involves ownership of both the process and products—who decides what is put into collections such as portfolios and who has the final say in evaluation of these materials? Teachers and students will have new grounds on which to negotiate the assessment process, until now not part of the school scene.

Parents can be drawn into assessment activity in a way that is not possible in the old models. First and foremost, parental knowledge of their children is valued and incorporated in assessment activities in the classroom. A partnership evolves in which home and school information is used to inform the context of schooling. Including parental knowledge of home-related growth provides teachers with contextualized data on the developing student, giving information on transfer of learning.

A caution: All students and parents are not equally able to participate in these activities. Differences in parent participation in schools has been related to both socioeconomic status and race (Graue, 1991; Lareau, 1989). These differences have a tremendous effect on the resources available to families and teachers in the educational process. Just as instructional activities must be developed to be culturally relevant, inclusive assessment activities must take into account the relationship between individuals and the school as an institution. This puts an additional responsibility on teachers to facilitate diverse kinds of participation, respecting the many kinds of information and insights that are offered.

Finally, teachers must find new ways to communicate the progress of their students to audiences outside the classroom. Administrators, who formerly could rely on the authority of standardized test scores to judge the relative effectiveness of teacher practice, will now need to trust a more holistic and ongoing process that relies on many samples of student performance. One advantage is that a principal will find it harder to make sense of students from a look at test forms in an office down the hall—it will become almost mandatory for administrators to visit classrooms regularly. The job will be easiest for teachers if their principal supports such efforts, but will require much work if the promise of this new model of assessment is to be fulfilled.

In this chapter, we have proposed a model for assessment that stretches commonly held ideas about testing practices. We suggest a more dynamic and interactive activity that joins efforts by teachers, parents, and children to get a better understanding of where students are going educationally. We have attempted to expand the purposes, ways, and uses for knowing your students, which redistributes the responsibility for generating tasks, products, and interpretations away from an anonymous authority to participants in the setting. These ideas are presented because we are convinced of the need to reform current testing practices. The old models have excluded teachers, parents and students from constructing assessments appropriate for their experiences and it is time to change.

Acknowledgment

We are indebted to the many teachers and instructional facilitators from Blue Ridge County, Virginia, schools who taught us about assessment by example. We also would like to acknowledge the support lent by the Commonwealth Center for the Education of Teachers at the University of Virginia.

References

Baker, E. L., & Stites, R. (1991). Trends in testing in the USA. *Politics of Education Association Yearbook, 139–157.*

Brown, A. L., & Palincsar, A. S. (1989). Guided, cooperative learning and individual knowledge acquisition. In L. B. Resnick (Ed.), *Knowing, learning, and instruction: Essays in honor of Robert Glaser* (pp. 393–451). Hillsdale, NJ: Lawrence Erlbaum.

Cambourne, B., & Turbill, J. (1990). Assessment in whole-language classrooms: Theory into practice. *Elementary School Journal, 90,* 337–349.

Clark, C. M. (1988). Asking the right questions about teacher preparation: Contributions of research on teacher thinking. *Educational Researcher, 17*(2), 5–12.

Darling-Hammond, L. (1991). The implications of testing policy for quality and equality. *Phi Delta Kappan, 73*(3), 220–225.

Ellwein, M. C. (1992, April). Watching teachers, watching students. In *More than just measurement: Assessment in the context of instructional practice.* Symposium conducted at the annual meeting of the American Educational Research Association, San Francisco.

Ellwein, M. C., & Glass, G. V. (1989). Ending social promotion in Waterford: Appearance and reality. In L. A. Shepard & M. L. Smith (Eds.), *Flunking grades: Research on retention practice and policies* (pp. 151–173). London: Falmer Press.

Erickson, F. (1987). Transformation and school success: The politics and culture of educational achievement. *Anthropology and Education Quarterly, 18,* 335–356.

Garcia, G. E., & Pearson, P. D. (1991). The role of assessment in a diverse society. In E. Hiebert (Ed.), *Literacy for a diverse society: Perspectives, programs, and policies* (pp. 253–278). New York: Teachers College Press.

Glaser, R., Lesgold, A., & Lajoie, S. (1987). Toward a cognitive theory for the measurement of achievement. In J. C. Conoley (Ed.), *The influence of cognitive psychology on testing.* Hillsdale, NJ: Lawrence Erlbaum.

Gnezda, M.T., & Bolig, R.(1988). A national survey of school testing of pre-kindergarten and kindergarten children. Washington, DC: National Forum on the Future of Children and Families, National Research Council.

Gomez, M. L., Graue, M. E., & Bloch, M. N. (1991). Reassessing portfolio assessment: Rhetoric and reality. *Language Arts, 68,* 620–628.

Graue, M. E. (1991, April). Construction of community and the meaning of being a parent. In *Connecting to culture, constructing the self—or teaching/learning in a social/cultural perspective.* Symposium conducted at the annual meeting of the American Educational Research Association, Chicago.

Gullickson, A. R. (1984). Teacher perspectives of their instructional use of tests. *Journal of Educational Research, 77*, 244–248.

Gullickson, A. R. (1985). Student evaluation techniques and their relationship to grade and curriculum. *Journal of Educational Research, 79*, 96–100.

Gullickson, A. R. (1986). Teacher education and teacher-perceived needs in educational measurement and evaluation. *Journal of Educational Measurement, 23*, 347–354.

Gullickson, A. R., & Ellwein, M. C. (1985). Post-hoc analysis of teacher-made tests: The goodness of fit between prescription and practice. *Educational Measurement: Issues and Practice, 4*(1), 15–18.

Haney, W., & Madaus, G. M. (1989). Searching for alternatives to standardized tests: Whys, whats, and whithers. *Phi Delta Kappan, 70*, 683–687.

Heller, K. A., Holtzman, W. H., & Messick, S. (1982). Placing children in special education: A strategy for equity. Washington, DC: National Academy Press.

Johnston, P. (1987). Teachers as evaluation experts. *The Reading Teacher, 40*, 744–748.

Koretz, D. (1988). Arriving in Lake Wobegon: Are standardized tests exaggerating achievement and distorting instruction? *American Educator, 12*(2), 8–15, 46–52.

Lamme, L. L., & Hysmith, C. (1991). One school's adventure into portfolio assessment. *Language Arts, 68*, 629–640.

Lareau, A. (1989). *Home advantage.* London: The Falmer Press.

Linn, R. L. (1986). Educational testing and research needs and policy issues. *American Psychologist, 41*, 1153–1160.

Linn, R. L., Graue, M. E., & Sanders, N. M. (1990). Comparing state and district test results to national norms: The validity that everyone is above average. *Educational Measurement: Issues & Practice, 9*(3), 5–14.

Lissitz, R. W., Schafer, W. D., & Wright, M. V. (1986, April). *Measurement training for school personnel: Recommendations and reality.* Paper presented at the annual meeting of the American Educational Research Association, San Francisco.

McDermott, R. P., & Goldman, S. V. (1983). Teaching in multicultural settings. In L. v. d. Berg-Eldering, F. J. M. de Rijcke & L. V. Zuck (Eds.), *Multicultural education: A challenge for teachers* (pp. 145–163). Dordrecht, Holland: Foris.

McLean, L. (1990). Time to replace the classroom test with authentic measurement. *Alberta Journal of Educational Research, 36*(1), 78–84.

National Commission on Excellence in Education (1983). *A nation at risk: The imperative for educational reform.* Washington, DC: Author.

Oakes, J. (1985). *Keeping track: How schools structure inequality.* New Haven: Yale University Press.

O'Sullivan, R. G., & Chalnick M. K. (1991). Measurement-related course work requirements for teacher certification and recertification. *Educational Measurement: Issues and Practice, 10*(1), 17–19, 23.

Resnick, L. B. (Ed.) (1989). *Knowing, learning and instruction: Essays in honor of Robert Glaser.* Hillsdale, NJ: Lawrence Erlbaum Associates.

Rottenberg, C., & Smith, M. L. (1990, April). *Unintended effects of external testing in elementary schools.* Paper presented at the annual meeting of the American Educational Research Association, Boston.

Schafer, W. D., & Lissitz, R. W. (1987). Measurement training for school personnel: Recommendations and reality. *Journal of Teacher Education, 37,* 57–63.

Shepard, L. A. (1989). Why we need better assessments. *Educational Leadership, 46*(7), 4–9.

Shepard, L. A. (1991). The influence of standardized tests on early childhood curriculum, teachers, and children. In B. Spodek & O. N. Saracho (Eds.), *Yearbook in early childhood education* (pp. 166–189). New York: Teachers College Press.

Shepard, L. A. (1991). Psychometricians' beliefs about learning. *Educational Researcher, 20*(7), 2–16.

Shepard, L. A., & Kreitzer, A. E. (1987). The Texas teacher test. *Educational Researcher, 16*(6), 22–31.

Sleeter, C. E., & Grant, C. A. (1987). An analysis of multicultural education in the United States. *Harvard Educational Review, 57,* 421–444.

Smith, M. L. (1991). Put to the test: The effects of external testing on teachers. *Educational Researcher, 20*(5), 8–11.

Stiggins, R. J. (1988). Revitalizing classroom assessment: The highest instructional priority. *Phi Delta Kappan, 69,* 363–368.

Stiggins, R. J., & Bridgeford, N. J. (1985). The ecology of classroom assessment. *Journal of Educational Measurement, 22,* 271–286.

Vygotsky, L. S. (1978). *Mind in society.* Cambridge: Harvard University Press.

Wiggins, G. (1989). A true test: Toward more authentic and equitable assessment. *Phi Delta Kappan, 70,* 703–713.

Williams, R. L., Mosby, D., & Hinson, V. (1976). Critical issues in achievement testing of children from diverse educational backgrounds. Paper presented at the invitational Conference on Achievement Testing of Disadvantaged and Minority Students for Educational Program Evaluation. Washington, DC: U.S. Office of Education.

Wise, S. L., Lukin, L. E., & Roos, L. L. (1991). Teacher beliefs about training in testing and measurement. *Journal of Teacher Education, 42,* 37–42.

Chapter 6

◆ ◆ ◆ ◆

Reconstructing Bilingual Education from a Multicultural Perspective

Toni Griego-Jones

University of Wisconsin-Milwaukee

Introduction

Bilingual education is not a subject or content area, but is an approach to educating students, much like multicultural education is an approach to perceiving education. All subject areas and field experiences discussed in this book are a part of bilingual teaching and can be viewed from a bilingual education perspective as well as from a multicultural and social reconstructionist perspective.

The simplest and most common way of defining *bilingual education* is to say it is education that uses two languages in teaching. The two languages are usually a child's native language and a second language that the child is learning. To understand bilingual education in today's public schools then, we must understand what using more than one language for instruction has historically meant in our society and schools.

Contrary to popular notions, the United States has always been a multilingual, multicultural society. From its beginning as a nation, people from many different language groups have made up American society and use of various languages in schools has often been a source of conflict between linguistic minorities and the linguistic majority. For teachers, the importance of understanding the ongoing struggle over the use of languages other than English in schooling is twofold: First, it helps put current controversies over bilingual education in perspective, and second, those of us who work with children and their families must realize the symbolic power of language in society as well as its instructional function if we are to succeed in educating children.

The following section reviews the history of using non-English languages in schooling. The ability to use non-English languages was never the result of a pedagogical conviction that children benefit from instruction in languages they understand (Andersson & Boyer, 1978). Instead, such use has been the result of language minority groups' struggle for access to education and their desire to instill pride of their cultural heritage in their children. When language minority groups had the political influence to demand instruction in their languages, local schools responded.

Teachers might want to deal only with instructional and curricular aspects of educating children, but they cannot escape the social and political struggles surrounding use of non-English languages in public schools.

Historical Perspective on Non-English Languages in Schooling

Tracing the use of languages other than English in our country, we find that before the arrival of Europeans in the New World, more than 500 American Indian languages were spoken in North America. Many of these are still in use today. When Europeans arrived in the 1500s, it was Spanish speakers who, by colonizing the American Southwest and Puerto Rico, firmly entrenched their language in what is now the United States. Spanish continues to be a dominant language in these areas today. Throughout the 1600s immigrants from almost every northern and western European nation flowed into the Eastern seaboard. At the time of the American Revolution (when English was established as the dominant language of the new country), German, Scotch, Irish, Dutch, French, Swedish, Spanish, Portuguese, Danish, and Welsh were widely spoken in the 13 colonies (Andersson & Boyer, 1978; Castellanos, 1985; Crawford, 1989).

When the new country was established with English as the dominant language, the freedom to use other languages in public education became a matter of political conflict. When a language minority group was large enough and politically powerful enough, it was able to insist that its language be used in private or public schooling. In the 1700s and 1800s, Germans were the largest non-English group and, consequently, schools using German as the exclusive medium of instruction or in various combinations with English were common until the late 1800s.

During that time, American public schools were locally controlled and therefore responsive to political pressure from ethnic groups attending them. This allowed immigrant groups to incorporate their linguistic and cultural traditions into schools and make the preservation of their cultural identity a legitimate responsibility of public education (Castellanos, 1985). This preservation of cultural identity usually took the form of instruction in a group's native language in schools, either exclusively or in combination with English.

Spanish became an important language when the United States acquired the Southwest part of the country from Mexico in 1848. The U.S. expansion to the West and Southwest in the mid-1800s was accompanied by immediate confrontation between Spanish-speaking residents of those regions and the English-speaking newcomers. This cultural and linguistic clash still exists today in schools and other public arenas. The use of Spanish in public places, including schools, has been prohibited by law at various times. Students who knew only Spanish were effectively excluded from instructional programs when schools refused to use Spanish for instruction (Carter, 1970; Johnson & Hernandez, 1970; Obledo & Alcala, 1980). Not only were students denied access to instruction, they also were punished in school for speaking Spanish.

Although controversy and sporadic use of languages other than English in schools have always been a part of our history, the widespread use of bilingual programs in public schools did not occur until the 1960s. Several factors— the development of a bilingual model in Florida by Cuban refugees, rising Hispanic political influence, and the Civil Rights struggle—converged to bring about deliberate development of instructional programs using a non-English language as a medium of instruction in public schools.

The influx of Cuban refugees to the United States in the late 1950s and early 1960s brought an educated middle class with experienced teachers to the United States. They helped develop a bilingual program for Cuban and American children at The Coral Way Elementary School in Dade County, Florida. With private funding from the Ford Foundation, the school developed a model of bilingual education that used Spanish to teach Cuban children. And, for the first time, a bilingual program also emphasized the benefit of learning a second language for speakers of English.

The academic success of the Coral Way experiment provided fuel for Hispanic political advocacy groups, who had long demanded bilingual programs. The program in Florida gave impetus to the political struggle in other parts of the country by showing that a bilingual approach (using two languages) could successfully educate language minority children in an English-speaking society. Hispanic pressure groups began to push for national bilingual programs and their increasing political influence helped bring about the passage of the federal Bilingual Education Act of 1968. Federal and state legislation during the 1970s also brought guidelines for programs, funding for teacher training, materials and curriculum development, and various types of monitoring and evaluation.

A third factor, the Civil Rights movement of the 1950s and '60s also called attention to inequities in schooling for ethnic and language minority students. The Supreme Court decision in *Brown v. Board of Education* (1954), which highlighted inequity in schooling for African American children, also helped point out inequities in schooling for other people of color, including language minority children. Attention began to focus on the needs of students of color, and bilingual programs were offered as a way of addressing instructional needs of language minority or non-English speaking children.

Other court decisions, including the landmark *Lau v. Nichols* (1974), focused exclusively on inequity in education of ethnic and language minority students. Although no specific programs were suggested by the courts to overcome the inequities, the use of the students' native languages for instruction was promoted by the insistence that children must understand instruction for instruction to be equitable. Consent decrees effectively created a presumption in favor of bilingual education (Andersson & Boyer, 1978) and guidelines developed in 1975 by the U.S. Office of Education (commonly called the Lau Remedies) further promoted the use of native languages for instruction in public schools.

Although well intentioned, the casting of bilingual education as a "remedy" for inequities resulted in a mindset that still persists in public schools: that languages other than English are deficiencies and something that should be purged. Students' native languages are often viewed as barriers keeping them from participating in the mainstream culture instead of as valuable communication vehicles for instruction. Unfortunately, something as potentially enriching to education as bilingual programs came to be regarded by educators, the public, funding sources, and even students as remedial or compensatory in nature, as programs aimed at removing language deficiencies in students and getting them ready to learn in "regular" educational settings.

In 1971, 30 states had legislation allowing bilingual instruction, while 20 others prohibited it (Ovando & Collier, 1985). By 1983 all 50 states permitted bilingual education, and some even mandated it through state legislation. In 1991, however, a number of state legislatures were caught up in the English-only debate and some have allowed bilingual education laws to lapse or be repealed. Spanish and English have figured as the most prominent languages in these debates, but other languages, notably German and Chinese, have also been part of the fray.

The Current State of Bilingual Programs in the United States

The most salient characteristic of bilingual programs in the United States today is simply the tremendous variation among them. It is difficult to describe them because of the extreme differences in student composition, program organization, teaching methodologies and approaches, and teacher backgrounds and skills across varying bilingual programs. Probably the only thing they have in common is that they are all aimed at developing proficiency in English. A 1978 U.S. Department of Education study of districts with bilingual programs found that every district's goal was to develop English to a level enabling students to participate in all-English classrooms (Hakuta & Gould, 1987).

Beyond that one general goal of developing English proficiency, the programs differ in their commitment to teaching other subject areas, developing children's native languages, and using children's native languages in instruction. For example, 91 percent of districts in the study discussed previously claimed their goal was to teach content areas in languages that students understand so they do not fall behind in school while learning English. Only 15 percent of the districts listed the maintenance of the students' native language as a goal.

Another variation within bilingual programs is that bilingual teachers often differ from district administrators and policymakers in what they think is important for children. Surveys of bilingual teachers indicate that they, too, want students to learn English, but they place a greater value on developing students' native languages and the learning of content areas (Ada, 1986; Clark & Milk, 1983; Garcia, 1988; Rodriguez, 1980).

Organizational Models

Bilingual programs are generally sorted according to their main goals and fall under transitional or developmental categories. Most programs are of the transitional type. Their main goal is to bring students to a minimum proficiency in English as quickly as possible without regard for native language development or even content area learning. The strongest emphasis of transitional bilingual programs is on the acquisition of English and, subsequently, of the mainstream American culture. Students' native languages are used for instruction only until they have acquired a minimal level of English proficiency, at which time they enter English-only classrooms.

Developmental bilingual programs not only teach children English but also actively develop students' native languages. Sometimes these programs are called Maintenance programs because they seek to maintain the native language while adding a second one. The goal of these programs is to develop proficiency in both languages to the point of developing fluent bilinguals. Some developmental programs, called Two-Way Bilingual programs, include native English speakers as a part of their program design, and their goal is to develop bilingualism in both English speakers and other language speakers.

Students in Bilingual Classrooms

Because modern bilingual programs were cast as remedies for non-English speaking children, only a few programs enroll English speakers: those with the stated purpose of developing bilingualism in all students (Two-Way bilingual programs) and those under desegregation orders. Consequently, most bilingual classrooms are made up exclusively of minority, non-English speaking children. Most of these students are Spanish speakers, but in a few areas of the country, there are programs for Chinese, Vietnamese, and Hmong.

An estimated 4 million people speak more than 120 major languages in the United States today (Delgado-Gaitan & Trueba, 1991) and most large urban systems claim students from at least 70 language groups. Districts try to serve students from non-English homes either through bilingual programs or through English as a Second Language programs. Bilingual programs are usually implemented when school districts have large numbers of one language group and ESL programs are used when districts have fewer numbers from many language groups.

Even with the expansion of bilingual and ESL programs over the years, some non-English students are not in either type of program. Only those students with the *least* proficiency in English are assigned to these programs. Placement in a program is exclusively based on students' knowledge of English. Little consideration is given to native language proficiency or subject matter knowledge in placing or grouping students. They are classified strictly according to their level of English proficiency. Those with the lowest scores on English proficiency measures are targeted for bilingual or ESL programs. When students reach a minimal proficiency level in English they are "exited" from bilingual or ESL programs into "regular" classrooms.

Federal and state legislation mandating programs for those least-proficient students refer to them as limited English proficient or LEP students. Educators have generally adopted that label. Most recent national school enrollment information indicates that 2.2 million, or 5.7 percent of children in public schools fit the U.S. government's definition of limited English proficient (U.S. Department of Education, 1991, p. 10).

The limited English proficient (LEP) count is an underestimate of the number of students from non-English speaking homes who could benefit from bilingual programs. There are many children for whom English is a second language who do not receive help in schools. For example, in California, where the largest number of language minority students reside, one explanation for chronic underachievement of students in some high schools was that many students not identified as LEP, in fact, had difficulty with English because it was their second language (California Department of Education, 1990). The failure to correctly diagnose students' needs has also resulted in an inordinate number of language minority students being placed inappropriately in special education programs for learning disabilities (Baca & Cervantes, 1989; Cummins, 1981; Ortiz & Yates, 1983).

Surveys show that less than a quarter of students for whom these programs were intended are actually in bilingual programs. So, where are the rest of the students who need bilingual programs? A 1978 national survey of 1.7 million limited English proficient students age 5–14 indicated that 23 percent were in bilingual classrooms, 11 percent were in English classrooms with ESL support, and 58 percent were in exclusively English-medium classrooms (O'Malley, 1982).

The fact that many, if not most, language minority students are in regular English-only classrooms has implications for "regular" teacher education. So far, teacher preparation has never included information on how to effectively educate students from non-English home backgrounds. Changing demographics and the small numbers of students served in bilingual/ESL programs demand that all teachers, not just bilingual and ESL teachers, need to understand second language acquisition. Indications are that almost half of the nation's teachers (42.2 percent) have had experience with language minority students, but only 7 percent of them were in bilingual or ESL classrooms (Wagonner & O'Malley, 1985).

Curriculum and Instruction in Bilingual Classrooms

Bilingual programs are housed in "regular" school buildings, preschool through high school. In large districts that have significant numbers of non-English speaking students, bilingual elementary schools often have at least one bilingual classroom at each grade level and secondary schools offer bilingual core content area classes.

Curriculum

The core curriculum in public school bilingual classrooms is the same as that for any other classroom. The only significant curricular difference is the focus on language development (ESL and the appropriate native language) and attention to the cultural heritage of the targeted language minority group. Besides teaching language, science, math, social studies, art, and music, bilingual teachers must facilitate language learning in everything they do. They are concerned with how best to teach non-English speaking students the full range of subjects while developing native and second-language skills. What are the most effective ways to create environments that can accomplish all that bilingual classrooms demand?

Instruction

Bilingual programs in the 1970s reflected practices found in foreign language teaching—drills and memorization of dialogues—and emphasized studying the structures of language. Recently, bilingual teachers have been experimenting with more natural approaches to facilitating language acquisition. Research in second language acquisition has produced sound theoretical bases for using more active, student-oriented approaches, such as total physical response, individualized instruction, language experience, and a whole language approach. Many teachers subscribe to a natural approach that creates a nonpressure environment that allows learning a second language much as students acquired their first language. Others emphasize a functional approach that centers on English skills necessary for success in academic settings (Ovando & Collier, 1985; Wong-Fillmore & Valadez, 1986).

Because bilingual teachers are part of the larger teaching force, they are also involved in the panoply of strategies and methodologies that other teachers are. Any and all approaches current in the teaching of subject areas can be found in bilingual classrooms.

Classroom Management

This is a key issue for teachers juggling two languages of instruction and planning for individual students' abilities and achievement within each language. Programs are experimenting with a variety of management approaches such as alternating days, half days, or weeks for using each language, team teaching using native speakers (teachers) of each language, bilingual teachers working with paraprofessionals, and mainstreaming students for content area subjects and a host of other management plans.

Bilingual Teacher Preparation

Delivering a school's curriculum in two languages requires that a teacher have a high level of proficiency in the native language of the students as well as in English. This level of bilingualism is difficult to achieve and teachers vary considerably in target language and English proficiency. Some are native speakers of the language of the students. Others are native English speakers who have learned the language of their students as a second language.

Although bilingual teachers are in demand in public schools, higher education has been slow to respond to this demand. Most teacher preparation programs that do exist were initially funded by Title VII of the Bilingual Education Act and are still heavily dependent on federal funding. Because bilingual education is inherently an interdisciplinary field, drawing expertise from education, social sciences, and language studies, bilingual teacher preparation programs use faculty and courses from a variety of departments. Programs are usually found in education departments, most in curriculum and instruction or elementary education (Johnson & Binkley, 1987).

Due to outside funding and the broad, widely encompassing nature of the field, bilingual teacher preparation has not been easily incorporated into teacher education in colleges and universities. Scholarly research in second language acquisition, bilingualism, or language minority concerns in general is woefully underfunded and unappreciated at the university level. As in public schools, there is an acute shortage of faculty for bilingual teacher preparation programs.

Beyond language proficiency, university preparation for bilingual teaching involves studying first and second language acquisition theory and practice (usually requiring some study of linguistics), cross-cultural studies focusing on the target language group, methods courses, and field experiences in bilingual classrooms. Certification requirements vary nationwide but the endorsement to teach in bilingual classrooms is usually an addition to a teacher's elementary or secondary license. Since 1976, when the first training programs under the Bilingual Education Act began, there has been a dramatic increase in the quality and numbers of professionally prepared teachers, but numbers still fall short of the increasing need (Ovando & Collier, 1985; Wagonner & O'Malley, 1985; National Forum on Personnel Needs for Districts with Changing Demographics, 1990).

Demographic trends in public school populations, the demand for qualified bilingual teachers, and subsequent pressures on teacher preparation programs can only increase. Population growth trends show language minority student populations increasing in all school districts that have traditionally enrolled concentrations of language minority students. Now, language minority students are also enrolling in districts that have never had significant numbers. Furthermore, more native languages are represented in school populations than ever, and language minority students are increasing even in districts that are experiencing decreases in enrollment. All this results in projections calling for as many as 175,000 bilingual teachers in the United States in the next several years, assuming a 20-to-1 student-teacher ratio (National Forum on Personnel Needs for Districts with Changing Demographics, 1990).

The numbers and spread of language minority students suggest that *all* teachers in public schools will need to know something about second-language learning and about the cultural backgrounds of language minority students (Diaz-Soto, 1991; Griego-Jones, 1991; Nieto, 1992). To adequately prepare teachers, bilingual and non-bilingual, colleges and universities must adjust teacher preparation programs to include knowledge and skills involved in teaching language minority students.

Bilingual Education That Is Social Reconstructionist

A multicultural and social reconstructionist approach has been defined as one that addresses societal issues that affect students and helps them learn to work collectively for change (Sleeter & Grant, 1988). Social reconstructionist classrooms encourage students to take an active stance on issues and to be in charge of their own lives.

With this definition in mind, reflection on the history and current status of bilingual education produces questions related to goals and practice in bilingual programs:

- Are the goals and strategies of bilingual education compatible with a social reconstructionist philosophy and approach?
- Is the organization and place of bilingual education in public schooling compatible with a multicultural and social reconstructionist philosophy?
- Does the current state of bilingual education reflect a social reconstructionist philosophy?
- Does bilingual teacher training promote this type of approach? If not, what would have to happen for bilingual education to reflect social reconstructionist thinking?
- How would the structure and organization of bilingual programs have to change?

In keeping with the definition of multicultural and social reconstructionist thinking, two aspects of bilingual education will be considered to answer the questions posed. First, we will reflect on bilingual classrooms (the students and curriculum) and second, on bilingual teacher preparation.

Bilingual Classrooms

Students Perhaps the most important aspect to be viewed from a social reconstructionist perspective is the student composition in bilingual classrooms. There is a tendency to label any classroom that is not White, middle class, and English speaking as multicultural. So, for some people, bilingual classrooms appear to be inherently multicultural settings because they are populated by non-mainstream language minority students.

But on second glance, we see that most bilingual classrooms are actually monocultural, containing only students from *one* language and culture group, usually a Hispanic student population. The practice of assigning only language minority students to bilingual programs seems contrary to multicultural and social reconstructionist thinking.

The isolation of language minority children and lack of attention to interrelationships between language groups keep bilingual programs from fulfilling their potential as social reconstructionist programs when they fail to teach language minority children (or the few majority students in them) how to effect social change and intercommunication between groups. Emphasis in curriculum and instruction in bilingual classrooms has been on helping minority students cope with what they will find when they move into the mainstream. Little thought is given to how to change things that are inequitable in that mainstream they will be entering.

To change this orientation in bilingual classrooms means more than teaching political awareness and strategies for social change. It means a complete reorientation and commitment to social change rather than an absolute acceptance of the social order as it exists. Acceptance of the existing social order is manifest in bilingual classrooms in the preoccupation with "transitioning" students.

The problem with that orientation is that it puts the burden of maintaining social order on the language minority child and relieves the rest of society from its responsibility to contribute to social equilibrium. All the attention is focused on how the minority child can fit in to the larger society, never considering that what might need to be done is to adjust the mainstream as well.

Curriculum Bilingual classroom curricula do include study of the target population's history and cultural heritage, but again, the emphasis is on building pride and self-esteem so that language minority students can cope with mainstream society and be "successful." There is nothing multicultural about focusing on transition of one ethnic and linguistic group into the majority society to the exclusion and devaluation of the minority group. It seems contradictory that bilingual programs claim to value language minorities' language and culture and then spend their time in the classroom pushing students to leave their language and culture and move into another. Instead of framing the classrooms as opportunities to add another language and culture, they are cast as transition "holding tanks" for students until they have acquired a minimal level of English.

Even though most bilingual classrooms may not be achieving their potential from a social reconstructionist perspective, it can be argued that the programs are examples of social reconstructionism at work because they are a response to the inequitable education of a segment of students. However, when bilingual programs are viewed only as vehicles for ridding students of their native languages and cultures, they function as tools of oppression in their role of superassimilator as much as they are vehicles for empowering language minority students.

Bilingual Teacher Preparation The second aspect of bilingual education, teacher preparation, also needs adjustment if bilingual education is to become social reconstructionist. Even bilingual educators think small when they allow themselves to be caught in the trap of "remedial" schooling for "limited" students. The orientation toward limited students binds educators' thinking as well as that of the public. They are often caught in a missionary mode of remediating children instead of remediating society. Somewhere a noble purpose was derailed.

The reorientation of bilingual teachers is key to enabling bilingual education to be social reconstructionist. Teacher education is the most feasible way to alter current practice in bilingual classrooms because it is the most manageable point of departure. Short of massive change in societal attitudes, preparation of knowledgeable, committed teachers is a most effective tool for change in public education (Fullan, 1982; Joyce, 1990; Lieberman, 1988). Thus, bilingual teacher preparation will have to undergo a reorientation to bring about a revolution in the classroom.

What little is known about bilingual teacher preparation suggests the programs do not show how to teach students cross-cultural communication and how to influence social change. Studies that analyzed skill areas and competencies facilitating intercultural communication found that bilingual teacher training programs did not include these kinds of skills (Chu & Levy, 1988; Clark & Milk, 1983). Teacher preparation in general perpetuates the status quo rather than preparing activist change agents. Bilingual teacher preparation, by and large, is no different.

In answering the question about whether bilingual education as it exists in public schools today is multicultural and social reconstructionist, the answer would have to be yes and no. Yes, because the very existence of bilingual programs is an example of social reconstruction. But in examining components of public school bilingual classrooms and bilingual teacher preparation the answer is no.

Becoming Social Reconstructionist Many strategies can be suggested for teaching in a multicultural and social reconstructionist manner, but bilingual classrooms are in the unique position of offering one megastrategy, that of learning a second language. There is no more effective, potent strategy for facilitating understanding of another culture than learning its language. The capacity to alter human experience by entering the mind and heart of another cultural group through language makes the development of classroom activities incorporating cultural awareness into the curriculum seem like tinkering.

The ability of language to empower individuals and groups, as well as to shut them out, has been at the root of the controversy throughout our history. The empowerment quality of language has tremendous implications for social reconstructionist theory. What better way to empower language minorities than to give knowledge of the dominant society's mode of communication and thought? On the other hand, what better way to enable language *majority* group students to understand other cultures than to put them in the position of having to articulate their thoughts through another's language? Bilingual classrooms are able to use that most powerful tool of language to transform human experience, and make lessons about oppression and social reconstruction take life for each student (Cziko, Lambert, & Gutter, 1979–80; Lambert & Tucker, 1972; Nieto, 1992; Wong-Fillmore & Valadez, 1986).

Restructured Bilingual Classrooms

Distinguishing characteristics of multicultural and social reconstructionist classrooms would be found in students, curriculum, and teachers. In bilingual classrooms that reflect social reconstructionist philosophy, there would be two language groups represented. Classrooms would not be limited to language minority students, but would include English speakers. Since most language minority students are Spanish speakers, the non-English group would likely be Spanish speaking, but any other language group could make up the non-English component. Two-Way Bilingual models fit this student composition requirement and hold promise for teaching in a social reconstructionist manner. They develop students' native languages and cultures as worthy in themselves, not just as vehicles for transition, and they do this for both language groups. This mixture of students makes bilingual classrooms more viable places to learn intercommunication.

Many suggest that the hope of the future for bilingual education lies in the expansion of Two-Way program models (Hakuta, 1986; Ovando & Collier, 1985). This undoubtedly is the preferred model of bilingual educators, but they are not always in charge of their own destiny in schools. Society may be willing to allow experiments, but wholesale bilingual schooling for minority and majority students may be a long way off. Those who have struggled through the evolution of bilingual education know that, in fact, bilingual education advocates started with visions of bilingual benefits for all students, but have had to settle for less (Andersson & Boyer, 1978; Fishman, 1982).

A solid research base is being developed by anthropologists, sociologists, and educators on the process that language minority children go through in learning a second language and assimilating into a new culture. But there is little research in the United States on language majority children learning another language, particularly a minority language that is less valued by the larger society. Those interested in social reconstructionism should promote research on the effects of learning other languages for English-speaking students. What can majority language students learn about themselves and their relationships to other culture groups? How does the status of minority languages affect their learning those languages, especially if majority speakers are required to learn that language not just as a subject, but as a second language?

The distinction between learning a foreign language and acquiring a second language lies in the amount of exposure a learner has to native speakers of the target language (Ovando & Collier, 1985) and the purpose for learning the new language. Learners of a second language need to become proficient and functional in their new language usually because they are going to have to live and communicate with native speakers of their new language. This is why we talk of language minority students in the United States learning English as a second language, not as a foreign language. Foreign languages are usually learned out of their cultural context and away from native speakers of the language. Second languages become part of a learner's daily repertoire for communication, a ready alternative to their native language.

Learning a second language to the proficiency of a native speaker sets up expectations that the learner's command of the cultural code of a language group will also be proficient. It is this facility in culture as well as language that bilingual classrooms can facilitate by mixing linguistically and culturally different groups. Delgado-Gaitan and Trueba (1991) state:

> Language, as the instrument par excellence for social intercourse, is essential in establishing the parameters of membership in social groupings and in opening the lines of communication. Not only through its spoken and written forms, but through kinetic, paralinguistic and other forms of face-to-face communications, language ultimately establishes social relationships and ongoing meaningful exchanges. (p. 25)

Language development would be the overriding focus of multicultural classrooms, native language as well as the second language. Communicative competence, which is vital to bringing about social change and mutual understanding, would be the expected outcome for the two language groups in multicultural and social reconstructionist classrooms.

Besides strong emphasis on native development of each language, curriculum would include structured learning of a second language from the first day of elementary school. Increasing exposure and formal instruction in the second language throughout elementary grades would bring students to middle school prepared to attend classes in either language. A sample progression is outlined in Table 6.1.

TABLE 6.1 Sample plan for second language instruction

Level	Native Language	Second Language
Pre-Kindergarten	All content areas taught to each group in native language by a native language teacher	Informal, consistent exposure to second language through contact with each other (e.g., play, games, movies)
Primary 1–3	Subjects (language arts, math, science, social studies) taught in native language	Continue informal mixing
	Continue teaching language arts in native language	Art, music, p.e. in second language
Upper elementary 4–5	As students gain proficiency in second language, begin to teach math, science, etc., in second, alternating with native language	Continue with above
	Continue native language arts	Introduce formal time for 2nd language and ensure opportunities for using it (contact with other language speakers)
Middle school 6–8	Continue native language arts	Continue formal study of second language
	Alternate teaching of all subjects in the native and second language	

Two language groups would be represented in the classroom. The combination of focusing on each native language group to develop strong native and cognitive skills and then mixing the two groups to provide opportunities to learn the second language (informal and formal) requires close collaboration between a team of two teachers.

Each teacher must be a native speaker of one language and have a working proficiency in the other, at least able to understand and communicate with children and parents. The native speaker of each language would instruct students of the same native language in core subjects and would teach his/her native language as a second language to the other group. Team teaching would require joint planning, instruction, and ongoing assessment to ensure learning of subject concepts and language specific to each content area.

Many different management schemes could be used to mix and alternate language groups. Whatever the scheme, the guiding principles would be to facilitate cognitive, linguistic, and social development in the native language (e.g., learning to read) *and* the constant, consistent acquisition of a second language through natural contact with other language speakers. As students' proficiency in the second language increases, alternating languages becomes easier. As students develop proficiency in the second language, it becomes more like teaching them in their native language. This level of proficiency will take at least four to five years.

It will be more difficult for majority English speakers to acquire a second language because they will not have it around them outside the classroom like minority language speakers will. An extra effort will have to be made to bring majority language speakers into contact with the minority language community outside the school.

Experience has also shown that attention will have to be given to upgrading the status of the minority language because societal attitudes toward it are pervasive and influence students' (majority and minority) attitudes toward using it and learning it. Discussion of minority language and its relative status in both language communities will have to be part of the study of the second language. Societal uses of and attitudes toward language will be part of the social studies curriculum.

These classrooms would not be remedial places to get rid of a language deficiency but enriching places where all students would learn a second language. Advocates of multicultural education have sometimes given suggestions for incorporating minority languages into daily classroom routines. Although well intentioned, this almost token attention to the native language of students in the classroom can contribute to the perception of minority languages as lower status. Learning a second language is difficult, serious business and involves personal, permanent behavior change.

Underlying most suggestions given for multicultural teaching in bilingual classrooms is the assumption that it is possible to teach multiculturally with only one population group (language minority children) in the classroom. The vision of multicultural and social reconstructionist classrooms proposed here does not accept that assumption. The difficulty with accepting the isolation of language minority students is the one-sided expectation of learners. Interaction and social change require more than commitment and understanding from one group of people. When language minority students meet the outside world, how are they perceived by the majority? What have majority children learned about language minority students that would enable a different type of interaction among them? If majority students have not been in classrooms with language minority students, chances are they have learned little that would change the current societal attitudes, specifically oppression of minority language speakers.

It is next to impossible to achieve the goals of multicultural and social reconstructionist philosophy without a mixture of students. Isolating language minority students only ignores the real conflict over power and oppression and does not come to grips with the powerful role language plays in society's ability to empower and oppress.

Curriculum in multicultural and social reconstructionist classrooms would include development of personal and family histories of all students in the tradition of the Foxfire Project (Wigginton, 1975). These personal stories would be the starting point for integrating subjects into a total curriculum that would revolve around the mixture of students in the classroom. Curriculum would reflect the heritages of students and the *current* situations of students, not just information about countries of origin of language minority children. All students would be involved in recording and documenting the developing history of individual class members and the group as a whole in American society.

The role of culture in determining human behavior would also be a part of the curriculum. Usually cross-cultural studies have been limited to the cultural traditions of particular language minority groups and not seen as the study of human behavior. Anthropology and sociology would be taught from elementary school through high school. Concepts from those fields would be adapted to the age group. A better understanding of the human condition would begin to shape a socially reconstructed sociopolitical context for public education.

The curriculum also would include study of oppression and inequity in education as well as in social, economic, and political arenas. In analyzing oppression and social inequity, students must deal with those concepts from their own backgrounds and perspectives. A White, English-speaking, middle-class child sees things, including oppression, through different eyes than a non-English speaking child of color. How can they understand oppression in the same way? Do they have to understand it to change the social order? Don't they both have to proactively work at changing society? It may be necessary to force the *experience* of being in another's culture, not just to *learn about* that culture. Learning a second language to fluency can give that experience.

Learning a second language is offered as a strategy for social reconstructionist classrooms knowing full well that the majority society has little interest in learning about minority cultures, much less in putting themselves in the uncomfortable, vulnerable position of learning a second language. The obvious question is why would the public want to do that? The shrinking world, economic competition, and multicultural reality of our nation and the world may not leave us a choice. Economic necessity alone may force our schools to teach other languages, not as elective subjects, but to a functional proficient level.

The Context of Bilingual Education

The historical and current sociopolitical context of the United States determines the organization and place of bilingual education in schools and bilingual teacher preparation programs in higher education. Reflection on the history of bilingual education in our country makes it clear that languages used in schools not only aid or hinder instruction, but also have the ability to provoke or subdue social protest and action. Use of languages other than English has incited public reaction in ways that few other educational strategies have because it is at once an instructional approach and an emotional symbol of resistance to oppression for minority groups.

Bilingual education is social reconstructionism at work, but the work is hindered because bilingual classrooms are not acknowledged as places to address oppression and inequity. Instead, they have become places to instruct minority students in the ways of the mainstream and discussions about bilingual education revolve around how best to transition minority students into those ways. Debates become clouded because they are supposedly framed in terms of effective education.

A more honest framework would acknowledge that the conflict is much deeper and basically one of status and power in society. The arena of bilingual classrooms, then, is a most appropriate one in which to address social reconstructionist theory. Clarification of terms and analysis of issues are the business of social reconstructionism and clarification of terms in any debate can only help bring it to a resolution.

Progress is being made as the question of power is more widely recognized and openly acknowledged today than even 15 years ago when Paulston (1980) astutely asked the following:

> Who stands to gain, where 'gain' can be operationalized as an indicator of which group benefits in the power struggle. The literature on bilingual education is noticeable for the almost complete absence of such questions. The pious assumption is of course that the children are the ones who stand to gain, with indicators like standardized test scores on school achievement and self-concept. (p. 57)

Years later, Hakuta (1986) stated the following:

> Bilingual education openly acknowledges the legitimacy of non-English languages in a centrally important public institution, and it appears to threaten the status of English. That is what critics are reacting to. Were it not for the symbolic status of bilingual education, one could easily imagine the assimilationists applauding the goals of the current bilingual programs. (p. 226)

Bilingual classrooms that acknowledge the conflict and strive to resolve it by mutual empowerment of students become social reconstructionist. Neutralizing the conflict by having students learn each other's cultural and linguistic code even as they jointly develop a new culture could be the result of bilingual classrooms. If everyone has something to gain from bilingual education, perhaps it may be a feasible option for reconstructing public education. If bilingualism were a goal for all students and if American society could accept the worth of *every* language as a communication system, many of the goals of social reconstructionism would be achieved. Bilingual education conceived as an educational approach for all students instead of as a remedial approach for some students would be the embodiment of social reconstructionist theory. The role that bilingual education has played in the struggle to empower language minority students should be expanded to empower all students to live and cope in a multicultural society.

References

Ada, A. F. (1986). Creative education for bilingual teachers. *Harvard Educational Review, 56*(4), 386–394.

Andersson, T., & Boyer, M. (1978). *Bilingual schooling in the United States* (2nd ed.). Austin, TX: National Educational Laboratory Publishers, Inc.

Baca, L. M., & Cervantes, H. T. (1989). *The bilingual special education interface.* (2nd ed.) Englewood Cliffs, NJ: Merrill/Prentice Hall.

California Department of Education. (1990). *Bilingual education handbook, designing instruction for LEP students.* Sacramento: California Department of Education.

Carter, T. (1970). *Mexican Americans in school: A history of educational neglect.* New York: College Entrance Examination Board.

Castellanos, D. (1985). *The best of two worlds.* Trenton, NJ: New Jersey State Department of Education.

Chu, H., & Levy, J. (1988). Multicultural skills for bilingual teachers: Training for competency development. *Journal of the National Association for Bilingual Education, 12*(2), 153–169.

Clark, E. R., & Milk, R. D. (1983). Training bilingual teachers: A look at the Title VII graduate in the field. *Journal of the National Association for Bilingual Education, 8*(1), 41–53.

Crawford, J. (1989). *Bilingual education: History, politics, theory and practice.* Trenton, NJ: Crane Publishing Company, Inc.

Cummins, J. (1988). From multicultural to anti-racist education. In T. Skutnabb-Kangas & J. Cummins (Eds.), *Minority education: From shame to struggle* (pp. 127–157). Philadelphia: Multilingual Matters.

Cziko, G. A., Lambert, W. E., & Gutter, R. (1979–80). French immersion programs and students' social attitudes: A multidimensional investigation. *Journal of the National Association for Bilingual Education, 4*(2), 19–33.

Delgado-Gaitan, C., & Trueba, H. (1991). *Crossing cultural borders.* New York: The Falmer Press.

Diaz-Soto, L. (1991). Understanding bilingual/bicultural young children. *Young Children, 46*(2), 30–36.

Fishman, J., & Keller, G. (1982). *Bilingual education for Hispanic students in the United States.* New York: Teachers College Press.

Fullan, M. (1982). *The meaning of educational change.* New York: Teachers College Press.

Garcia, E. (1988). Effective schooling for language minority students. In National Clearinghouse for Bilingual Education (Ed.), *New Focus* (pp. 1–12). Occasional papers in bilingual education. Arlington, VA: Editor.

Griego-Jones, T. (1991). Rethinking programs for language minority students. *The Journal of Educational Issues of Language Minority Students, 9,* 61–74.

Hakuta, K. (1986). *Mirror of language.* New York: Basic Books, Inc.

Hakuta, K., & Gould, L. J. (1987). Synthesis of research on bilingual education. *Educational Leadership, 44*(6), 38–45.

Johnson, D. M., & Binkley, J. L. (1987). Management and organizational structure in university bilingual education programs: A national survey of Title VII. *Journal of the National Association for Bilingual Education, 11*(2), 95–116.

Johnson, H. S., & Hernandez, W. J. (1970). *Educating the Mexican American.* Valley Forge, PA: Judson Press.

Joyce, B. (Ed.). (1990). *Changing school culture through staff development.* Alexandria, VA: Association for Supervision and Curriculum Development.

Lambert, W. E., & Tucker, G. R. (1972). *Bilingual education of children: The St. Lambert experiment.* Rowley, MA: Newbury House.

Lieberman, A. (Ed.). (1988). *Building a professional culture in schools.* New York: Teachers College Press.

National Forum on Personnel Needs for Districts with Changing Demographics. (1990, May). *Staffing the multilingually impacted schools of the 1990s.* Washington, DC: U.S. Department of Education.

Nieto, S. (1992). *Affirming diversity, the sociopolitical context of multicultural education.* New York: Longman Publishing Group.

Obledo, M., & Alcala, C. (1980). Discrimination against the Spanish language in public service: A policy alternative. In D. J. R. Bruckner (Ed.), *Politics and language: Spanish and English in the United States* (pp. 155–162).

O'Malley, J. M. (1982). *Children's English and services study: Educational and needs assessment for language minority children with limited English proficiency.* Rosslyn, VA: InterAmerica Research Associates.

Ortiz, A. A., & Yates, J. R. (1983). Incidence of exceptionality among Hispanics: Implications for manpower planning. *Journal of the National Association for Bilingual Education, 7*(3), 41–54.

Ovando, C., & Collier, V. (1985). *Bilingual and ESL classrooms: Teaching in multicultural contexts.* New York: McGraw-Hill.

Paulston, C. B. (1980). *Bilingual education: Theories and issues.* Rowley, MA: Newbury House.

Rodriguez, A. M. (1980, July). Empirically defining competencies for effective bilingual teachers: A preliminary study. *Bilingual Education Paper Series of the National Dissemination and Assessment Center, 3*(12).

Sleeter, C. E., & Grant, C. (1988). *Making choices for multicultural education.* Englewood Cliffs, NJ: Merrill/Prentice Hall.

U.S. Department of Education. (1991, June). *The condition of bilingual education in the nation: A report to the Congress and the president.* Washington, DC: U.S. Department of Education, Office of the Secretary.

Wagonner, D., & O'Malley, M. (1985). Teachers of limited English proficient children in the United States. *Journal of the National Association for Bilingual Education, 9*(3), 25–42.

Wigginton, E. (Ed.). (1975). *Foxfire 3.* Garden City, NJ: Anchor Press Edition.

Wong-Fillmore, L., & Valadez, C. (1986). Teaching bilingual learners. In M. C. Wittrock (Ed.), *Handbook of Research on Teaching* (pp. 648–685). Englewood Cliffs, NJ: Merrill/Prentice Hall.

Chapter 7

◆ ◆ ◆ ◆

Multicultural Concerns and Classroom Management

Mary Lou Fuller

University of North Dakota

Introduction

Multicultural Education and the Population of Students

Stephanie Olsen is preparing to graduate. After 12 years of public school in the small city where she grew up and 4½ years of college, she is ready for her first elementary teaching position. She is both excited and apprehensive—excited at the idea of having her own classroom, and apprehensive because many of the positions advertised are in classrooms that differ dramatically from those she knew as a student and those she worked in during her field experiences. Stephanie has done well in her teacher education program, but she wonders whether she can meet the educational needs of these diverse classrooms. She is particularly concerned about how she will handle classroom management.

Stephanie was fortunate to attend a college of education requiring a course in multicultural education in her program. In this course, she learned that multicultural education is not a kind of education, but rather an orientation toward the educational process that is sensitive to the diverse backgrounds students bring with them to school (Sleeter & Grant, 1988).

In her teacher education program, Stephanie learned that many children in the public schools come from backgrounds different from her White, middle-class upbringing. She also learned that in 23 of the 25 largest school districts in the United States, children of color constitute the single largest population served (Gay, 1989).

These schools have changed markedly over the past half century, reflecting an increase in the number of people from culturally diverse populations in the United States. These changes will continue. In fact, relatively higher birth rates and increased immigration mean that by 2010, between 33 percent (Commission on Minority Participation, 1988) and 38 percent (Hodgkinson, 1989) of all K–12 students in the United States will be children of color (Griffith, Frase, & Ralph, 1989).

She also learned that while socioeconomic levels are less noticeable than skin color or language, they are equally important. In particular, teachers must consider issues associated with poverty because they permeate the lives of both children and their families. Ignoring poverty, Stephanie has learned, means ignoring important issues in the lives of one-fourth of all children in the United States currently, and as many as one-third of all children by 2000 (Haberman, 1989).

Stephanie's concerns about encountering diversity in her classroom are understandable. What can she do to prepare for the diversity of the student populations she'll be teaching? An important part of the answer lies in her developing a multicultural perspective—a perspective she can use in managing her classroom, among other things.

The purpose of this chapter is to help Stephanie, other teachers, and preservice teachers consider classroom management from a multicultural perspective. Because an in-depth exploration of all the cultures Stephanie might encounter is impossible, we will present another way for her to approach learning about children of other cultures and other socioeconomic groups. It is a process she can use to gather information and interpret experiences.

To help readers take a multicultural approach to classroom management, this chapter describes the nature of classroom management (with particular reference to discipline), and how it is affected by multicultural concerns. We present examples of cultural behaviors and then demonstrate the process of drawing management implications. In addition to classroom management, special attention is directed toward parental involvement because it is an important part of a child's educational experience generally and classroom management specifically. To be a good teacher, Stephanie will need to develop ways of working with parents whose cultures differ from hers, and some of those ways are considered in this chapter. Finally, we offer specific suggestions designed to help teachers learn about the cultures of their students.

Classroom Management and Discipline

In her classroom management course, Stephanie learned that attitudes toward the treatment of children have changed dramatically over time. During the Middle Ages, children were routinely beaten in the mistaken belief that they were inhabited by evil spirits who could be exorcised by corporal punishment—hence the expression "beat the devil out of that child." Canings (beatings) were the most common method of classroom control well into this century; corporal punishment is still legal in most of the United States. Now, though, there is less concern about evil spirits and more interest in children's needs as a way of understanding their behavior.

Stephanie Olsen shares that interest; that is why she was pleased that the course considered issues such as what classroom management is and the goals it seeks to address. Unfortunately, her course was like most others in that it did not address multicultural issues. This is unfortunate because she will need to consider these issues in her classroom if she is to address the needs of diverse student populations. Indeed, discussing those interactions is one of the goals of this chapter.

What Stephanie needed before she could appreciate the multicultural concerns of classroom management and discipline was a broader societal and educational view, a view that is multicultural and social reconstructionist in nature. She needed this view because before she could understand any individual child in her classroom, she needed an appreciation for and understanding of societal equality and cultural pluralism. This is because schools must "prepare citizens to work actively towards social structural equality; promote cultural pluralism and alternate life styles; [and] promote equal opportunity in the school" (Sleeter & Grant, 1993, p. 211).

Multiculturally sensitive classes based on a social reconstructionist perspective address inequities related to such diversities as race, class, gender, and disability. These courses help preservice teachers consider such crucial issues as tracking, learning styles, cooperative learning, resources available to students, pedagogy, meaningful curriculum, student culture, and of course, classroom management. In addition, they help develop the responsibility to work actively toward equality for all children.

Further, before Stephanie can appreciate the multicultural concerns of classroom management and discipline, she needs to consider the nature of classroom management and why it is an important concern. She also needs to see how classroom management differs from discipline and examine the various models of discipline. Finally, she must develop an understanding of the possible effects of cultural diversity on classroom management.

The Importance of Classroom Management

Classroom management is an integral part of all classroom activities. While the presence of good management does not guarantee a successful lesson, its absence means that even the best lesson will be lost. This is because successful classroom management helps create an environment where learning can take place.

It is the responsibility of teachers to make certain that the classroom environment is both conducive to learning and comfortable for students. Glasser (1986) points out that unless this happens, "teachers and parents needn't bother telling students how valuable school is to them: Unless classroom management works well, students will be dissatisfied; and if they are not satisfied in school, they will get little from the time they spend there" (p. 54).

One aspect of classroom management, discipline, is of particular concern to educators and parents. Each year since 1969, Phi Delta Kappa has sponsored a Gallup Poll of the public's attitudes toward education. One question asked is, "What do you think are the biggest problems with which the public schools in this community must contend?" In most years, the public has listed discipline as the No. 1 problem (Gallup & Clark, 1987) and teachers agree (Elam, 1989). In addition, student teachers ranked discipline as the greatest stress factor in their teaching (Abernathy, Manera, & Wright, 1985).

The Panel on the Preparation of Beginning Teachers (chaired by Ernest Boyer) identified three major areas of expertise needed by beginning teachers such as Stephanie: knowledge of how to manage a classroom, knowledge of subject matter, and understanding of their students' [cultural and] sociological backgrounds (Jones & Jones, 1995). To be truly effective, a teacher must approach these inter-related areas of expertise from a multicultural perspective.

Of 82 classroom management textbooks published between 1980 and 1991, 70 make no mention of multicultural concerns, 9 make only brief reference to them, and only 3 deal substantially with the issue.[1] Only one of these books took a multicultural approach, *Trouble-Free Teaching* (Grossman, 1990), while the other two focused on classroom management related to a single culture. In *Ribbin' Jivin' and Playing the Dozens* (Foster, 1986), the author talks about classroom management as it pertains to African Americans, and Lockart (1981) examines barriers to teaching Indian groups in *Resolving Discipline Problems for Indian Students*.

The Nature of Classroom Management

Too often educators look for "the answer" to classroom management concerns. Preservice teachers and practicing teachers alike enter classroom management courses looking for a specific formula that will result in the perfect classroom. For a formula for classroom management to work, however, all ingredients— including students—must be constant and unchanging. And because there are no absolutes when dealing with people, it is impossible for any formula to work with regularity.

But generalizations can be made about people's physical/socioemotional development needs, which Stephanie studied in educational psychology courses. This body of knowledge, when combined with data on family, economic, and cultural background, can help Stephanie develop basic understandings about students. It is these understandings—interpreted by teachers in terms of their personal philosophies and some basic rules of good organization—that result in good classroom management practices.

Classroom Management and Discipline: How Do They Differ?

Educators often err in using the terms *classroom management* and *discipline* as synonyms. This is an error because classroom management is much broader in scope than discipline; classroom management includes everything teachers do to increase student involvement and cooperation in classroom activities and to establish productive working environments for children. Classroom management is "the orchestration of a classroom . . . : planning curriculum, organizing procedures and resources, arranging the environment to maximize efficiency, monitoring student progress, anticipating potential problems" (Lemlech, 1988, p. 3).

Discipline is narrower in perspective. It deals with how children behave in the classroom and the teacher's ability to influence that behavior. Unfortunately, many people think discipline is characterized by autocratic authority and thus means punitive action or rigid control.

This authoritarian view stands in opposition to a more positive and productive definition of discipline: Discipline should help children move toward self-control. It is a way of helping children assume responsibility for their behavior. The ideas of dignity and respect—for both self and others—are inherent in this approach, as is the idea that children should behave in manners appropriate to them and the settings in which they find themselves.

This approach is more compatible with a multicultural perspective than is autocratic authority because it is governed by the behavioral norms of the group rather than a single set of expectations applied to all children in all settings. In this more humanistic, less punitive model, children are responsible to the group and to themselves for their behavior.

What is more, logical consequences follow from and are directly related to all of each child's behavior. Logical consequences express the reality of the social order, acknowledge mutual rights, and separate the deed from the doer (Albert, 1989; Dinkmeyer, McKay, & Dinkmeyer, 1980; Dreikurs, Grunwald, & Pepper, 1982). For example, a student who pours red paint on the floor would be expected to clean it up (as opposed to the punishment of missing recess, or writing something 500 times). A student who continually disrupts the lunch room might give up the right to eat there (as opposed to the punishment of staying after school, or being deprived of fun activities).

Logical consequences also follow appropriate behaviors but in less obvious ways. For example, while it is generally easy to spot the consequences of a negative behavior (the child who disrupts the class is removed), the positive consequence is less conspicuous, but just as valuable (the child who behaves in an appropriate manner not only benefits from the activity but also experiences the satisfaction of group acceptance and the pleasure of participation). In other words, the principle of logical consequences applies to all behavior, not simply transgressions.

By applying logical consequences to all behavior, this management approach helps children learn to make good decisions, be productive, interact well with others, and make good use of their educational environments. Responsibility for helping children learn these skills is shared by adults at school, adults at home, and the child. Through logical consequences, the child comes to realize that self-discipline is "a method of teaching appropriate behaviors and making wise decisions. . . ." (Keating, Pickering, Slack, & White, 1990, p. 3).

As an educator, Stephanie must employ a model of classroom management that is congruent with multicultural principles. Because multicultural education requires teachers to consider students' cultural and social backgrounds, and these backgrounds bear on how children will understand and interact with the environments in which they find themselves, the relationship of multicultural education and classroom management is obvious. "The key of the multicultural curriculum [and the key to classroom management] should be to help students develop decision-making and citizen-action skills" (Banks, 1991, p. 34).

Banks' description of multicultural goals supports Glasser's view of classroom management: Given both views, students are rational and capable of being responsible for their own behavior. Teachers need to help students learn to make good choices that will produce good behaviors since reasonable consequences follow both good and bad behaviors (Glasser, 1977).

Appropriate classroom behaviors are generally those agreed upon by the dominant culture, and often these are accepted less because they are meaningful to the children in the classroom and more because they carry the weight of tradition. For example, we know children learn best when they are actively involved in their learning, and yet in many classrooms "silence is golden" seems to be a whisper from the ghosts of teachers past when children's needs were less well understood than they are now.

Classification of Discipline Models

Theories of discipline are based on a variety of belief systems conceptualized in overlapping ways. No one theory is applicable to all cultures, or even to a single culture on all occasions. Skillful teachers select the model most philosophically congruent with a given culture and augment it with attributes from the other models when they address children's needs. Later in this chapter, this practice is demonstrated several times.

Wolfgang and Glickman (1980) classified discipline theories into three categories: "interventionist," "non-interventionist," and "interactionist."[2] While these categories are derived from psychological theories of child development, the authors build on these categories to include teacher behaviors useful in classroom management. Aspects of these belief systems are displayed in Table 7-1.

More specifically, interventionists maintain classroom discipline by planning and organizing the learning environment to shape students' behaviors in predetermined ways. Teachers adopting this view maintain complete authority over what happens in the classroom and it is the teacher's standards (and culture) that determine the criteria for acceptable behavior. Consequently, the interventionist model tends to perpetuate the values of the dominant culture.

In contrast, non-interventionists believe the teacher must play a more supportive role in helping students arrive at their own solutions to discipline problems. This position is humanistic in nature and is more concerned with inner feelings and processes than with observable behaviors. This model is culturally sensitive in that it places a high value on the whole child and factors, such as ethnicity, that influence children. The strength and weakness of this model both stem from its concentration on the individual child with proportionately lesser interest in the group. While individuals are given due and deserved attention, the dynamics of the classroom (working together for the benefit of the individual and the whole) are short-changed. This is a problem for children coming from cultural backgrounds where the group is more highly regarded than the individual. Many Hispanic and American Indian children, for example, might be confused by a non-interventionist approach to classroom management. This point will be discussed later.

TABLE 7.1   Aspects of Interactionist, Interventionist and Non-Interventionist Approaches to Classroom Management

	INTERVENTIONIST	NON-INTERVENTIONIST	INTERACTIONIST
Primary responsibility for control	teacher	student	student and teacher
Development of rules	teacher	student with teacher guidance	teacher with some student input
Primary focus	major focus on behavior	major focus on inner feelings and thoughts	initial focus on behavior; secondary focus on feelings and thoughts
Importance of individual differences	minor emphasis	major emphasis	moderate emphasis
Time until intervention	teacher moves quickly to redirect behavior	allow time for student to control own behavior	allow some time for student to control own behavior but protect group
Types of intervention used	rewards, punishments, token economy, contracting	nonverbal moves, conferences, communication, skills, "I" messages	coping skills, consequences, group meetings, anecdotal records

Finally, the interactionist model views student behavior as the responsibility of both the teacher and the student; power and control are shared, and students learn they have both the freedom to choose how they will behave and the responsibility to respect the rights of others. This view of behavior emphasizes the dynamics occurring between children and their environments and is particularly sensitive to cultural and multicultural concerns. It prizes the individual, is concerned with each child's relations with the group, and values the group as a whole. It operates much like a pluralistic society in that the integrity of both the individual and the group is important.

Cultural Diversity

Successful classroom management requires more than a model; it requires cultural sensitivity, because it is impossible for teachers to address the needs of children whose backgrounds they do not understand and appreciate. Stephanie does not wish to be this kind of teacher, and so, under her professors' guidance, she sought ways to understand cultures other than her own.

First, she studied her own culture, because without an understanding of her own cultural behaviors, values, and traditions, it is difficult for her to see how her background affects her views of people with other cultural behaviors, values, and traditions. Without this conscious awareness, her own background will color her perceptions of her students' behaviors, and result in her making ethnocentric judgments about her students. At a minimum, these judgments will hinder communication; at worst, they will cause irreparable harm to the relationships she is working to establish with her students.

For example, people in some cultures are brought up to be most considerate of others ("Don't make noise too early, you will wake the people in the next campsite," and "Play outside with your friends so your brother can study") while in other cultures, youngsters are taught to be most tolerant of others ("Don't let the radio bother you," and "Learn not be distracted by other people—the world can't stop because you have to do your homework") (Grossman, 1990, p. 82). If students from both groups are in her class, and Stephanie is unaware of their differing expectations, encouraging consideration of others will be confusing to some students while tolerance of others will be confusing to the second group. It is only through an understanding of the needs and expectations of both groups that Stephanie can tailor her efforts to be appropriate for all her students.

Considering Socioeconomic Grouping, Assimilation, and Culture

Diversity is as great within a given culture as it is among cultures. This means that to appreciate people from a specific culture, a variety of factors must be considered. The two most significant for classroom management are socioeconomic group and the degree of assimilation exhibited by a child.

Socioeconomic Grouping

Stephanie must understand that one's socioeconomic group is perhaps as predictive of behavior as is culture. It reflects financial assets, prestige, and power (Webb & Sherman, 1989), because as a rule, power and prestige are closely tied to financial assets. Further, one's socioeconomic group is strongly influenced by economic resources that determine the options people have (such as educational opportunities, health care, etc.). This is of particular importance when considering non-mainstream cultures, because they are apt to have access to fewer economic resources (Bianchi, 1990). In terms of both economic resources and the options they allow, Hispanic, African American, and Euro-American children of a given socioeconomic group may well have more in common with one another than with children of their own cultures who are of different socioeconomic groups. Stephanie is aware of her limited exposure to ethnic/racial groups, but she is less aware of her lack of exposure to diversity associated with socioeconomic grouping. This means she probably lacks vital information she'll need to create a learning environment appropriate for students from different socioeconomic groups.

Assimilation

The other important aspect of culture is the degree of assimilation exhibited by a child. Assimilation indicates the degree to which a person moves from one culture to another—usually from culture of birth into the mainstream culture. For example, the more assimilated an American Indian child, the further he or she has moved from the traditional culture towards that of the dominant culture. But even if students are closer to being members of the mainstream than their traditional culture, knowledge about their traditional culture is important because it will help the teacher better understand the background influences on the students' behavior and attitudes.

Because there is great diversity within cultures, it is impossible to describe each in its entirety; it is similarly impossible to produce a single generalization describing all the people in a culture. Descriptions exist about cultures and the people who participate in them, of course, and overgeneralization about them is called *stereotyping*. Stereotypes are harmful because they deny that variability exists within a culture and its people and, in so doing, limit what the observer can see and expect of the people observed.

One way in which stereotyping causes problems for both teachers and their students grows from the fact that only a single description exists, and it is forced to apply in all circumstances. The result is that simple explanations are offered for what in fact are complex cultural phenomena. When teachers use stereotypes, they overlook the complexity of factors that influence behavior and thus cannot recognize patterns in their students' actions. This means behaviors not fitting the stereotype will appear haphazard and uninterpretable and, when this happens, teachers will be disadvantaged in planning management strategies. This, in turn, leads to ethnocentrism. The following paragraph provides an example.

As a beginning teacher, I taught first grade on an Indian reservation. It was the start of school, and children from several classes were lining up in front of their respective classroom doors. There were the usual happy sounds of children giggling, greeting friends, sharing news with teachers, and—suddenly—total silence. One of the teachers had grabbed a student and was vigorously shaking him for some unknown offense. As though her behavior was not already culturally (or for that matter generally) inappropriate, she yelled, "When I speak to you, you show me the respect of looking me in the eye." How incredible that must have sounded to the child, who was trying to do exactly that—show his respect. He had been taught that to be respectful, he should not look directly into the eyes of people in positions of authority. So the teacher's statement was as confusing to him as if she had told Stephanie as a young child, "When I speak to you, you show me the respect of sticking out your tongue." Later, when the teacher and I talked about what had happened, she blamed the district for not having informed her about the cultural characteristics of her students. She was right, of course; people who prepare teachers and people who employ teachers have a responsibility to inform them about the children they'll be teaching. But when she accepted a position with that reservation school district, she had an overriding responsibility to inform herself. In other words, though everyone—except the children—had responsibilities to make certain that this teacher was well informed, it was first and foremost up to the teacher to learn about her students. Similarly, it is up to Stephanie to learn about the students who will be in her classroom.

Classroom Management and Cultural Groups

Stephanie does not want to risk unwittingly committing a cultural blunder that might label her as tactless, insensitive, or thoughtless. She wants to be sensitive to her students and their families' cultural needs, but she is uncertain how to gather the information she needs. How can a beginning teacher like Stephanie learn about the behaviors, values, and traditions of a particular student group? Collecting information about a culture is the first step. The second step is drawing implications from this information, and identifying issues that pertain to classroom management.

Following are some exercises in drawing such implications about various cultural groups. These exercises are not in-depth examinations of each of these cultures; rather, they are demonstrations of how Stephanie can translate information about students' cultures into culturally sensitive classroom management practices. In doing this, she must keep in mind that group membership is not about absolutes, but rather the multiple dimensions of peoples' lives and the roles that race, class, gender, sexual orientation, and language background all play in a person's development. Again, it is the process—not the cultures presented—that is being examined.

There is diversity within any group, and so while children may appear alike, they nevertheless may vary greatly. For example, Carlos Canas and Lucy Gonzales are both Mexican American. They live in the same neighborhood, attend the same school, and are in the same grade. However, the language of Lucy's home is Spanish while Carlos knows only a few Spanish words. Lucy's family celebrates with joy and enthusiasm many of the holidays of Mexico while Carlos' family celebrates the holidays of the mainstream society.

Amy Yazzie and Billy White Bear are another example. Amy is a Navajo child who was born and still lives in Los Angeles while Billy White Bear is a Sioux who lives on a reservation in North Dakota. These two children live culturally different lives as American Indian children. Billy's parents are culturally traditional, while Amy knows very little about her cultural heritage. Besides cultural diversity, the children also experience environmental diversity: Amy lives in a metropolitan area and Billy lives in one of the most sparsely populated areas in the United States.

The resources available to a child's family must also be considered. For example, an African American child in an upper middle-class neighborhood may have more in common with the Euro-American child next door than with another African American child who lives in a federally subsidized housing project.

In short, while Stephanie must learn all she can about the cultures in her school community, she must also guard against overgeneralizing this information as she strives to understand her students. In the following paragraphs, we present a few examples of how Stephanie might take into account who her students are and how she can sensitively meet their needs in her classroom.

Hispanics

Background   Stephanie starts at the library where she finds that Hispanics are the largest group of people of color in this country; there are now 20 million Hispanics in the United States (Valdivieso & Davis, 1988). Even though there is considerable diversity within the Hispanic community due to ethnic origin (the community includes Mexicans, Puerto Ricans, Cubans, and others), there is also diversity attributable to socioeconomic group and the degree of assimilation. Nevertheless, Hispanics share some broad cultural values and a common language.

Cultural Traits Central to the life of many Hispanic students are the family, community, and ethnic group. The family is the most valued of these highly prized institutions and family inspires great loyalty. Hispanic parents tend to be affectionate and nurturing, and the extended family plays a more active role in the lives of Hispanic children than in the Euro-American family (Riding, 1984). Indeed, grandparents, aunts, uncles, and cousins are a particularly important part of the Hispanic concept of family. Age and gender are usually important factors in determining each individual's status, and sex roles are often more clearly defined than in the larger society (Dodd, Nelson, Peralez, 1989; Riding, 1984; Castaneda, 1974).

Hispanic children often develop a strong sense of community. They are generally taught to be cooperative and to have a strong sense of group (Connoly & Tucker, 1982). This means that, as students, Hispanic children tend to be more warm, concerned about others, and physically affectionate than children in the mainstream society (e.g., touching is an important part of interpersonal communication in the culture). A required distance between people (also called *personal distance*) can be much less than in the mainstream society, and handshakes are frequent among acquaintances while hugs are common among family members and close friends (Dodd, Nelson, & Peralez, 1989).

Classroom Management Implications Because Hispanic children usually respect adults and have respect for age, the teacher is expected to play a positive role and be an authority figure. And with status as an adult and an authority figure, the teacher receives respect.

In organizing classrooms, Stephanie will want to remember that, while stressing competition and individualism is the tradition in most U.S. schools, many Hispanic children will feel more comfortable in a cooperative environment (Melendez, Melendez, & Molina, 1981). The wise teacher will plan accordingly for Hispanic children because tensions caused by differences between cultural preference and the tradition of the school can only result in frustration for both the students and the teacher.

Stephanie will want to create a sense of community in her classroom by adopting a cooperative attitude toward classroom behaviors. This can be done by pointing out that good behavior reflects on the whole class and, whenever possible, by implementing group problem solving. Glasser's (1977, 1986) earlier works and his control theory, as well as Johnson, Johnson, and Holubec's (1986) cooperative learning, would be appropriate resources in largely Hispanic classrooms. The interactionist model described earlier is generally culturally sensitive to this population. The teacher plays an active nurturing role similar to a parent and the "sense of group" is encouraged and supported.

Teachers will want to be physically affectionate with their students in age- and gender-appropriate ways. This includes a hand on the arm while talking, a pat on the shoulder while passing, a hug to comfort or affirm, a smile across the classroom. All in all, Hispanic children will benefit from a warm, friendly classroom.

Because the power of the group is strong, it is often demeaning for the Hispanic child to be publicly disciplined. Further, the purpose of discipline should always be to change a behavior (as opposed to punishing a child) and should be done away from the group whenever possible.

Southeast Asians and Asians

Background Asians make up a highly diverse segment of the U.S. population. As is the case with all ethnic groups, this diversity can be better understood through studying the history, experiences, and cultures of these groups. Chinese, Japanese, and Filipinos, for example, have a long history in this country, characterized by loyalty and significant contributions to U.S. society.

At the same time, the response to their contributions and loyalty has often included racism and discrimination. For example, the Immigration Act of 1882 was aimed at Chinese, Japanese were interred from 1942 to 1946, and anti-Filipino sentiments were rampant in 1920 (Banks, 1991). Over time, these three groups came to be recognized as important segments of American society.

Asians are the fastest growing group in the United States (O'Hare & Felt, 1991). This is because of the large number of Southeast Asians (such as Cambodians, Vietnamese, and Laotians) who have arrived more recently. Because many Southeast Asians have not been in the United States very long (they came after being displaced by the Vietnam War), they are less well acculturated. At the same time, their children are less understood by the public schools both because the cultures of these "new" Asians are different from mainstream American society and because their children are apt to be members of refugee families.

Because these children are less understood, they are the group we will address in this exercise. Note, though, that many of the cultural characteristics we will consider could describe many Asian groups, not just those from Southeast Asia.

Cultural Traits Southeast Asians highly prize the family, and children generally see themselves as representatives of their families; they may perceive their accomplishments and failures as bringing honor or shame to their homes. These children are often under pressure to perform well, and if they do poorly they are apt to blame themselves rather than existing conditions (Kang-Ning, 1981).

Southeast Asians often have a great respect for education. Their cultures traditionally place a great emphasis on hard work and success at school, and young people are expected to actively and seriously pursue educational opportunities (Knoll, 1982).

Most Southeast Asians also seek harmony with others, with nature, etc. They generally think carefully before speaking (Kang-Ning, 1981), and Southeast Asian children often have a tradition of being polite and respectful to people in positions of authority—such as teachers (Kang-Ning, 1981). These children tend to wait to be called on rather than volunteering responses to questions. Further, while they may not take initiative in classroom settings, they follow directions well (Wong, 1978).

Classroom Management Implications Fulfilling adult expectations at home and at school is apt to be an important part of the traditional Southeast Asian student's world; therefore, open-ended situations in which it is not clear to the children what is expected of them may result in confusion. These situations might be academic assignments or behavioral expectations. Clearly defined expectations will help Southeast Asian students feel more secure, and a posted list of classroom rules may be helpful. In the absence of this kind of structure, disciplinary problems may develop because students may not know the limits of their freedom and their responsibilities (Kang-Ning, 1981).

Children sitting quietly and listening: How could there be a problem here? But the stereotype of the Southeast Asian-American student as polite and hard working does bring them problems. Because teachers expect docility and passivity, Southeast Asian students who "act out" are frequently treated more harshly than other children (Divoky, 1988). Furthermore, the Euro-American's direct style of communication may appear to these children to be impolite and ill considered (Nguyen, 1986). At worst, it might be hurtful.

While Asian students have been called the "model minority," the problem with this label, as with all labels, is that it limits how teachers see them. For example, because of their unobtrusive behavior, it may be easy to overlook children with certain kinds of problems.

As noted, many of the more recently arrived Southeast Asians are refugees and immigrants and have a set of adjustments to make that are not required of native-born students. Divoky (1988) notes that immigrants from war-torn countries bring with them experiences that may include both trauma and its aftermath. Questions to be asked about all incoming students include, "What are these children's prior experiences?" and "How are these experiences alike or different from those educational experiences they'll encounter here?" "Were their educations interrupted, for example, and what expectations do they have of teachers now?"

While children of Southeast Asian cultures are apt to be seen as integral parts of the family, they are still recognized as individuals with the potential to bring honor or shame to their families. Thus the performance of each individual child—as opposed to the group—is valued.

Cooperative discipline is an appropriate model to use in working with children from Southeast Asian cultures because it is cognitive (logical) in nature, allows teachers to play strong leadership roles, is structured, and allows each child some control in creating inner harmony.[3] Albert's (1991) *Cooperative Discipline* (not to be confused with cooperative learning) is based on Rudolph Dreikurs' work (Dreikurs, Grunwald, & Pepper, 1982), and strongly supports the notion of logical consequences. It provides students with a process of determining the appropriateness of their behavior. As with Hispanic children, the principles of the interactionist model are generally the most sensitive to the needs of Southeast Asian children. Though these two groups may benefit from the same theoretical model, the specific organizations may differ. Southeast Asian children customarily feel most comfortable with a more structured classroom environment. Additionally, they might benefit from the positive reinforcement component of the interventionist model.

American Indians

Background There are at least 300 recognized Indian tribes and 252 Indian languages in the United States (Bearcrane, Dodd, Nelson, & Ostwald, 1989). As with other groups, there is great diversity among groups and individuals within groups. Some individuals live on reservations, some in rural communities, and some in urban areas (10 percent of school-age American Indian children are born and reared in cities). Although tribes may have unique languages and customs, they share some basic values (Fuller & Casaus, 1987).

Cultural Traits The family is usually an important institution within the culture, and the extended family plays a particularly important role in the life of the American Indian child. In some tribes, aunts play roles similar to mothers, uncles may have some of the responsibilities the dominant culture assigns to fathers, and cousins may be treated like siblings. Occasionally, a grandmother or aunt may actually rear the child (American Indian Education Unit, California State Department of Education, 1982). American Indian parents also tend to be permissive and accepting of their children.

Emphasis is often placed on the group and the importance of maintaining harmony within the group; the needs of the group are often considered over the needs of the individual. Because of strong feelings of group solidarity, cooperation—and not competition—is the desirable mode of operation (California State Department of Education, 1982). Relatedly, American Indian children are often hesitant to show themselves as superior, especially if it presents someone else in a poor light (Fuller & Casaus, 1987).

Furthermore, American Indian children often feel more comfortable participating in class after they have had time to consider their responses or practice their skills (Sanders, 1987). They also are apt to delay answering questions (Sanders, 1987).

Classroom Management Implications American Indian children tend to be more comfortable in classrooms that are cooperative in nature and that use small group activities as instructional techniques. Thus while a child might feel uncomfortable being singled out for praise, this child will feel pride when their group receives recognition. Because the group is so important, there is pain in being reprimanded in front of peers. In accord with the cooperative preference of this group, the whole class should be involved in identifying desirable class behaviors and then helped to formulate rules to accomplish those goals. The skillful teacher will then refer to those rules as "our class rules."

Teachers in traditional classrooms usually allow for a brief response time and assume that students who know will respond immediately. More response time should be allowed for American Indian students, and, moreover, they should be given many opportunities to practice an activity by themselves before they are expected to show mastery of it. The culture enjoyed by American Indian children is generally congruent with the non-interventionist model because of its emphasis on the whole child, and the interactionist approach because of its concern for the group. Although these two models have different philosophical goals, they share a humanistic perspective. In this way, they differ from the interventionist model, which takes a behavioristic approach.

In planning her room, Stephanie will have the same basic goal for all her students—to create a positive learning environment where children respect themselves and others. But the management strategies she uses will differ depending on her students' cultural characteristics. Further, Stephanie's strategies will have to be based on an understanding of her students' culture, and she will be required to translate that understanding into good classroom management. This may well mean addressing the needs of several cultures together.

Parental Involvement

Importance of Involving Parents

Stephanie is ambivalent about working with the parents of diverse student groups. On one hand, she knows that parental involvement is an important part of successful classroom management and that this will be an excellent opportunity to learn about her students. But on the other hand, she is afraid her lack of cultural knowledge might result in some great faux pas that will offend the parents and embarrass her. The best approach to this problem is to learn as much as possible about the children's families and cultures before meeting with their parents. General information can be collected through reading, as described in the following pages, and more specific information can be provided by administrators and other teachers at the school.

It is important for Stephanie to collect that information, too. It helps her approach and understand her students' families, and teachers and parents have an important common bond: They both care about the children. It is for this reason that they should work as a team to provide the best education possible for those children. There are some things teachers can do to create a productive educational team: First, they should remember that these parents are sending them the best they have. Second, they should convey to parents a genuine appreciation of their children. Third, they need to create an environment where parents and teachers must work at understanding the parents' situations including family structure, socioeconomic level, work demands, culture, and so on.

It is also important for Stephanie to understand that lack of information about cultural differences will affect her ability to work productively with parents. Teachers too often assume that parents of color are not as interested in their children's academic performances as Euro-Americans, and this is blatantly untrue. Parents of color do want to be involved in their children's educations, but often describe feeling uncomfortable in their children's schools. In addition, they report seldom being invited to participate (Chavkin, 1989).

The public schools, as institutions, represent the values and behaviors of the White middle class and are designed for children from this community. And they generally work well for these children as home-school relationships are based on this cultural tradition. As with any tradition, it works because those involved understand and are comfortable with it.

Consequently, parents from other cultures may operate under a distinct disadvantage when dealing with the schools; they may not know, understand, or feel comfortable with the traditional home-school relationships that work so well for the dominant community. And because behavior, attitudes, and achievement are all positively influenced by parental involvement, it is to the school's advantage to create constructive relationships with all parents. An important step in doing this has educators informing themselves about the educational experiences and cultural patterns of the diverse groups of parents served by the schools.

The illustrations that follow are not in-depth representations of different cultural groups; rather, they are examples of situations with potential for cultural misunderstandings. The purpose of these descriptions is to create an awareness of potential areas of conflict that may impede home-school relations.

Asian (primarily Indochinese)

Many factors influence whether Indochinese parents will feel comfortable with home-school relations in the United States, factors including the parents' educational backgrounds, the size of their native community, etc. Further, while teachers expect caring parents to be involved in their children's educations, active parent involvement is counter to these parents' experiences. In their native countries, school officials and teachers decided all matters—from curriculum to discipline—without regard to parental concerns or desires (Morrow, 1991). In other words, Indochinese parents' expectations for parental involvement differ significantly from those of the school and, as a result, both parents and educators may be confused by each others' motives and behaviors.

In addition, the dominant culture's manner of communicating may cause problems. Unintended messages may be conveyed by the manner in which teachers communicate with Indochinese parents. Because the parents are particularly sensitive to nonverbal messages, they may construe a teacher's folded arms or other casual gestures as indications of indifferent attitudes (Yoa, 1988). It is wise for new teachers to ask about these things before meeting with parents.

Finally, Indochinese and the dominant U.S. culture may have contradictory goals for students. Where the educational system sees *good students* as well rounded with interests and skills in a variety of areas, Indochinese parents are more apt to have a narrower definition of the term. They actively encourage their children to be serious about academics, and they may not value extracurricular activities such as sports, drama, or field trips. They may see these activities as play, and to them, play is a reward for exemplary performance or hard work (Kang-Ning, 1981), not a routine part of children's lives.

American Indians

American Indian parents have a short tenure as invited partners in the educational system. The Bureau of Indian Affairs (BIA) and parochial boarding schools were the primary educational institutions for their children until well into the 20th century. Because the historical goal of these institutions was to "civilize the savage" (cultural genocide), parents (as representatives of the "undesirable" culture) were actively discouraged from participating in their children's educational experiences. In addition, the distances from the children's homes to the boarding schools and lack of transportation further complicated home-school relations. Thus, even though most contemporary American Indian children live with their parents and attend schools in their communities, and even though the goals of the schools have changed dramatically, there is not a historical tradition of home-school relations (Little Bear, 1986). Unfortunately, the old BIA practice of excluding parents from reservation schools has been continued by many public schools. Parents are made to believe they have no responsibility for the education of their children—that's the job of the school (Chavers, 1991). This attitude is both counter to promoting parental involvement and tragic.

Another factor interfering with the working relationship between American Indian parents and educators is the role of the extended family. Because the extended family plays a more meaningful role in the child's life than is the case in much of mainstream society, the responsibility for rearing an American Indian child is shared by a number of family members. Grandmothers, aunts, and uncles all may have serious responsibilities for and to the child so that parents *and* other relatives may attend school conferences, or the child may at different times live with different family members. The schools often misinterpret this as lack of parental concern or avoidance of parental responsibility. It is neither.

African American Parents

Presenting cultural patterns for African American students and their parents is difficult. Most studies in the literature are more than a decade old, and the research tends to consider lower socioeconomic level, inner-city children. The problem is that these studies do not consider either the 45 percent of the population who are middle or upper class or those who are low-income and live in rural areas (Blackwell, 1985). Nevertheless, this literature can be used to examine briefly a continuing problem in African American home-school relations.

Educators often make erroneous assumptions about a particular group of parents, and these faulty assumptions then become the basis for interpreting the parents' behavior. Lightfoot (1978) discusses this problem in her book *Worlds Apart: Relationships Between Families and Schools*.

> Despite the passionate dreams of Black parents, teachers continue to view them as uncaring, unsympathetic, ignorant of good education for their children and unconcerned about their children's academic success in school. Often they perceive the parents' lack of involvement in ritualistic school events and parent conferences as apathy and disinterest and rarely interpret it as an inability to negotiate the bureaucratic maze of schools or as a response to a long history of exclusion. (p. 166)

Children learn and grow best in schools where the parents and teachers understand one another, share similar visions, and collaborate on guiding children—as is the case in the suburban schools. Lightfoot (1978) also observes that, for a long time, we have understood that the magic of suburban schools is not merely the relative affluence and abundant resources of the citizens (nor their Whiteness), but also the consonance between what the parents want for their children and what teachers believe is educationally sound.

James Comer has successfully achieved this consensus in schools with large African American enrollments (Stocklinski & Miller-Colbert, 1991). In the Comer Model, the parent is a respected, integral part of the program. This model is centered on the idea that if parents, teachers, and staff share control of a school, they will convey a positive attitude to the children, who will then be motivated to learn. The success of these schools demonstrates the power of an educational system in which parents and teachers combine their efforts.

In each of the situations described, the parents' roles in home-school relations were misunderstood. The Indochinese parents' view, for example, came from their experiences with authoritarian schools in their native countries, and the American Indian parents' perceptions are reflected in the U.S. government's historical rejection of them in the educational process. And finally, many African American parents' attitudes emerged from the erroneous assumptions education institutions made about them in the past. In all three cases, parents came to school with attitudes and behaviors which were interpreted according to standards for parents whose culture was that of the school; instead, the school should have tried to understand the parents' expectations, needs, and concerns. To be a good teacher, Stephanie will have to recognize that her students' parents may see their roles in relationship to the school as different from what she has known. This means she must work with them to facilitate a positive home-school relationship.

Suggestions for New Teachers

Chances are that Stephanie will sign a contract with a school district that has a diverse student population whose cultures differ significantly from hers.

Clearly, she must become as well informed as possible about the culture of her students; it is as unprofessional to enter a classroom without knowledge of the students' culture as to agree to teach a subject for which one is unprepared. Being a professional educator doesn't mean Stephanie is an expert in every aspect of education, but it does mean that she is prepared to teach the students in her class. She will enter her classroom well informed about her students' cognitive, socioemotional, developmental, and cultural needs, in addition to being knowledgeable about the subject matter.

Gathering Information for the Culturally Diverse Classroom

Stephanie already feels comfortable with her general knowledge of the children she'll teach in terms of what she has learned about their cognitive and social-emotional development. But she knows little about them culturally—except that their backgrounds are different from hers, and that she must know more about them if she is to be a good teacher.

Stephanie can begin her search for information by finding answers to the questions that follow. They are designed to help her collect information about people whose cultural backgrounds are different from her own. The answers to these questions are a starting point; Stephanie will temper what she learns from her answers with the experience she gains teaching here.

Specific Questions to Ask About a New Culture

1. **What is the group's history?** While Stephanie will not become a scholar on the history of a given group, she can become well informed by reading some general books and articles. She'll be able to recognize names, places, and events that are important to the group in question. She'll be especially interested in learning how historical events influence the ways in which members of this group see things now.

2. **What are the important cultural values of the group?** Stephanie will learn about values that are important to the group. Do they value family issues over individual concerns? How do members of the group view themselves and others?

3. **Who are outstanding individuals who claim membership in this group?** There will be artists, writers, inventors, historical figures, athletes, and others who are members of the group and who have standing in the local, national, and international communities. Knowing who these people are is helpful to a teacher, because it makes it easier to understand who children are talking about and who can act as positive role models. Furthermore, teachers can help the other children in the class appreciate the leaders of different cultural communities.

4. **What are the group's major religions and beliefs?** The answers provide information on values and events in children's lives and are important in explaining to other children what their classmates are doing and how they see things.

5. **What are the current political concerns?** Knowing about these issues means knowing about what is important in the children's home community. Sometimes these concerns will affect the school directly, sometimes they will not; but in all cases, they are issues the children will hear about in the neighborhood and at home.

6. **What are the group's political, religious, and social celebration days?** These are events that are important to the community and, as such, are days children will discuss at school. Good teachers will make use of this information in understanding their students and in planning curriculum.

7. **What are the educational implications of the answers to the preceding questions?** Very often, the answers are important because they affect individual students, and because they have a bearing on the entire class. It is important to know when students will miss school for religious holidays that are not part of the Christian calendar just as it is important to discuss the political issues facing a specific group with all the students in the class. Because everyone should have an appreciation of the issues facing students of color, integrating these issues into the curriculum is a good instructional strategy.

Finding the Answers, or, How Does a Teacher Go About Gathering This Information?

Much of the information Stephanie needs to begin with is available in the library. In addition to looking up books and journal articles, she can do an Educational Resource Information Center (ERIC) computer search at a college or university library. She can also look up titles in the Current Index to Journals in Education (CIJE), and Resources in Education (RIE). Stephanie can also view videotapes and films. A good listing of these can be found in *Teaching Strategies in Ethnic Studies* (Banks, 1991).

It is to Stephanie's advantage to live as close to the cultural community of her students as possible, for there is an understanding that comes from being a member of a community that cannot be acquired by commuting. For example, teachers who live on American Indian reservations have a much better understanding of their students and the community than those who commute. But whether Stephanie chooses to live within the community or commute, she can attend community activities. If the cultural community publishes an English-language newspaper or magazine, she can subscribe. And of course, she can continue the reading she's begun.

If the population has a large number of immigrants, Stephanie might also contact the agencies providing services to the group. These people can offer much information she'll find useful—both about the groups of people and about ways to work successfully with them.

If the community has cultural centers and museums, Stephanie can visit those (initially on her own, but also later with her students on field trips). Those visits will provide her with information about the people she's interested in, and give her a chance to talk with people who work there. They should be knowledgeable about the population and might suggest ways she might come to better understand the group.

Stephanie should accept invitations to visit her students' families on special occasions. These might be religious observations, or they might be more secular holiday celebrations. In any event, they are opportunities for Stephanie to see people in the community setting, learn about them, and enjoy herself.

Stephanie should also consider learning the language spoken by the group whose children she's teaching. This communicates a message to her students and their families about how she feels about them. It also allows her to communicate with them in a manner otherwise impossible. Even if she doesn't become proficient, she will have gained insights into her students' lives as well as demonstrating her respect for them.

In addition to these "do's," there are some "don'ts" teachers need to be aware of. It is not a good idea to ask too many questions initially, because many cultures feel uncomfortable with newcomers who press too hard for information or inclusion in the community. The community will let her know through its behavior when a more active role is appropriate.

Getting Started

For classroom management to be meaningful, it must be culturally sensitive. In the absence of this sensitivity, both the students and the teacher will feel confused and frustrated as they approach one another. Also, the expectations of most classroom management programs are based on the behaviors of mainstream society, which are often not applicable to children of diverse cultures. Consequently, Stephanie will need to become culturally acquainted with her students, their families, and communities, and then determine which classroom management approaches will be most culturally appropriate for her student population.

Stephanie will select the model of classroom management that best meets the needs of her students. And she will do so with the understanding that there is no "formula" of classroom management applicable in all classrooms. After selecting the most culturally appropriate model, Stephanie will modify it to meet the needs of her particular classroom. In addition, Stephanie will encourage parental involvement for she knows that parental involvement will enhance her classroom management. All of these activities will help Stephanie develop classroom management skills resulting in a positive learning environment for her and her students.

Notes

1. All the books' tables of contents were checked to see if they contained chapters dealing with this subject, and then their indexes were searched for shorter references to multicultural concerns and related topics (e.g., culture, ethnicity, poverty). Seven books mentioned the subject briefly, with 6–10 pages being the longest reference.

2. It should be noted that in Wolfgang and Glickman's 1986 edition of *Solving Discipline Problems*, these three models have been renamed "Rules/rewards—punishment," "Relationship—listening," and "Confronting—contracting," respectively. I have chosen to use the original terms because they are more descriptive of the phenomena they describe.

3. It is not clear if Dreikurs' four goals of misbehavior are appropriate explanations of misbehavior for non-Euro-Americans.

References

Albert, L. (1989). *Cooperative discipline: How to manage your classroom and promote self-esteem*. Circle Pines, MN: American Guidance Service.

American Indian Education Unit, California State Department of Education (1982). *The American Indian education handbook*. Sacramento, CA: State Department of Education.

Abernathy, S., Manera, E., & Wright, R. E. (1985). What stresses student teachers most? *The Clearing House, 58*(8), 361–362.

Banks, J. A. (1991). *Teaching strategies for ethnic studies*. Boston: Allyn and Bacon.

Bearcrane, J., Dodd, J. M., Nelson, J. R., & Ostwald, S. T. (1989). Educational characteristics of Native Americans. *Rural Educator, 11*(3), 145–149.

Bianchi, S. M. (1990). America's children: Mixed prospects. *Population Bulletin, 45*(1). Washington, DC: Population Reference Bureau.

Blackwell, J. A. (1985). *The black community: Diversity and unity*. (2nd ed.) New York: Harper Row.

Castaneda, A. (1974). The educational needs of Mexican-Americans. In J. Castaneda & L. Robbins (Eds.), *The educational needs of minority groups*. Lincoln, NB: Educators Publications.

Chavers, D. (1991). Indian education: Dealing with a disaster. *Principal, 70*(3), 28–29.

Chavkin, N. F. (1989). Debunking the myths about minority parents. *Horizons, 67*(4), 119–123.

Connoly, L. H., & Tucker, S. M. (1982). *Motivating the Mexican American student*. Las Cruces, NM: ERIC Clearing House on Rural Education and Small Schools (ERIC No. ED 287-0657).

Dinkmeyer, D., McKay, G. D., & Dinkmeyer, D. (1980). *Systematic training for effective teaching*. Pine Circle, MN: American Guidance Service.

Divoky, D. (1988). The model minority. *Phi Delta Kappan, 70*(3), 219–222.

Dodd, J. M., Nelson, J. R., & Peralez, E. (1989). Understanding the Hispanic student. *Rural Educator, 10*(2), 8–13.

Dodd, J. M. (1981). Towards special services: Minus prejudice. *Educational Considerations, 8*(13), 8–13.

Dreikurs, R., Grunwald, B. B., & Pepper, F. C. (1982). *Maintaining sanity in the classroom*. New York: Harper Row.

Elam, S. (1989). The second Gallup/Phi Delta Kappa poll of teachers' attitudes towards the public schools. *Phi Delta Kappan, 70*(10), 785–798.

Foster, H. L. (1986). *Ribbin', jivin' and playin' the dozens*. Cambridge, MA: Ballinger Publishing Co.

Fuller, M. L., & Casaus, L. (1987). Culture, school and the family. *PTA Today, 12*(5), 23–25.

Gallup, A., & Clark, D. (1987). The 19th annual Gallup poll of the public's attitudes towards the public schools. *Phi Delta Kappan, 69*(1), 17–30.

Gay, G. (1989). Ethnic minorities and educational equality. In J. A. Banks & C.A. McGee Banks (Eds.), *Multicultural education: Issues and perspectives* (pp. 167–188).

Glasser, W. (1977). 10 steps to good discipline. *Today's Education, 66*, 60–63.

Glasser, W. (1986). *Control theory in the classroom*. New York: Harper Row.

Griffith, J. E., Frase, M. J., & Ralph, J. H. (1989). American education: The challenge of change. *Population Bulletin, 44*(4), 16.

Grossman, H. L. (1990). *Trouble-free teaching: Solutions to behavior problems in the classroom*. Mountain View, CA: Mayfield Publishing Company.

Haberman, M. L. (1989). More minority teachers. *Phi Delta Kappan, 71*(10), 771–776.

Johnson, D. W., Johnson, R. T., & Holubec, E. J. (1986). *Revised circles of learning: Cooperation in the classroom*. Edina, MN: Interaction Book Company.

Jones, V. F., & Jones, L. S. (1995). *Comprehensive classrooms: Creating positive learning environments*. (4th ed.) Boston: Allyn and Bacon.

Kang-Ning, C. (1981). Education for Chinese and Indochinese. *Theory Into Practice, 20*(1), 35–44.

Keating, B., Pickering, M., Slack, B., & White, J. (1990). *A guide to positive discipline: Helping students make responsible choices*. Boston: Allyn and Bacon.

Knoll, T. (1982). *Becoming American: Asian sojourners, immigrants, and refugees in the western United States*. Portland, OR: Coast to Coast Books.

Lemlech, J. K. (1988). *Classroom management: Methods and techniques for elementary and secondary teachers*. New York: Longman.

Levin, J., Nolan, J. F. (1991). *Principles of classroom management*. Englewood Cliffs, NJ: Prentice Hall.

Lightfoot, S. L. (1978). *Worlds apart: Relationships between families and schools*. New York: Basic Books.

Little Bear, D. (1986). Teachers and parents working together. In J. Reyhner (Ed.), *Teaching the Indian child*. Billings, MT: Eastern Montana College.

Lockart, B. L. (1981). *Resolving discipline problems for Indian students: A preventive approach*. Las Cruces, NM: Educational Resource on Rural Education and Small Schools.

Melendez, D., Melendez, D. C., & Molina, A. (1981). Pluralism and the Hispanic student: Challenge to educators. *Theory Into Practice, 20*(1), 7–12.

Morrow, R. D. (1991). The challenge of Southeast Asian parental involvement. *Principal, 70*(3), 20–22.

Nguyen, L. D. (1986). Indochinese cross-cultural adjustment and communication. In M. Doa & H. Grossman (Eds.), *Identifying, instructing and rehabilitating Southeast Asian students with special needs and counseling their parents*. (ERIC ED 273 068).

O'Hare, P. O., & Felt, J. C. (1991). *Asian Americans: America's fastest growing group*. Washington, DC: Population Reference Bureau.

Riding, A. (1984). *A distant neighbor*. New York: Random House.

Sanders, S. (1987). Cultural conflicts: An important factor in academic failures of American Indian students. *Journal of Multicultural Counseling and Development, 15*(2), 81–90.

Sleeter, C. E., & Grant, C. A. (1988). *Making choices for multicultural education: Five approaches to race, class, and gender*. Englewood Cliffs, NJ: Merrill/Prentice Hall.

Sleeter, C. E., & Grant, C. A. (1993). *Making choices for multicultural education: Five approaches to race, class, and gender*. (2nd ed.) Englewood Cliffs, NJ: Merrill/Prentice Hall.

Stocklinski, J., & Miller-Colbert, J. (1991). The Comer process: Moving from "I" to "we." *Principal, 70*(3), 18–19.

Valdivieso, R., & Davis, C. (1988). U.S. Hispanics: Challenging issues for the 1990s. *Population Trends and Public Policy*. Washington, DC: Population Reference Bureau, Inc.

Webb, R. B., & Sherman, R. R. (1989). *Schooling in society*. (2nd ed.) Englewood Cliffs, NJ: Merrill/Prentice Hall.

Wolfgang, C. H., & Glickman, C. D. (1980). *Solving discipline problems: Strategies for classroom teachers*. Boston: Allyn and Bacon.

Wolfgang, C. H., & Glickman, C. D. (1986). *Solving discipline problems: Strategies for classroom teachers*. (2nd ed.) Boston: Allyn and Bacon.

Wong, M. K. (1978). Traditional Chinese culture and the behavior patterns of Chinese in American classrooms. In *Second annual forum on transcultural adaptation (proceedings): Asian students in American classrooms*. Chicago: Illinois Office of Education.

Yoa, E. L. (1988). Working effectively with Asian immigrant parents. *Phi Delta Kappan, 70*(3), 223–225.

◆ ◆ ◆ ◆

The true aim of everyone who aspires to be a teacher should be not to impart his own opinion, but to kindle minds.

Frederick W. Robertson

You may write me down in history
With your bitter, twisted lies,
You may trod me in the very dirt
But still, like dust, I'll rise.

Maya Angelou

I finish a unit on "racism and Native Americans" for an education class and receive a low grade because my project is called "inappropriate subject material" to be taught to children. I am outraged. My classsmates treat my anger and insight with pity; I know they see me as having emotional problems, or, at best, as being politically extreme…

Rosemary Gonzales

Nothing in life is to be feared. It is only to be understood.

Marie Curie

Part 3

◆ ◆ ◆ ◆

The Subject Matters

Chapter 8

◆ ◆ ◆ ◆

Telling and Critiquing Stories of Our Teaching—for Literacy[1]

Mary Louise Gomez

University of Wisconsin-Madison

The ability of story (prose and poetry) to transform the storyteller and the listener into something or someone else is shamanistic. (Anzaldua, 1988, p. 30)

My 9-year-old daughter Lily[2] has always loved books and stories. In preschool, she never napped. Rather, she gained permission to lie on her cot and "read" a bagful of picture books that I brought from home every day. We have always shared a few books, or a chapter or two, before bedtime. Four years ago, as she struggled to conquer her fears of being in a new school—where noisy "big kids" were in the halls and on the playground—she began to plead for one last story before she slept—"one from the mind"—as she said.

So, each night during that kindergarten year, after we read a few books, and talked about her day, Lily and I composed stories about a hero named Peter, whom we had originally come to know as a character in a favorite book. Now, he romped through our collaborative stories as a citizen of Blueberry Land, Triangle Land, or some other exotic and faraway place. In the pattern of these shared tales, Peter's primary role was to enter a story just when the troublesome children of a kind king or queen required rescuing. Regardless of how careless a story's royal offspring had been in leaving a gate unlocked or wandering too far from their caretakers, Peter was always able to save them. Each day when the monsters were conquered and the kingdom was safe, Peter returned home to his mother. Then our chapter closed, and Lily drifted off to dream.

Anzaldua (1989) says such stories magically link tellers and listeners. They provide solace from the frightening demons that lurk in children's dark bedrooms late at night. Stories also draw us to adventure from which we would otherwise be barred by time, geography, or physical prowess. And they help to "render the horizons of others more accessible" as "we seek to understand landscapes other than our own" (Barone, 1987, pp. 14–15).

Stories make permeable the boundaries of our own and others' life experiences (Smith, 1991), and enable the appraisal of these experiences (Rosen, 1985). Through telling and listening to stories, individuals are able to "put the personal and particular into perspective" (Rich, 1979, p. 43) and to fashion "alternative notions of truth and representation" (Helle, 1991, p. 50). As people, we interpret and secure, challenge and reinterpret our experiences through storytelling.

Narayan (1991) sums the responses of researchers from anthropology, philosophy, psychology, and theology to the question "What happens when we tell stories?" when she writes: "By arranging the flux and welter of experience around a narrative line, we make sense of our pasts, plan for our futures, and comprehend the lives of others" (p. 114). Narayan views stories as opportunities for tellers and listeners to take an alternative perspective on our experiences, to see our lives as composed of stories that can be "observed" and evaluated (p. 125).

Rosenwald and Ochberg (1993) argue that it is the storyteller in particular who has the potential to be transformed through tales:

The stories people tell about themselves are interesting not only for the events and characters they describe but also for something in the construction of the stories themselves. How individuals recount their histories—what they emphasize and omit, their stance as protagonists or victims, the relationship the story establishes between teller and audience—all shape what individuals can claim of their own lives. Personal stories are not merely a way of telling someone (or oneself) about one's life; they are the means by which identities may be fashioned. It is this formative—and sometimes deformative power of life stories that make them important. (p. 1)

Rosenwald and Ochberg remind us that stories are fashioned by the individual teller within the social and institutional discourses available to her as they acknowledge the possibilities for self-understanding that are inherent in the stories we tell.

I have never spoken directly with Lily, my storytelling partner, about the parallels between her fears of "big kids" who fill school hallways with their large, jostling bodies and who accidentally bump into her when she is least expecting it—and the children of Blueberry and Triangle Land who are stalked by creatures prowling the royal woods. Yet, her requests for our jointly constructed stories began after she had first expressed her fears of the sixth-, seventh- and eighth-graders at her school, and ended later that winter when she became more comfortable with their presence.

Unlike the children in our stories, she had no Peter to rescue her. However, through the telling, I believe Lily came to see that she could conquer her fears and rescue—or transform—herself as we made the strange familiar in our tales. Through telling her stories, Lily gained an alternative perspective on her experiences, one in which she saw herself, like Peter, as someone who could "conquer demons" and return safely home.

Many times since we told the "Peter stories," I have thought about how beneficial the storytelling was for Lily as she became accustomed to a new school, and for me as a mother who wanted to support her in meeting this challenge. Our storytelling was facilitated by the bonds that connect us, as mother and daughter; as people who share a language background, socioeconomic group, gender, and ethnicity; as people who daily work and play together.

As a teacher educator and teacher, I dream of ways I and my colleagues in classrooms around the country might similarly support and sustain children's learning and adults' understandings. Yet, I recognize that it is unrealistic to expect that teachers and students in the United States today share many of the situations that link my daughter and me. Opportunities for teachers to know the feelings and imagine the experiences of the children in our classrooms are inhibited as the student population becomes more diverse and the teacher population remains homogeneous. (See Gomez, 1994, for a discussion of how United States teachers' race, socioeconomic group, gender, sexual preferences, and language backgrounds affect their perspectives on diverse student populations' abilities to learn.)

As the differences between those teaching and those taught continue to grow, the barriers to understanding one another appear to become greater. The possibilities for teachers forging personal relationships with students and for developing curricula and instructional practices that assist students' learning and meet their needs for academic success become narrowed.

Delpit (1988) contends that teachers can develop personal relationships with students and meet their academic needs only when we become "vulnerable enough to allow our world to turn upside down in order to allow the realities of others to edge themselves into our consciousness" (p. 297). Delpit says we have to develop an insiders' perspective on children's lives if we are to help them learn in school. As teachers, we must see school and its demands from the perspective of children and their families as well as from our own.

In this chapter, I discuss how telling stories of my teaching has allowed me to turn my teaching world upside down and develop new perspectives on my practice. A focus on these stories is teaching for "literacy," an idea that encompasses the teaching of the technical skills of reading, writing, listening, and speaking, but is also more than that. Like Giroux (1993), I see literacy as a means of organizing, inscribing, containing, and contesting meaning.

Telling Teaching Stories: My Own

For the past few years, I have been asking the question (Gomez & Tabachnick, 1992; Abt-Perkins & Gomez, 1993, Gomez & Abt-Perkins, in press): What happens when teachers tell stories about themselves and their work? I have found that in telling teaching stories—narratives in which a teacher and her classroom practices play a central role—that individuals can conduct a self-critique of their complex interactions with others in a fresh light. In particular, I am trying to understand how telling teaching stories to their peers (over time and in a supportive setting) can help teachers puzzle through their behaviors toward different students; question accepted schooling practices; unpack the social, economic, and institutional forces against which children and their families struggle; and devise new ways to teach that invite all children to learn.

While I have been a storyteller and writer since childhood, I began to explore formally what Anzaldua (1988) calls the transformative and magical power of personal narrative in the 1980s. Then, through a confluence of teaching and research opportunities, I began considering the potentials of storytelling for teaching. Later in this chapter, I tell about one way I began to consider how telling stories of teaching might affect teachers' thinking and actions.

In 1989, two colleagues, Bob Tabachnick and Ken Zeichner, asked me to write a chapter for their book focused on inquiry-oriented teacher education. They asked me to write about a university course I taught that focused on teaching language arts in the elementary school. They were interested in the social justice orientation of the course—how I taught and how students responded to my teaching. They wanted to know what grounded my teaching—why I taught in particular ways, what drove my choices for reading and activities.

I pulled out old paperbacks and recalled reading about teaching and school reform when I was in my 20s—works by Axline (1964), Dennison (1969), Featherstone (1971), Holt (1964, 1967, 1974), Koch (1970), Kohl (1967), Kozol (1967), and Stuart (1970a, 1970b). I also thought about the influence of my father, Manuel Gomez, who explained by his words and actions what he saw as each person's obligation to care for others. I remembered children whom I had taught—in particular, David, who was a first-grader in Black River, Vermont, in the 1970s. I contemplated how I had felt called to teach by the promise it held for changing children's lives. I remembered how I had tried to live out my ideals as a student teacher with David and his friends, and I wrote the following story:

> Twenty years ago in a small Vermont milltown where the looms had long been silent, I was a student teacher. My experiences that year mark my teaching to this day, for it was then that I became David's foster mother. I was drawn to David from the moment I entered his first-grade classroom for my year-long student teaching. David was small and brown; his eyes were large and liquid, sorrowful. He could not identify the letters of the alphabet in September, nor could he do so in May. David's biological mother was a single parent and an alcoholic; she was an absent and sometimes abusive parent. While she was hospitalized during the winter that year, David came to live with me and my husband.
>
> Like many of his peers at Black River School, David and his mother lived in terrible poverty produced by the closing, decades earlier, of the town's factories. Frequently hungry and sleepy, he and his classmates walked from flats adjacent to the railyard to the town's one elementary school. There, Ms. Paterson, their teacher, and I attempted to construct a sanctuary from life as these children knew it. We made cakes for our parties—photographing each step of the preparation and writing group-constructed tales of the work. We made centers for the children's listening, clay modeling, housekeeping, exploration with magnets, and dramatic play. We threw the preprimers and primers for the basal reading series in the closet and gathered books from the town and school libraries for reading. First in the school to put aside textbooks and to teach in ways that we believed were child-centered, we became an admired team.
>
> Late in the springtime, when my student teaching—evaluated as highly successful by all—was nearly completed, David's mother was discharged from the hospital. The state social services department required that we return David to her. Soon afterwards, my husband and I finished graduate school, and we moved away, leaving David in Black River. Neither the social worker assigned to David nor his mother encouraged us to remain in contact with him. So, unhappy about returning him to his flat by the tracks, I buried myself in my new teaching job in the Midwest and did not write or call. I have thought a lot about David in the past years. He would be in his mid-twenties now—about my age when he lived with me. (Gomez, 1991)

My reflections about my student teaching in Black River helped me understand how, in attempting to create a sanctuary from their lives outside of school, Ms. Paterson and I failed to build the critical links that bind children's homes to their school classrooms. Missing from our teaching was recognition that all children come to school with knowledge, skills, and experiences upon which we can draw, build, and expand. Our reading and writing program focused on activities and ideas that Ms. Paterson and I chose because we thought the children would enjoy and learn from them. We chose the themes, the books to read, and the forms that the writing would take.

Ms. Paterson and I did not invite the children and their families to make this school their school because we wanted to replace what they brought to school with what we knew and valued. We failed to value the stories of David and his friends, other than to confirm our own vision of their families' pathology. We did not learn to listen to the children's voices and the voices of their families. Therefore, we could not, in Erasmus' (1989) words, "extend, rather than limit the possibilities these children [brought] to school" (p. 274).

I began to see my intentions as a teacher and the outcomes of those intentions in fresh light. My writing was a telling of my teaching stories, or personal narratives of classroom life. The telling provided me with the time and opportunity to revisit my practices with an imagined sympathetic audience of peers. The telling provided me with multiple perspectives on my work: the perspective of an insider on my teaching as a person who wanted to make children's lives better. It also provided me with the perspective of an outsider, someone who could see that my idea of making children's lives better was to make their lives more like the one I had experienced in a working-class family with middle-class aspirations. I had interpreted a better life as a middle-class life.

In responding to the request to write about why and how I taught a university course, I engaged in self-critique. I interrogated my intentions and what grounded them. I looked closely at how I had enacted those intentions. I analyzed their outcomes for the children. I saw how what I had thought about as classroom teaching grounded in concerns for social justice was actually entrenched in middle-class perspectives on what children should know and learn and do.

Telling Teaching Stories: With Prospective Teachers in an Experimental Program of Teacher Education

During the same period in which I wrote the book chapter, Bob Tabachnick and I were co-directing an experimental multicultural program of teacher education called Teaching for Diversity (1987–92). In the same years, I was developing a graduate course called Teaching Writing to Diverse Learners (now more aptly titled Literacy, Culture, and Schooling). The teacher education (and accompanying research) was aimed at helping prospective teachers prepare for U.S. elementary classrooms where privileged children primarily from White, middle-class backgrounds sit side by side with peers from low-income families, who are often also families of color. Our program was predicated on multicultural and social reconstructionist theories.[3] Our objective was to prepare teachers who were committed to and successful at teaching everyone's children.

Our program spanned the three semesters that the university students were enrolled in course work and field experiences. The students mirrored their peers in the U.S. teaching population: most were White, middle-class, suburban- and rural-born, English-speaking, heterosexual females. Students worked in one of two schools with children from a variety of socioeconomic backgrounds—50 percent of whom in each building were children of color. Most children in these two schools spoke English as a first language; however, there were children from many different language backgrounds enrolled in English as Second Language programs in each building.

Each semester, we led weekly seminars with two teachers from the schools. Over time, we found that our weekly meetings provided opportunities for students in our cohort group to get to know one another well. We also found that the conversations, while guided by readings and assignments, were most exciting and challenging when students talked to one another about their teaching and their understandings of it.

We began to explore how focusing on telling teaching stories in the seminars provided the student teachers with the opportunity to do what I had done for myself in my writing—to critique their classroom practices in relation to their goals for themselves and their students and in relation to the outcomes of their work. We wanted prospective teachers to recognize links between classroom action and children's lives outside of school. We wanted them to see how their perspectives on and interpretations of children's motives and behavior are rooted in their race, socioeconomic group, gender, and sexual preferences just as the children's actions are also rooted in their backgrounds and experiences. We wanted our students to understand how they as teachers and how schools as institutions transformed the multi-faceted, complex dilemmas that families confront into school problems. We wanted prospective teachers to see themselves as a community that had collective responsibility for and investment in the children in their care. Through storytelling, we aimed to question our teaching goals; to consider effective alternatives to our teaching practices so that we continually focused on who the children were and what strengths as well as needs they brought to school; and to reconsider our role and behavior as individual teachers. We tried to see ourselves as members of not only a classroom community of children to which we were obligated, but also to see ourselves as members of a school community and of larger communities outside of school to which we were obligated for social action and justice.

Bobby Jo Johnson's Story

This story illustrates how, through telling teaching stories, prospective teachers were challenged to think about teaching for a literacy focused on increasing children's skills of reading and writing and also consider literacy as a way that people made and challenged meanings. Bobby Jo Johnson, the narrator of this story, is a White woman born in rural Wisconsin and raised on a farm as the youngest of 11 children. She was 25 years old and a candidate for a second bachelor's degree (her first was in economics) as an elementary teacher when she enrolled in our program, Teaching for Diversity.

In a pedagogical autobiography Bobby Jo wrote at the beginning of the program, she said that until she had completed her first university degree she had not thought much about teaching because she thought "money was a critical factor" in her life. However, as she grew older, and was not happy with who she was or what she was doing, she decided she wanted to be a teacher and "make a difference in the lives of [her] students and help as many children as [she] could be lovers of learning." Bobby Jo wanted to be like her favorite teacher, Mrs. Southfield, from second grade. She said,

> I want to be the Mrs. Southfield for every student I have. I want to reach out to the students and help them discover new, exciting interests; to create an environment where all feel welcome and safe so that they can be comfortable in their learning. But, most of all, I want to be thoughtful and reflective enough to see my weaknesses and mistakes I make in order to correct them. This is what I believe a good teacher does.

At the end of October 1992, during her final field experience as a student teacher, Bobby Jo chose to teach a multiweek unit focused on the presidential election to her fourth-grade students. She did so because the elementary school was located in the politically active eastern corridor of the city and the children in her class talked continually about the election. Many of the girls in the class were especially concerned about the stand that each candidate took on a woman's choice to control child-bearing. On their own initiative, several girls were tracking how the candidates represented their views at various campaign stops and with different constituent groups.

As she began planning for the unit, Bobby Jo asked the children to write down questions they had about elections, particularly presidential elections. She used the girls' questions about women's choice as an example of the things the children might wonder about. Once all students had posed their queries, she used them as jumping-off points for the centers that she and a peer, Margaret Smith, who taught another fourth-grade class across the hall, would develop with their cooperating teachers.

Eight centers were developed for the two classes. One featured campaign booths for each candidate where the platforms of Bush, Clinton, and Perot were available for students to read and analyze. Later, the children would stage a mock debate with the data they gathered from the center. At other centers, children could design and construct campaign buttons, banners, and slogans for their favorite candidate/s or about some issue, like children's rights to vote. In other centers, children voted in mock election booths, read biographies of each candidate, and analyzed data from various nations regarding who could vote and how voting rights had been determined.

As the days passed, and the actual election drew near, Bobby Jo observed that most of the fourth-graders appeared interested and engaged in the activities. She also observed that the children who had been labelled emotionally disturbed, four of whom were students in her class, seemed to be having fewer self-control problems—fighting, name-calling and general, "goofy" off-task behavior—than usual. Bobby Jo said,

> I know we have talked a lot about starting from what kids know and like and do and all that. But, for the first time, I saw how putting everything together . . . in one big unit for over an hour a day made all the difference for kids who usually can't make it all day in our room without some scene and Bob [guidance counselor] or Laurie [the educational assistant] coming on the run. Kids like Marvin and Corry and Danny, who are always popping off at someone or yelling, "I ain't gonna do that [four letter word]!" are hanging in there. Now, maybe they're not reading all of the words in the biographies or the campaign literature, but they are listening to the tapes I made and sitting there and when we talk about the centers, they have something to say. They're not just hanging over their desks with their heads down or trying to make Rollie cry or get angry by snapping a rubber band her way. Marvin was here all day for three days running. Amazing!
>
> What gets me is how during all of this good learning, I hear how we're going to do more testing with Marvin [an African-American boy] so we can label him CD (cognitively disabled) along with ED (emotionally disturbed). I got so excited today because the learning disabilities staff is trying to tell us that he's done so low on the testing for learning disabilities that . . . I don't want to say it, but that he's mentally retarded. And I'm like . . . there's no way [that is so]. I said that I can prove they are wrong. For one thing, I mean I've watched him listen to a tape and follow along to the reading. I mean I cued him for the first few lines. And when I looked back, he was already on the second column. And, you know, he is able to follow and write the words. This election unit [I taught] really helped me to see how smart he is because all the different learning stations let him use what he knew and what he was interested in knowing. I am going to go to the m-team meeting and argue for Marvin. We need to be better teachers. It's not Marvin— yes, he's certainly got his problems, but we shouldn't label him and say it (not learning) is his fault.

Bobby Jo's descriptions of Marvin as a child who *could* learn and her analyses of who should take responsibility for teaching that would help him build on his interests and the ways he learned best unleashed a torrent of comments from her listening peers. Several other students also gave examples of children of color in their classrooms who were "in a queue" for appointments with various psychologists and learning specialists for testing that would almost certainly result in their being labeled cognitively disabled or emotionally disturbed.

Belinda Davis told about Latanya, an African American child in her kindergarten class, who was struggling with many challenges, including young parents who were jailed. Latanya loved school and was a favored friend of many children in the class. She was small in stature and active—always in motion—and had a sweet disposition. She and some of her siblings were lovingly cared for by their grandmother.

Latanya could not identify any alphabet letters when she came to school in September and did not know how to read or write her name. By December,

Latanya could identify many, but not all of the alphabet letters and could write her first name (inconsistently), but not her last. Nonetheless, Belinda saw Latanya as making great progress in both her development of the traditional compartmentalized kindergarten skills of reading and writing and in the ways she talked about and drew about her understandings of the books read to the class, the trips they took around the city, and the classroom activities of measuring, counting, and cooking in which the children took part. Like Bobby Jo's pledge to Marvin, Belinda vowed to keep Latanya from being labeled *disabled*.

"Disabled, yeah," she said, "let's be honest, they want to call her retarded and put her in a special class away from the other kids! I'm going to fight as hard as I can. I'm so disappointed, you know. Even my principal (an African American woman whom Belinda greatly admired) seems to support this testing. I think people just kept talking to her about what's wrong with Latanya and she has started to believe it or wonder about it, too." Belinda felt sad and angry, but also stronger as she realized she was not alone in challenging how low-income children of color in her school were slotted for labeling and "treatment." Knowing that her peers agreed that Latanya and Marvin were smart and could do well in school gave Belinda confidence that she could struggle with Bobby Jo on the children's behalf.

Bobby Jo summed up what she learned from the unit and the story she had told about it to us all a few days after it was completed:

> I chose to teach this unit about the election because it was all around them. Lots of kids' parents were campaign workers and the news about the election was everywhere—on their lawns, in their mailboxes, on television, at their dinner tables. What I did not anticipate was how teaching about the election helped me understand how I could stand up and fight for a child's right not to be called disabled. I actually had records of what Marvin could do when he was interested in what he was learning.

Bobby Jo's story helped her understand what had made the difference in literacy learning for Marvin. He could read and write when he was interested, when the tools to support his reading and writing were in place, and when he could contribute to class conversations. Bobby Jo's peers, like Belinda, saw more clearly how they, too, might question ongoing school practices of slotting and labeling learners—especially children of color who were often testing targets—and to find ways to act against these for children's benefit. Together, they saw how different meanings and responsibilities for literacy teaching and learning could be assigned that might not result in some children's categorization.

Telling Teaching Stories: In a Graduate Course with Practicing Teachers

The graduate course I was developing at the same time focused on helping practicing teachers develop commitments to reflection and to understanding teaching as a negotiation of meanings. My purpose was to support teachers' reflections on what teaching for literacy meant and on how they might enact a pedagogy that supported their best intentions, despite the societal and institutional constraints on doing so. The syllabus told participants that the course was designed to do the following:

1. Help us understand the perspectives different people have of themselves, of others, and of their experiences with literacy—particularly as these experiences demonstrate the varied ways people are literate and how their literacies conflict with or are not recognized or are not enhanced by schools, schooling, and teachers.

2. Help us develop understandings about ourselves and the personal and professional perspectives that we bring to teaching for and about literacy with different students. Our understandings will develop in part through critical reflections conducted by telling stories about our teaching, our students, and ourselves.

3. Provide opportunities for us to examine, re-examine, and alter the perspectives we bring to schooling different people, and to alter the practices we conduct—in a community of teachers engaged in the same endeavor.

4. Provide opportunities for us to read, discuss, and write about theories of narrative and link them to our understandings of ourselves as teachers and of the roots and outcomes of our literacy teaching.

Through the course, I hoped to heighten teachers' awareness of literacy teaching and learning as activities, on which so much emphasis is placed in schools, teacher education, and in the assessment of individuals. Those activities include reading, discussing, and answering questions about the work of published authors and writing stories, poems, and essays. I also hoped to encourage thinking about ways that people make, negotiate, and contest meanings among others, across time, and in various places.

My intention was that participants acknowledge the sources of their own understandings of what it means to be literate, to examine how they have enacted these understandings, and to envision new practices that open their classrooms to dialogue and debate. In the class, I ask students to read theoretical pieces in which teachers and researchers (e.g., Lisa Delpit, Ann Haas Dyson, Bernardo Ferdman, Paulo Freire, Martin Nystrand, Denny Taylor) lay out their perspectives on teaching for literacy as a potentially dialogic and liberating process, and personal narratives in which poets, essayists, artists, and others from diverse backgrounds (e.g., Michelle Cliff, Mary Crow Dog, Carlos Fuentes, Paula Gunn Allen, David Mura) tell their stories of becoming literate.

The course has four key activities: Students write and share their literacy autobiographies, write weekly journals or reflective essays about the readings, construct projects in which they link their theories about how literacy is encouraged and constrained at home and at school with their practices as classroom teachers or teacher educators, and write and share stories of their teaching with the group.

The readings serve as jumping-off points for the discussions as teachers explore how their personal perspectives on learners and the mandates of schools as institutions often deny the knowledge and skills people bring to classrooms, as we reify particular, school-based proficiencies of reading and writing. Through our discussion of the readings and through the telling of our teaching stories, we explore ways we might enter into relations with children premised on efforts at mutual understanding—respecting, supporting, and sharing their social realities as much as we can as teachers.

Some class members are classroom teachers working on their master's degrees. They most often tell stories of their current work with children and their daily struggles to help children learn to read and write—and to learn *through* reading and writing. Other master's and doctoral students are on leave from or have left public school teaching to pursue college and university careers. Often, they are employed in our university teacher education program supervising the field of experiences of prospective teachers. These students generally tell two sorts of stories, those in which they examine their past classroom teaching and those in which they examine their work with prospective teachers.

My goal as the course instructor is to provide an environment where people with diverse backgrounds and experiences can come together to tell teaching stories—to support one another as they challenge their personal perspectives and the institutional perspectives on teaching, learning, and learners, and to critique their own and each other's classroom practices. The following pages contain stories from teachers enrolled in the course. They show how an opportunity to reflect on one's perspectives and practices with an audience of supportive peers can help us reconsider our understandings of teaching.

The stories are from a semester in which 15 graduate students (13 women and 2 men) from diverse backgrounds were enrolled in the course; three were working as classroom teachers at the time. The group ranged in age from 23 to 48. Two of the students were international students for whom English was not a first language. Three of the students from the United States identified themselves as persons of color (one African American woman, one bilingual Latina and one Latino who spoke conversational Spanish as well as his native English); all others identified themselves as White, native English speakers. All but one were either classroom teachers or had been classroom teachers. These cursory descriptions are offered to give readers a glimpse of the varied backgrounds and experiences the students brought to the course and our discussions.

We met every Tuesday evening for 15 weeks for 2½ hours. While we often told brief stories about ourselves as we explored our understandings of the readings, I also asked that the individuals write personal narratives about their practices three times during the semester. I asked that each person who felt comfortable in doing so read them to the group members, who would comment on the narratives or question the teller. The following stories were told one evening in the 10th week of the semester.[3] They were the second occasionof the semester in which we had told teaching stories. Students were asked to write about their current or past literacy teaching in light of our conversations and the interpretations of the reading we had conducted over the prior weeks.

Lesley Colabucci's Story

One of the first to tell her story was Lesley Colabucci, a master's degree candidate in multicultural education. Lesley, a recent graduate of an eastern university teacher education program, was a teaching assistant in a course on teaching children's literature in which prospective teachers were enrolled. While Lesley usually spoke confidently and easily, she hesitated as she began her story.

> I'm "out there" a bit on this one. I am going to tell you about my teaching last year while I was a student teacher in a first-grade class. I have thought about this one child, Billy, a lot and I have told stories about him to many people. But now I see differently my teaching of him and the responses of children in the class to him. I think while it may not sound like it at first, this is a story about literacy, about making and challenging meaning and about a discourse that I and the children in my class developed when Billy challenged us.

Lesley told us how, in the third week of school, Billy came to her class. He had moved frequently in his life because his parents had separated when he was very young and he had lived alternately with his mother, in a foster home, and with his father. Billy had been sexually abused on many occasions by adults in parental or guardianship roles. He created problems in the class by masturbating openly and frequently; by urinating on other children; by stealing other children's belongings; by eating crayons, pencils, and other supplies; and by licking the carpet, floors, and chalkboard.

Lesley said that for several weeks, she and the other children were upset by Billy's behavior and did all the things people do in school when someone does not follow the rules. Lesley felt compelled to send Billy to the office when he did not comply with her requests to stop stealing other children's belongings or urinating on his peers. Daily, Billy pushed the boundaries of Lesley's patience as well as the patience of her cooperating teacher and the other children. The following lines from Lesley's written story illustrate how, over time, the children and teachers found a way to live with and talk about Billy:

> Then, on the last day of full-time teaching, Billy mooned the class. . . . I won't even begin to get into stories of Billy masturbating in class, of little girls coming up to me to complain (My common response was, "Well, [name of child complaining], what do you think we should do about that?"), of Billy pulling shards of rusted metal out of trash cans, of Billy stealing things from everyone.

And I don't even really know how to get into explaining how we, as a class, coped with everything. But we did. So, on the last day of my teaching that fall, when Billy mooned the class, I knew that we had developed a discourse of our own, a literacy of sorts. Here's how it worked:

We were sitting around singing and playing the drums. I was sitting in the front of the room and students were taking turns coming up in two's to beat the rhythm of the song on the drum. I was pretty much lost in the music and fun of it all, to be honest, so I was shocked when Frederica came up and quietly tapped me on the shoulder.

"Yes, Frederica?"

"Billy just mooned the class."

"Oh."

"I don't think anyone else saw."

"Okay, well thanks for telling me."

"Sure."

At the end of the day, I told the county psychologist, who happened to be around, about the incident, and before Frederica left I made sure she was okay and told her to tell her mom to call me if she was concerned. . . . As I was driving home that day I felt better than I ever had about myself as a teacher. Now I see that my students and I had developed—no, created—our own literacy. We knew what to do now when Billy was having trouble. We didn't have to cringe or cry or scream or get upset or bother him in any way. We simply had to make sure he wasn't hurting himself or anyone else and go on with what we were doing.

This isn't to say that we decided to ignore or marginalize Billy; we worked as hard as we could to include him and to help him cope. The key was we knew how to cope as a class. How to express ourselves about Billy in a way that freed *us* up for learning. I don't know if *Billy* will *ever* be *free* (Lesley's emphasis).

Lesley later told me that when she realized she had to write a story for our class, she opened her "Billy" file. Previously, she had written poetry about Billy and letters to him that she had never mailed. But, until that night, when she began to plan what she would tell us, she had not thought about the class responses to Billy as a form of "containing" and making new meanings, as being experiences of meaning. "Then I knew," she said, "as I wrote, that we had made new meanings and contested old ones, about Billy, about what it meant to be him and how we could respond differently."

Someone asked Lesley, "What happened, to Billy and everyone, after you left the class?" She continued her story:

One day, later that spring, I came back to visit the children. I walked in on Mrs. Norris [my cooperating teacher] just as tears began streaming down her face. I stood in awe for I don't know how long. Linda was a terrific and experienced teacher. I had attributed my failures with Billy to my amateur-ness so this made no sense to me. Finally, a student spoke out, "Mrs. Norris has allergies." The student and I stared at one another for a minute, knowing allergies had nothing to do with it. I didn't even have to look at Billy to know. Then, I began singing, *If You're All for Freedom,* a Sweet Honey in the Rock version of *If You're Happy and You Know It,* that my students loved. Linda crept quietly out of the room without notice. She returned in time for the last chorus:

> If you're all for freedom, clap your hands (clap, clap)
> Stomp your feet (stomp, stomp)
> Shout hooray ('Hooray!')
> > Billy had a huge smile on his face as he clapped and stomped and shouted, "Hooray!"

Our university class was quiet for a long time after Lesley concluded. We were thinking about Billy, and Lesley, and what they had both learned that year. Lesley believes that in some ways, Billy found a place for himself in that classroom, a place to learn. She believes that in telling her story to her peers in the class, she acquired new perspectives on her practices. Lesley saw herself again from the viewpoint of an insider to her teaching experience, someone who was angry that Billy was abused and suffered and who was distressed at how Billy's misery manifested itself in classroom behavior that upset everyone, including him.

She also developed an outsider's perspective, one that enabled her to see how over time, she and the children had developed a way of responding to Billy's behavior that made a place for everyone in the classroom to learn academic knowledge and skills, as well as to acquire more personal understandings of suffering and how people live with it. While Lesley still saw many of her individual interactions with Billy and their outcomes as a failure due to her status as an "amateur," she also recognized that she and the children had negotiated new meanings for what they had formerly seen as a child's "bad" behavior.

As listeners, we also developed new understandings of teaching. Another student in the course said to me later:

> I cannot get Lesley's story out of my head. I have tried, because it is so tragic and it is hard to keep thinking about it. Every time I think about Billy and how Lesley and the children learned to think about him and what he did, I see how I do the same things. I make a child's actions, especially when they are "bad ones," into something so important that the only way we can all think about Barika or Sam is to think about what they do wrong and how mad they make all of us. Then, that's who Bari and Sam are, who they become for everybody, "bad." But Lesley helped her kids think about Billy in a different way as a person who was hurt. . . . Maybe it's good [she smiled] I can't stop thinking about Billy.

Martha Scheibel's Story

With uncharacteristic hesitation and a flushed face, Martha Scheibel, a White, 42-year-old special education teacher with two decades of experience broke the silence that evening:

> Well, I came to understand something new myself when I was thinking about this assignment. I am going to tell you a story about my son, Benjamin. It's also about

understanding . . . that comes out of the thinking I did preparing to tell you this story tonight. This is hard for me. It is so close, so . . . personal.

A few weeks ago Daniel [another class member] spoke about how he was concerned that we were addressing the reading of the texts in a superficial way that distanced us from the people and ideas about which we read. I was thinking about what he said and I am going to tell . . . something about my 13-year-old son.

Martha told about two assignments that one of her teen-age sons, Benjamin, recently had been given in school. One was to read a mystery book and write a report about how that book exemplified the elements of texts in the mystery genre. As an elementary-grade student, Benjamin had loved reading and being read to. But now he resisted reading at every turn. He grudgingly accepted Martha's maternal efforts to help him complete the assignment and agreed to read a 100-page mystery featuring the relationship between two brothers.

Martha tells how, in struggling with Benjamin, she developed a new understanding of literacy teaching and learning in school and why it so often does not connect with students:

A few weeks ago, Benjamin's language arts teacher presented a unit to his seventh-graders on people with disabilities in observance of National Americans with Disabilities Week. One of the assignments was to write a multifaceted paper about people with disabilities and about what the kids perceived to be their own disabilities.

Benjamin came to me in the kitchen to discuss his writing. We talked and he wrote thoughtfully about how important it is not to group people with disabilities. He wrote persuasively that the person should come before the disability. He didn't understand how he could write about advantages of being disabled, as the teacher had asked, because he thought the advantages were "not worth it." I agreed. "My disability is that I hate to read and that's what you have to do in school."

This lone sentence in my son's writing was the most powerful. The reality I confronted that day will be etched forever in my mind. What could I say? *You can read! Do it more and then you will like it. Oh, come on, Benjamin, at least you can do it! Imagine not being able to read! You just have to put forward a little effort. Change, Benjamin; it's your problem.*

I had heard his complaints before about how hard it was, how boring it was, how long it takes. He and I talked to teachers about his struggles. *Was I truly listening? Was he really saying I hate to read all this meaningless stuff; I'm at a disability, and there's nothing I can do about it? Wouldn't Benjamin change if he could?* The truth that became a reality for me that day is what Denny Taylor calls the ultimate irony . . . "that when children are given the opportunity to create an authentic foundation for their own existence they do not fail" (1993, p. 26). Taylor says that "we consistently underestimate the enormous potential of children to participate in the construction of their own learning environments." She says we "ignore their abilities" and interests and "blame them" when they "get it wrong."

"So Benjamin," I queried, "when is that mystery book report due?"

"Day after tomorrow."

"So, you've finished the book?"

"Page 30."

"Thirty pages more to read?"

"Nope, seventy."

Silence. . . . I'm thinking. *He doesn't care about filling in the blanks on the book report form. I wonder if he knows what the elements of a mystery are? He doesn't care about getting the assignment handed in on time or maybe at all. So, I stopped. I resisted the ultimatums and the lecture and the consequence giving.*

"Seventy pages. That would be thirty-five a night, unless we just can't put it down!" I said with a grin. "Meet you in your room tonight after dinner."

Benjamin and I read that forsaken mystery together. My boys had broken it to me a few years back that they were too old to be read to. Sadly for me, our nightly reads had ceased. But, somehow Benjamin did not resist this reading. He turned over and around on the single bed next to the one I was stretched out upon as I held the book, straight-armed, above my eyes.

We talked about how the author kept us hanging on. We talked about the characters and the plot and tried to predict who killed Nick's brother. We talked about how hard it would be if Benjamin or his brother died "for real." Together, we filled in the lines of the book report. The warm memories of reading together when my kids were little came back to me. Somehow, I don't think Benjamin hated to read this time.

As I read my own book in bed that night, I heard a quiet knock on my door.

"Thanks for helping me, Mom."

When Martha finished, we asked what she had discovered—about herself, about Benjamin, about schooling? She said she didn't have any simple answers. However, she had learned for certain that the assignments Benjamin was given in school were not encouraging him to read. Rather, they pushed him away from reading as he was asked to dissect the books he read for information his teacher deemed important. Often the reading was accompanied by equally tedious writing assignments that were not connected in any way to the lives and interests of adolescents. She pulled a copy of one of Benjamin's seventh-grade English assignments from her folder:

Look at this! It is titled *Unfinished Stories* and the directions read: "Use the writing checklist below to finish one or more of the stories that follow." Printed on the bottom and back of the handout are two very short stories, one called *Steep and Deep* that opens an adventure at a quarry, and the other called *Race to Taylor's Island* in which some teen-agers encourage others to race in a 3-mile swim across dangerous water. In addition to the opening paragraphs of a story, there is a short "cast of characters" for each story and questions to think about as you write. These include the following:

Have I written emphatically by:

1. Using active verbs?

2. Trimming overweight sentences and paragraphs?

3. Using precise and peppy words?

4. Using fresh figures of speech and no cliches?

Have I created good dialogue by:

1. Using idioms, if appropriate for a character?
2. Matching the character's speech and personality?

The more I have thought about Benjamin since he wrote that he hated to read, the more carefully I have read the assignments he gets. I wanted to yell from the rooftops. How can a child know what an "overweight sentence" is when he wrote it and thinks it is good? Why should my kid use peppy words if the story is sad? How could my kid know if an idiom is appropriate for a character or if the character's speech matched his personality when he didn't name or decide on the characters himself? His teacher did, and now all Ben and his friends can do is play a guessing game. How would "Mrs. Olga Beadle, an elderly woman who believes the quarry holds a startling secret" speak? Or, how would "'Scuba' Maynard, a professional underwater diver" talk? Peppily, no doubt!

Martha's words rang in our ears. A few of us wriggled in our chairs as we recalled devising similar assignments for our students. Surely, we chuckled, we hadn't asked anyone to "trim an overweight sentence"; we must have been more "sophisticated" than *that*. Martha's story reminded us how, as teachers, we have been seduced into thinking that by providing students with opportunities to read real novels, to write their own stories with scaffolds like story starters, and to self- and peer-edit, that we are connecting their lives outside school with those they live within its walls. As we listened to Martha, we recognized that Benjamin did not need to change or be fixed; he did not have a disability. We saw how Benjamin's teacher, like many of us, approached literacy teaching as a series of what Reder (1994) calls "a set of decontextualized information processing (e.g., encoding and decoding) skills, which the individual learns and then contextualizes by applying them to a progressively wider range of activities" (p. 40). We understood how teaching this way fails to acknowledge who children are and what they bring to school; teaching this way fails us all.

Telling Teaching Stories: Conclusion

Perhaps Maxine Greene (1982) sums best what Bobby Jo, Lesley, Martha, and I—and our listeners—learned from telling stories of our literacy teaching:

Teaching for literacy conceives learning as action rather than behavior. The notion of action involves the reflective taking of initiatives: trying out what has been learned by rote, acting on the so-called competencies. This is in contrast to an unreflective, semi-automatic movement through predefined sequences of what is sometimes optimistically called "mastery." A concern for beginnings, for action rather than behavior, is different than an occupation with end points, with predetermined objectives. Indeed, once teachers approach their students as novices, as newcomers to a learning community extending back through time and ahead into a future, they may well open themselves (as well as their students) to all sorts of untapped experiential possibilities. (p. 326)

I believe, like Greene, that teaching that conceives of action taken for fresh starts, just-glimpsed opportunities, and plain hopefulness is what counts in literacy curricula and instruction and in teacher education. This is not a naive view of the possibilities that lie before us; rather, it is a planned and committed endeavor in which concerns for social justice and equity ground the hard work of teachers, children, and families. It is an endeavor aimed at *all* children becoming bi- or tri-dialectal in English as they read, write, listen and talk—for real purposes—with one another and their teachers, families, and other community members. It is an endeavor that can reap the richest and most fruitful harvest in our country's educational and social life as we offer teachers of all children occasions to tell stories of our learning and rethink our perspectives and our practices.

Acknowledgment

I thank Wayne Otto for his comments on an earlier draft of this manuscript. I am grateful to my students Bobby Jo Johnson, Lesley Colabucci, and Martha Scheibel, and to my daughter Lily Gomez Sasse for allowing me to retell their stories.

Notes

1. A draft of this paper was presented at the American Educational Research Association meeting in New Orleans, April 1994.

2. The names of all children and teachers in this paper who either tell stories or appear as "characters" in stories are pseudonyms except for the names of my daughter, Lily Gomez Sasse, and graduate student Lesley Colabucci.

3. The experimental teacher education program Teaching for Diversity (1987–92) was grounded in multicultural and social reconstructionist principles that suggest teachers become engaged in (1) self-reflection concerning how cultural identity frames personal development; (2) examination of the activities of classroom life as situated in a larger sociocultural milieu; and (3) collaboration with others for thinking about and conducting social action. For discussion of multicultural and social reconstructionist principles grounding teacher education, see Zeichner & Tabachnick (1991); for a critique and analysis of various approaches to multicultural education, see Sleeter & Grant (1987).

References

Abt-Perkins, D., & Gomez, M. L. (1993). A good way to begin—Examining our personal perspectives. *Language Arts, 70*(3), 193–202.

Anzaldua, G. (1988). The path of the red and black ink. In S. Walker & R. Simonson (Eds.), *The Graywolf annual five: Multicultural literacy* (pp. 13–28). St Paul, MN: Graywolf Press.

Axline, A. (1964). *Dibs: In search of self.* New York: Ballantine Books.

Barone, T. (1987). Educational platforms, teacher selection, and school reform: Issues emanating from a biographical case study. *Journal of Teacher Education, 38*(2), 12–17.

Delpit, L. (1988). The silenced dialogue: Power and pedagogy in educating other people's children. *Harvard Educational Review, 58,* 280–298.

Dennison, G. (1969). *The lives of children: The story of the First Street School.* New York: Vintage Books.

Erasmus, C. C. (1989). Ways with stories: Listening to the stories aboriginal peoples tell. *Language Arts, 66,* 267–275.

Featherstone, J. (1971). *Schools where children learn.* New York: Discus Books.

Giroux, H. (1993). Literacy and the politics of difference. In C. Lankshear & P. McLaren (Eds.), *Critical literacy: Politics, praxis, and the postmodern* (pp. 367–378). Albany: State University of New York Press.

Gomez, M. L. (1991). Teaching a language of opportunity in a language arts methods course: Teaching for David, Albert, and Darlene. In B. R. Tabachnick & K. M. Zeichner (Eds.), *Issues and practices in inquiry-oriented teacher education* (pp. 91–112). London: The Falmer Press.

Gomez, M. L. (1994). Teacher education reform and prospective and novice teachers' perspectives on teaching other people's children. *Teaching and Teacher Education, 10*(6), 1–16.

Gomez, M. L., & Tabachnick, B. R. (1992). Telling teaching stories. *Teaching Education, 4*(2), 127–138.

Gomez, M. L., & Abt-Perkins, D. (in press). Sharing stories of teaching for practice, analysis, and critique. *Education Research and Perspectives.*

Greene, M. (1982). Literacy for what? *Phi Delta Kappan, 63*(5), 326–329.

Helle, A. P. (1991). Reading women's autobiographies: A map of reconstructed knowing. In C. Witherell and N. Noddings (Eds.), *Stories lives tell: Narrative and dialogue in education* (pp. 48–66). New York: Teachers College Press.

Holt, J. (1964). *How children fail.* New York: Dell Publishing Co., Inc.

Holt, J. (1967). *How children learn.* New York: Dell Publishing Co., Inc.

Holt, J. (1974). *Escape from childhood: The needs and rights of children.* New York: Ballantine Books.

Koch, K. (1970). *Wishes, lies, and dreams: Teaching children to write poetry.* New York: Vintage Books.

Kohl, H. R. (1967). *36 children.* New York: New American Library.

Kozol, J. (1967). *Death at an early age.* New York: Bantam Books.

Narayan, K. (1991). According to their feelings: Teaching and healing with stories. In C. Witherell & N. Noddings (Eds.), *Stories lives tell: Narrative and dialogue in education* (pp. 113–135). New York: Teachers College Press.

Reder, S. (1994). Practice-engagement theory: A sociocultural approach to literacy across languages and cultures. In B. Ferdman, R. M. Weber, & A. Ramirez (Eds.), *Literacy across languages and cultures* (pp. 33–74). Albany: State University of New York Press.

Rosen, H. (1985). *Stories and meanings.* Sheffield, U.K.: National Association for the Teaching of English.

Rosenwald, G. C., & Ochberg, R. L. (1992). Introduction: Life stories, cultural politics, and self-understanding. In G. C. Rosenwald & R. L. Ochberg (Eds.), *Storied lives: The cultural politics of self-understanding* (pp. 1–18). New Haven: Yale University Press.

Sleeter, C., & Grant, C. A. (1987). An analysis of multicultural education in the United States. *Harvard Educational Review, 57*(4), 421–444.

Smith D. (1991). Hermeneutic inquiry: The hermeneutic imagination and the pedagogic text. In E. G. Short (Ed.), *Forms of curriculum inquiry* (pp. 187–209). Albany, NY: SUNY Press.

Stuart, J. (1970a). *The thread that runs so true.* New York: Charles Scribner's Sons.

Stuart, J. (1970b). *To teach, to love.* Baltimore: Penguin Books.

Taylor, D. (1993). *From a child's point of view.* New York: Teachers College Press.

Zeichner, K. M., & Tabachnick, B. R. (1991). Reflections on reflective teaching. In B. R. Tabachnick & K. M. Zeichner (Eds.), *Inquiry-oriented practices in teacher education* (pp. 1–21). London: The Falmer Press.

Chapter 9

◆ ◆ ◆ ◆

Mathematizing and the Democracy: The Need for an Education that is Multicultural and Social Reconstructionist

William F. Tate IV

University of Wisconsin-Madison

What people chose to count and measure reveals not only what was important to them but what they wanted to understand and, often, what they wanted to control. Further, how people counted and measured reveals underlying assumptions ranging from plain old bias—the historian's easy target, when it is detected—to ideas about the structure of society. In some cases, the activity of counting and measuring itself altered the way people thought about what they were quantifying: numeracy could be an agent of change. (Cohen, 1982, p. 206)

How one is categorized is far from a merely academic or even personal matter. Such matters as access to employment, housing or other publicly or privately valued goods, social program design and the disbursement of local, state, and federal funds, or the organization of elections (among many other issues) are directly affected by racial classification (Omi & Winant, 1986, p. 4).

Scholars who challenge the implicit, unspoken assumption of objectivity in effect claim that knowledge depends on the interaction between the one who sees and what is seen. Reality is not discovered but constructed and invented and this process of invention needs itself to be included within the search for knowledge. (Minow, 1987, p. 175)

The above remarks suggest that the use of mathematics is connected to issues of economic power and social control. Traditionally, mathematics has been described as a discipline unconnected to human affairs. Mathematics is defined as "the science of numbers and their operations, interrelations, combinations, generalizations, and abstractions and space of configurations and their structure, measurement, transformations, and generalizations" (Merriam-Webster, 1993, p. 217).

Further, mathematical constructs are rigorously exact, precise, and certain. Many in the mathematics community believe in the absolute objectivity, neutrality, and exactness of mathematics. However, Ernest (1991) pointed out that this view of mathematics that promotes itself as value-free is actually value-laden. He stated:

Abstract is valued over concrete, formal over informal, objective over subjective, justification over discovery, rationality over intuition, reason over emotion, general over particular, theory over practice, the work of the brain over the work of the hand, and so on. These constitute many of the overt values of mathematicians, as well as being shared by much of British and Western scientific culture. (p. 259)

Ernest's remarks provide a backdrop for discussing the following question: Should schools prepare students to question the assumptions of objectivity and neutrality that accompany the use of mathematics in our multicultural and democratic society? I contend curriculum and instruction that present mathematics as objective, value-free, and neutral is problematic. I will argue throughout this chapter that mathematics is embedded in the nexus of society's power relations. Thus, mathematics as a tool to guide social decision-making is influenced by the values of those who use it in human affairs.

Understanding Mathematics in Society: Mathematizing

An important way for students to understand mathematics is to know how and why critical issues are mathematized. Putnam, Lampert, and Peterson (1990) described mathematizing as the building of quantitative models to represent nonquantitative relationships. They said mathematizing assumes the following:

> [A] certain view of the social and physical world, which asserts that the important *elements* [emphasis added] of situations can be represented by numbers and relationships among numbers. In Western society, this view is somewhat of a given, certainly among particular segments of the population who use mathematics to formulate and solve problems and others who *consume* [emphasis added] their work. (p. 98)

How does the mathematizer select the important elements of a situation? Einstein provides some insight into this question:

> To the discoverer . . . the constructions of his imagination appear so necessary and so natural that he is apt to treat them not as the creations of his thoughts, but as given realities. . . . The stereotypical categories that we use are rarely without some point of tangency with reality (biological, social, medical), but their interpretation is colored by the ideology that motivates us. (cited in Minow, 1987, pp. 173–174)

The selection of "appropriate" variables/categories to represent a situation is a subjective process (Omi & Winant, 1986). Further, choosing the "proper" mathematical technique to model and analyze a situation is a subjective process. The mathematizer can use multiple mathematical techniques to model the same situation. Each technique can provide a different result. This allows mathematizers to choose a result more consistent with their preordained set of beliefs. In essence, mathematics can be used to "scientifically" reconstruct situations that serve purposes of the mathematizer (Gould, 1981).

Quantitative methods built on assumptions of objectivity and neutrality can mask the subjective and nonneutral position of the mathematizer (Rosenberg, 1992). The philosophical underpinnings associated with mathematics, objectivity and neutrality are transferred to the value-laden reconstructions of reality made by the mathematizer. This allows the mathematizer to offer solutions to social problems under the guise of being neutral, objective, and fair. I will use personal experience to illustrate how the mathematizer's ideology influences the reconstruction and interpretation of situations.[1]

College admission requirements that use a combination of test scores and high school class rank are an example of a mathematized method for sorting people into categories (Putnam et al., 1990). When I was an undergraduate, the university administration recommended raising the mandatory ACT score by three points for incoming freshmen. The proposed higher admission requirement was part of a plan to enhance the national status of the campus. Many students favored the proposed change. They argued that improving the national status of the institution would enhance their opportunities for employment and graduate school admission.

But a group of students, including myself, was concerned with how the new policy would affect the number of culturally diverse students admitted to the institution. We formed a committee to analyze the policy. The committee decided to determine how the proposed policy would affect the admission status of African American freshmen admitted to the university in the prior five fall semesters. African American students were chosen because the university's administration had made public statements about the need to increase the presence of this group on campus. We believed there was a potential conflict between the proposed admission policy and the university's public stance on African American students.

We applied the new admission criteria to the previous five incoming freshmen classes admitted for fall semester. This analysis revealed an estimated 300 of 1000 African American students previously admitted would have failed to gain admission.[2] This would have represented a 30 percent reduction of African American freshmen admitted to the university in the previous five fall semesters.

We presented our results to the university administration. To our surprise, the university's department for institutional research had performed the same mathematical procedure on all fall semester admittees from the past five incoming freshmen classes.[3] The institutional research group's analysis provided the total number of incoming freshmen admitted during the previous five fall semesters who would not have gained admission under the new proposal. They categorized these students into three groups—White, African American, and "other." The institutional research figures confirmed the findings of our student group. That is, 300 of the 1000 African American students would not have been admitted under the proposed admission requirements. In addition, the university institutional research group found that 2,000 of the 10,000 White students and 500 out of the 2,000 students categorized as "other" would not have been admitted under the proposed entrance requirements.

The institutional research group argued that only 300 of the total 2,800 students not admitted under the proposed entrance requirement would have been African American. Thus, African Americans represent only 10.7 percent of those students who would not have been admitted using the proposed entrance requirements as compared with 2,000 of 2,800 or 71.4 percent of White students. The university research group argued that the percentage of African American students that would not have been admitted was small compared with the percentage of White students.

For both sides involved in the college admission debate, the selection of variables and the analysis performed on these variables were linked to the ideology of each group. Thus, each group responded to several important questions related to using mathematics in the democracy. For example, what methods of mathematical analysis will best support your group's position? What variables should be included within the analysis to strengthen your group's argument? How can you minimize the appearance of variables that may weaken your group's argument? Will percentages or aggregate numbers leave a more striking impression? All these questions are integral aspects of using mathematics in a multicultural democracy.

Imagine if the university's institutional group had reported their findings without the input of our student group's analysis. For instance, the university institutional group could have reported that 2,800 freshmen admitted to the university over the previous five fall semesters would not have gained admission under the proposed entrance requirements. Further, only 10.7% of those not admitted were African American. In comparison, 71.4% of those not admitted were White students. Would reporting the data in this fashion cause an uproar in the African American student community? Not likely. In fact, it would have probably moved White students to protest against the policy recommendation. Few people are educated to investigate the ideology that motivates the production of mathematical analysis.

In the end, our student group won the debate. We argued that the new admission policy would have resulted in 300 of 1,000 African Americans not gaining admission, a 30 percent reduction, as compared with 2,000 of 10,000 White students, a 20 percent reduction. Clearly, the proposed policy would have more negatively affected African American freshmen enrollment. Although the university institutional report was mathematically accurate, it did not accurately represent the effect of the proposed admission requirements. Instead, it represented the viewpoint of the university policy-makers.

Without the activism and the mathematical input of the student group, an admission policy recommendation would have been enacted that was inconsistent with the university's policy statement on African American student enrollment. Earlier, I asked the question: "Should schools provide students a mathematics education that prepares them to question the assumptions of objectivity and neutrality that accompany the use of mathematics in our multicultural and democratic society?" I submit that by failing to do so, mathematics teachers will continue to produce a society of mathematical consumers.

The college admissions debate introduces discussion of a mathematics education designed to prepare students to be producers and critics of mathematics in society, rather than consumers. More specifically, this discussion will look to principles of multiculturalism as a guide for mathematics teaching that prepares students for the challenges of the democracy.

The word *multicultural* may evoke different images both within and across the various learning communities in education. For instance, the concept of multiculturalism has been interpreted differently in the mathematics education community than by scholars who argue for an education that is multicultural and social reconstructionist. This approach to mathematics education specifically addresses the issue of preparing students to be critical activists within the democracy. Therefore, to facilitate communication and understanding between mathematics educators and educators who advocate the multicultural and social reconstructionist approach, the next section of this chapter examines the interrelationship of Eurocentrism and multicultural mathematics education. Included in this discussion are past multicultural recommendations within mathematics education. The final section of this paper is a discussion of two philosophical tenets—centricity and conflict—that undergird a new vision of mathematics education that is multicultural and social reconstructionist.

Eurocentricity and Multicultural Approaches to Mathematics

Eurocentricity is premised on White supremacist notions whose purposes are to maintain White privilege and advantage in education, economics, and other areas of human affairs (Asante, 1991). The Eurocentric principles underlying the use of mathematics cast this discipline as "elite knowledge" appropriate only for those with privileged status, White males (Cohen, 1987; Kamens & Benavot, 1991). Joseph (1987) argues that the current structure of mathematics education is based on the following tenets derived from Eurocentrism:

1. The inclination to not locate mathematics within a capitalistic base and thus to connect its advancement with the economic, political, and cultural venues of society.

2. The belief that mathematics should be confined to an elite group thought to possess the requisite talent denied a majority of society.

3. The widespread agreement among mathematicians that mathematical discovery can only follow from deductive logic believed to be a product of Greek mathematics; thus, empirical methods are viewed as having little mathematical value.

A great deal of the multicultural movement within mathematics education is defined by its opposition to the second Eurocentric principle. That is, multiculturists believe mathematics education should be expanded beyond just the elite few (Cuevas, 1984; Ethington, 1990; Johnson, 1984; Research Advisory Committee, 1989; Reyes & Stanic, 1988).

More specifically, the multicultural approach in mathematics education has focused on (1) working with culturally diverse students to improve affective factors (e.g., self-esteem and attitude), (2) adding more diversity to the mathematics teaching work force, and (3) introducing multicultural elements into mathematics textbooks. (See McLeod, 1992; National Research Council, 1989; Valverde, 1984. This body of literature delineates an approach to mathematics education principled on all students learning the traditional curriculum in traditional classrooms and being successful in the society as it is currently configured.)

In contrast, educators advocating a multicultural and social reconstructionist approach look to restructure the traditional curriculum by integrating into it social issues involving inequality based on race, socioeconomic group, disability, and gender. The primary objective of the curriculum is to prepare students to be citizens able to reconstruct the democracy based on egalitarian precepts. According to Grant and Sleeter (1989), meeting this objective would involve the following:

- Promoting and celebrating America's cultural diversity.
- Helping all children achieve academic success.
- Structuring classrooms like a real democracy to situate students in realistic opportunities for decision-making.
- Developing curricula directly related to the students' lived reality.
- Encouraging social action by involving students in social issues.

Some mathematics educators have made efforts to address one or more of the above themes. However, a paradigmatic tension exists between the philosophy of traditional approaches to mathematics teaching and multicultural approaches. According to Kuhn (1970), normal science is based on "one or more past scientific achievements, achievements that some particular scientific community acknowledge for a time as supplying the foundation for its further practice" (p. 10). The foundation of practice in more traditional approaches to mathematics is derived from the Eurocentric influences described earlier. Joseph (1987) provides further insight into the political implications of Eurocentrism in mathematics:

> Now an important area of concern for anti-racists is the manner in which European scholarship has represented the past and potentialities of non-White societies with respect to their achievement and capabilities in promoting science and technology. The progress of Europe and its cultural dependencies [including the United States] during the last 400 years is perceived by many as inextricably—and even causally—linked with the rapid growth of science and technology. So that in the minds of many, scientific progress becomes a uniquely European phenomenon, to be emulated only following the European path of social and scientific development. (pp. 13–14)

Joseph argues that the void of non-European contributions in the mathematics curriculum is a function of two issues of power. First, for one group to maintain control over another group, the knowledge of the dominant group must be perceived as most relevant (Apple, 1979; 1992). If the basis of control is scientific knowledge, as was the case with Europe over its colonies, then Eurocentric mathematical principles must be imposed over those of non-European groups.

The second issue of power concerns the group associated with the development of mathematical knowledge. If mathematics were associated with non-Europeans it would imply that they were capable of creating their own technology-based economies. This implication is counter to the stereotypic mythmaking used to justify the oppressive actions of European domination (Crenshaw, 1988; Jefferson, 1954). For example, Thomas Jefferson argued that people of African descent were incapable of mathematical reasoning. He used this argument to legitimize the unequal social status of African Americans (i.e., slavery). Jefferson's reasoning was not only morally questionable, he was also inaccurate in his position on African Americans and mathematics (Van Sertima, 1988). A body of scholarly work now exists that documents how people of African descent and other cultural backgrounds have contributed to the development of mathematics.

Ethnomathematics

Many scholars view mathematics as an abstract subject devoid of connections with the capitalistic base, while for many cultural groups mathematics is directly linked to the structural development of their societies. The study of how various groups and cultures in the world develop and use mathematics is called *ethnomathematics* (Nunes, 1992). D'Ambrosio (1985) defined ethnomathematics as the art of comprehending, describing, coping with and managing both natural and socially constructed systems—using techniques such as counting, measuring, sorting, ordering, and inferring—developed by well-defined groups like nations, professional classes, children in various age groups, labor groups, and so on. Ethnomathematics provides a lens to view mathematics as a cultural product. Further, ethnomathematics illustrates the validity of the mathematics produced by a wide variety of groups.

For example, Zaslavsky (1991) describes how the Chokewe people of Angola and Zaire use networks to symbolize their beliefs about the beginning of the world. Networks are finite mathematical graphs. In Western society, finite graphs are used to represent telecommunication systems, highways, and other technological applications. For Zaslavsky and others who incorporate ethnomathematics into their classroom instruction, it is important that all students understand how mathematical representations like networks are connected to the lives of people in various cultures and societies.

Critical Mathematics Literacy

I contend the Eurocentric bias has resulted in censorship of the ethnomathematics of the United States. Schools do little to prepare students for the role of mathematics in a capitalistic/democratic society. Frankenstein (in press) argues that the applications of mathematics taught in schools impart a vision of neutrality and naturalness to specific social configurations that helps obscure the class structure of society. Frankenstein states the following:

> Mathematical disempowerment works by presenting math applications that support a particular interpretation and organization of society; and by omitting information that shows the usefulness of statistical data in understanding economic, political, and social issues; and by ignoring data that presents alternative explanations and visions about the structure of society. (pp. 5–6)

In response, Frankenstein has developed a critical mathematical literacy (CML) program. Students learn how and when mathematics is used as a result of studying situations in which mathematics is a product. CML provides students an opportunity to analyze data on wealth distribution, the exploitative activity of multinational organizations, and the connection between race, gender, and socioeconomic exploitation. One theme of the curriculum is "welfare for the rich" or government transfer of monies from the poor to the rich. For example, Frankenstein's students study the mathematics embedded within the Neil Bush Silverado Savings and Loan scandal.

The situational contexts of CML allow students to construct and reconstruct real, not just "realistic," mathematical applications. This process allows students to connect mathematics to other knowledge they have about society. Frankenstein suggests this connection catalyzes discussion about the subjective aspects of mathematics. Students begin to see mathematics as context specific. For example, they realize categories are socially negotiated and that reality can be obscured by categorizing data in a certain way.

Many educators may question how ethnomathematics and critical mathematics literacy help students understand mathematics. I contend that there are several reasons these approaches are important:

- Both allow students to gain a sense of how mathematics is developed and used in real settings.
- Both approaches connect mathematics with other subject areas such as history, social studies, economics, anthropology, medicine, and potentially any other domain. The mathematics education reform establishment has argued that this is an important component of numerical literacy (National Council of Teachers of Mathematics, 1989).
- Both challenge the Eurocentric premise that mathematics is a neutral norm devoid of connection to human affairs.
- Ethnomathematics documents the development and creation of mathematics by many cultures and groups.
- Both ethnomathematics and critical mathematical literacy provide teachers of mathematics a literature base to broaden their understanding of how mathematics is used in real contexts.

A mathematics education that is multicultural and social reconstructionist should build on these strengths.

Mathematics and Multicultural and Social Reconstructionist Education: The Philosophical Underpinnings

Centricity is the first component of a mathematics education that is multicultural and social reconstructionist. This component distinguishes the multicultural and social reconstructionist mathematics approach from ethnomathematics and critical mathematics literacy, in that centricity is a paramount consideration.

A mathematics education that is multicultural and social reconstructionist centers the student in the knowledge-acquisition process. Students bring culturally relevant knowledge and experiences to classrooms that traditional mathematics pedagogy and other multicultural approaches often fail to acknowledge and build on. The danger of not building on students' experiences and communities is the loss of opportunities to illustrate the subjective aspects of mathematics. Elsewhere I captured this point in a story about a group of African American students from a middle school who responded "strangely" to a question on a school district mathematics test (Tate, 1994). The structure of the test item was similar to the following:

> It costs $1.50 each way to ride the bus between home and work. The weekly pass is $16.00. Which is a better deal, paying the daily fare or buying the weekly pass?

The school district's test designers constructed the problem assuming the students solving the problem correctly would choose the option of "paying the daily fare." Implicit in the test item design is that all people work five days a week. Also implicit is that the worker has only one job. Yet, these assumptions are not congruent with the realities of many culturally diverse students (Darity & Meyers, 1989). Therefore, it should not be shocking that a large percentage of the students from this particular middle school chose the "buying the weekly pass" option. When school officials questioned the children about their answers they found many students had personalized the solution process. For example, the students commented on the ability of more than one family member to use a weekly pass. Students also mentioned using the weekly pass on Saturday and Sunday.

For many culturally diverse students the financial provider(s) in their family have several part-time jobs—on both weekdays and weekends. For these students, selecting the weekly pass is economically appropriate, thus mathematically logical. I argue the correct answer should have been connected to the specific context of the students' lives. Stiff and Harvey (1988) note that students who center their lives and experiences within the process of acquiring mathematical competency risk being penalized for focusing on "tangential matters." As a result many culturally diverse students view mathematics as a subject appropriate only for White males and they fail to see the usefulness and relevance of the subject (Johnson, 1984).

The failure to provide all students with curriculum and instruction based on their experiences, cultures, and traditions is a major impediment to an empowering education (Asante, 1991; Cummins, 1986; Secada, 1991; Stanic, 1991; Stiff & Harvey, 1988; Woodson, 1990). Asante (1991) argues that an empowering education would be premised on centricity. He states the following:

> Centricity refers to a perspective that involves locating students within the context of their own cultural references so they can relate socially and psychologically to other cultural perspectives. Centricity is a concept that can be applied to any culture. . . . For White students in America this is easy because almost all the experiences discussed in American classrooms are approached from the standpoint of White perspectives and history. (p. 171)

The centric perspective provides a framework for analyzing why many of the Philadelphia middle-school children responded incorrectly to the test question. First, the students had to understand that the mode of response should reflect the lived realities of a "mythical" White, middle-class household. Second, the students had to understand the mathematics involved in solving the problem using the White, middle-class perspective as a frame to guide the solution process. This dual level of consciousness must occur if the student is to solve the problem based on the Eurocentric assumptions.

Is the first level of consciousness fair or empowering to students whose experiences are outside the White, middle-class realm? Harvey (1984) provides an appropriate response to this question:

> The advocacy of the values and lifestyles of the dominant White culture is not and cannot be psychologically beneficial to Blacks. The dominant cultural value system, and that of the school admonishes Black students for being what they are while physical and social reality prevents them from being anything else. (p. 446)

To take advantage of the diversity in a single classroom, the mathematics teacher using a multicultural and social reconstructionist approach would allow each student to solve problems using their lived reality. Of course, the mathematical processes used to solve a problem should be consistent with the parameters of the student's life. Further, the multicultural and social reconstructionist approach to mathematics education would advocate students solving the same question from the perspective of different members of the class, school, or society.

This would be important for two reasons. First, students would have an opportunity to solve the same question using different contextual backgrounds. The solution processes for each context provide the students invaluable insight into the subjective nature of mathematics. More specifically, it would show students that mathematics is embedded in contexts and, as a result, doing mathematics is context dependent. Second, students could relate and compare their experience with a variety of groups.

Conflict and Mathematics

The second philosophical principle guiding multicultural and social reconstructionist mathematics education is drawn from conflict theory. *Conflict theory*
provides an explanatory framework for understanding how social systems
work. The major premise of this theory is that society distributes its rewards
through various social structures and according to the laws that govern these
various structures (Appleton, 1983). Social conflicts are a product of groups
attempting to secure a favorable position over other groups in the allocation of
these rewards (Allen, 1974; Bell, 1992; Marable, 1983).

One way educational systems secure a favorable position for particular
groups is by failing to provide *all students* with instruction that prepares them
to expose and reconstruct inequitable conditions. I emphasize "all students"
because some students are provided an education principled on a reconstructionist philosophy. For example, Kozol (1991) documented how a White, upper
middle-class group of fourth-graders expanded the concept of "right" after
learning about the Bill of Rights and how greed and domination could affect
the implementation of the current definition. In the same school, a sixth-grade
class learned to question the scientific findings of researchers. One sixth-
grader wrote the following:

> Gregor Mendel . . . the Austrian monk who founded the science of genetics, pub-
> lished papers on his work with peas that some experts say were statistically too
> good to be true. Isaac Newton, who formulated the law of gravitation, relied on
> unseemly mathematical sleight of hand in his calculations. . . . Galileo Galilei,
> founder of the modern scientific method, wrote about experiments that were so
> difficult to duplicate that colleagues doubted he had done them. (Kozol, 1991, p.
> 97)

The students of this school are being provided with an education that
attempts to demystify the scientific method and begins to prepare them to
understand and challenge the use of science in society. Apple (1979) offers two
reasons for students to have an education that includes an opportunity to
explore the role of conflict in the scientific enterprise. Both reasons apply to
mathematics.

First, mathematical production is a function of conflict. Knowledge production is conducted by groups or communities of scholars. Like all communities, the mathematics community is governed by both stated rules and a covert
value system (Ernest, 1991). Within this community, individuals and groups of
mathematicians have a significant history of struggle over what is appropriate
knowledge for the discipline. These struggles also include conflicts over data
interpretation, credit for discovering ideas, censorship, and many other issues
(Eves, 1983). The very nature of mathematical production seems to involve
conflict. Yet, school mathematics is presented as a body of static ideas and procedures. Hidden from the student is the role and need for conflict to advance
mathematical thought.

A mathematics education that fails to prepare students for the conflict involved with mathematical production is problematic for a second reason. The use of mathematics in our democratic/capitalistic society is almost always linked to one group or individual attempting to secure resources over another. For example, in Major League baseball fielding, averages from .99 to 1 are excellent. Fielding averages less than .96 are considered poor. Suppose you are an agent for a professional baseball player. You are responsible for presenting an arbitrator information on the player's fielding performance as compared with that of an All-Star player.

Do the graphs in Figure 9.1 represent the same information? If you said yes, you are correct. But which graph should be presented by the player's agent? Which graph should be presented to the team? Which graph is more accurate? Why? If you knew nothing about good or bad fielding averages, what would you have concluded? This example represents how the same information can be "mathematized" and made to appear more consistent with the needs and ideology of the mathematizer.

Ask yourself the following question: "When do you count just for the sake of counting?" The answer: in school. The remainder of the time, counting and other mathematical activities are performed to move forward or block a particular agenda. Mathematics education should prepare students to recognize that the role of mathematics in the society is to both initiate and resolve conflicts. Further, students should be prepared to initiate and resolve conflicts "centric" to their lives using mathematics.

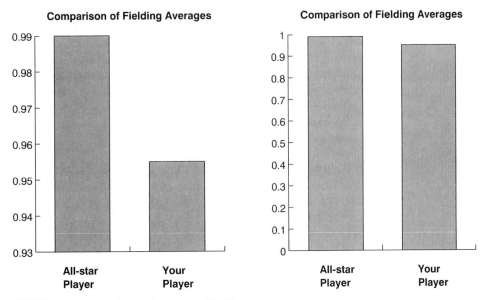

FIGURE 9.1 A comparison of two players' fielding averages

Final Note

Would you want to be represented by an attorney whose legal education consisted only of memorizing the laws, codes, and regulations of your state? Most likely not. Imagine having this attorney prepare an argument on your behalf in a case involving several types of institutions in our society—a government entity, a citizen's group, and a large corporation. You would want the attorney to understand the vested interests of each institution and to integrate this background information with the law to formulate a strong case in your behalf. This implies that an attorney must have knowledge of the legal system and of the many different institutions that interact within this system. Further, the attorney's reasoning is guided by the context and factors of each case. Merely memorizing the law is inadequate for this profession.

The same issues that apply to an attorney's professional knowledge base apply to the knowledge base of a multicultural and social reconstructionist mathematics teacher. First, mathematics teachers, like attorneys, must work to understand and build on the background, experiences, and culture of their clients/students. Thus, both professions require a centric perspective.

Second, both the lawyer and the multicultural and social reconstructionist mathematics teacher are preparing their clients for the conflicts of the democracy. The multicultural approach calls for providing students with a mathematics education that prepares them to make decisions on complex political issues that arise within our democratic society. The multicultural approach to mathematics not only requires teachers to have a thorough knowledge of the connections across mathematical topics, but also insists that they know how and why mathematics is used in particular social contexts.

Many students leave school unprepared to use mathematics in real situations. Just as legal education provides the law student an opportunity to apply the law in realistic settings of the profession (e.g., mock trials, internships, and summer clerkships), multicultural and social reconstructionist mathematics teachers must structure the educational environment so students have opportunities to construct mathematical understanding within realistic settings where mathematics is a product. The key phrase here is "educational environment." For the multicultural mathematics teacher, the world is your educational environment.

Acknowledgment

The author wishes to thank Carl Grant, Mary Gomez, and Kimberly Cash Tate for their remarks and feedback on this chapter.

Notes

1. Delgado (1990) argues that people of color speak with experience that our society is framed by oppression. This framework gives their stories a common

structure warranting the term *voice*. A growing body of literature incorporates voice to explain the experience of culturally diverse people. These scholars use parables, chronicles, stories, counterstories, poetry, fiction, and revisionist histories to illustrate the irony and contradictions of certain policies in education (Tate, in press). In this chapter, I use voice scholarship as a vehicle to illustrate the contradictions within the traditional mathematics education paradigm.

2. The data provided here are rounded estimates. Please note admission data by race are not mandatory information on most college admission applications. Thus, both the university administration and the student group extrapolated their estimates for the sake of discussion.

3. One member of the student group informed the school administration of our mathematical methods and conclusions.

References

Allen, R. (1974). *Reluctant reformers: The impact of racism on American social reform movements*. Washington, D.C.: Howard University.

Apple, M. W. (1979). *Ideology and curriculum*. New York: Routledge.

Apple, M. W. (1992). Do the standards go far enough? Power, policy, and practice in mathematics education. *Journal for Research in Mathematics Education, 23,* 421–431.

Appleton, N. (1983). *Cultural pluralism in education: Theoretical foundations*. New York: Longman.

Asante, M. K. (1991). The Afrocentric idea in education. *Journal of Negro Education, 60,* 170–180.

Bell, D. (1992). *Faces at the bottom of the well: The permanence of racism*. New York: Basic Books.

Cohen, P. C. (1982). *A calculating people: The spread of numeracy in early America*. Chicago: University of Chicago.

Crenshaw, K. W. (1988). Race, reform, and retrenchment: Transformation and legitimation in anti-discrimination law. *Harvard Law Review, 101,* 1331–1387.

Cuevas, G. (1984). Mathematics learning in English as a second language. *Journal for Research in Mathematics Education, 15,* 134–144.

Cummins, J. (1986). Empowering minority students: A framework for intervention. *Harvard Educational Review, 56,* 18–36.

D'Ambrosio, U. (1985). Ethnomathematics and its place in the history and pedagogy of mathematics. *For the Learning of Mathematics, 5,* 44–48.

Darity, W. A., & Meyers, S. L. (1989). *The problem of family structure, earnings inequality and the marginalization of Black men*. Unpublished manuscript.

Delgado, R. (1990). When a story is just a story: Does voice really matter? *Virginia Law Review, 76,* 95–111.

Ernest, P. (1991). *The philosophy of mathematics education*. Bristol, PA: Falmer.

Ethington, C. A. (1990). Gender differences in mathematics: An international perspective. *Journal for Research in Mathematics Education, 21,* 74–80.

Eves, H. (1983). *An introduction to the history of mathematics*. (5th ed.) New York: Saunders.

Frankenstein, M. (in press). Equity in mathematics education: Class in the world outside the class. In E. Fennema, W. G. Secada, & L. Byrd (Eds.), *New directions for equity in mathematics education*. Madison, WI: Wisconsin Center for Education Research.

Gould, S. J. (1981). *The mismeasure of man*. New York: W. W. Norton.

Grant, C. A., & Sleeter, C. E. (1989). *Turning on learning: Five approaches for multicultural teaching plans for race, class, gender, and disability*. Englewood Cliffs, NJ: Merrill/Prentice Hall.

Harvey, W. B. (1984). The education system and Black mental health. *Journal of Negro Education, 53,* 444–455.

Jefferson, T. (1954). *Notes on the state of Virginia*. New York: W. W. Norton.

Johnson, M. L. (1984). Blacks in mathematics: A status report. *Journal for Research in Mathematics Education, 15,* 145–153.

Joseph, G. C. (1987). Foundations of Eurocentrism in mathematics. *Race and Class, 27,* 13–28.

Kamens, D. H., & Benavot, A. (1991). Elite knowledge for the masses: The origin and spread of mathematics and science education in national curricula. *American Journal of Education, 99,* 137–180.

Kozol, J. (1991). *Savage inequalities: Children in America's schools*. New York: Crown.

Kuhn, T. (1970). *The structure of scientific revolutions*. Chicago: University of Chicago.

Marable, M. (1983). *How capitalism underdeveloped Black America*. Boston: South End.

McLeod, D. B. (1992). Research on affect in mathematics education: A reconceptualization. In D. A. Grouws (Ed.), *Handbook of research on mathematics teaching and learning* (pp. 575–596). Englewood Cliffs, NJ: Merrill/Prentice Hall.

Merriam-Webster's Collegiate Dictionary. (1993). (10th ed.) Springfield, MA: Author.

Minow, M. (1987). When difference has hit home: Group homes for the mentally retarded, equal protection and legal treatment of difference. *Harvard Civil Rights—Civil Liberties Law Review, 22,* 111–190.

National Council of Teachers of Mathematics (1989). *Curriculum and evaluation standards for school mathematics*. Reston, VA: Author.

National Research Council (1989). *Everybody counts: A report to the nation on the future of mathematics education*. Washington, D.C.: National Academy.

Nunes, T. (1992). Ethnomathematics and everyday cognition. In D. A. Grouws (Ed.), *Handbook of research on mathematics teaching and learning* (pp. 557–574). Englewood Cliffs, NJ: Merrill/Prentice Hall.

Omi, M., & Winant, H. (1986). *Racial formation in the United States*. New York: Routledge.

Putnam, R. T., Lampert, M., & Peterson, P. L. (1990). Alternative perspectives on knowing mathematics in elementary schools. In C. B. Cazden (Ed.), *Review of research in education* (pp. 57–152). Washington, D.C: American Educational Research Association.

Research Advisory Committee (1989). The mathematics education of underserved and underrepresented groups: A continuing challenge. *Journal for Research in Mathematics Education, 20,* 371–375.

Reyes, L. H., & Stanic, G. M. A. (1988). Race, sex, socioeconomic status, and mathematics. *Journal for Research in Mathematics Education, 19,* 26–43.

Rosenberg, A. (1992). *Economics—Mathematical politics or science of diminishing returns?* Chicago: University of Chicago.

Secada, W. G. (1991). Agenda setting, enlightened self interest, and equity in mathematics education. *Peabody Journal of Education, 66,* 22–56.

Stanic, G. M. A. (1991). Social inequality, cultural discontinuity, and equity in school mathematics. *Peabody Journal of Education, 66,* 57–71.

Stiff, L. V., & Harvey, W. B. (1988). On the education of Black children in mathematics. *Journal of Black Studies, 19,* 190–203.

Tate, W. F. (1994). Race, retrenchment, and the reform of school mathematics. *Phi Delta Kappan, 75*(6), 477–485.

Tate, W. F. (in press). From inner city to ivory tower: Does my voice matter in the academy? *Urban Education.*

Valverde, L. A. (1984). Underachievement and underrepresentation of Hispanics in mathematics and mathematics-related careers. *Journal for Research in Mathematics Education, 15,* 123–133.

Van Sertima, I. (1988). The lost sciences of Africa: An overview. In I. Van Sertima (Ed.), *Blacks in science: Ancient and modern* (pp. 7–26). New Brunswick, NJ: Transition Books.

Woodson, C. G. (1990). *The mis-education of the Negro.* Trenton, NJ: African World Press. (Original work published 1933.)

Zaslavsky, C. (1991). Multicultural mathematics education for the middle grades. *Arithmetic Teacher, 38,* 8–13.

Chapter 10

◆ ◆ ◆ ◆

Learning Science as a Transformative Experience

Jean Lythcott

Teachers College, Columbia University

James H. Stewart

University of Wisconsin-Madison

Imagine that, when you turned 21, your parents passed on to you an artifact, an object from an ancestor, a long-gone member of the family tree. Maybe by this time, exactly who she was has been forgotten—someone's great-great-great-aunt, perhaps, or great-great-grandmother. No one knows why the piece had importance to the original owner, and so no one is really sure what it is. But the tradition of handing it on to the eldest child has been preserved, and you are the current recipient.

You examine it and find it to be a little odd in today's world. You cannot connect with it, you cannot make meaning out of it. Unable to be situated into a real experience, it doesn't seem to fit into your life in any meaningful way. The threads of connection with its origins are gone, reduced to a tradition of passing it along, intact, unspoiled by its sojourn with successive recipients. What are you to do with it, except to put it away safely, to pass it along in turn when your time comes?

School science is often like such a tradition—the respectful passing along of decontextualized words and sentences from the past. These words are revered—not to be changed, worked with, nor fitted into the lives of children; they are only to be respectfully received by children from their elders. Listen to the words of science as they exist in the public domain of texts:

> A solid is a state of matter in which a substance has a defined size, shape, and well-defined surface that separates it from all other matter (p. 332), and a liquid is a state of matter in which the molecules are free to move from place to place but remain essentially a fixed distance from each other; liquids have a definite volume but they assume the shape of the container in which they rest. (Boeschen, Gerard, & Storin, 1983, p. 330)

These sentences and definitions are terse distillations of meaning that are stripped of the situations in which they were made. They are the decontextualized, abstracted cores of the rich original meaning. This is the language of science that is often taught in schools: sets of words and sentences with their fullest original meanings gone into history.

These pieces of language are our cultural inheritance, passed down to us from the centuries of work, of meaning making, by hundreds of people of different nations, in different contexts, with different materials, asking different questions. The artifacts that are these textbook words and phrases, with their stark, strange and isolated beauty, have over time become disconnected from the meanings of a cultural past. In science classrooms, the time-honored activity of learning to recite these definitions is like the tradition of a simple passing along of an inheritance. And what is a youngster to do with such strange things that have so little apparent connection with life being actively lived? How can such artifacts help children make meaning of their world and of themselves in that world? How can receiving these inheritances enable youngsters to transform themselves, to be able to make changes in their own lives and in the lives of others?

Now, leaving this metaphor and creating a different vision, put down this book and collect the following materials:

- ½ cup of corn starch—any brand from the grocery store will do
- 4 tablespoons cold water
- A coffee mug or teacup
- A sturdy spoon
- A small container of any kind, but much smaller than the mug—a plastic margarine container works just fine

Put the corn starch into the mug, and pour in the cold water. Stir lightly. Adjust the mixture by adding more water or more corn starch until it is runny when you are not stirring it, but dry and sort of hard when you push it with the spoon. Now scoop the mixture out of the mug with your hand and play with it, in your hands, on the table, in the small container, feel it, drop it, snap it, see what it will do.

You might be thinking, "If I just read ahead I can avoid the nuisance of having to do all of this." Maybe so. But if you don't take the time out to experience this stuff you will miss out on something important. By reading ahead you will, in some important respects, only be taking part in the passing on of the ritual.

This playing, and feeling, and watching, can spawn conversations that mirror the connections of meaning that grow between the player, the stuff and the events. Listen to snippets of classroom conversation about this mixture: "It's weird, I mean it's cool stuff—sometimes it's wet, sometimes it's dry"; and "It's like hard and soft, back and forth. When you press it, it becomes hard and solid, then it gets wet and runny again"; another says, "It's wet and dry together like it's a liquid but then you pick it up and it turns solid; it's funny." Someone notices something a little different from the others: "It spreads out and it's shiny and loose when it's wet and when it hardens it's not shiny anymore." Now a discussion leader asks: "Tell me how you know when it's being a solid? What is it that let's you know that it is a solid?" and the same question concerning "liquid." The answers come back: "When it's solid you can break it, it just snaps in two, clean; liquids won't do that"; another sees that "When it's a solid the powder, I mean the extra starch, can't penetrate the edges"; someone says, "It has, like edges, that are stiff, not flowing"; and then, "You know it's solid when it keeps its own shape, it'll just stand there on its own. You put it in the little jar and for a minute it stands up firm, but then it starts to run down and fills the jar to its shape."

Now the conversation moves to consider the liquidness issue: "It doesn't have a shape when it's liquid, well not like the solid, but it does when it stops spreading out on the table"; another person notices something else: "When it pours out of your hand, you know it's liquid. You can pour it and it'll leave part of itself behind; that's a liquid because a solid moves all together in a lump."

What the youngsters knew before they began, each knowing different things from lives lived outside of science class, is crucial to the connections out of which meaning is made. Playing with the corn starch mixture is an experience; it is a context of objects and events out of which children make new meaning for the terms *solid* and *liquid*. When allowed to speak in their own language, respected and encouraged to grope for expression of what they think, individuals are free to make meanings for *solid* and *liquid,* to comment and converse about specific bits of the experience that strike a cord of recognition with something they already knew.

Listening to the conversation, one can hear the understandings that the students have. One can hear the general understanding of the students that things are either solid or liquid, they cannot be both at the same time; and one can hear the understanding that for a solid to change into a liquid, and vice versa, is an unexpected event.

Meaning, moreover, is an individual's personal property in this situation. The one who speaks of solids breaking is not the one who speaks of it having its own shape, nor is it the one who sees that the corn starch powder cannot penetrate the edges of the solid. The one who saw "pouring" as the liquid leaving behind some of itself is not the one who was struck by it filling the shape of the small container. In this science classroom, the personal contributions of the youngsters are not merely allowed or tolerated, as in a theater of free classroom discourse. Rather they are the crux of the meanings that the science definitions to come will shadow.

The teacher learns what her students notice, hears the language they use, and begins to negotiate meaning with them: "So, you know a solid is different from a liquid, you know that solids have fixed edges and so they have a distinct and definite size and shape—the powder cannot penetrate the edges. A solid has well-defined surfaces; it takes up a space that nothing else can occupy—we call that its volume."

"You have noticed that nothing about a solid moves, it stays still. But a liquid moves by itself—something about the liquid is in motion, pushing the edges of the liquid until it meets the walls of the container and can't go any farther. Somebody noticed that when you hold your hand like this, the liquid pours off it; some of it moves and some of it stays behind. The liquid can separate itself; we can think of the liquid being made of tiny pieces that are always moving."

As the meaning is negotiated, the language moves away from the corn starch mixture. It becomes increasingly detached from and reliant on the particular events and experiences. As the conversation becomes increasingly abstract, the meanings can be connected with a multitude of events not yet experienced nor even imagined. The science definitions are used, worked with. Each person owns the terse abstractions in a personal way. Rather than inheriting knowledge, the corn starch players, children and teacher, were the makers of the knowledge they now own. In this way, the science lesson has included children's ideas and experiences as essential to science learning. This is not an easy task for children—making meaning. And it can feel like a discovery to a particular child.

In science class, then, we can provide some experiences and conversations so that youngsters can make the grounded connections that are the stuff of understanding. Returning to the metaphor, these inheritances from the past, these science definitions, will not be strange artifacts to be merely received and put into storage. They have become things with meaning, related and fitted by the youngsters into what they already know. Now they can speak in the language of science; they can use the special words and phrases of science. When they do so the words and phrases function as language cues to a rich nexus of connections with things and events. The words become included in their life; so, students come to speak not about science, but *in* science.

Our intention has been for you to see the group of children in your imagination. We invited you to join into conversation with us and negotiate meaning about science teaching. This is an impossibility in reality, but perhaps not so in the imagining. What we have been talking about is teachers learning how to teach their students science, starting with materials, events and changes, with something engaging to think and talk about, then listening to their students.

Teachers who have invited children to bring what they know to the table can then negotiate meaning with them from their current understanding. We have been talking about the distinction between a view of science as an artifact to be received and as decontextualized language for which meaning must be created. We have acknowledged that children and teachers use everyday processes and knowledge of some piece of the world to negotiate and construct new abstracted meaning, in the language of science. It is always the case that youngsters know something that can serve as the foundation for building new ways of explaining and questioning, for noticing new issues, for new language and new meaning.

Our discussion has not concerned the traditional divisions in science education of content versus process; not only do both count, but they are also inseparable. Classifying, for example, is often described as a science process. In playing with and talking about the corn starch mixture, the youngsters clearly had already classified matter into solid and liquid, but they extended and abstracted that classification through making new decontextualized meaning for the categories in the science class.

The process of classification they used in everyday life was also used in science, but to make science meaning, the content and the process were inseparable. Observation is also often mentioned as a science process. The youngsters were certainly observing. They were noticing specific features of the stuff and the changes that occurred. But observing the characteristics that count in science requires one to know what science has said to look for. One child noticed that when the mixture became a liquid, it was shiny. That child had observed a characteristic that was indeed interesting and accurate. Whether the observation is useful in science can only be determined from knowing ahead of time what to look for. Only the science meaning for the distinction between solid and liquid tells one whether or not the observation "shiny" is valuable in making science meaning.

This making of meaning is the basis for the current push for "hands-on" activities in science classes. This is a phrase that makes us laugh a little, for it seems sometimes as if there is an idea that knowledge leaks into children's minds through their fingertips. Science meanings do not emerge from events and experiments. Meaning must be made. No one can see the atoms or molecules of solids and liquids, for example, by observing, touching, and manipulating materials in "hands-on" activities. These particles that scientists have proposed exist have to be imagined by each learner. Students get to this imagining by thinking and conversing and struggling for meaning with teachers and with each other about the way things work.

But it is important to understand that although the starting point for learning clearly is real things, "hands-on" activities could be useless as the source of science learning if "minds-off" occurs at the same time, or if children are left to play without the invitation to negotiate science meaning with us. The kind of free, respected discourse in the previous comments of the students does not occur automatically when a fun activity is brought into the classroom. It has to be nurtured by a teacher who knows that children's ideas together with the events and objects at hand are the starting points for learning. In fact, such conversation can be closed down before it has even begun. Suppose a science specialist, a discussion leader, enthusiastically introduced the corn starch and water task to a group of fifth-graders with the following:

> Today—listen up class—you will be making a non-Newtonian fluid, spelled n-o-n N-e-w-t-o-n-i-a-n f-l-u-i-d [writing the letters carefully on the blackboard]. This is a very strange fluid which you will find does not behave according to the regular scientific laws of solid and liquid matter. . . .

Oh, the students will probably enjoy playing with the stuff and experiencing its weirdness, regardless of what the leader says. Nevertheless, in this introduction it is clear the task is not expected to be connected to real life, especially not that of the children. Rather, it seems to be a science classroom event which has relevance only in the classroom and has no real connection with life on the outside. Framed in this way, there is no valuing of the voices of the children as a necessary contribution to understanding science, and no notion that the diversity of experience of family, traditions, and culture of a youngster count for anything. Such a teacher has instantly framed school science, not as a connection between, but as a clash of, the cultures of science and children.

Science as Meaning Making

Let us turn our attention to some other events and phenomena. There is a kind of meaning making that should go on in science class, different from the solid-liquid negotiations. It is the struggle to understand in an entirely new way something that seemed already clear. Through open, nonjudgmental conversations with young people, science education researchers have heard the fullness of the ideas students have that are their way of explaining and describing the world.

For example, children do have ideas about why a thrown ball flies the way it does, how they know that fire is alive, what is going on when iron rusts, where the light goes when the switch is turned off, why the moon looks different on successive nights, and why a child resembles her or his parents. Most of these ideas are, not surprisingly, inconsistent with scientific ideas. We know from research data that youngsters often continue to explain events with similar ascientific ideas both before and after completing a course in college physics, for example, or a sixth-grade science class about atoms. Traditional science teaching does not seem to enable them to make new scientific understanding or to substantively change the ideas they brought with them to science class.

Traditional science teaching, the inheritance of ritual words, focuses on children getting the artifacts of language, then putting them away somewhere safe and secure. Of course, they easily get lost (buried in the attic), or perhaps were never put away because teacher said one thing and child understood another. The attic is a useful metaphor for the mind, for we know that trying to put something into memory is no guarantee that it can be retrieved, nor is it a guarantee that it will still be there in a few days, or that it even made it to the attic. Let us consider the last of these possibilities.

We all, children and adults alike, interpret and translate what is said through our existing knowledge about the way the world is. When people hear the proverbial someone shout "Fire!" in the proverbial crowded theater, they do not hear a call to set off their muskets. In science class, this interpretation issue can cause a lot of misunderstanding. We see and hear with what we know. The meanings that people already have get in the way of making different meanings, especially if they are not encouraged to struggle to make the distinctions. Without a negotiation of meaning, without conversation in which children can work with new meanings and their pre-existing meanings in a context of real experience, no teacher can ever know what sense children are making of the science language they use.

Often it is this negotiation of meaning that is particularly and precisely necessary in science, when what youngsters know in everyday life is at odds with what science states to be the case. There are many instances of this: In everyday life it suits us to talk of *heat* as stuff that flows out of an open door on a winter day, or *cold* as stuff that flows out of a refrigerator left open, because it seems intuitive that a thing doesn't move unless something pushes or pulls it. When we see a baseball moving, for example, we say the pitcher gave it force that is causing it to move; and children so often seem to be a blend of the features of their parents that it seems as if some mixing of fluid, like blood, makes us who we are. In each instance, however, science disagrees. Under these circumstances, when making a science understanding is contradictory to one's own beliefs, building that new understanding takes a lot more negotiating and struggling to make meaning than in the solid-liquid example.

Here is another activity; you'll need to collect the following items:

- A hard-boiled egg still in its shell
- A large, empty glass bottle, such as an apple juice bottle, the opening of which is too small for an egg to pass through
- A small piece of paper—newspaper is fine
- A match

Twist the paper loosely to make a taper about 3 inches long that you can eventually light with the match. Peel the egg. Light the taper and stuff it, flame down, into the glass bottle. Immediately set the peeled egg upright (either way up is fine) onto the bottle opening and watch.

You'll see the egg perhaps wobble a little, the flame will go out, the jar will fill with smoke, and the egg will get sucked into the bottle with a distinct squeeze through the neck, an "ooomph" sound, and a satisfying thump onto the bottom of the bottle. There is no doubt that you will both see and hear the egg being sucked into the bottle. Even though for science there is no such thing as a "suck" force, scientists and science teachers, being also regular people, do see and hear the egg being sucked in.

This is the point about "hands-on" alone being insufficient. To make science meaning about this egg and bottle experience we have to be able to interpret this activity and re-interpret it, to impose new meaning on it. Because they have scientific understanding, science teachers can decide to see this event a different way, to observe not that the egg was sucked in but that it was *blown* into the bottle by the air outside. Knowing this, science teachers can ask the youngsters if it is possible to get the egg out again by blowing air into the bottle—the usual answer is "NO!" Demonstrating that, in fact, the unexpected happens and that one can indeed blow the egg out of the bottle begins a conversation driven by the youngsters' need to know.[1]

Even in this demonstration, where the everyday explanation is inconsistent with science, children will tell you words and understandings that are a useful foundation for negotiating new meaning. Your students may say the same or very different things from the children we have heard. It is likely, however, that you will hear some of the same things, for example, such as mention of a vacuum. You will negotiate the understanding that the burning paper heated the air in the bottle; that the hot air expanded and pushed up out of the bottle—making the egg wobble a bit on the way out—so there was then less air per volume in the bottle than in the outside air; that less air per volume means a lower air pressure when the temperature is the same; that when the flame went out because of lack of oxygen, and the air in the bottle cooled down again, the air outside the bottle moves to get back into the bottle to equalize the pressure. Because the egg is in the way, the air moving back toward the bottle pushes the egg into the neck, sealing it, so that no more air can get in. Eventually the air pushes the egg ahead of it into the bottle. The egg moved because it was pushed by the air that had the greater pressure. It is blown out again by exactly the same process, using the same understanding: Blowing a lot of air into the bottle creates greater pressure inside the bottle than outside, and this time the air pressure pushes the egg in the opposite direction.[2]

The conversation that students must have to make this meaning for themselves is rich, complicated, and time consuming. They have to make some of this fit with what they already knew; they have to acknowledge that the science explanation is a long chain of argument, one piece connecting to and supporting the rest. They have to dissociate the original explanation from the new understanding they are building. They will want to make new experiments, they will want to test out their ideas, and they will want to investigate predictions.

These explorations determined by the children are times and places for them to converse with the data they get, and to check out their understanding, their explanations, and the connections. They will each be interested in different issues, and when allowed to set out on their own trail of questioning and answering, they will struggle to make meaning of science and to make science have meaning to them. Clearly, they must be the ones to decide that trail. In trying to answer their own questions it is common sense that what happens will be meaningful to them. Eventually, like the teacher, the youngsters will be able to choose to see the egg either being sucked into the bottle or blown in by the air.

The understandings built around science's way of looking at the egg and bottle event connect with so many other daily life issues: vacuum cleaners; the movements of air masses that make weather and climate; pressure, temperature, and volume relationships in balloons and tires; and ear problems on airplane take-offs. If the teacher continues class negotiations to consider these phenomena, the students will continue to construct ever larger and more secure connections of words and relationships. The conversation of science learning often takes the form of arguing from, about, and with "evidence." At other times, it takes making the familiar unfamiliar through the use of analogy, metaphor, and models. As teachers, we must foster connections between what children think and what they see, and between what they see and what they think.

We have said that youngsters come to us with a rich set of understandings about the world they know. We have used a principle of a constructivist perspective about learning to say that what is already known is used to interpret new situations and new information. Because many times ideas that work in ordinary life are different from explanations that scientists make, teaching science is often about learning to see the old things from a new perspective. And we have acknowledged that this is not easy.

Becoming a Teacher of Science

Let us consider the issue of people making themselves teachers. Everyone, having lived in classrooms as students for 12 or so years, has beliefs and understandings about the way teaching is supposed to work. As you read our words, your understanding of them is guided by those understandings about teaching that you already have. You may be understanding as we do; you may be struggling to see science class in a new way. Whatever is going on, we do hope you are talking, questioning, and struggling to figure out what you think we are saying.

A major assumption guiding this chapter is that changes in the way we teach science must occur. The real reason for re-thinking science education is that there is such powerful evidence that what is going on is not working at all well. There is a loss of interest and lack of achievement in science by students at every level of education from Ph.D. programs to elementary schools. There is a loss of knowledge about science to American students who could, through science, gain new understandings about being in charge of their own lives. Equally distressing is a loss of U.S. women and students of color with a rich diversity of knowing and questioning to science. The numbers tell a sad story. There are concerted calls for change in science classrooms and lecture halls, to stem this loss. These calls include the specific issues of women and students of color for several reasons, not the least of which is that they suffer the greatest loss.

But the hard question must be asked: Is it really possible to have hordes of young folk loving and achieving in science in schools and colleges? This question is at the heart of the matter, of course, because for those who believe that girls, children of color, or even most children do not have what it takes to truly understand science, then there is no point in trying to create change. If one believes as we do, however, that most children can build a science way of looking at the world, then one has to ask what continues to exclude so many from science at each point in the education process. Let us look at the probable areas of exclusion.

All of the discussion about the necessity for inviting and including children's whole selves into science rests on the assumption that all children can create meaning, can cross the boundary of science by extending themselves into that world. Not everyone agrees on this assumption. The opposite opinion is more common: that real science is accessible only to the few children who are headed in this direction and motivated to do the hard work that is required.

The belief that science is for the very few is pervasive. Society has conferred on science an extremely high status, the status of high culture. Through science we have gained so much control over aspects of our world that brought human misery and travail; many scourges and hardships have been tamed through the interaction of science, technology and social forces. Science's status is not inappropriate. High culture status involves the specialized activities, rituals and language of a social, cultural and intellectual elite. This high culture defines what a scientist is: in all things, a superbly logical skeptic who accepts conclusions as facts only as they are reasoned from evidence; who thinks and acts in a peculiar way following the method demanded by the culture, the "scientific method"; who speaks fluently in a language so specialized that it is difficult to converse with nonscientists—to "come down to their level"; and who probably dresses in a white coat with sharpened pencils in the top pocket.

Within this view of science and scientists, inspiring children in a multi-ethnic classroom to belong to this cultural group is often attempted by displaying pictures of scientists of color or women scientists. In texts and on wall posters are hung the portraits of those who "made it." Such portraits of the privileged few can be helpful in providing a source of youngsters' imaginings of themselves as adults. When they accompany a high culture view of science, however, they can carry the connotation that crossing the boundaries into that cultural group requires that one's old home self must be discarded, left behind, as unbecoming and unnecessary to science culture status.

It is not enough to post pictures of people, disembodied from their lives, if inspiration is the intent. There must be a different view of science that includes our origins, our cultural selves. There must be a sense that gaining a scientific cultural self does not require that we discard what we are. Transformative and emancipatory education, a process through which children shape their own lives, can neither entail nor ever suggest the essential loss of self.

There is no doubt that the scientific lens on the world has generated some powerfully reliable and productive knowledge. But we believe it is a serious error to put science on an intellectual pedestal as the best, or the only useful, lens on the affairs of our world. If we can see science not as high culture, but as just one of many ways of illuminating our world, then the ways of, for example, poets, historians and artists can be recognized as equally worthwhile.

This view immediately opens the door of science to everyone who would like to cross the threshold. Such an educative stance allows teachers to ground children's school science experiences in their own beginnings; to let youngsters stretch toward the unknown future of their well-educated selves, with the connections between new learning and family and tradition providing secure support in that reach. Education in action involves transformation of self that is a change, not a loss; an evolution from origins, not a discarding of them. By recognizing science as just one of the many valuable ways in which human beings have made sense of the world, we can take a step toward letting children know that this science world is one in which they can live, work, and grow.

Revisiting to reconstruct one's view of the nature of science, however, is only one fundamental requirement for transformative science education. There is another boundary that excludes many children. This boundary concerns beliefs about the nature of children as learners. Many educators set out their task by identifying in the regular population what is wrong with individual children: This child lacks skills in reading, this one lacks a proper home background, this one lacks basic intelligence. In traditional classrooms, the view of children as units of deficiency makes a perfect partner with the view of science as high culture. Students described as deficient in this or lacking in that, who need remediation for some shortcoming, are clearly excluded from membership in high culture science. Such boundaries dictate that those assumed to have deficiencies cannot possibly excel in or even understand this very difficult subject. They are counseled out of science or they exclude themselves. If they do find themselves in science classrooms, all that is left for them is the receipt and memorization of language, busywork and the role of following scripts for experiments and investigations—at the end of which they are told what they are supposed to have found.

The inclusion of children, with all the richness of their lives outside school, into making meaning for themselves in science class springs from the understanding that children are whole, knowing contributors to the process and that science is no mysterious elite thing but one glorious example of human, collective meaning making.

Questions need to be addressed, however, regarding our sense of children bringing themselves and all they know to active conversation about things and events, and negotiating to make new meaning. How much meaning? What contextualized meanings are appropriate? Lost to most everyone except historians of science is the rich set of contexts in which science meaning makers worked in their times; therefore, the original richness out of which the abstracted cores of meaning were distilled is also lost.

It took science hundreds of years to create the most basic of the definitions or words we use today. These include *matter, mass, force, atom, element, compound, inheritance* and *evolution*. Scientists long ago were either struggling to resolve the problems they had set for themselves by sharpening the meanings of their language, or inventing new words and relationships to answer the questions they had asked. A full understanding, then, will surely include the knowledge of those problems, those answers, and those questions.

Gaining contextualized meaning, however, does not require a reinvention of the original contexts from history. Much as we might like to, we cannot usefully imagine that a fourth-grader, or a brilliant 12th-grader, is able to reinvent the triumphs of reason and imagination of adult scientists such as Best, Carver, Curie, Dalton, Darwin, or Margulis. They are unlikely to be able to rediscover the foundations of science for themselves. It is futile to attempt to have every child recreate the intellectual pieces of the struggles after meaning that occurred among scientists over hundreds of years—they are after all just children living in today's, not yesterday's, world. But, if science is to become part of their lives, they do have to create some meaning for themselves, in some real context.

Keeping in mind the twin boundaries of high culture science and deficient children views, let us explore one way in which those are expressed. Some teachers phrase their curricular tasks in terms of how deeply children can be expected to enter the science world: Chemistry requires math, and children shouldn't study chemistry unless they did well in algebra; what children can do in science depends on their comprehension skills.

Other teachers phrase their curricular tasks in the language of the abstracted cores: I think we should teach photosynthesis; they really should have studied Newton's laws; little kids have to know about atoms and molecules early on, because they are the basis of everything. These teacher phrases make us believe science teaching and learning is being squeezed into science's world.

Still other teachers do the reverse as they squeeze science into their world of teaching and learning. These teachers phrase their curricular task in the language of events and contexts: These kids are on ice skates almost as soon as they can walk, so we ought to explore collisions and movements like hockey pucks—and force, momentum, and energy; this garbage disposal issue is something they all live with one way or another so let's have them explore decomposition and combustion, and let's see what directions they want to take; perhaps we could get them talking about a litter of kittens to get at how and why they look like their parents. For teachers to squeeze science into their own world of teaching and learning is to be powerful people, with a sense of daring, and a willingness to risk. It is to take ownership; it is to deny boundaries. Moreover, it is to invite students to be powerful, to own their work, to include them in making something work.

Does this happen? Yes! In a New York City middle school, Kahla, an African-American student who had not distinguished herself as an efficient, academic performer, was a part of such a world with such a science teacher. She had told her teacher earlier that she "hated" science, but that he should not take it personally. The teacher, a beginner, was determined to invent an activity that would sponsor meaning making with his charges. They had completed several days of work on the pieces of a topic that is very intricate, specialized and complex—protein synthesis.

He framed the task this day as the need to have them tell the whole complicated tale all at once. He brought in a variety of shapes cut from construction paper of different colors and arranged them with tape on the board. The students were first asked to name the pieces with the biological structure that they represented, a piece of a DNA molecule, a ribosome, and so forth. Then he asked them to go up to the board, one at a time, and move the pieces around—without saying anything. Their task was, by changing shapes and moving them around, to recreate the story that biologists have written about how a protein is made—without saying a word. Everyone was invited to participate to begin the story, to move the next piece along, or to edit the unfolding story by undoing previous moves if that seemed called for. At one point in the story line, Kahla stood up and moved a couple of pieces to edit the story, then turned to face her classmates. Putting her hands on her hips, she said something like this: "Well, what I know is that the DNA in the nucleus can't come out of it and go over there, it's the mRNA that does that; then it goes to the ribosome and the tRNA brings its amino acid tails over to it, and they line up to make the protein. Now I may be wrong, but that's what I know!" Whether or not as a reader of this chapter, or as a visitor in the room at the time, you understand what she said, the point is that it was clear she understood. And that is what counts. She owned that story; she knew it with such clarity that she had to have made meaning out of it for herself.

When youngsters are invited to bring themselves into the arena, and when what they have to say is honored and respected, being there has significance: not the significance of being present at a traditional ritual, but the significance of pushing oneself to do something meaningful.

In another classroom, a Latino child was following his teacher's directions to make an event happen. He had a zipper bag with a small container filled with a white solid (ammonium chloride), and some water. He maneuvered the small container so the solid dropped into the water and dissolved. The bag became very cold. In the milling of students working with this investigation, the boy walked over to his teacher:

STUDENT: "This stuff is crazy cold! Hey, couldn't we use this in air-conditioning?"

TEACHER: "It's an interesting idea, what do you have in mind?"

STUDENT: "Well, this stuff'll give you your cold that you want . . . you'd have to have a blower to move the air and. . . . Hey, how much is this stuff anyway? Is it expensive, like, for a lot of it? And you'd blow the room air across this packet like, bigger than this one, it'd be in the bedroom but it could be like [stretching his arms wide] and the warm air will get cool! Hey, how long does it stay cold anyway? D'you think it's still cold enough? What do you do with it when it's done, anyway? Can you start it up again?"

TEACHER: "What do you think you want to do to find out?"

The conversation was not about endothermic and exothermic reactions—the intended learning. But can anyone deny the meaningfulness of it? Can you imagine how not to be invited to make these connections with his outside school life would have felt? His participation in the negotiation of meaning that followed seemed like a most natural transition from his own world across the threshold into the science of energy changes in chemical reactions. In classrooms such as these, children make science meaningful, both in the ways and in the direction toward decontextualized science knowledge that we intend, and also, when invited to take ownership, in the myriad individualistic ways that we cannot predict.

A Classroom of Science Teachers

Throughout this chapter we have talked of science in different ways and at different levels of organization, as decontextualized words and relationships, as explanations for phenomena, and as a way of seeing the world differently. Now we consider another task of scientists: inventing and refining models to explain the world. We do this in the context of people becoming transformative science teachers. To address the education of science teachers is to engage the question of how teachers can create classrooms in which the science taught is related to the particular concerns of their youngsters.

Picture a classroom in which the students are prospective elementary school teachers. They have organized themselves into groups of three or four and each group is examining a half-gallon, milk carton-shaped container filled with liquid laundry soap. They have been asked to do what they each consider to be a central activity of scientists: to make observations about the carton, to gather data about it without tearing it apart. So they did: "It's a half-gallon container." "It's white, with blue lettering." "The contents slosh around in there." "Let's try pouring some of the detergent out." "It looks like liquid soap. But, hey, it stopped coming out as we poured!" "Try to pour it again. About the same amount came out—how does it happen?" "Look, it says there are 48 fluid ounces in here, but it sure looks like the same size as a milk carton." "Can we pour the detergent back in?" "What will happen if we hold the container completely upside down?" "Suppose we pour out of the side?" "No, let's pour it out of the side opposite the spout." "Hey, look, there is something across the top about an inch down from the top of the spout."

They continue making observations, with each observation suggesting new things to be done to the container, in turn producing new observations. They are interrupted by their instructor, who comments on the high quality of their observations but suggests that there is more to science than making observations or collecting data. She asks them to imagine what they might see if they could get inside the container, explaining that much of science involves the invention of underlying models or theories of what is not visible to explain what is visible (when was the last time you saw an electron in the same way that you saw a pizza?).

The prospective teachers, still in groups, are now challenged to invent mechanisms (models) to explain their observations. They are also asked to come up with at least one test of each model: If the world inside the carton is like X, then if you do Y to it, you expect Z to happen. In animated groups they draw, they build three-dimensional objects, they argue, they negotiate, they revise, they collect more observations, they make their own meanings. Then they share their models with the other groups. "Hey, that one is not like ours at all. How does that flap work?" "How would your design allow only a measured amount of detergent to come out?" "What's the right answer?" "When are we going to open up the boxes so we can see what is really in there?" (They never do open the cartons.)

For two hours they have been doing things that are similar to what scientists do—they posed problems for themselves, they attempted to solve the problems that they had posed, they had to persuade other groups that their models worked, and, in many cases, they had to revise their models based on the critiques of their colleagues. They had, for a brief time, been part of a scientific community, sharing with each other, not wanting to give up their own ideas that had been a challenge to create, realizing that their prior experiences (with sugar dispensers that poured a measured amount of sugar; attachments for the tops of liquor bottles that poured measured amounts; valves and floats from experiences with toilet bowl mechanisms) influenced what problems they posed and how they began to think about the mechanism that was at the heart of their explanatory models. They begin to talk about how what they have done is like what those who study atomic structure, or genes, must do.

They begin to wonder if it would be best to open the carton for their own students or even if something like this could be done with elementary school students: "Could fourth-graders really do what we have just done?" "Would they enjoy it?" "What might they learn from doing it?" Gradually they begin to wonder if it would be possible to teach "real" science, and not just the fun activity of the detergent container, using this model-building approach. The only answer from their instructor is "Try it and see what happens."

There are skeptics: "This may be OK for middle or high school kids but it will never work with kindergartners or first-graders." But many are willing to see what would happen during the next few weeks they are teaching in schools.

One woman, teaching about the human body to first-graders, decides to take the challenge, and rethinks how she might do a standard activity usually done as a teacher-directed demonstration. Centered on the movements of the upper arm, this demonstration involves showing students two pieces of wooden doweling hinged together with screw eyes and with large rubber bands connecting them. The dowels represent the humerus and the combination of radius and ulna, while the rubber bands represent the muscles of the arm that allow it to bend at the elbow.

Rather than passing on this piece of her science education inheritance to her students, she takes a model-building approach. She describes this to her colleagues in the science methods course, painting a vivid picture of her classroom. She had asked her first-graders to bend their arms in different ways and describe what happened. Then, she asked them to feel the muscles on the front of their upper arm and their lower arms as they bent their arms at the elbow. They did the same thing with the muscles at the back of the arm.

The children made all sorts of observations, including ones that she had not made herself or had ever read about in the textbooks that she had consulted in preparing her lesson. She was learning from 6-year-olds; because they were all experiencing on their own, they were not limited to what the textbook writers said as important. She was surprised and in some ways worried as the "world" of the arm and elbow seemed so much more complex than she had imagined. On the other hand, the complexity did not seem to bother her first-graders.

As they assembled in small groups after making observations, she asked them what materials they thought they would need to make something that worked like an arm. The students came up with many materials, such as soda straws with bendable elbows, tape, string, and aluminum foil tubes. She gave them a couple of days to collect the necessary materials and then set them to work building. And they did, for a longer time than first-graders are supposed to be able to attend to anything. They built working models, they revised them when they didn't work like they thought that they should, and they learned a lot about muscles and bones.

But they also learned other lessons they may not have been able to articulate: They were learning that as science learners they could be successful. And they were learning about science; that is, in the world and in themselves. As this prospective teacher described her experiences to her colleagues, she was having a bigger effect on them than the methods professor—she had been successful, she had created a classroom where children were creating meaning for themselves. It was in her own words "The highlight of my practicum teaching."

It is possible to see classrooms in a new way. It is possible to suspend belief in children as units of academic deficiency and in science as something only for the peculiarly bright, to imagine inclusive places without boundaries, where teachers and children learn together, making science meanings and meanings of science together. In these inclusive places it is expected that everyone will have something to contribute to the collaborative tasks of investigating something real, of creating, refining, and eventually decontextualizing reliable and powerful understandings.

Even though a primary emphasis of science education in the elementary school may be on the conceptual and intellectual activities associated with investigations and model building, we need to recognize that there is more to science, and much more to teaching science to elementary school children than just the conceptual. Rachel Carson, author of *Silent Spring* (1962), the book that helped raise a nation's awareness and conscience about the frailty of the natural environment, wrote another book, *The Sense of Wonder* (1984), that contains rich insights about science teaching from perspectives other than the conceptual/intellectual. We'll end this chapter on science teaching in the elementary school with a quote from *The Sense of Wonder*. The spirit of Carson's thoughts, if we could make them come alive in our own teaching, would go to great lengths toward alleviating the "crisis in science education":

> A child's world is fresh and new and beautiful, full of wonder and excitement. It is our misfortune that for most of us that clear-eyed vision, that true instinct for what is beautiful and awe-inspiring, is dimmed and even lost before we reach adulthood. If I had influence with the good fairy who is supposed to preside over the christening of all children I should ask that her gift to each child in the world be a sense of wonder so indestructible that it would last throughout life, as an unfailing antidote against the boredom and disenchantments of later years, the sterile preoccupation with things that are artificial, the alienation from the sources of our strength.
>
> If a child is to keep alive his inborn sense of wonder without any such gift from the fairies, he needs the companionship of at least one adult who can share

it, rediscovering with him the joy, excitement and mystery of the world we live in. Parents [and we would add teachers here too] often have a sense of inadequacy when confronted on the one hand with the eager, sensitive mind of a child and on the other with a world of complex physical nature, inhabited by a life so various and unfamiliar that it seems hopeless to reduce it to order and knowledge. In a mood of self-defeat, they exclaim, "How can I possibly teach my child about nature . . . why, I don't even know one bird from another!"

I sincerely believe that for the child and for the parent [or teacher] seeking to guide him, it is not half so important to *know* as to *feel* . . . Once the emotions have been aroused . . . a sense of the beautiful, the excitement of the new and the unknown, a feeling of sympathy, pity, admiration, or love will emerge . . . then we will search for knowledge about the object of our emotional response. Once found, it has lasting meaning. It is more important to pave the way for the child to want to know than to put him on a diet of facts he is not ready to assimilate. (1984, p. 45)

Science teaching that has the possibility of enabling young and old to transform themselves into owners and makers of their own life's path begins at that spot, paving the way for them to want to know, and supporting them in their efforts to create understanding.

Notes

1. To blow the egg out, first remove the charred paper remains from the bottle, then tip the bottle upside down and shake the egg into position to come out of the neck. Holding the bottle like that blow into it as much air as you can with one breath. Remove the bottle from your mouth and the egg will drop out.

2. Sometimes, people make the argument that the burning paper uses up the oxygen and so reduces the amount of air in the bottle. Because carbon dioxide gas and water vapor are products of combustion (the oxygen is just recombining with other atoms, not being "consumed") this is not a particularly persuasive argument.

References

Boeschen, J. A., Gerard, J. A., & Storin, D. J. (1983). *Physical science.* San Diego, CA: Coronado.

Carson, R. (1962). *The silent spring.* Boston: Houghton Mifflin.

Carson, R. (1984). *The sense of wonder.* New York: Perennial Library.

Chapter 11

◆ ◆ ◆ ◆

Teaching Social Studies for Decision-Making and Action

James A. Banks

University of Washington

Social studies, like multicultural education, is a field characterized by competing paradigms, diverse approaches and methods. It also is filled with debates about how social studies teaching in the nation's schools can best help students to develop citizenship skills and abilities (Armento, 1986; Barr, Barth & Shermis, 1977; Shaver, 1977, 1991).

Most social studies educators agree that citizenship, or the development of effective citizens, should be the major goal of social studies teaching. However, educators have conflicting conceptions and ideologies about what constitutes an effective citizen and what kind of curriculum can best develop citizens for a democratic nation-state (Marker & Mehlinger, 1992). The wide array of social studies scope and sequence schemes and proposed plans for the field reflects the disagreements and tensions within it (Bragaw, 1986). See *Social Education* (1986) for a range of scope and sequence proposals.

A number of writers have developed typologies that categorize the diverse approaches and traditions within the social studies. One of the most frequently cited typologies is the one developed by Barr, Barth & Shermis (1977). They categorize the literature and theories of the social studies into three traditions: (1) social studies taught as citizenship transmission, (2) social studies taught as social science, and (3) social studies taught as reflective inquiry. In the first tradition, citizenship is developed by efforts to instill particular values into students. In the second, it is developed by teaching students the key concepts, theories, and methods of the social science disciplines, including history. In the third tradition, citizenship education focuses on decision-making and solving problems that people face in a democratic society.

This is a useful way to conceptualize developments within social studies education. However, like all typologies, its categories are interrelated. They do not encompass all the approaches and developments in the field, especially those that have emerged since the 1960s. Newer approaches include the interdisciplinary conceptual approach developed by Taba (1967) and her colleagues, and the decision-making and social action approach conceptualized by theorists such as Banks with Clegg (1973) and Newmann (1975). Also new is the critical theory, postmodern approach developed by theorists such as Popkewitz (1977) and Cherryholmes (1982), and based on the work of Habermas (1968).

Overview

In this chapter, I describe four major periods in the development of social studies education in the United States:

- The traditional or pre-revolutionary period that extends from the time that the National Council for the Social Studies was founded in 1921 until the publication of *The Process of Education* (Bruner, 1960).
- The era of the social studies revolution of the 1960s and '70s.

- The public issues and social participation period of the 1970s and '80s.
- The resurgence of history and the rise of multiculturalism today.

Next, I describe what should be the goals of social studies education in a pluralistic democratic society and a decision-making/social action model designed to attain them. Finally, I discuss a lesson developed and taught with this model.

It is important to keep in mind that when one of the four periods ended, the developments related to it did not end abruptly. Rather, many trends and elements from the previous period continued into the next. However, the characteristics of the new period became the dominant ones.

Also keep in mind that social studies education in the United States can be viewed and conceptualized on at least five different dimensions: (1) research and theory, (2) state and school district policies and curriculum guides, (3) social studies textbooks, (4) inservice development and training programs for social studies teachers, and (5) actual classroom practices.

What happens at one level can differ greatly from what is happening at another. For example, one cannot assume that just because many articles and books were being written about conceptual teaching by experts during the 1960s and '70s that most teachers in the classroom were teaching concepts. As a matter of fact, research indicates this was not the case. Even during the height of the social studies revolution of the 1960s and '70s, when conceptual teaching was emphasized by many social studies theorists, most teachers in U.S. classrooms continued to teach in traditional ways, such as emphasizing facts and isolated historical events (Shaver, Davis, & Helburn, 1979).

The Pre-Revolutionary or Traditional Period

Before the 1960s, the social studies was dominated by history and geography. The emphasis was on the development of national patriotism and the memorization of isolated facts about events, places, and people. Yesterday's social studies classrooms were dominated by textbooks, teacher talk, student passivity, recitation, and stories about the historic deeds of the United States and the glorious accomplishments of Western civilization. An important goal of the social studies was to develop patriotic, loyal, and unquestioning citizens. Consequently, little attention was devoted to the nation's problems for fear that its warts might show and undermine the development of patriotic and loyal citizens.

Because little attention was devoted to the nation's problems or the problems related to the growth and development of Western civilization, groups that were the society's victims or on the fringes received scant attention in the curriculum and in textbooks. When they were included, they were viewed primarily from the perspectives of upper-class European and European-American males. Consequently, the struggles, victories, hopes, and voices of groups on the margins of society, such as women, people of color, and low-income people, were largely invisible in the pre-1960 social studies curricula, textbooks, and programs (Banks, 1969).

American Indians appeared in traditional social studies textbooks either as groups that were impediments to the spread of European civilization from the east to the west, or as "good" Indians—allies who taught the Europeans how to farm and survive in America. In the first case, American Indians had to be removed so that Western civilization could advance, such as the Cherokees in 1838–39. In the latter case, they were celebrated and venerated, such as Pocahontas and Sacajawea.

African Americans and Hispanics appeared in traditional social studies curricula largely in contexts in which they interacted with or became problems for the Europeans in America. Little attention was devoted to African Americans as institutional builders and as shapers of their own fates and destinies. Content about African Americans was limited primarily to slavery and to a discussion of two or three heroes who made contributions to society but did not challenge the prevailing social and political structures. In the 1950s and '60s, those who appeared in textbooks most frequently were individuals such as Booker T. Washington, George Washington Carver, and Marian Anderson. More radical African Americans such as W. E. B. DuBois, Marcus Garvey, and Ida B. Wells rarely appeared in social studies curricula and textbooks during the 1950s. Most of the content about Mexican Americans in social studies curricula and textbooks of yesteryear dealt with the events that led to the Texas secession from the Mexico union and the United States-Mexican War.

International studies emphasized the study of European nations. Consequently, little was studied about nations in Asia and Africa. There was little emphasis on active learning strategies, teaching students to question what they read or reviewed, critical thinking, or social action and participation.

The Expanding Communities of Human Beings

During the past 70 years, a rather standardized social studies curriculum has developed within the elementary and secondary schools in the United States. History and geography have dominated social studies during most of this period. In the primary grades, students have studied the communities closest to their experiences, such as the family, the school, the neighborhood, and the state. In the middle and upper grades, students studied communities further away from their immediate experiences, such as the state; the region; other nations in the Americas; and finally nations in the world, including Europe, Africa, and Asia.

The concept of studying communities close to the child first and branching out later became the dominant curriculum pattern in social studies in the United States. Hanna (1963) helped popularize this pattern, which became known as *The Expanding Communities of Humans* curriculum framework. This curriculum framework has remained tenacious throughout all periods of social studies curriculum reform in the United States and is the most common social studies curriculum framework in the United States today. Superka, Hawke, and Morrissett (1980) found that the topics listed below were the most frequently taught at the grade levels indicated. This sequence is very similar to the Expanding Communities of Humans pattern.

Grade	Topic
Kindergarten	Self, school, community, home
1	Families
2	Neighborhoods
3	Communities
4	State history, geographic regions
5	United States history
6	World cultures, Western hemisphere
7	World geography or history
8	American history
9	Civics or world cultures
10	American history
11	American government

The Social Studies Revolution of the 1960s and '70s

In September 1959, about 35 scientists, scholars, and educators gathered at the Woods Hole conference center in Cape Cod, Massachusetts, to discuss how science education might be improved in the nation's schools. Based on this 10-day meeting of eminent American scholars and educators, Bruner (1960) wrote a book destined to revolutionize thinking about teaching and learning not only in the sciences but in all subject areas, including the social studies. In this book, *The Process of Education,* Bruner presented his now-famous contention, "Experience over the past decade points to the fact that our schools may be wasting precious years by postponing the teaching of many important subjects on the ground that they are too difficult. . . . The foundations of any subject can be taught to anybody at any age in some form" (p. 12).

Bruner also argued that the fundamentals of every discipline can be reduced to its *structure,* by which he meant its key concepts, key generalizations and principles, key questions that the discipline asks, and its unique modes of inquiry or investigation. Bruner said the structure of each discipline could be identified and that this structure could be taught to all students in some form, regardless of age or stage of development.

By stating that the key ideas of each discipline could be identified and by arguing that these key ideas could be taught to young children, Bruner seriously challenged the leading ideas of developmental psychologists at the time as well as the existing social studies curriculum that had been popularized in the writings of Hanna (1963). *The Expanding Communities of Humans* framework is based strongly on developmental ideas, e.g., children should study the family before they study the larger community.

Based on the idea of the structures of the disciplines and other key ideas set forth by Bruner, social scientists such as historians, geographers, sociologists, anthropologists, and political scientists became heavily involved in the development of social studies curriculum projects during the 1960s and 1970. Major goals of these projects included helping students to do the following:

- Learn the structures of the social science disciplines.
- Learn the methods that social scientists used to gather data and study society and how to use these methods.
- Learn key concepts and generalizations in each of the social science disciplines.
- Become actively involved in social studies learning.

Bruner was involved in one of these projects, which was designed to teach anthropology to elementary school students. The program was called *Man: A Course of Study*. Bruner described the emphasis in the course:

> The content of the course is man: his nature as a species, the forces that shaped and continue to shape his humanity. Three questions recur throughout: What is human about human beings? How did they get that way? How can they be made more so? (Dow, 1969, p. 4)

To develop a better understanding of what makes people human, the students start by studying salmon, herring gulls, and baboons. The Netsilik Eskimo is studied as an example of a human culture. The course consists of a variety of instructional materials, including films made especially for the project. It deals primarily with the first question raised in the quote from Bruner.

Like any educational movement that tries to change the schools from the outside, the social studies revolution of the 1960s and '70s had mixed results. It created vigorous discussion, debate and innovation in the social studies and had significant influence on social studies curriculum development at the state and school district levels and on textbook writing. It also had a significant influence on the research, teaching, and writing of social studies literature by scholars and university professors.

However, the influence of the *new social studies*, as it was called, on classroom teachers and actual classroom practice was far less than its architects had envisioned. Most of the social studies projects of the 1960s and '70s were conceptualized by academics and scholars who taught at universities. Few classroom teachers were involved in their creation. Consequently, many teachers had a difficult time understanding and using many of the materials or did not believe they withstood the test of the classroom. Many of the project materials also required extensive inservice training and staff development. Some of the programs, however, such as *Man: A Course of Study* and Senesh's economics program for the elementary grades, *Our Working World*—which was published as a textbook series—became quite popular.

There are probably many complex reasons that schools largely resisted the social studies curriculum reforms of the 1960s. The reformers erred when they assumed that they could create teacher-proof materials and engineer a social studies curriculum revolution from outside the school culture. Teacher development and involvement are essential to the effective implementation of curriculum reforms and projects. This basic principle of curriculum reform was largely ignored by the social scientists who led most of the social studies curriculum projects of the 1960s.

The social scientists who dominated the curriculum reform projects of the 1960s neither understood nor fully appreciated the complex culture of the school. School cultures have their own ethos, symbols, norms, values, and traditions. Like other cultures and institutions, a school is not easily changed or reformed, especially by outsiders who neither understand nor appreciate its culture and institutional structure. Probably the most important reason that the social studies curriculum reforms of the 1960s failed to become institutionalized on a large scale is the tremendous holding power and tenacity of the culture of the school (Cuban, 1991).

The Public Issues and Social Participation Period of the 1970s and '80s

Between 1960 and 1980, social movements that pushed for civil rights and social reform were prominent in the United States. These movements included the quests for the rights of groups of color such as African Americans and Hispanics, the rights of women, the rights of people with disabilities, and protest over the war in Vietnam. During this period, the United States enacted some of its most enlightened legislation that protected the rights of women, people of color, and people with disabilities, including the Civil Rights Act of 1964, the Bilingual Education Act in 1968 (Title VII of the Elementary and Secondary Education Act), and Public Law 94-142 in 1975, the Education for All Handicapped Children Act.

During the 1970s and '80s the social reform and civil rights movements influenced the social studies curriculum. Many theorists began to criticize Bruner's structuralist position and argued that it was not sufficient to teach students the key ideas and methods of the social sciences. Bruner's critics argued that the main goal of social studies education should be to develop reflective citizens for a democratic society (Newmann with Oliver, 1970; Oliver & Shaver, 1966). To become effective citizens, students needed to learn how to apply social science knowledge to the solution of social problems in society, such as racial discrimination, discrimination against women, and the improvement and protection of the environment. The citizenship and public issues curriculum theorists also argued that students need to take social action to improve society and develop a sense of political efficacy.

Theorists such as Banks with Clegg (1990), Metcalf (1971), Newmann with Oliver (1970), and Oliver and Shaver (1966) developed theories, materials, and strategies for teaching students to master more than just social science knowledge. Students also would be taught to analyze and clarify their values, identify courses of actions to take, consider alternative actions, and take actions that are consistent with the knowledge and values they have derived and clarified.

Oliver and Shaver (1966) developed a theory of teaching public issues to high school students and published data on the results of their experimental public issues curriculum. Newmann with Oliver (1970) developed theories and strategies for involving students in social action and civic participation. In its *Curriculum Guidelines for the Social Studies,* the National Council for the Social Studies (1979) stated, "Extensive involvement by students of all ages in their community is essential. . . . The involvement may take the form of observation or information-seeking, attending meetings, and interviews. It may take the form of political campaigning, community service or improvement, or even responsible demonstration. The school should not only provide channels for such activities, but build them into the design of its K–12 social studies program" (p. 266).

The Resurgence of History and the Rise of Multiculturalism

The current period of social studies education in the United States is characterized by diverse and conflicting trends. One major development is the resurgence of what is called "back to the basics," which is a return to an emphasis on history and geography that was dominant during the Pre-Revolutionary period described earlier. This trend grew out of the criticisms by popular writers, who were sometimes joined by historians, who argued that students do not know the basic facts of U.S. history, such as when the Constitution was ratified or when the Civil War occurred.

Hirsch (1987) made this argument in *Cultural Literacy: What Every American Needs to Know.* This book was on the *New York Times* best-seller list for almost six months. Its popularity indicated that it articulated important concerns among U.S. citizens about what students were learning in school. Another popular book by Hirsch, Kett & Trefil (1988), *The Dictionary of Cul-*

tural Literacy: What Every American Needs to Know, also became a best seller. Ravitch and Finn (1987) extended the argument in their book *What Do Our 17-Year-Olds Know?* They describe how students gave many incorrect answers to multiple-choice test items that assessed their recall of factual knowledge in history and literature. Ravitch has argued that the replacement of history teaching with the teaching of the social studies is the main reason that students do not know the basic facts about history and geography.

Writers such as Ravitch, Finn, and Hirsch think the teaching of factual history should be emphasized in the schools. The new framework developed and adopted by the state of California, our largest state with more than 30 million people, is history-oriented and incorporates many of Ravitch's ideas (California State Department of Education, 1987). She was one of the major writers of the California curriculum framework.

Another major development in U.S. social studies education today is inconsistent with the emphasis on factual history. There is a trend toward infusing multicultural content and perspectives into the social studies curriculum. A multicultural social studies curriculum describes concepts, events, and ideas not only from the point of view of mainstream Americans but also from the perspectives of ethnic groups of color such as African Americans and Hispanics as well as from the perspectives of women (Banks, 1991).

Major school districts such as those in Portland, Oregon, and New York City have adopted guidelines for infusing multicultural content into all areas of the school curriculum, including the social studies. State departments of education, such as those in Washington and New York state, also have developed guidelines in multicultural education. In July 1989, the State Education Department in New York published a social studies curriculum document recommending ways to make the curriculum multicultural: *A Curriculum for Inclusion* (New York State Department of Education, 1989). This report evoked a major national debate in the nation's newspapers and magazines that indicated that Americans are sharply divided on how to describe the balance between national unity and ethnic diversity in the school curriculum. Another document published by the New York State Department of Education (1991), more moderate in tone and language than the earlier document, also evoked considerable controversy and debate in the popular press.

Multicultural education is a growing development in the nation and will increasingly become integrated into the social studies curriculum in future years. Many of the nation's most prestigious colleges and universities, such as Stanford, the University of California-Berkeley, the University of Wisconsin-Madison, and the University of Minnesota-Twin Cities, require all undergraduate students to take courses in ethnic studies.

A major factor stimulating the growth of multicultural education in the United States is the nation's changing demographics (Banks, 1991). The growth rate in the nation's population of color is much greater than the growth rate of the nation's White population. Most (about 85%) of the legal immigrants to the United States today are coming from nations in Latin America and Asia. Only about 11% of them are coming from Europe. By 2000, one out of every three Americans will be a *person of color* (e.g. African American, Hispanic, Asian, American Indian, etc.). By 2020, if current growth trends continue, students of color will make up about 46% of the nation's school-age youths. Because of the nation's changing demographics, more and more Americans are realizing that in order to prepare the nation's students for the America of tomorrow, ethnic content and content about women must permeate the total school curriculum, including the social studies.

The growing awareness among educators that the knowledge, attitudes and skills that constitute multicultural education are needed to keep our society democratic and free is another factor that is contributing to the growth of multicultural education. Multicultural education is an education for freedom in three important senses: (1) it enables students to freely affirm their ethnic, racial, and cultural identities; (2) it provides students with the freedom to function beyond their ethnic and cultural boundaries; and (3) it helps students develop the commitment and skills needed to participate in personal, social, and civic action that will make our nation and world more democratic and free (Banks, 1991/1992).

Goals for Social Studies in a Democratic Pluralistic Society

A major goal of social studies education in a multicultural society should be to help students attain the knowledge, skills, and attitudes needed to participate in the mainstream society. Although social participation is an important goal of social studies in a democratic, pluralistic society, it is not sufficient. Social studies also should help students attain the knowledge, attitudes, and skills needed to help transform and reconstruct society. Problems such as racism, sexism, poverty, and inequality are widespread and permeate many of the nation's institutions, such as the work force, the courts, and the schools. To educate future citizens to merely fit into but not transform society will result in the perpetuation of these problems, including the widening gap between the rich and the poor, racial conflict and tension, and the growing number of people who are victims of poverty and homelessness.

A society that has sharp divisions between the rich and the poor, and between Whites and people of color, is not a stable one. It contains stresses and tensions that can lead to societal upheavals and racial polarization and conflict. Thus, citizenship education for the 21st century must not only help students to become literate and reflective citizens who can participate in the mainstream society, it must also teach them to care about other people in their communities (Kohn, 1991) and to take personal, social, and civic action to create a humane and just society (Banks, 1990).

Teaching Decision-Making and Social Action

I have developed a model for teaching decision-making and social action in the elementary and high school grades. This section describes the model, and the next section describes a lesson taught by a teacher using it.

This model, summarized in Figure 11.1, assumes that the main goal of the social studies is to help students acquire the knowledge, skills, and values needed to make reflective personal and public decisions so they can take action, consistent with American values—such as equality, justice, and human dignity—that will improve and reform society. One essential component of decision-making is knowledge.

Knowledge for Reflective Decision-Making

There are many different types of knowledge and ways of validating beliefs and observations. Knowledge that forms the basis of reflective decisions must be scientific knowledge—it must be derived using a process that can be replicated by others, and it must be public as opposed to private. Knowledge used in reflective decisions must also reflect the experiences and perspectives of a wide range of groups within a pluralistic society. Knowledge that only reflects elite groups or ignores the perceptions and experiences of various racial, ethnic, and gender groups cannot result in decisions that reflect the best interests of the commonwealth or civic community.

The Decision-Making Process

Figure 11.1 illustrates the major components and process of a social studies curriculum that focuses on reflective decision-making and social action. The unit begins with a decision-problem. The knowledge needed to make the decision is derived with a process of social inquiry. Value inquiry related to the decision-problem leads to clarified values. The knowledge and clarified values are interrelated to make a decision that is implemented by action.

There are various kinds of knowledge and paradigms as Kuhn (1970) points out in his book *The Structure of Scientific Revolutions*. Some knowledge and paradigms challenge the current social structure and support reform of institutions; other knowledge and paradigms reinforce the prevailing social-class structure and institutional arrangements within society. Kuhn also describes how difficult it is for new knowledge systems or paradigms to challenge or replace existing ones. When this occurs, Kuhn says, a scientific revolution has taken place.

There are many examples of paradigms, theories, and concepts created by elite social scientists that have resulted in decisions and policies detrimental to

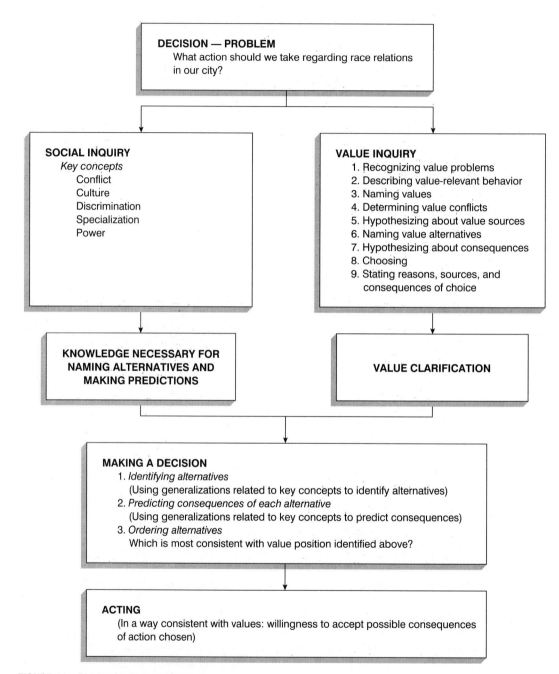

FIGURE 11.1 The decision-making process

Note. From *Teaching Strategies for the Social Studies: Inquiry, Valuing and Decision-Making* (4th ed.) (p. 457) by J. A. Banks with A. A. Clegg, Jr., 1990, White Plains, NY: Longman. Reprinted by permission.

people of color or different ethnic groups, such as African Americans, Hispanics, and American Indians. Such paradigms and theories include Phillips' conception of the contented slave (1918), Jensen's theory of the intellectual abilities of African Americans (1969), and conceptions about culturally deprived children that were developed in the 1960s (Riessman, 1962). The cultural deprivation concept has reemerged in the 1990s in the form of *at-risk* students (Richardson, 1990). The *at-risk* and *culturally deprived* concepts are not identical, but they are similar in several important ways: Both are labels that tend to blame the victim for their situations; both become stigmas for the individuals and groups labeled with the terms.

Value Inquiry and Reflective Decisions

To make reflective decisions, students must have clarified and thoughtfully derived values. An important goal of a curriculum focused on decision-making is to help students identify the sources of their values and determine how they conflict, identify value alternatives, and choose freely from them (Banks with Clegg, 1990). However, students should be required to justify their moral choices within the context of higher societal values such as human dignity, justice, and equality. If students are not required to do that, value teaching will run the risk of becoming relativistic and ethnically neutral (Banks with Clegg, 1990).

After students have mastered interdisciplinary knowledge related to a concept or issue such as racism or sexism, they should participate in value or moral inquiry exercises. The goal of such exercises should be to help students develop a set of consistent, clarified values that can guide purposeful and reflective personal or civic action related to the issue examined. This goal can best be attained by teaching students a method or process for deriving their values within a democratic classroom atmosphere. In this classroom, students must be free to express their value choices, determine how those choices conflict, examine alternative values, consider the consequences of different value choices, and defend their moral choices within the context of human dignity and other American values. Students must be given an opportunity to reflectively derive their own values so they develop a commitment to human dignity, equality, and other democratic values. They must be encouraged to reflect upon their value choices within a democratic atmosphere (Banks with Clegg, 1990).

Teachers can use the following value model to help students identify and clarify their values so they can make reflective moral choices. It consists of these steps:

1. Defining and recognizing value problems.
2. Describing value-relevant behavior.

3. Naming values exemplified by the behavior.

4. Determining conflicting values in behavior described.

5. Hypothesizing about the possible consequence of the values analyzed.

6. Naming alternative values to those described by behavior observed.

7. Hypothesizing about the possible consequences of values analyzed.

8. Declaring value preferences; choosing.

9. Stating reasons, sources, and possible consequences of value choice: justifying, hypothesizing, predicting. (Banks with Clegg, 1990, p. 445)

Decision-Making and Action

After students have gathered knowledge, using a scientific process and making sure it represents diverse perspectives and points of view, they should make a decision regarding actions they take related to the topic, problem, or issue they have studied. In making a decision, they should use the knowledge they have attained to make a list of alternative actions, to predict the possible consequences of each alternative, and to order the alternatives. They should ask, "Which of the alternatives are most consistent with our values?"

The students should take action only after they have thought carefully about the alternatives, weighed and ordered the alternatives, and considered their possible consequences. The action the students take may be *personal, social,* or *civic.* One possible form of action is inaction. Lewis (1991) has developed a helpful guide to social action activities for students. Primary-grade children who have studied a unit on stereotypes may decide to stop using words and phrases that stereotype American Indians and African Americans. Middle-grade children who have studied a unit on prejudice may decide to read several books on various ethnic and racial groups or to make a friend from another racial, ethnic or religious group.

Junior high school students may decide to do volunteer work for a candidate in a local election who advocates racial equality after they have studied a unit on contemporary race relations. High school students may design, administer, and publish the results of a districtwide survey on racism, as was done by a group of high school students in the Ann Arbor, Michigan, School District (Polakow-Suransky & Ulaby, 1990). In this ambitious project, the students administered the survey to all high school students in the district. Their response rate was 57.4 percent, or 2,006 students. Two of the students published an article based on their survey in the *Phi Delta Kappan*, a widely circulated national educational journal. They also presented their findings to the school board and made recommendations. These are among the recommendations:

- Arranging immediate follow-up activities to the survey—including workshops, class discussions, and assemblies—in all high schools.

- Reevaluating the district's policies on tracking, with the goal of discontinuing the practice.
- Requiring students to take a course that would expose them to issues related to racial oppression in the U.S.
- Establishing a task force to evaluate the entire high school curriculum from a multicultural perspective and to draw up guidelines for dealing with the "racial incidents" involving students and school personnel. (Polakow-Suransky & Ulaby, p. 605)

Making Decisions and Taking Action: A Classroom Example

Mr. Carson, a junior high school social studies teacher, used the Banks decision-making model to teach a unit on the civil rights movement. Mr. Carson wanted his students to acquire an understanding of the historical development of the civil rights movement and to analyze and clarify their values related to integration and segregation. He also wanted them to conceptualize and perhaps take some actions related to racism and desegregation in their personal life, the school, or the local community. Mr. Carson teaches in a predominantly White suburban school district near a city in the Northwest that has a population of about 500,000. The metropolitan area in which Mr. Carson's school is located has a population of about 1 million.

The Long Shadow of Little Rock

Mr. Carson used the Banks value inquiry model to help his students analyze the value issues revealed in Chapter 8 of *The Long Shadow of Little Rock* by Daisy Bates (1987). In this well-written and moving chapter, Mrs. Bates describes the moral dilemma she faced as head of the National Association for the Advancement of Colored People (NAACP) in Little Rock, Arkansas, when Central High School was desegregated. Nine African American high school students enrolled in Central High School during the 1957–58 school year.

Mrs. Bates was the leading supporter and organizer for the nine students. Her husband, L. C. Bates, was a journalist. They owned a newspaper, *The States Press*. In Chapter 8 of *The Long Shadow of Little Rock,* Mrs. Bates describes how a middle-aged White woman came to her home at 3 p.m. one day and told her to call a press conference and announce that she was withdrawing her support for the nine students and was advising them to withdraw from Central High School and return to the Negro schools. The woman said she represented a group of "Southern Christian women." Mrs. Bates asked the woman what would happen if she didn't do what she told her to do. She looked Mrs. Bates straight in the eye and said, "You'll be destroyed—you, your newspaper, your reputation. . . . Everything."

During a long, anguished night, Mrs. Bates wondered whether she had the right to destroy 16 years of her husband's work—the newspaper. Yet she believed she could not abandon a cause to which she and many other African Americans were deeply committed. By morning, Mrs. Bates had made a difficult and painful decision. She called her visitor and told her no. Later, she told her husband what she had done. He said, "Daisy, you did the right thing." Mrs. Bates' visitor kept her promise. Major stores and businesses withdrew their advertising from *The States Press,* forcing it to close. The Bates family suffered financial and personal turmoil because of the newspaper's closing and because of threats and attempts on Mrs. Bates' life.

Using the Banks value inquiry model, these are some of the questions Mr. Carson asked his students:

Defining and Recognizing Value Problems

1. What value problem did Mrs. Bates face after she was visited by the woman?

Naming Values Exemplified by Behavior Described

2. What did the visitor value or think was important? What did Mrs. Bates value? What did Mr. Bates value?

Hypothesizing About the Source of Value Analyzed

3. How do you think Mrs. Bates' visitor developed the values she had? How do you think Mr. and Mrs. Bates developed the values they showed in this selection?

Declaring Value Preferences: Choosing

4. Try to put yourself in Mrs. Bates place on Oct. 29, 1959. What decision would you have made?

Stating Reasons, Sources, and Possible Consequences of Value Choice

5. Why should Mrs. Bates have made the decision you stated above? What were the possible consequences of her saying "no" and saying "yes" to her visitor? Give as many reasons as you can about why Mrs. Bates should have made the decision you stated above.

Keep in mind that Mrs. Bates knew if she said yes to her visitor she would probably have been able to keep her property, but that the nine students probably would have had to return to Black schools and that segregation would have been maintained in Little Rock. On the other hand, by saying no, she risked losing all of her property and her husband's property, including his newspaper. Also, consider the fact that she did not involve him in making her decision.

Decision-Making and Citizen Action

After Mr. Carson's students had derived knowledge about the civil rights movement of the 1950s and '60s, and clarified their values regarding these issues, he asked them to list all the possible actions they could take to increase desegregation in their personal lives as well as in the life of the school and the community. Mr. Carson was careful to explain to the students that action should be broadly conceptualized. He defined action in a way that might include personal commitment to do something, such as making more friends from different racial and ethnic groups; making a commitment to watch the movie *Roots* and then discussing it with a friend; or reading a play or book to better understand another racial or ethnic group, such as *A Raisin in the Sun* by Lorraine Hansberry or *Beloved* by Toni Morrison. These are some of the possible actions the students listed:

1. Making a personal commitment to stop telling racist jokes.
2. Making a commitment to challenge our own racial and ethnic stereotypes either before or after we verbalize them.
3. Compiling an annotated list of books about ethnic groups that we will ask the librarian to order for our school library.
4. Asking the principal to order sets of photographs that show African Americans and other people of color who have jobs that represent a variety of careers. Asking the principal to encourage teachers to display these photographs on their classroom walls.
5. Observing television programs to determine the extent to which people of color, such as African Americans and Asian Americans, are represented in such jobs as news anchor and program host. Writing to local and national television stations to express our concern if we discover that people of color are not represented in powerful and visible roles in news or other kinds of television programs.
6. Contacting a school in the inner-city to determine if there are joint activities and projects in which we and they might participate.
7. Asking the principal or the board of education in our school district to require our teachers to attend inservice staff development workshops that will help them learn ways to integrate content about ethnic and racial groups into our courses.
8. Sharing some of the facts that we have learned in this unit—such as that by 2000, one out of three Americans will be a person of color—with our parents and discussing these facts with them.

9. Making a personal commitment to have a friend from another racial, ethnic, or religious group by the end of the year.

10. Making a personal commitment to read at least one book a year that deals with a racial, cultural, or ethnic group other than my own.

11. Do nothing, take no actions.

The Decision-Making Process

After the students had completed the list of possible actions (including no actions), Mr. Carson asked them to consider the possible consequences of each of the actions identified, such as:

If I Take No Action

Then I will be doing nothing to improve race relations in my personal life, in my school, my community, or my nation.

But I will not risk trying to do something that could fail. I will also be indicating to others, by my behavior, that I am not concerned about improving race relations in my personal life, my family, school or community.

If I Make a Personal Commitment to Tell No More Racist Jokes

Then I will be improving my personal behavior that relates to other racial, ethnic and cultural groups. I will also demonstrate to others that I am concerned about improving race relations in my personal life.

But I will be doing little directly to improve the behaviors of other people in my family, school and community.

After the students had worked in groups of five to identify and state the possible consequences of various courses of actions, Mr. Carson asked them to select one or two personal or group actions they would like to take related to the problems they had studied in the unit. Mr. Carson also asked the students to be prepared to defend or explain the course of action or actions they chose, to tell whether it was feasible for them to carry out the action or actions, and to provide a timeline for its initiation and completion (if possible). These are among the actions the students chose:

- Kathy and Susan decided to read the play *A Raisin in the Sun* by Lorraine Hansberry to get a better understanding of the experience of African Americans in the United States.

- Clay, Pete, Tessie, Rosie, and Maria decided to prepare an annotated list of books on ethnic cultures and ask the school librarian to order them for the school library. The group planned to ask Mr. Carson to help them find resources to prepare the list of books.

- Roselyn decided to improve her understanding of ethnic cultures by reading these books during the year: *Let the Circle Be Unbroken* by Mildred D. Taylor, *A Jar of Dreams* by Yoshiko Uchida, and *America Is in the Heart* by Carlos Bulosan.

- Aralean, Juan, James, Angela, and Patricia decided to develop a proposal that would require teachers in the district to attend multicultural education workshops. They would develop their plan with Mr. Carson and present it to the principal and then to the Board of Education for possible adoption.

Toward Developing Effective Citizens

Social studies education in the United States is characterized by many conflicting conceptions, paradigms, and ideologies that mirror the tensions, value conflicts, and developments in U.S. society. Although educators hold conflicting conceptions about what should constitute social studies teaching, they agree that the development of effective citizens should be the goal of social studies education.

Barr, Barth & Shermis (1977) have identified three major traditions within social studies education. The goal of each is to develop effective citizens. They are: (1) social studies taught as citizenship transmission, (2) social studies taught as social science, and (3) social studies taught as reflective inquiry.

Approaches and theories that have developed since the 1960s are not adequately reflected in the Barr, Barth & Shermis typology. These newer approaches include the interdisciplinary conceptual approach, the decision-making and social action approach, and the critical theory paradigm based on the work of Habermas (1968).

In this chapter, I identified and described four major periods in the development of social studies education in the United States, described a model for teaching social studies that focuses on decision-making and social action, and described a social studies lesson on race relations that is organized around the teaching model presented.

Social studies teaching, research, and practice reflect the major social, political, and economic developments in U.S. society. Because social studies deals with the nature of people in society, the social studies curriculum is more likely than other subject areas to mirror the debates, controversies, and tensions within society. The social studies curriculum will continue to reflect the major issues and tensions within American life, as well as mirror the nation's ideals, goals, aspirations, and conflicts. The development of reflective and active citizens who can contribute to and participate in making our nation more democratic and just should be the major goal of social studies education as we enter the 21st century.

Acknowledgment

A section of this chapter is adapted with permission of the publisher from James A. Banks, A curriculum for empowerment, action, and change. In C. E. Sleeter (Ed.) (1991). *Empowerment through multicultural education.* (Pp. 134–139). Albany: State University of New York Press.

References

Armento, B. J. (1986). Research on teaching social studies. In M. C. Wittrock (Ed.), *Handbook of research on teaching* (pp. 942–951). New York: Macmillan..

Banks, J. A. (1969). A content analysis of the Black American in textbooks. *Social Education, 33,* 954–957, 963.

Banks, J. A. (1990). Citizenship education for a pluralistic democratic society. *The Social Studies, 81,* 210–214.

Banks, J. A. (1991). *Teaching strategies for ethnic studies* (5th ed.). Boston: Allyn and Bacon.

Banks, J. A. (1991/1992). Multicultural education: For freedom's sake. *Educational Leadership, 49* (4), 32–36.

Banks, J. A., with Clegg, A. A. (1973). *Teaching strategies for the social studies: Inquiry, valuing, and decision-making.* Reading MA: Addison-Wesley.

Banks, J. A., with Clegg, A. A. (1990). *Teaching strategies for the social studies: Inquiry, valuing and decision-making* (4th ed.). White Plains, NY: Longman.

Barr, R. D., Barth, J. L., & Shermis, S. S. (1977). *Defining the social studies.* Bulletin 51. Washington, D.C.: National Council for the Social Studies.

Bates, D. (1987). *The long shadow of Little Rock: A memoir.* Fayetteville, AK: The University of Arkansas Press.

Bragaw, D. H. (1986). Scope and sequence: Alternatives for social studies. *Social Education, 50,* 484–485.

Bragaw, D. (Ed.). (1986). Scope & sequence alternatives for social studies. *Social Education, 50*(7), 484–534.

Bruner, J. S. (1960). *The process of education.* New York: Vintage Books.

California State Department of Education (1987). *History-social science framework for California Public Schools, kindergarten through grade twelve.* Sacramento: The Department of Education.

Cherryholmes, C. H. (1982). Discourse and criticism in the social studies classroom. *Theory and Research in Social Education, 9,* 57–73.

Cuban, L. (1991). History of teaching in social studies. In J. P. Shaver (Ed.). *Handbook of research on social studies teaching and learning* (pp. 197–209). New York: Macmillan.

Dow, P. B. (1969). Man: A course of study: An experimental social science course for elementary students. *Man: A course of study talks to teachers.* Cambridge, MA: Education Development Center, p. 4.

Habermas, J. (1968). *Knowledge and human interests.* Boston: Beacon Press.

Hanna, P. R. (1963, April). Revising the social studies: What is needed. *Social Education, 27,* 190–196.

Hirsch, E. D., Jr. (1987). *Cultural literacy: What every American needs to know.* Boston: Houghton Mifflin.

Hirsch, E. D., Jr., Kett, J. F., & Trefil, J. (1988). *The dictionary of cultural literacy: What every American needs to know.* Boston: Houghton Mifflin.

Jensen, A. R. (1969). How much can we boost IQ and scholastic achievement? *Harvard Educational Review, 39,* 1–123.

Kohn, A. (1991). Caring kids: The role of schools. *Phi Delta Kappan, 72,* 496–506.

Kuhn, T. S. (1970). *The structure of scientific revolutions* (2nd ed., enlarged). Chicago: The University of Chicago Press.

Lewis, B. A. (1991). *The kid's guide to social action.* Edited by P. Espeland. Minneapolis: Free Spirit Publishing, Inc.

Marker, G., & Mehlinger, H. (1992). Social studies. In P. W. Jackson (Ed.), *Handbook of research on curriculum* (pp. 830–851). New York: Macmillan.

Metcalf, L. W. (Ed.). (1971). *Values education: Rationale, strategies, and procedures.* Washington, D.C.: National Council for the Social Studies.

National Council for the Social Studies. (1979, April). Revision of the NCSS Social Studies Curriculum Guidelines, *Social Education, 43,* 261–278.

Newmann, F. M. (1975). *Education for citizen action: Challenge for secondary curriculum.* Berkeley, CA: McCutchan.

Newmann, F. M., with Oliver, D. W. (1970). *Clarifying public controversy: An approach to teaching social studies.* Boston: Little Brown.

The New York State Department of Education. (1989, July). *A curriculum for inclusion.* Report of the Commissioner's Task Force on Minorities: Equity and Excellence. Albany: State Department of Education.

The New York State Department of Education. (1991, June). *One nation, many peoples: A declaration of cultural interdependence.* Report of the New York State Social Studies Review and Development Committee. Albany: State Department of Education.

Oliver, D. W., & Shaver, J. P. (1966). *Teaching public issues in the high school.* Boston: Houghton Mifflin.

Phillips, U. B. (1918). *American Negro slavery.* New York: D. Appleton and Co.

Polakow-Suransky, S., & Ulaby, N. (1990, April). Students take action to combat racism. *Phi Delta Kappan,* 601–606.

Popkewitz, T. S. (1977). The latent values of the discipline-centered curriculum. *Theory and Research in Social Education, 5,* 41–60.

Ravitch, D., & Finn, C. E., Jr. (1987). *What do our 17-year-olds know? A report on the first national assessment of history and literature.* New York: Harper & Row.

Richardson, V. (1990, Spring). At-risk programs: Evaluation and critical inquiry. In K. A. Sirotnik (Ed.), *Evaluation and social justice: Issues in public education* (pp. 61–75). San Francisco: Jossey-Bass.

Riessman, F. (1962). *The culturally deprived child.* New York: Harper and Row.

Shaver, J. P. (Ed.). (1977). *Building rationales for citizenship education.* Bulletin 52. Washington, D.C.: National Council for the Social Studies.

Shaver, J. P. (Ed.). (1991). *Handbook of research on social studies teaching and learning.* New York: Macmillan.

Shaver, J. P., Davis, O. L., Jr., & Helburn, S. W. (1979). The status of social studies education: Impressions from three NSF studies. *Social Education, 43,* 150–153.

Superka, D. P., Hawke, S., & Morrissett, I. (1980). The current and future status of social studies. *Social Education, 44,* 362–369.

Taba, H. (1967). *Teachers' handbook for elementary social studies* (Introductory ed.). Palo Alto: Addison-Wesley.

Chapter 12

◆ ◆ ◆ ◆

The Social Reconstruction of Art Education: Teaching Visual Culture

Kerry Freedman

University of Minnesota

The Social Reconstruction of Art Education: Teaching Visual Culture

Issues of culture are fundamental to art education. The focus of these issues has changed historically in relation to shifting views of art and culture and changing ideas about the purposes of art in school. Since public school art began in the 19th century, the meaning of culture has ranged from a particular notion of good taste and refinement reflected by fine art to a more general milieu or social context in which artistic production and appreciation take place.[1]

This chapter is about representations of culture in art education. Culture, including visual culture, can be represented differently depending on when and where people live, who they are, and how they think. My purpose is to challenge how art is commonly depicted and taught in schools, and to suggest more equitable and enriching ways of teaching and thinking about art.

This chapter has three sections. The first section focuses on the relationship of past and present myths of art education to issues of equity. The second section concerns how cultural knowledge is shaped by art curriculum and instruction. In the third section, recommendations for practice at the elementary and middle-school levels are presented.

Conceptions of Equity: Past and Present

Historically, equity has been dealt with in art education through a focus on two issues: (1) the role of the individual as a self-expressive maker of art and (2) the reflection and reproduction of a "common" culture through common art experiences for all students (Freedman, 1989a). Embedded in art education of the past has been the assumption that focusing on individual self-expression at one level and on promotion of a common culture at another level would override cultural differences and promote equity.

The focus on individualism has resulted in children's cultural commonalities, as well as their differences, being ignored. Except for the similarities among children that have been assumed biophysical and developmental, each child has been viewed as natural, entirely unique, and without attributes of culture.

Late 19th and early 20th century models of artistic ability were borrowed from eugenics to classify children's art abilities based on race, class, and gender (Chalmers, 1992; Freedman, 1989a). More contemporary models of artistic development have represented the characteristics of children's drawings as universal. Only recently have these models been questioned as research has shown that similarities between children's drawings are often copied from common cultural sources (see Wilson & Wilson, 1977) and vary between cultures (see Brittain, 1990). When children enter school, for example, they have similarities in gendered experience, cultural tradition, and socioeconomic group. Children's artistic production and learning are also bound by the commonalities of schooling. Differences in children's art cannot be entirely individualistic or universal, because they reflect these cultural similarities and differences.

The focus on individualism in school emerged based on 18th-century Enlightenment philosophy and the writings of Rousseau, Pestalozzi, and Froebel. Later, the philosophical notion of individualism in children became mingled with clinical psychology, resulting in a therapeutic purpose for art education by the 1920s. Progressive educators promoted a therapeutic art instruction that was assumed to keep children "natural" and untouched by society and culture (see Rugg & Schumaker, 1928). However, the notion of what was natural was culturally based on ideas of self-expression in the fine-art community, the upper middle-class interests of progressive private schooling, conceptions of childhood in social science, and a political economy of freedom and social mobility.

While the art of a few various cultures began to be included in some art education literature early in the 20th century, and grew particularly in the 1930s, and in the '40s as America began to adopt a more global perspective after World War II, the post-war model for art instruction was that of the fine artist. By the end of World War II, American art educators had become captivated by an ideal of the autonomous fine artist who worked alone in a studio, freely self-expressing and intuitively creating. The ideal was merely symbolic; fine artists are actually part of a professional community that is shaped by cultural norms and values.

Guided by the image of individualistic art, art educators became even more immersed in the practice of therapeutic art education in the hope of confounding the development of authoritarianism in children and nurturing a perceived naturally democratic personality (Freedman, 1989b). This model was tempered somewhat in the 1960s, when art educators began to place a greater emphasis on incorporating formal instruction in other fine-art disciplines, such as art history and criticism (Barkan, 1965), and a multicultural perspective (McFee, 1961), into instruction. Since that time, art education has shifted to include more multidisciplinary art content, but has continued to focus largely on the Western, male-dominated, fine-art community.

The assumption that the dispersal of "common" culture would benefit all has been maintained in art education through the promotion of Western models of aesthetic value and an appreciation of work produced by a male-dominated fine-art community. A purpose of such an education in the United States has been to instill in students a knowledge and appreciation of the symbols of socioeconomic success and the values held by people who have been such successes (Freedman, 1989a; Hamblen, 1990). These values have been seen as cultural capital necessary for social mobility.

This purpose of art education is now viewed as problematic for at least three reasons. First, while teaching common culture has been represented as democratic because it appears to make the elite available to everyone, the notion of elite reflects a power structure not conducive to democratic life. The aesthetic values of a few are instilled in all; they are presented as universal and, in their presentation, become "common." In this way, elite values influence what is valued in non-Western and nonmainstream cultures. It is a strength of education to enable the appropriation of knowledge by those who are excluded to provide avenues for empowerment; however, art education has been reproductive in that it has acculturated students without providing the critical foundation necessary for analyzing underlying assumptions of the aesthetic values taught in school.

Second, visual culture ("common" or otherwise) is continually fragmented and dispersed. When art is not examined from a multicultural perspective, the pluralism that exists in life is not acknowledged and the impossibility of real and stable cultural boundaries is ignored. Modern fine art exemplifies this ongoing transformation because it has been greatly influenced by non-Western sources and is intertwined with traditions of popular art. For example, Picasso was influenced by African masks, Van Gogh by Japanese block prints, and American Indian artist Randy White was influenced by Georgia O'Keeffe and James McNeill Whistler when he painted a picture of O'Keeffe in a pose similar to that of the painting known as "Whistler's Mother."[2] However, these types of cultural conjunctions are rarely presented in school.

Third, the assumption that a common culture can be distributed to students contains a certain irony when juxtaposed with traditions of individualism. It is an illusion to assume that students can adopt a universal model of aesthetics when they are viewing art, yet conceive unique ideas when producing art. Students gain experience in relation to their cultural context and cannot simply put it aside when the demand to view or produce art is made.

Myths of Art Education: The Old and the New

Two decades ago, Eisner (1973–1974) revealed the mythological character of seven beliefs that contributed to the focus on therapeutic self-expression in art education:

1. Children should be left on their own to work with art materials.
2. The purpose of art instruction is to develop children's general "creativity."
3. Artistic process, not product, is important.
4. Children perceive the world more clearly than adults.
5. Children's art should not and cannot be evaluated.
6. Teachers should not talk about art because talk ruins the effect of art.
7. Good art education for young children should provide the widest range of materials and studio activities possible.

Eisner argued that educators should replace these myths with art knowledge and discontinue the practice of determining curriculum based on this mythology.

Consistent with Eisner's aims, educators have shifted toward a greater emphasis on looking at and talking about art in school. However, there has been a continued absence of attention paid to issues concerning the art of multiple ethnic, gender, and socioeconomic groups, as well as other vital cultural issues, such as the ecological implications of art and the visual effects of the mass media. This absence suggests that several new myths of art education need to be examined. The following seven myths reflect current debates concerning multiculturalism in art education.[3]

Myth 1: Art has inherent value. Philosophers since Kant have argued that aesthetic value is inherent within a "masterpiece" and that an educated person will be able to appreciate that value. The irony of this argument is that an education in artistic production and valuing is necessarily socially constructed. It is in relation to time, place, and even social group that art is valued. When the contexts of production and valuing are the same (that is, when the artist and the viewer have the same values), the value may *appear* to be within the work of art; but when the context of valuing is different from the context of production, it is more easily understood that value is largely determined based on issues external to any particular work of art. If this were not the case, European art once considered great, such as Raphael's madonnas, would always be considered great. Though Raphael's paintings were admired in his time, there have been times during which they were shunned. Impressionist paintings, once ridiculed, have gained favor.

Even members of the professional art community from the same time and place do not always agree on the value of any particular work of art. The value of a work of art also changes as it moves from one cultural context to another. For example, ceremonial objects used in different cultures and objects traditionally considered decorative that are made by women have only in the last century been viewed as art in European-American culture.

Myth 2: Art is a universal language. While art may take similar forms in several cultures, the context of production, the intent with which things are made, and the uses to which they are put differ dramatically in different contexts. As in the case with language, technical similarities may exist across the arts of different cultures, but the differences in meaning may be profound and require a specific education to be understood. Even the expressive qualities of art that are often considered universal may be culturally specific. Recent cross-cultural studies of emotion indicate that there are cultural differences in people's capacities for emotion and the characteristics of their emotional states (Schweder & Levine,

1984). Profound differences such as these influence the production and appreciation of art.

Myth 3: Art can be studied effectively without studying the context of production and appreciation. It may be possible to appreciate, at some superficial level, an artifact from another culture just by looking at it, but one cannot understand it without information about the culture. For example, the pair of beaded earrings meant to be worn during a ritual dance in motion in the sun or before a campfire at night—where they disappear, leaving only light sparkling around the dancer's head—are transformed when placed in a museum case or a photograph. The transformation occurs because the new context shapes what viewers *see* as art.[4]

Myth 4: There are hard and fast distinctions between fine art and other forms of visual production. Although there are dramatic differences between the art forms of different cultures, older, dichotomous categories (such as fine art/non-fine art) may no longer be helpful in understanding these differences. It is no longer easy to view cultures as totally separate because they interact on many levels and through many media. Fine artists borrow imagery from popular culture, men borrow from women, and artists in the United States borrow from other countries. Contemporary visions of art and culture are too complex to be represented dichotomously.

Myth 5: The interpretation of art is the domain of experts. Many people believe that instruction should focus on the opinions of experts in fine art. At least two dilemmas surface resulting from this myth. First, experts in the professional art community do not always agree with each other. For example, women art historians often disagree with men in their interpretations of paintings of and by women. Second, people knowledgeable about art may not be part of the fine-art community. For example, those who have a deep understanding of an American Indian culture in which art is integrated into everyday life, particularly a member of that culture, can provide information and aid understanding about art.

Myth 6: All art can be understood through certain analytical (Western) aesthetic models. Modern Western models of aesthetics focus on an analysis of objects influenced by Western science and are based on Western conceptions of taste and beauty. However, these models are often treated in curriculum as if they enable objective description; that is, the models give the impression that aesthetics is not socially constructed and culturally located. Currently, most art curricula are based on simplified versions of formalistic and expressionistic notions of aesthetics. Formalism is a pseudo-scientific conception of aesthetics primarily concerned with the abstract qualities of art. It focuses on the analysis of physical and perceptual characteristics of art objects. It involves the reduction of form to elements (such as line, shape, and color) and principles (such as rhythm, balance, and unity) of design.

In contrast, expressionist aesthetics focuses on characteristics considered either unique and personal (different for everyone) or universal (the same for everyone). This notion of aesthetics involves an analysis of artistic production that is concerned with the individual self-expression of an artist. Subject matter of a work of art and cultural context (including purpose, social effect, etc.) are usually considered peripheral to these two perspectives. Hence, these models of aesthetics do not include an analysis of the context of production and appreciation (function, underlying assumptions, social effect, etc.) because they do not take into account the multiple cultural influences on art (or on the creation of models themselves).

While these models appear to simply facilitate an analysis of what is contained within a work of art, they actually condition the ways students approach visual culture. The focus on these models in education prepares students to approach art as a series of objects about form and feeling isolated from context. The assumption that any object can be effectively analyzed using such models carries with it the idea that the artifacts of any culture can and should be taught about as if they were Western (male) fine art. This form of acculturation does not promote an understanding of the peculiarities of fine art and aesthetics, nor does it maintain the integrity of other forms of visual culture and alternative ways of understanding.

These Western models of aesthetics also facilitate an education based on a "disinterested" aesthetic experience, which is the form of elation one may feel when encountering a work of art. Such an experience is supposed to defy simultaneous human (personal, social, economic) interests and elevate people to a higher plane of existence. Whether any experience is possible for one isolated from interests is highly debatable, but regardless, this level of experience is merely a perceptual coupling with a work of art, about which the viewer may know nothing. It is only the first simple step toward developing an understanding of visual culture and having the much richer aesthetic experience that comes with depth of knowledge.

Myth 7: Art education should always start with the object. It is understandable that the efforts of several decades to move art education away from a focus on the production process, mythological notions of self expression, and "the child," have resulted in the emergence (actually reemergence) of this myth.

The professional art community is also currently challenging the notion of individual self-expression and focusing to greater extent on the many communities (professional, cultural) and conditions that make production and appreciation possible.

Information about community and cultural conditions is vital to art knowledge. To start with the object is starting in the middle of the story. This strategy for teaching may convey to children that commodities have privilege over people, purposes, and processes.

Recently, there has been pressure on art educators to overcome these myths and move toward a greater focus on multiculturalism. Several perspectives on the topic have emerged as a result of this pressure. The following sections will discuss these approaches and make recommendations for the future.

Teaching Cultural Fragments

Much of the discussion about diversity and reform in art education has focused on change in curriculum. A pervasive view is that teachers should simply supplement published or unpublished curricula that are largely built on models of the disciplines of Western fine art with multicultural content. Stuhr (1991) has equated this activity with the first level of Sleeter and Grant's (1987) multicultural approaches to education.

In part, the pervasive use of this approach to art education is due to the ways government and school district officials have responded to demands for equitable schooling. Their attempts at multiculturalism have often been couched in terms of fair "distribution" or "treatment," suggesting that what is needed is a certain number of lessons about a particular culture or a special (perhaps therapeutic) set of activities where women and people of color are concerned.

In school, the legislation becomes reduced to a requirement that curriculum contains a specified number of artifacts made by women and people of various cultures. For example, a school district in Minnesota requires that each art lesson taught must include examples of art made by people of at least three different cultures, one of which can be "women." This inclusion may be helpful, but it misses the point of teaching art in a socially sensitive and responsible manner.

The ideal purpose of including these artifacts in curriculum is to promote learning and understanding about disenfranchised groups and inform students about the aesthetic contributions of world cultures. However, art curricula have been published in which non-Western art has been disassociated from its cultural context and analyzed using modernist, Western models of epistemology and aesthetics. The use of these models and quota systems often becomes patronizing and results in inappropriate juxtapositions of culture that misinform students and further disenfranchise the groups curriculum is to support. This occurs, in part, because the *technical* and *formalistic* attributes of artifacts are often focused on in art curriculum, making vitally different cultural artifacts appear to be similar. It also occurs because art is taught with a discourse of extreme individualism, without attention to the ethnocentrism of this idea.

For example, in a second-grade art textbook used by many districts in the United States, a picture of a Navaho woman weaving on a loom is juxtaposed with a close-up photograph of the woven plastic strips of a lawn chair that might be found at a local department store (Chapman, 1987). Rather than addressing the important differences in function, design, and production reflected in these images, the text highlights the relatively less important similarities in the physical structure of "woven" objects. Perhaps a better comparison might be between the Navaho image and a picture of the conceptual work of art titled *Powow Chair* by American Indian artist Edgar Heap of Birds, which consists of a lawn chair placed on a box of dirt taken from the reservation where the artist resides. According to the artist, this piece was produced to respond to stereotypical questions, such as whether American Indians sit cross-legged during powwows.

In another example, a published curriculum contains a slide of two Northwest Coast Indian totem poles showing one in the background and a part of one in the foreground (Alexander, 1988). The photographer has shown what is important in Western aesthetics: the pole in the background is shown so that the form as a whole can be seen, and in the foreground we see an individual face carved into a pole that has been framed as if it were a portrait (a Western art form). In neither pole are we able to see the interrelationship of figures as one meets another, an important visual and spiritual aspect of the totem in native culture. Curricula are filled with such juxtapositions that reflect a reconstitution of culture as mainstream Western aesthetic theory is drawn upon for interpretation and analysis.

Instruction also has an effect on the way we represent culture in art education. Instruction, as well as curriculum, is often more fundamentally about the structure of schooling and teachers' beliefs than about cultural knowledge and identity. The following vignettes taken from schools illustrate these dynamics in art instruction.

▼ Vignette 1

A third- and fourth-grade class is making papier mache masks. The teacher is using a published art curriculum that includes reproductions of masks from various countries and cultures. As recommended in the curriculum, she points out some of the physical characteristics of the masks in the pictures and tries to connect the lesson to the life of the students by calling their attention to wearing masks on Halloween. The teacher must make the presentation brief so the students have time to work on their masks. When asked what he has learned about masks as the hour draws to a close, a boy responds, "All people, all over the world, go trick-or-treating."

Vignette 2

A second-grade class has just completed a lesson on the environment. The word "recycle" is still printed on the board and the teacher has placed a recycle bin across the room from the garbage can. The classroom teacher tells the students that the art teacher will arrive soon and that they will be doing a clay project. The art teacher has 45 minutes in each room of two schools, once a week, to set-up, teach, and clean up an art lesson. She has more than 600 students and little opportunity to know what they do outside their art period. When she enters the room, the students are spreading newspapers out on their desks in preparation for the lesson. At the end of the lesson, the art teacher tells the students to quickly throw their newspapers in the garbage can because she must get to her next class. Some of the students begin approaching the garbage can, but others appear to be wandering around the room with their paper and not following her directions. To spur them on, the art teacher asks the class, "Now, what are we going to do with our newspapers?" A boy raises his hand and says, "Recycle."

Vignette 3

In a middle-school class, the girls are required to make tissue paper flowers and the boys are assigned intricate pencil drawings of cars. When queried about the two assignments, the teacher responds that after many years of teaching, he has learned that the girls like to make tissue paper flowers and boys prefer to draw cars. He states that it is important to him to teach fairly and that this is the only fair way to teach. "Besides," he adds, "tissue paper is expensive and this solves part of my budget problem."

As Sleeter and Grant (1987) point out, the problem with education is usually assumed to be found in the occurrences that take place in a classroom, rather than being inherent in the structure of schooling. It is also assumed that individual teachers are the agents of change toward multiculturalism. However, these vignettes illustrate that the interests of teaching multicultural art often conflict with other interests of schooling and that the complexity of teaching about diversity and ecology cannot be handled by individual teachers or solely on the level of written curriculum development. Multicultural art education demands a deeper understanding by all concerned with schooling, as well as by the public. The character of instruction and institutional boundaries of schooling, even aspects of schooling that seem neutral such as scheduling, must be reconsidered if such an understanding is to be reached.

The vignettes also give attention to the importance of specificity and the rejection of metanarrative in teaching. Students get mixed messages and fragmentary information which become a misrepresentation when the art of any group is used stereotypically or presented as historically static. It is an important part of the social reconstruction of art education to give clear messages to students about social responsibility. These messages must maintain the integrity of difference, yet attend to equity and global concerns.

It is becoming increasingly difficult to think of cultures from being separate. Consider, for example, the daily interactions of Japanese and American culture. The television show *Dallas* is seen in Japan and *karaoke* takes place in country-western bars in Texas. A Japanese corporation is largely responsible for the restoration of Michelangelo's ceiling of the Sistine Chapel and a growing number of Western "masterpieces" have been purchased by Japanese businesses (Januszczak, 1990).

There is concern about a negative effect on the national economy from the sale of better-quality Japanese automobiles in the United States. In the name of patriotism, we are pressured to buy lesser-quality American cars. Ironically, Japanese car companies are located in the U.S. and employ American citizens and vice versa. In school, multicultural education, which should promote understanding and acceptance has developed a new twist: students now learn about Japanese culture to give the United States a competitive advantage.

While many cultures currently interact, we must struggle to maintain the notion of different artistic traditions in historically separate cultures for the sake of identity. *Identity* is defined, in part, by tradition. It is also important for students to study these historical differences so they can better understand the multidirectional influence that results when cultures touch. Students should understand when and where cultural connections have occurred, because these connections produce cultural change and transform art.

Recent shifts in the fields of sociology and anthropology provide guidance for our thinking about the complexities of multicultural art education. The phrase *ethnographic surrealism* (Clifford, 1988) has been used to represent the ways in which anthropologists develop an understanding of culture. This use of the term *surrealism* refers to the combining of fragments of various cultures in a type of conceptual collage, where pieces are brought into a common space and work together to provide a new meaning for the whole. As teachers, we must ensure that the collages we present do not denigrate cultural groups or nature.

This new vision of anthropology includes a reconceptualization of time as a multidimensional space where various cultural and socioeconomic groups coexist. Rather than a linear, progressive series of events acted upon only by people in power, time is shaped by crises that ensue when cultures, classes, and other social groups collide. From this perspective, history is not viewed only as being in the past; rather, it is seen as being a cultural structure, which conceptually locates and shapes us. The structure restricts the possibilities for change while being its medium. Modernism, for example, is part of the structure that at one level has provided the possibility for art to become part of schooling, while at another level has denied the relevance of art for the general public.

Fine-art disciplines, such as art history, have begun to include these new anthropological and sociological perspectives; yet art teachers are still teaching art history based on 19th century models. These models are rooted in Western notions of individual and periodic style, in contrast to, for example, the maintenance of tradition through style as seen in some American Indian cultures (Freedman, 1991). It is important to understand the profession of art history and other fine-art disciplines as distinctive cultural practices constructed within a particular historical period.

A more equitable and reasonable approach to multicultural art education requires a general social reconstruction of the field, wherein all art can be seen as visual culture that is socially constructed and meaningful. This type of art education requires that Western art be anthropologized, made exotic and peculiar, and that the contexts and implications of any art be studied as part of the knowledge necessary to understanding social life.

Recommendations for Practice

Change in art education can promote the transformation of cultural representations in school at large (see Lanier, 1969; Neperud, 1988; Stuhr, Petrovich-Mwaniki, & Wasson, 1992). Such a transformation, toward the social reconstruction of art education, could improve schooling in general. If we are to see a social reconstruction of art education, we must be culturally sensitive in our own teaching and ready to oppose institutional structures that push us toward presenting inappropriate understandings of art. Also, preservice and in-service teachers must be made aware of the enriching possibilities of new theoretical contexts for art education and gain a deeper knowledge and appreciation of the importance of teaching visual culture.

It is also imperative that socially reconstructed art curricula be developed. These curricula must reflect an awareness of the power of juxtaposition and include a serious consideration and valuing of all types of art. They must be designed to present a collage that illuminates and demonstrates an awareness of the fragile and fragmentary state of culture and teaching. This requires that the study of art be seen as fundamental to the study of culture and that culture is foundational to art.

Foundations to Understanding: Elementary School Art

To carry out such reconstruction, practical responses to the myths of multicultural art education must begin at the elementary school level. Each of the following guidelines for practice responds to one of the myths discussed above.

Response to Myth 1. We must illustrate to students that while the creation of visual culture is a basic part of human existence and certain psychophysical or perceptual responses to art may be commonly shared, the value of any particular work of art is largely socially constructed. Part of teaching art should be teaching why certain works of art have been valued in the past and why we study them today. They should also be made aware of the reasons that some art valued today was not valued in the past. Students can begin to learn at an early age about the connections between art and life by studying the art of a few cultures in depth. Only by understanding some works of art in depth can students begin to understand why a particular work of art, and art in general, is valuable.

Response to Myth 2. To develop the understanding that there are many languages of art, children should experience art broadly as well as deeply. They should become acquainted with the art of many cultural groups, and by both women and men. They should also become aware that some art and architecture is made in accordance with nature. During elementary school, children begin learning distinctions, categories, and generalizations of many types; it is important that they become aware of the variety of styles, subjects, forms, meanings, and purposes of visual culture. By developing an awareness of these facets of visual culture, students can begin to recognize differences as well as similarities in art. For example, teachers should help students understand that there are different cultural representations of the same subject matter (such as people or animals) and why those differences exist.

Response to Myth 3. Art can only be studied effectively by including the study of production and appreciation contexts. Without cultural context, only a small part of any art form can be understood. Therefore, beginning in the elementary school, children cannot be taught art by activity or product-oriented method alone. Looking at and talking about art is as important as making it. To contextualize art at the elementary-school level, art can be taught in conjunction with other subjects. However, an interdisciplinary approach to art is appropriate only when art concepts are focused on, not merely as support for a science, mathematics, social studies, or English lesson.

Art concepts connect the work of art to its context and include what various art forms look like, how they are similar and different, how and why they were made, and how they were used and viewed. Even young children can think and talk about art concepts that range from the elements and principles of design to concepts emerging from large, philosophical questions that have been debated for centuries, such as, "What is art?" and "How is art different in different places?" Art concepts should be introduced to students in their first year of school and advance in complexity throughout their school years.

Response to Myth 4. The boundaries between art forms are blurred. While classifying and categorizing promotes concept development in students, dichotomies should be used cautiously. Art instruction must be broadened to include many types of visual culture, including visual forms that affect mainstream culture but are not considered fine art, such as the mass media. A fruitful way to distinguish between art forms is to specify how they are meant to be seen or used. For example, some art is meant to be hung on a wall in a gallery or museum, some is meant to be used in a ceremony, and so on. A general connection between the art objects and activities of various cultures may be seen as "making special" (Dissanayake, 1988). Children should be taught that there are few universals, but that in many cultures, art is a way of making some part of life special and not to be forgotten or neglected. This is an important point to be made not only to students, but to teachers, administrators, and parents, because art is so often ignored in school.

Response to Myth 5. Interpretations of art can come from a variety of sources. Bringing expert knowledge into the classroom is important, but it must be remembered that experts disagree on occasion and that people knowledgeable about art may not be members of the professional fine-art community. Focusing on differences of opinion in the professional community can help students see that there are multiple ways of looking at things and that we need not always look for consensus in the classroom. However, it is vital to have students, at any age, justify their interpretations of art as a way of enriching critical thought. People who are well versed in knowledge about the art of any culture, particularly a member of that culture, should be called on to provide students with information and aid their understanding. A student's own cultural context can also provide important contributions to instruction.

Response to Myth 6. Different notions of aesthetics exist in different cultures and these differences should be included as part of curriculum. Comparing artifacts from different cultures must be done carefully, because what may be similar in appearance may be fundamentally different in purpose and meaning. By pointing out these differences, teachers can help children see that an understanding of art requires a search beyond appearance. This does not mean every teacher must know all about every culture. Teaching some cultural examples in depth can give students skills in investigation and help them develop a sensitivity to aesthetic differences.

Often, artists and guest speakers from museums and local arts organizations are available to visit classrooms and talk about the art of a particular culture. It is also important to make even young children aware that artists borrow their imagery from many sources and that there are cross-cultural currents in art. These currents are apparent even in television shows and advertisements that children see every day. Consider, for example, the use of art vocabulary and artists' names in the *Teenage Mutant Ninja Turtles* cartoons.

Response to Myth 7. Although the study of visual culture necessarily involves the consideration of objects, it should not necessarily begin with a focus on the physical object per se. Rather, objects should be contextualized so that students can develop an understanding of the conditions (cultural, social, political, economic, environmental) that made the production of the object possible. Teaching visual culture should start with the context of production, but also with the context of appreciation. For example, students should understand why their curriculum includes the study of certain aspects of visual culture and not others, where such visual culture would be found and how it would be used outside a classroom (in a museum, place of worship, ceremony, dwelling), and how visual culture changes by being brought into a classroom (such as through reproduction). Contextual information is not peripheral to visual culture, it is integral and therefore fundamental to study. Students cannot understand an art object without having a sense of the people and purposes that are part of it.

These recommendations for the social reconstruction of art at the elementary-school level should be carried over into the middle school with some additional emphases and more complex concepts and activities. The focus of these additions can involve the larger sense of community and culture, including peer culture held by middle-school students, and draw on their capacity for a more sophisticated analysis.

Enriching Apprehension: Critique and Community at the Middle School Level

As students reach adolescence, they become more socially and critically aware. They begin to place a greater emphasis on social rules and mores, and in the process, question as well as accept cultural similarities and differences. This awareness can be enhanced through the development of critique capabilities in art education.

Among the difficulties teachers find with early adolescent critique is that students tend to be concerned with being correct and how they are seen in the eyes of their peers. Students at this age tend to prefer realism in art and are often frustrated when they are unable to produce art that is highly realistic. However, creating a safe environment for writing and talking about adult art can help students understand that multiple representations and interpretations are acceptable and enriching.

Middle-school students can take part in a more sophisticated level of critique and reflection than younger children. They are more aware of social conditions, influenced by local and media culture, and are immersed in the culture of their peers. Culturally sensitive art educators recommend that these students use sociological and anthropological methods, such as interviewing artists in the community to bring local art into the classroom (see Chalmers, 1981; Congdon, 1989; Stuhr et al., 1992; Wasson, Stuhr, & Petrovich-Mwaniki et al., 1990). Students can investigate topics concerning community art, such as where art is located, who makes art, and why art is made.

Students should be encouraged to develop a critical awareness of visual culture they encounter every day, such as film and television. For example, they can use methods from feminist critique to become more aware of the influences of gender in art (see Garber, 1990; Hicks, 1990), an emerging interest in adolescence. Through these investigations, students can develop an understanding of how social groups and cultural issues are represented in art. These investigations should include student as well as adult interpretations of art and critical analyses of how art is used in daily life. Teachers can approach these topics, for example, by having students write a dialogue between themselves and a person in a work of art, or by selecting an advertisement that includes a painting or sculpture and asking the students to explain how and why the advertiser used art to sell something.

Adolescents tend to be particularly interested in the symbolic and metaphorical attributes of art. Instruction in these attributes illustrates to students that art goes beyond the formal qualities of the objects themselves. To understand these aspects of art and maintain the integrity of the artist and culture, the context of production should be taken into account. For example, there is a popular art movement in Shaba, the copper-production region of Zaire, that cannot be understood without study of the artists' context (Brett, 1987). These artists create at least three different types of paintings: *Things Ancestral, Things Present,* and *Things Past* (Szombati-Fabian & Fabian, 1976). Paintings of Things Ancestral refer to early tribal life and customs; they include romanticized images of everyday activities, such as hunting. Things Present are representations of contemporary urban industrial life, such as the copper smelting industry. Paintings of Things Past involve historical topics from the time following contact of the Shaba people with outsiders; it includes images of Arab slave traders and Belgium colonialism. I have seen African art ridiculed and judged as simplistic by middle-school students when the art was analyzed using the formalistic approach prevalent in U.S. schools. However, the same students were intrigued by art from Africa when it was considered in relation to the aesthetic and iconographic context in which it was produced.

Critique of student art can also promote inquiry into issues of culture. This can be done individually or in a group, it can be initiated by students or teacher, and it can be done during or after production. Ongoing critique is part of any good art lesson and the types of critical analysis used in art education are useful methods for developing reflective general educational practice (Eisner, 1982, 1985; Schon, 1987).

When students are producing art, teachers should promote the articulation of art concepts used by students in their work, including the reasons the artist made certain decisions, what appears to be successful about the art and why, and how it can be improved. Through in-class critique, educators can provide students with ways to consider, assess, and act on situations that can help them to make positive changes in their art and in their attitudes about art made by others. Student interaction during critique disperses control and responsibility in the classroom and promotes student interpretation as part of the construction of knowledge.

Reconstituting Cultural Knowledge

Cultural knowledge is reconstituted in a classroom. Even when students actually write stories, play music, and make art in school, these are done within the confines of an institution, a classroom, and an assignment. In the reconstitution, we give the knowledge a new meaning. We cannot give it back its original form; however, we can use this new knowledge as a vehicle for the contemplation of life and of what it means to be of a certain gender or culture. We can also use it to understand how culture shapes artistic production and appreciation.

The social reconstruction of education involves a fundamental revaluing of art in curriculum. Art should no longer be thought of as a frill attached to the curriculum to meet the therapeutic activity needs of students imposed by dull, academic school subjects. Beginning in elementary school, art should be at the center of a curriculum on culture because understanding the characteristics of artifacts, ceremonies, costume, and other aspects of visual culture is fundamental to understanding human existence.

Notes

1. People use many different words to represent visual culture. In some cultures, a word similar in meaning to the word *art* does not exist. In mainstream American culture, a range of phrases are used to make distinctions between art forms that serve different purposes and have different socioeconomic locations, such as *fine art, commercial art, folk art,* and *popular art.* Also, some phrases are now viewed as demeaning to nonindustrial cultures, such as *primitive art.* For the purposes of this chapter, I use the phrase *fine art* to denote the work produced by those in the professional community (in advanced industrialized countries) who seek gallery, museum, and other collection recognition. The phrase *Western art* refers to artwork produced as part of the mainstream culture of European and European-American countries. The phrases *art* and *artistic production and appreciation* refer to the visual culture of any group.

2. The title of Whistler's painting is *Arrangement in Grey and Black.*

3. The word *multiculturalism* may be misleading because it suggests to some people that only issues of race and ethnicity are of concern. However, I am using the term in this chapter to signify a general social reconstruction of art education that would effectively respond to a broader notion of culture and include issues of ethnicity, gender, socioeconomics, ecology, mass media influence, etc.

4. The example of the earrings came from a personal communication with Patricia Stuhr.

References

Alexander, K. (1988). A world of art: Grade six. *Learning to look and create: The SPEC-TRA program*. Palo Alto, CA: Dale Seymour.

Barkan, M. (1965). Curriculum problems in art education. *Seminar on Research and Curriculum Development*. State College, PA: The Pennsylvania State University.

Brett, G. (1987). *Through our own eyes: Popular art and modern history*. London: GMP.

Brittain, W. L. (1990). Children's drawings: A comparison of two cultures. In B. Young (Ed.), *Art, culture, and ethnicity* (pp. 181–192). Reston, VA: National Art Education Association. (Reprinted from *Journal of Multicultural and Cross-cultural Research in Art Education*, Fall, 1985.)

Chalmers, F. G. (1981). Art education as ethnology. *Studies in Art Education, 22*(3), 6–14.

Chalmers, F. G. (1992). The origins of racism in the public school art curriculum. *Studies in Art Education, 33*(3), 134–143.

Chapman, L. H. (1987). *Discover art: Grade 2*. Worcester, MA: Davis.

Clifford, J. (1988). *The predicament of culture: Twentieth century ethnography, literature, and art*. Cambridge: Harvard University Press.

Congdon, K. G. (1989). Multi-cultural approaches to art criticism. *Studies in Art Education, 30*(3), 176–184.

Dissanayake, E. (1988). *What is art for?* Seattle, WA: University of Washington Press.

Eisner, E. W. (1973–1974). Examining some myths in art education. *Studies in Art Education, 15*(3), 7–16.

Eisner, E. W. (1982). *Cognition and curriculum: A basis for deciding what to teach*. New York: Longman.

Eisner, E. W. (1985). *The art of educational evaluation: A personal view*. London: Falmer.

Freedman, K. (1989a). Dilemmas of equity in art education: Ideologies of individualism and cultural capital. In W. G. Secada (Ed.), *Equity in education* (pp. 103–117). London: Falmer.

Freedman, K. (1989b). Art education and changing political agendas: An analysis of curriculum concerns of the 1940s and 1950s. *Studies in Art Education, 29*(1), 17–29.

Freedman, K. (1991). Recent theoretical shifts in the field of art history and some classroom applications. *Art Education, 44*(6), 40–45.

Garber, E. (1990). Implications of feminist art criticism for art education. *Studies in Art Education, 32*(1), 17–26.

Hamblen, K. A. (1990). Beyond the aesthetic of cash-culture literacy. *Studies in Art Education, 31*(4), 216–225.

Hicks, L. E. (1990). A feminist analysis of empowerment and community in art education. *Studies in Art Education, 32*(1), 36–46.

Januszczak, W. (1990). *Sayonara Michelangelo: The Sistine Chapel restored and repackaged*. Reading, MA: Addison-Wesley.

Lanier, V. (1969). The teaching of art as social revolution. *Phi Delta Kappan, 50*(6), 314–319.

McFee, J. K. (1961). *Preparation for art* (2nd ed.). Belmont, CA: Wadsworth.

Neperud, R. W. (1988). Conceptions of art in the service of art and aesthetic education: A critical view. *Arts and Learning Research, 6,* 95–102.

Rugg, H., & Schumaker, A. (1928). *The child-centered school: An appraisal of the new education.* Yonkers-on-Hudson, NY: World Book.

Schon, D. A. (1987). *Educating the reflective practitioner.* San Francisco: Jossey-Bass.

Sleeter, C. E., & Grant, C. (1987). An analysis of multicultural education in the United States. *Harvard Educational Review, 57*(4), 421–444.

Stuhr, P. (1991). Contemporary approaches to multicultural art education in the United States, *INSEA News, 1,* 14–15.

Stuhr, P., Petrovich-Mwaniki, L., & Wasson, R. (1992). Curriculum guidelines for the multicultural classroom. *Art Education, 45*(1), 16–24.

Shweder, R. A., & Levine, R. A. (Eds.). (1984). *Cultural theory: Essays on mind, self, and emotion.* Cambridge: Cambridge University Press.

Szombati-Fabian, I., & Fabian, J. (1976). Art, history, and society: Popular painting in Shaba, Zaire. *Studies in the Anthropology of Visual Communication, 3*(1), 1–21.

Wasson, R., Stuhr, P., & Petrovich-Mwaniki, L. (1990). Teaching art in the multicultural classroom: Six position statements. *Studies in Art Education, 31*(4), 234–246.

Wilson, B., & Wilson, M. (1977). An iconoclastic view of the imagery sources of the drawing of young people. *Art Education, 30*(1), 5–11.

Chapter 13

◆ ◆ ◆ ◆

Multicultural Approaches to
Music Education

Julia Eklund Koza

University of Wisconsin-Madison

When music educators and classroom teachers talk with each other about multiculturalism, they may be speaking different languages. The term *multicultural* may have a different meaning for music teachers than it does for educators who take a multicultural and social reconstructionist perspective. Therefore, so that elementary classroom teachers may better understand their colleagues who are musical educators, I begin this chapter with a comparison of definitions of multicultural education.

Next, I review the history of multicultural music education as traditionally defined and describe the current state of multiculturalism within the discipline. In the final section of the chapter, I discuss a new vision of music education that is multicultural and social reconstructionist, with an eye on implications for instruction and curricular content. My goal is to offer an analysis of the successes and shortcomings of music education's past and current multicultural initiatives in an effort to enlighten the discussion of a new and broadened definition.

Defining Multiculturalism

According to Sleeter and Grant (1988), multiculturalism encompasses the "education policies and practices that recognize, accept, and affirm human differences and similarities related to gender, race, handicap, and [social] class" (p. 137). Multiculturalism is, to Sleeter and Grant, a "different orientation toward the whole education process" (p. 175).

A social reconstructionist perspective adds the element of social criticism to multiculturalism; one goal of educators with a social reconstructionist perspective is to help children become citizens who will actively work to promote equality (Sleeter & Grant, 1988). In short, multiculturalism is a perspective that has far-reaching implications for all aspects of schooling, including instruction, curriculum, evaluation, home/school/community relationships, staffing, and extracurricular activities (Sleeter & Grant, 1988).

By contrast, the term has a more circumscribed meaning to most music educators. It refers to the teaching of ethnic music; the multicultural movement within music education traditionally has been concerned primarily with curricular content. This is not to say that music educators have been oblivious to issues surrounding social class, gender, and disability. However, in music education these topics are not generally found under the multicultural umbrella. Although some music educators are concerned with specific issues addressed in the multicultural and social reconstructionist realm, there is no concerted movement within the discipline to embrace the dramatic changes in schooling suggested by the latter. In fairness to music educators, many of them today are struggling for the survival of their programs. Unfortunately, given the conditions existing in most schools, few of them have time or energy to consider broader issues.

Multicultural music education as traditionally conceived has been surrounded by some ambiguity because the question of what constitutes ethnic music has been answered in a variety of ways. As Bessom (1972b) astutely pointed out, *all* music is ethnic; this observation has not informed past definitions, however. Thus, designating specific music as ethnic has also been a process of placing people into the categories of "we" and "they," of articulating which music is "theirs" and not "ours." Definitions of *ethnic* and *multicultural* provide a study in exclusion—whose music typically has been omitted from the canon.

High-art music from Europe and the United States has traditionally constituted "our" music; however, the boundaries between categories have always been blurred and have shifted over time. *Ethnic* has referred to such disparate fare as European folk songs, African American rap, ragas from India, and Ojibwa music for wood flute. The placement of European folk music in the multicultural category indicates that socioeconomic group, in addition to ethnicity, has been a factor defining the parameters of ethnic music. Although some music educators are gradually realizing that "they" can be "us," few have discussed or questioned the problematic and limiting nature of the current definition.

Multicultural Music Education, Past and Present

The Beginnings

Multiculturalism is a relatively new movement in music education, generating little interest until the late 1960s. Before that time, only a handful of visionaries saw value in teaching any music from outside the circumscribed borders of a Euro-American canon. For example, from 1914 to 1967, only six articles on the topic of multiculturalism appeared in music education's major trade publication, *Music Educators Journal*.[1] This small collection of articles is important, however, not only because the authors were progressive, but also because it reflects beliefs, values, and problems that have persisted to some degree to the present and are ultimately counterproductive to music education that is multicultural and social reconstructionist. Three of these beliefs and problems will be examined in greater depth: (1) a hierarchy that values Western high-art music above all others, (2) divisive distinctions between "our" and "their" music combined with ambiguity concerning what is "ours" and "theirs," and (3) belief in a myth of music as a universal language.

The first problem, a hierarchy that values Western high-art music above all others, fueled the belief that such music was the only worthwhile genre to study. Even the use of the term *high* indicates the privileged status these particular styles traditionally have been given. Using biased standards, and basing their judgments on incomplete and often inaccurate understandings of music of other cultures, many early musicologists and music educators concluded that the music of nearly all of the world's people fell short. High-art music was the bench mark against which all others were measured and invariably deemed inadequate. Music was sorted into "ours" and "theirs"—and "ours" invariably was better. Well-intended music teachers, whose practices reflected beliefs and values of larger segments of society, concerned themselves with cultivating good taste and exposing children only to music of the "highest quality"; however, the bounds of high quality were narrow.

Belief in the hierarchy was not always openly stated, but its influence is nonetheless evident in early writings about music. For example, the earliest music journal article to address multiculturalism portrayed practices that are grounded in hierarchial thinking. Appearing in 1933, it described an openness to ethnic music in the British schools established on colonized South Sea islands.

Beck (1933) gave a firsthand account of a music education program in an island school run by a British master. After the class had presented a lengthy concert of hymns and American songs in four-part harmony (hallmarks of Western music), one student was allowed to let out a "thrilling old Fijian war-whoop." This final demonstration was considered evidence of British sensitivity, the author concluding that the British "know how to colonize and yet retain the identity of the native" (p. 20).

On the one hand, this article opened the door to consideration of music outside the traditional Euro-American canon, and it emphasized the importance of valuing the culture students bring with them into the classroom. On the other hand, the ratio of indigenous music to Euro-American, and the ordering of selections such that the indigenous music came at the end of the concert (or perhaps *after* it), are telling commentaries on which styles were deemed most worthwhile by the concert's organizers. The well-intended author apparently did not find the school's imposition of large doses of Euro-American music problematic, nor did she notice any incompatibility between avowed ideology and actual practice.

This biased hierarchial structure was evident in other articles of the era. For example, a remarkably progressive author advocated studying American Indians of the southwest United States through an integrated approach reminiscent of John Dewey. Nonetheless, he differentiated between "primitive" people and their music and people of "higher culture"—American Indian music fell into the former category (Otterstein, 1938).

The same article contains another problem often found in early efforts: divisive distinctions between "our" and "their" music combined with ambiguity about which musics might be considered ethnic. Teachers were encouraged to introduce children to the people of other lands by singing folk songs from countries such as Holland and Switzerland (Otterstein, 1938). This is a curious suggestion, given the longstanding influence European styles have had on music in United States schools; it indicates that "folk" and "ethnic" may have had socioeconomic group overtones.

In addition to noting where the music of various people of the world was situated on the hierarchial structure, it is important to consider whose music was not mentioned at all. A 1947 article advocating ethnic music as a means of promoting "one world" included a description of a 20-unit audio-visual curriculum, each unit focusing on the music from a specific geographic region (Duffield, 1947). While the tiny countries of Belgium and Switzerland each were allotted one unit, the entire continent of Africa was overlooked.

A third problematic belief is the myth that music is a universal language capable of transcending the barriers of spoken or written word. This myth is but one of many overstated assertions about music's capabilities, some assertions being as old as the ancient Greeks. Many of these claims were drawn on by music educators of the 19th century in their efforts to convince skeptical school boards of the value of music in the curriculum. The legacy of these early music educators is apparent in writings from the first half of the 20th century; the universal language myth was popular then and lingers to some degree now.

Although music is a universal phenomenon, it cannot transcend social context, and thus, the culture that produces the music also constructs its meaning. Therefore, rather than sending a universally understood message, the music of a particular culture may strike an uninitiated listener as alien and incomprehensible.

A more romanticized notion of the powers of music was present in early discussions of multiculturalism, however. In 1945, shortly after the end of World War II, an article about using music to improve "intercultural relations" included a quotation from President Roosevelt:

> Because music knows no barriers of language; because it recognizes no impediments to free intercommunication; because it speaks a universal tongue, music can make us all more vividly aware of the common humanity which is ours and which shall one day unite the nations of the world in one great brotherhood. (Moses, 1945, p. 23)

The article said understanding cultural differences would foster sensitivity to others and that such sensitivity would effect global peace. Other sources have echoed similar sentiments. Calling upon "music's universal and unifying message," Duffield (1947) envisioned music as a tool that could bring about a "one world" consciousness (p. 21). Unfortunately, he did not spell out what music's universal and unifying message might be.

Despite the problems just discussed, these older articles are nonetheless extraordinary. Because their authors opened the door to the possibility of a broader concept of "legitimate knowledge" than had heretofore been envisioned, they courageously challenged "business as usual." However, they probably had little effect on schooling practices, and therefore to call these early efforts a movement is to perhaps overstate their effect.

Modern Multicultural Music Education

The birth of the modern multicultural music education movement came at about the same time as the Tanglewood Symposium in 1967. The symposium was sponsored by the Music Educators National Conference, the most prominent music teachers' organization in the United States. One purpose of the gathering was to suggest ways of improving music education in the face of rapid social change. The Tanglewood recommendation having the most far-reaching implications for multiculturalism declared the following:

> Music of all periods, styles, forms, and cultures belongs in the curriculum. The musical repertory should be expanded to involve music of our time in its rich variety, including currently popular teen-age music and avant-garde music, American folk music, and the music of other cultures. (*Music in America*, 1967, p. 2)

Early Problems With the Modern Movement   The mere suggestion of this ambitious goal did not effect a transformation overnight, however. Post-Tanglewood multicultural music education had a slow start; in addition to changes for the better, problems persisted. One of these problems arose because interest in multiculturalism grew at about the same time that music educators were beginning to apply a conceptual learning approach to music.

At that time, music educators usually translated *concepts* to mean the concepts surrounding the structural or formal elements of the music itself—i.e., melody, rhythm, harmony, timbre, texture, and form. Thus, forays into multicultural music often focused on teaching the elements of music through materials drawn from a variety of cultures. Educators spoke of common structural elements that provided a unifying thread for all music and that offered a framework with which to compare musical styles. Concept statements focusing on the structure of the music, such as "Music may move in relation to the underlying steady beat," were illustrated using music drawn from several cultures.[2] The structural concepts remained the same, only the musical examples changed. The common-elements approach was, in effect, an updated version of the universal language myth, except now the assumption was that the elements of music provided the unifying link.

One weakness of the common-elements approach is that it skirts the cultural context of the music being studied. Overlooking context can lead to incomplete and inadequate understandings; the common-elements approach has the potential to reduce music education to merely an intellectual exercise. Whether one considers the common-elements approach to be adequate depends on one's definition of understanding music. The unanswered question is whether the technical Euro-American understanding of how music works—derived from the common-elements approach—is sufficient if other understandings, ascribed by the cultures creating the music, are ignored.

For example, an advocate of the common-elements approach might teach a piece of Javanese gamelan music with the intention of helping children understand its formal structure. The goal of the lesson would be to learn that the particular piece exhibits a two-part form and that the gong marks out the structure by sounding on every 16th beat. What I question is not the accuracy of the information presented but rather the limited focus of the lesson. Concentrating primarily on structure and talking about it in this manner reflect Euro-American ways of understanding music. Familiarity with beliefs Javanese people hold concerning this music is at least as essential to a student's understanding as is knowledge of structure. The meaning of the piece begins to become clear only when the significance of the gong in Javanese culture is understood and when the function of this work in relation to puppet theater and dance is known.

Using only a Euro-American lens to view musical creations from other cultures unjustly privileges that way of seeing and thinking. Children may develop a limited idea of what a piece is about unless they explore other aspects of the musical event as well. The common-elements conceptual approach continues to be widely used today. It can be useful as long as teachers keep in mind that it is merely one culturally constructed and, therefore, limited way of thinking about music. It is not the only tool, nor necessarily the best one, that can be brought to bear on new and unfamiliar sounds. Unfortunately, in past practice its own cultural situatedness has often been overlooked by its proponents.

A second post-Tanglewood problem stemmed from the very ambitiousness of the goal established at the symposium to teach music of all cultures. To learn well the music of one culture is a formidable task; a thorough knowledge of all cultures is probably beyond the grasp of any human being. However, early proponents were ambitious and idealistic, and the common-elements approach lent itself to introducing musical appetizers from a wide assortment of cultures.

A shortcoming of this ambitious goal was the potential for superficiality. Multicultural curricula emerged that amounted to the musical counterparts of *Around the World in 80 Days*. For example, a 1972 issue of the *Music Educators Journal* devoted entirely to the subject of multiculturalism covered six continents in a little more than 40 pages (Bessom, 1972a).

The bold music teacher who decided to introduce the music of what was then called a "non-Western culture" often found few suitable materials.[3] Furthermore, what did exist frequently contained overgeneralizations and inaccuracies; the most acute problems tended to occur in introductory materials. For example, complex rhythms were sometimes ironed out, melodies were outfitted with harmonized piano accompaniments when neither harmony nor pianos were part of the culture, and musical instruments were incorrectly identified. Because some of these materials still occupy shelves in elementary classrooms and libraries, a teacher with no experience in the music of another culture should be especially cautious when consulting older sources.

Finally, multicultural music education was (and often remains) a low priority in colleges and universities that trained teachers. Thus, the notion of multicultural music education was handed to unprepared music teachers who had little or no experience with music beyond high-art forms from Europe and the United States. Until recently, few colleges required future music teachers to take a course in ethnic music; even jazz and popular music are relative new-comers to the college curriculum.

Because many teacher-training institutions placed a low value on the introduction of a wide range of styles, the teachers trained at these institutions, especially those who found employment in relatively homogeneous schools, gave multicultural music education a low priority in their own classrooms. One critic, commenting on the limited curricular fare found in many public schools, noted with acerbity:

> In the Western world the best music has always been made outside the schools and in important ways against the teaching of the schools. And much of the worst has been made in them. Should we not, perhaps, restrict music in the schools to the training of bands, choruses, and orchestras as we have done for the last several decades to the performance of fairly conservative repertoires and leave outside the school music activities something to rebel against? (Seeger, 1972, p. 111)

This remark invites contemplation on whether teaching the exciting music a multicultural curriculum can offer remains a low priority today—both in colleges and in elementary classrooms. At present, few music teachers are prepared to implement a multicultural curriculum, even as it is narrowly conceived within the music profession; the concept of multiculturalism has not filtered into musical training for elementary classroom teachers, either. Therefore, any collaborative attempt at multicultural music education in an elementary school will likely be a new learning experience—not only for the classroom teacher, but for the music specialist as well.

Strengths of the Movement Since Tanglewood

Much good came out of efforts to follow Tanglewood's recommendation. During the past 20 years, a greater emphasis has been placed on recognition of the respect for diversity. Thanks to efforts that began at Tanglewood, the hierarchy that valued high-art music above all others is gradually disappearing. For example, Anderson and Campbell (1989) emphasize that there are "many different but *equally valid* [italics added] forms of musical and artistic expression" (p. 1). Definition of the term *ethnic* has been reexamined as music educators acknowledge the ethnic diversity existing not only outside but also within the United States, and as they recognize the rich cultural heritages children bring with them into the classroom (see Anderson, 1991). Perhaps in recognition of the limitations of the common-elements conceptual approach, recent resources emphasize the importance to musical understanding of familiarity with cultural context (see Anderson & Campbell, 1989).

More and better resources are now available to teachers. Devoting the entire 1972 issue of the *Music Educators Journal* to ethnic music was a bold and unprecedented move; since that time, in addition to a second special issue appearing in 1983, the *Journal* has published a number of individual articles on the topic.[4] These recent articles, along with the ever-growing body of books on related subjects, can be invaluable resources for elementary classroom teachers. Perhaps the finest among recent publications is the book edited by Anderson and Campbell mentioned earlier. Its extensive bibliographies, discographies, and filmographies contribute to its usefulness.

Growth of interest in multiculturalism among music educators is reflected not only in the increased number of written publications available, but also in higher attendance at workshops on related topics. One recent conference was the Symposium on Multicultural Approaches to Music Education in Washington D.C. in 1990.[5] Because well-developed musical skills often are required of participants, these workshops may not be advertised to classroom teachers; however, some workshop organizers undoubtedly would welcome any interested teacher, and some classroom teachers may possess sufficient skill to succeed in even the most technical of workshops.

In the face of many changes, multicultural music education continues to be defined as the study of ethnic music, the focus of the movement remaining primarily on curricular content.[6] Anderson and Campbell (1989) note, "A multicultural approach to learning centers around organizing educational experiences for students that encourage and develop understanding and sensitivity to peoples from a broad spectrum of *ethnic* [italics added] backgrounds" (p. 1). As valuable as the multicultural music education movement has been, its limitations lie in its very definition.

Music Education That Is Multicultural and Social Reconstructionist

Turning away from the traditional definition of *multiculturalism* and adopting Sleeter and Grant's (1988) broader concept would necessitate changes not only in music content, but in many other facets of music education as well. Let us consider what some of these modifications might be and contemplate how classroom teachers would fit into this new model. I propose changes in four areas: (1) schooling at large, (2) the music education paradigm, (3) instructional practices, and (4) the music curriculum.

Multicultural Music Education and Schooling

Some changes in thinking about schooling at large would facilitate efforts to make music education multicultural and social reconstructionist. If, for example, schooling practices were informed by the following four assumptions related to music education, significant departures from "business as usual" would occur:

1. Music is worthwhile and deserves as large a share of time and other resources as any subject traditionally considered basic.

2. Any elementary classroom teacher is capable of creating an environment in which children can learn music.

3. The responsibility for helping children learn music rests on classroom teachers as well as on music specialists.

4. Compartmentalizing elementary subject areas, such that music is seen as a discipline apart from social studies, language arts, or physical education, is artificial and often unnecessary.

To elaborate, in current practice music is often considered a frill—a nicety, but not a necessity. As mentioned earlier, many music teachers today are struggling to keep their programs alive. While it may be argued that this struggle is a sign of the failure of music education to stay in touch with the needs of children, this explanation is too simplistic. The struggle to give music education legitimacy is at least 150 years old and was present when the subject was introduced into the public schools. The marginalization of music education has been a chronic problem, in part, an outgrowth of a pragmatism that saw no use for music.

The difficulties music educators historically have faced are reminders that schools sometimes can exclude or marginalize not only individual students but entire domains of knowledge as well. The struggle is a commentary on the values of those who decide what constitutes worthwhile knowledge; thus the marginalization of music is, in a broad sense, a multicultural issue. Values that marginalize music typically manifest themselves in meager allotments of time and other resources for elementary music education. Overburdened music teachers, some of them traveling from room to room with their supplies on a cart, often work in two, three, or more schools. Some of them see hundreds of children in one day, the average student-to-music teacher ratio being nearly 500 to 1.[7]

Honoring curricular areas other than the traditional "basics" is an acknowledgement that there are many ways of knowing. Valuing music, as well as the other arts, invites more pluralistic and diverse views about what it means to be intelligent. Valuing music education is a valuing of the affective component of living, of the emotional aspects of life often dismissed as feminine and, therefore, inconsequential. Finally, valuing music and other subjects that may not necessarily lead to gainful employment helps send the message that material wealth is neither the only nor the most important of life's treasures.

Music is often perceived to be such a specialized subject that only an expert, someone with supposedly innate music talent who has been extensively trained, is qualified to teach it. Given this assumption, elementary classroom teachers may feel ill equipped to offer any form of music education to their students. Aside from a few minutes per week with the music specialist, children may receive no regular music instruction, especially in upper elementary grades and middle schools.

Deferring completely to a music expert is a fairly recent practice in United States education. In the early part of the 20th century, music teachers were called supervisors, and their job was to oversee the music education provided by classroom teachers (Coffman, 1987). Unfortunately, as is frequently the case with established schooling practices, the current arrangement, with its total reliance on music specialists, is assumed to be the way things have always been done and, thus, should continue to be done. This is not to suggest that music specialists are unnecessary. Rather, given the inadequate conditions under which many of them work, the quantity and quality of elementary music education might conceivably be increased if classroom teachers decided that they can and will participate in this portion of schooling.

Even if a classroom teacher is willing to collaborate with a music specialist, scheduling may not permit these individuals to communicate the valuable ideas and information they can offer one another. In a considerable number of schools, the arrival of the music specialist signals welcomed preparation or release time for overextended classroom teachers. Little opportunity for collaboration between the classroom teacher and the music specialist may cause sharply delineated boundaries to appear between music and the rest of the elementary curriculum.

The four assumptions listed earlier are only indirectly related to multiculturalism. However, individual curricular areas do not exist in a vacuum, and the success of elementary music education that is multicultural and social reconstructionist depends on a reconsideration of more basic assumptions about the relationship between music education and elementary education in general.

Under the current conditions, many of the changes suggested by multicultural social reconstructionists would be difficult for music specialists to implement without outside assistance. For example, when music instruction occupies only 15 minutes of class time per week and is provided by a music specialist who sees 500 students in a week, it is no small task for that teacher to learn the names of all the students. Achieving the multicultural goal of tailoring instruction to each child and that child's particular interests and needs is probably impossible under such circumstances.

Developing a New Music Education Paradigm

What Is Music Education?   In addition to changes in schooling at large, modifications of the music education paradigm are needed. An analogy may help explain what I mean. I have lived in the Midwest all my life and have never seen a desert. Therefore, my concept of a cactus—my cactus paradigm— has been limited. I envision lanky, leathery green varieties or perhaps squat, spiny barrels. On a recent trip to a cactus display at the Mitchell Conservatory in Milwaukee, I was astonished by a variety called lithops, or Living Stones, which look like the small, smooth, brown pebbles that surround them. A marker at the location of these cacti was the first clue that my cactus paradigm was inadequate. I only saw a few lithops at first, but as my cactus paradigm gradually shifted, I realized that the garden floor was covered with them. As valuable and useful as my original paradigm was, it also limited my vision.

Applying the analogy to music, ideas about what constitutes music education, shaped by past experiences, may limit a person's vision of possibilities for the future. Developing a new paradigm may mean putting aside the notion that music education only means participating in large-group sing-alongs, playing the clarinet in the band, or learning to read standard musical notation. For example, because some music from outside the traditional Euro-American canon does not lend itself easily to large-group performances, multiculturalists may need to carefully reexamine music education's longstanding emphasis on large ensembles and whole-class activities. Furthermore, large-group activities such as band and orchestra involve the purchase of expensive musical instruments, and thus these activities can widen the gap between children who come from wealthy communities and those who do not.

Developing a new paradigm will mean dreaming beyond the boundaries of past personal experience, as well as of what currently constitutes standard practice. Redefining the music education paradigm opens the door to the possibility that classroom teachers, even those with little or no formal musical training, can create environments in which children learn music.

The limitations of a traditional music education paradigm were apparent in a recent incident involving a child, Katherine, who is deaf and was integrated into an elementary music class.[8] After several weeks of encouraging Katherine to sing, the music specialist learned from the classroom teacher that the rest of the teaching and support staff was trying to train the girl *not* to vocalize. Apparently the child's vocalizations were considered disruptive; an evaluation team decided the sounds would be a hindrance and an embarrassment to her in social situations. When the conflict of goals was discovered, one person on staff said she could not understand why a child with little residual hearing was placed in music in the first place and recommended Katherine be removed from the class.

If music education is understood to mean only singing, there may have been scant justification for placing this child in music. However, the incident prompted creative thinking on the part of the music teacher, classroom teacher, and support staff about what music education *might* mean and how a broadened definition might benefit Katherine as well as the rest of the class. It was determined that Katherine needed to work on physical coordination and on overcoming shyness. Instead of taking the child out of music, music education was adapted to the child. Everyone in the class learned to sign the songs they sang; Katherine helped teach the class (and the music specialist) how to sign. Dance, taught with a focus on rhythm and accompanied by acoustic instruments, was given more emphasis in the program. Acoustic instruments were chosen over recorded sounds because the former produce strong vibrations that can be felt and can reinforce any residual hearing a child might have.

The changes were not particularly radical, and many other creative possibilities can be imagined. Dancing and signed songs could have been incorporated into a play the children were writing. Class members could provide the background music and sound effects for the play, compose music for the dance, and choreograph it as well. Follow-up activities might include a field trip to see a signed choir or a performance by a troupe of dancers who are deaf. The possibilities are limitless.

However, the simple steps these teachers did take show that even minor modifications in a traditional music education program and small shifts in paradigm can result in an educational setting that is more useful and beneficial to all children. Also, a message was sent: This child is a valued member of the class and her contributions are important; she is entitled not only to be present in the classroom but also to learn, as is *every* child.

Changing the paradigm concerning what constitutes music education will require cooperation from music specialists; without a doubt, some of them will be hesitant to modify the current model. For example, some may contend that Katherine was not receiving a *music* education; instead, music was used as a tool to achieve other curricular ends. These educators are concerned that utilitarianism may compromise the music education profession and further erode its already small plot of turf. A few might argue, "The classroom teacher does not teach music, so why should I be concerned with social studies, or mathematics, or physical education? I have precious little time, and it should be devoted solely to music."

They make some good points. However, if one assumes that boundaries between subject areas are artificial and not always necessary or useful, that classroom teachers *will* teach music, and that music warrants a more prominent place in the curriculum, then these fears have a weaker foundation.

Who Is To Be Educated?   In addition to thinking about what might constitute music education, it is equally important to consider who is to be educated. "Music for every child and every child for music" has been a rallying cry for the profession for decades, but the ideal has rarely been practiced. In general, elementary music specialists have been more conscientious than their secondary counterparts in applying this universal philosophy to their teaching.

Even on the elementary level, however, some children slip through the cracks; children with disabilities are the most likely candidates. In some schools, children with disabilities may be excluded from music altogether; or if brought into the music class, they may be tacitly excluded by "business as usual" instruction that does not take into consideration their specific needs.

Failure to provide music education for all children becomes an even more serious problem in middle schools and high schools. Recent statistics indicate that only 22 percent of high school students are enrolled in music (Gerber & Hughes, 1988). Although many factors contribute to this low statistic—among them tight schedules and the elective nature of secondary music courses—the accusation that many middle and high school music programs are elitist and exclusionary cannot be ignored, especially given the strong emphasis these programs frequently place on polished performance of a restricted repertoire of musical styles.

The belief that musical talent is innate and differentially bestowed from one individual to another is a popular but not necessarily accurate assumption that can result in exclusion. This belief often divides children into "haves" and "have nots," effectively prohibiting the "have nots" from ever becoming a "have." In the past, this belief served as justification for giving music instruction to a select few. Today, most music educators advocate music for every child, regardless of perceived ability, but few have considered the possibility that musical talent may be a social and cultural construct; "giftedness" may have far more to do with experience and nurturance than with natural gifts.[9]

Traditional beliefs about musical talent can lead to tracking, especially on the middle and high school levels. Those who are perceived to have talent find themselves in a performance organization (band, choir, orchestra). If every child is required to take a music course, those who are viewed as lacking in talent may be relegated to a general music class.

A few critics may argue that championing music for all children is as insensitive to diversity and individual needs as any other global perspective. Perhaps a better way of stating the goal is that every child is entitled to music education tailored to the individual. This is a tall and expensive order, however, and given the current ratio of music teachers to students, it may remain out of the realm of possibility until "business as usual" changes. Taxed music specialists may have considerable difficulty achieving the goal of reaching every child, and this is one area where classroom teachers, who know students well, can offer invaluable insights.

Rethinking Teaching

The concept of education that is multicultural and social reconstructionist invites reexamination of who teaches, as well as how and where learning can take place. Children can learn from people other than teachers and in places other than classrooms. Multicultural education invites a softening of the boundaries between teacher and student, suggesting that we can all learn from each other and can teach each other. Softening the boundaries creates an environment conducive to cooperative teaching and learning. The music specialist and the classroom teacher can learn from each other; students can learn from other students; and teachers can be students themselves, learning much from the children they teach.

Softening the boundaries means that teachers relinquish the hat of the expert or, perhaps, pass the hat around. If one operates under the assumption that everyone has something to contribute—everyone has gifts—then classroom teachers having little or no experience with either traditional or multicultural music education also can make contributions, and they can create an atmosphere conducive to learning music. Classroom teachers do not even have to pretend they are music experts. However, from another perspective, nearly everyone has had a vast amount of experience with music—if not with music education. Most people are inundated by music daily, and thus, in some sense, we may all have much more expertise than we realize.

Classroom teachers who feel uncomfortable with their formal knowledge of music, especially of music from cultures unfamiliar to them, may find that inviting others to share in the teaching, including parents, community members, and the students themselves, can be a clever way of introducing students to a diverse array of music while simultaneously circumventing their own lack of expertise. Field trips can be invaluable, and such outings are another way of taking pressure off of classroom teachers to be music experts. Although music field trips often have meant visits to the symphony, the fare can be far more varied; outings can help students sample a marvelously diverse mosaic of musics from the United States, the world, and in many cases, from their own neighborhoods.

Rethinking music teaching such that it is multicultural and social reconstructionist invites examination of whether instructional emphasis should focus primarily on a child's needs and interests or on more global goals based on perceived needs and interests of children as a group. When a music teacher sees 500 students in one week, knowing individual needs, interests, and learning styles becomes nearly impossible. Traditionally, much of public school music education has focused on singing or playing in large performing groups. Only when these activities are no longer perceived as constituting the totality of music education will the student-music teacher ratio fall to a level where individual differences can shape curricular and instructional practices.

When resources have permitted, public elementary music education has also included individual instruction, typically in the form of private lessons on a band or orchestral instrument. Thus, public schools have sometimes made available to a larger segment of the population what historically has been a privilege of the wealthy: private instruction with its potential for adaptation to individual needs and interests. Although one-on-one instruction is not always individualized, greater possibilities for individualization exist when the student-to-teacher ratio is low. Unfortunately, the benefits of private instruction may still go largely to children in wealthy districts that can afford to pay the enormous costs incurred.

Given the status quo, classroom teachers will probably be more attuned to a child's needs and interests than will a music specialist; they may be in a good position to implement music curricula and instructional practices that focus on the individual. These practices need not be elaborate. For example, showing respect for the individual can manifest itself in such simple ways as honoring a child's preference not to sing solos by structuring activities so that children can make performance choices with which they feel most comfortable.

In addition to encouraging students to make choices for themselves, multicultural social reconstructionists also suggest that teachers be sensitive to the modalities through which a particular child learns most effectively. Sensitivity to modality has multicultural implications, not only because it focuses on the individual, but also because slavish dedication to one modality may be a sign of a monocultural bias. The fact that much of the world's population learns and transmits music exclusively "by ear" indicates that aural learning is a valid and effective practice; yet some music teachers consider it a less desirable way of learning than reading notes. Music from many cultures does not lend itself to being written down; in fact, "standard Western notation" often proves inadequate. Even music from a fairly mainstream style such as jazz is difficult to notate. Therefore, in some cases not only is written notation inconsistent with the usual manner of transmission, but it can be a hindrance.

Because learning through the specific visual mode of reading standard notation is privileged by many musicians in power, for example, those who will make decisions about which students will be admitted to the most prestigious music schools and conservatories, it may be argued that children who do not learn this skill will be handicapped. In effect, the ability to read music will separate children into "haves" and "have nots" and will deny "have nots" access to elite and powerful circles. This is a valid and troubling argument, indicating that even well-intended practices, such as acknowledging the equal validity of aural learning, may have negative consequences for individual students. If people in positions of power ever change their perspective, the shift may come too late for today's students.

The heavy reliance on visual learning notwithstanding, music education at its best, with its emphasis on "hands-on" experience, has been perhaps more sensitive to alternative learning styles than other curricular areas. Many students not succeeding in traditional academic courses have found a niche in music; this phenomenon may result from a longstanding emphasis in music on different ways of knowing and learning. One of the advantages of a multicultural approach is that music of other cultures may rely even more heavily on other learning modalities than methods of teaching Western high-art music do. Techniques of learning music borrowed from other cultures may be successful with students who are not gaining understanding through traditional methods.

Rethinking the Curriculum

Content That Is Diverse, Inclusive, and Respectful   Curricular modifications are needed in addition to instruction changes. One of these modifications involves placing greater emphasis on content that is diverse, inclusive, and respectful. Multicultural music education should focus on content representing the diversity of the community, the nation, and the world. This means the inclusion of contributions by people whose music has not been heard in schools in the past, the marvelously interesting music that Seeger, quoted earlier, indicated was being kept out of schools.

In addition to referring to music created and enjoyed by people of color within and outside of the United States, multicultural content can encompass contributions by women, people from many religious backgrounds, and people of various social classes, to name but a few. A multicultural perspective invites consideration of who traditionally has been left out of the collective "we" when people in the past have referred to "our musical heritage." Advocates of multiculturalism promote a further consideration of the question of what constitutes good music, while pointing out the narrowness of past definitions that limited the designation to works by dead, White, male, European composers.

Multiculturalism acknowledges that culture does not merely mean something "out there" and far away but also refers to the varied rich experiences children bring with them to school. Curricular content that is multicultural incorporates, respects, and connects to children's previous musical experiences. A multicultural curriculum begins with a specific child or some particular children and expands from there. These concepts invite contemplation of whether standardized curricula in music education, which are generally designed to fit all students in all situations, can now or ever be multicultural.

While familiarity with music of *every* culture is probably an unrealistic goal, it is possible to strive toward "polymusicality" for all children.[10] Polymusicality may be defined as the ability to speak and understand more than one musical language—to know the music from more than one culture. Such familiarity does not generally breed contempt; quite to the contrary, it increases the likelihood that children will enjoy, respect, and celebrate the rich diversity constituting human creative expression.

Recalling the difficulty early educators encountered when attempting to teach the music of all cultures prompts contemplation of whether the appetizer or the four-course meal tactic is more consistent with multicultural goals. In other words, is the breadth provided by a smorgasbord of musical tidbits from a large number of cultures worth the risk of superficiality? Would children be better served if music from a few cultures was discussed in depth and presented in such a way that students learned to remain open to new and unfamiliar experiences? I have no easy answer to these questions; regardless of whether we opt for breadth or depth, however, it is important to focus on instilling values that will foster openness to and respect for unfamiliar music encountered in the future.

Some critics argue that time away from traditional curricular content will be detrimental to the people who most need the empowerment that knowledge of the Euro-American canon can provide. For example, if the elementary music curriculum focuses on learning to play rock drums, or on the folk music of Ghana, or on rap, precious time will be taken away from the study of Bach,

Beethoven, and Brahms. The latter knowledge, because it is often more highly valued by people in positions of power in music, can open doors to students who possess it. Children from upper-class families will likely be exposed to this canon outside of school; others may not. This argument is valid and clearly points out the complexity of the issues at hand. One response might be that balance, rather than abandonment of the traditional canon, is the more prudent route; but this response leaves the question of what constitutes balance unanswered.

Content That Is Contextual and Integrated   Because music is not a universal language and does not speak for itself, multicultural music education must ever be mindful of situating music content within a larger context. Because musical meaning is socially constructed, mediation is often necessary when introducing children to music from cultures unfamiliar to them. Herein lies the beauty of integrating music with curricular areas such as language arts, social studies, foreign languages, physical education, and art. Education that emphasizes the interconnectedness between the arts and other aspects of life will help bring context into focus. Furthermore, in many cultures, music is inseparable from other aspects of life. Boundaries between content areas are somewhat artificial under any circumstances, but they can be especially counterproductive when the goal is multicultural education.

Content That Is Fair   In addition to calling for music curricula that reflect diversity and are contextual, multiculturalism advocates curricula that are fair to all. Equity issues related to music education curricula are legion; the following discussion will focus on just two areas: (1) content that is respectful of religious belief or unbelief, and (2) content that is equitable to both sexes.

Content That Is Respectful of Religious Belief/Unbelief   One "business as usual" music practice related to the issue of respect for religious belief/unbelief is the performance of music in conjunction with Christian sacred holidays. Although public schools in the United States are in theory nonsectarian, their roots lie in Protestantism; nowhere are these roots more obvious than in music education. Some teachers who would not dream of advocating prayer in public schools unflinchingly present wholly sacred Christmas concerts complete with crèches; they lead caroling sessions in classes, hallways, and neighborhoods. The fact that such customs are steeped in tradition lends an aura of legitimacy to them.

Such practices have been under fire for at least 20 years, however, and proponents of the traditional approach have presented a varied array of rationales for continuing "business as usual." Some of the most zealous supporters have contended that events such as Christmas concerts are part of an essential ministry to the unchurched. Others present less overtly biased arguments: For example, many assert that sacred music is a central part of the "Western musical heritage"; not to program Christmas music, they argue, is to deny children familiarity with some of the world's greatest art. Others contend that Christmas is as much a secular holiday as a sacred one and, therefore, Christmas carols are not actually sacred songs. Still other arguments are variations of "Majority rules" and "When in Rome, do as the Romans do."

Siding with proponents who say sacred music has great artistic value apart from its religious significance, courts and local school boards alike have continued to allow the performance of Christmas music in the public schools so long as the intent and effect are secular.[11] In the past, policies concerning the performance of sacred holiday music have given teachers considerable latitude. However, latitude was often interpreted by teachers to mean free license. Teachers used community response as a gauge for whether their curriculum was appropriate and fair; receiving no complaints meant curricular decisions were wise.

Complaints occasionally effected such minor changes as the inclusion of a Hanukkah song or two, but the balance of time and effort remained devoted to Christmas fare. Angered by complaints, some teachers, rather than taking a hard look at whether "business as usual" was a good idea, stubbornly insisted on doing everything they could get away with. However, as communities have become more culturally diverse, traditional practices have increasingly come under fire, a trend not likely to be reversed in the future.

From a multicultural perspective, a better question than "Is this permitted?" or "Will the community object?" might be "Is this fair?" Fair curricula assure that no child will feel embarrassed, isolated, or inadequate because of religious belief or unbelief. Put more positively, education that is multicultural affirms who the child is, as the child is.

Excusing children from musical activities that are contrary to their beliefs marks children and can create awkward and unhappy moments for the child who leaves. Such practices suggest that the curriculum is fine and that the problem lies with the child. The message is sent that majority rule means exclusion; this practice devalues the minority voice, especially when coupled with large doses of traditional fare.

The heated debate generated by the holiday music question suggests that the issues at stake are much larger than music, the debate evolving out of contrasting visions of society. Opposition to change probably is also fueled by fear. Rather than seeing a more balanced multicultural curriculum as a marvelous opportunity, promising rich reward in exchange for small concessions, many people, sadly, only see loss.

Few proponents of multiculturalism would argue that all Christian sacred music should be removed from the music curriculum; indeed, such music can be an enriching part of a child's education, *as can the music of other religions*. Instead of removal, the usual call is for balance, sensitivity to alternative voices, and thoughtful consideration to the possible consequences of current practices.

If one proceeds on the assumption that sacred music can be taught without proselytizing, and if one opts to keep sacred music in the public school curriculum, then many alternative voices, still silenced by current practice, must be given a fair and respectful hearing. In a nation as diverse as the United States, monocultural public school practices such as caroling, giving Christmas concerts, and confining the study of sacred music almost exclusively to Christian music are anachronistic, insensitive, and exclusionary. If the music associated with every other major world religion is not to be given a fair share of time, then Christian music belongs in church, not in school.

Equitable Music Content: The Gender Component

Sex equity is another content issue meriting attention from multicultural music educators. Because all of us have grown up in an environment that in many ways tacitly accepts sexism, it is sometimes difficult for us to see "business as usual" practices as unfair; subtle and overt sexism can slip into curricular content unnoticed.

In the United States, longstanding sex stereotypes exist concerning participation in music activities. Boys may be reluctant to join in because they have been subtly or explicitly taught that music, specifically singing, is feminine. For example, the stereotype persists that "real men" do not join choir. Despite the feminization of the discipline, however, many musical activities, notably composing and conducting orchestras and bands, have traditionally been reserved for males. Furthermore, except for an occasional vocalist, the performance of rock music and jazz are exclusively male domains.

Stereotypes concerning musical instruments also exist. For example, the flute, clarinet, violin, and harp are considered feminine, while drums, trumpets, trombones, tubas, and string basses are deemed masculine (Abeles & Porter, 1978; Griswold & Chroback, 1981). A recent study of the representation of females in music textbook illustrations indicates that textbook content is seriously flawed because it tends to reflect traditional music-related stereotypes (Koza, 1991). Such research raises the question of how teachers might proceed, given the problematic nature of available resources.

First, teachers can examine materials carefully. In addition to including equal numbers of females, and being free from stereotypes that might appear in resources from any curricular area, music materials should portray people of both sexes participating in a wide variety of musical activities and playing a variety of instruments. When analyzing how males and females are represented, it is important to consider not only the written text and illustrations but the musical examples as well. As appealing as it may be to teach favorite songs from one's own childhood, it is nonetheless critical for teachers to first think about whether song texts portray males and females in ways that are considerate, respectful, and fair. For example, "Peter, Peter, Pumpkin Eater," is a traditional favorite in the repertoire of beginning pianists and is based on a familiar nursery rhyme:

Peter, Peter, Pumpkin Eater,
Had a wife but couldn't keep her.
Put her in a pumpkin shell,
And there he kept her very well.

It is tempting to say, "This is just a cute silly song; it is absurd to eliminate it from a young pianist's repertoire on the grounds that it is unfair." However, consider another perspective. In addition to playing the traditional role of breadwinner, Peter is the active problem-solver in the song. All we learn about his wife is that she is kept. Apparently she does not even have a name, and nobody asked her how she felt about being cooped up in a vegetable. Rather than eliminating the song altogether, teachers might invite children to think about Peter's wife and consider her viewpoint on the events. In the spirit of "Fractured Fairy Tales," children could write their own second and third verses in which Peter's beleaguered wife gains an identity and a voice.

If teachers who advocate a multicultural approach that is social reconstructionist use biased materials, they might carefully consider how to incorporate them in ways that are consistent with a goal of being fair and sensitive to all children. A thoughtful question is, "Who might be harmed or served by this representation, especially if it is presented without question or comment?"

One alternative to removing materials is to critique them. For example, excerpts from Broadway musicals long have been a popular part of upper elementary and middle school music curricula. However, female roles in these musicals have often been stereotyped. Teachers can use these musicals as a springboard for critical analysis and class discussion of equity issues. Against-the-grain performances are another effective way of problematizing sexist roles.

Content With a Focus on Social Issues

Finally, it is important to keep in mind that music, because it is a social construct, is intricately related to the society from which it has sprung. Therefore, music is never politically neutral nor value free. This also means that music can be related in many ways to social issues. A music curriculum that is multicultural and social reconstructionist can highlight this relationship in countless ways, four of which will be briefly discussed. Curricular content can focus on such topics as (1) current practices within the field of music and how they are related to larger social problems, (2) social issues and problems of a particular society or culture as reflected in its music, (3) how music is used to sell social and political ideas, and (4) the role music has played in efforts to effect justice and change.

First, students can explore the effect that social problems have on the field of music itself. Questions such as "Why are there no women in this book about famous composers?" or "Why haven't more boys signed up to sing in choir this year?" or "Why are there no people of color in this picture of a symphony orchestra?" can lead to exploration of how larger social issues affect the discipline itself. They can provide students with opportunities to think carefully about their own beliefs and values, and they can be starting points for an array of follow-up projects. For example, such questions might lead to a search for music by women composers represented in the Top 40, or to interviews of classmates and parents asking them why boys often do not join choir, or to a letter-writing campaign asking an orchestra association why no persons of color are employed by their organization. Music can be a starting point for efforts to teach children how to not only analyze and critique, but also debate, coalesce, and take action.

Students can also analyze and critique music with an eye on how it may reflect social issues and problems. For example, an analysis of a rock video or a television commercial can include questions about how women, people of color, or people of various social classes are portrayed in the images and text. Then, in addition to asking questions typical of musical analysis, such as queries on instrumentation or tempo, the issue of how the music itself reinforces the portrayals can be addressed.

Third, students can analyze how music is used to sell not only products—ranging from deodorant to presidential candidates—but ideas as well. For example, propagandists often use music to sell ideas; such sales tactics rely heavily on codes of shared meaning. Children who have watched television in the United States have a vast repertoire of sonic experiences from which they can draw when thinking about what it is in the music itself that prompts particular associations, and when considering how the code of shared meaning is sometimes used to manipulate people.

Finally, students can investigate the role music has played in efforts to effect social and political change. Campaigns that have striven for justice, such as the suffrage, civil rights, and labor movements, have often used music as a way of rallying and sustaining supporters. Sometimes music has come to represent the movement itself. For example, *We Shall Overcome* is one symbol of the efforts of the Civil Rights movement in the United States. Knowing this music and understanding its significance can help introduce children to people and ideas that have challenged "business as usual."

Keeping the Focus on People

Instructional practices and curricular content are, without question, important for educators to consider. However, from a multicultural and social reconstructionist perspective, the central focus of any educational endeavor must always be on people. If in the past music education has sometimes become preoccupied with content and method, and if it has grown isolated from elementary education at large, then multiculturalism can offer a new path.

The inclusivity suggested by multiculturalism can mean welcoming pluralistic content into the curriculum, and, more importantly, opening doors to diverse people, ideas, and ways of doing things. Classroom teachers represent one group of people with a wealth of experiences to bring to a new music education paradigm that is both multicultural and social reconstructionist.

Changes in "business as usual" are clearly needed. Sweeping change cannot be effected by music specialists or classroom teachers alone, however, because schools, like classrooms, do not exist in a vacuum. If music education is to survive and if it is to become multicultural and social reconstructionist in the broadest sense, administrators, legislators, taxpayers, and parents must look deep within themselves and reconsider many time-honored beliefs and values.

Beliefs and values shape goals, mold policies, and govern priorities; they determine, for example, whether instruments of human destruction or instruments of human expression will receive more resources, whether people or things are given first priority. If equity and justice for all people were placed at the top of the list of goals, both for individual curricular areas and for public education as a whole, then a new perspective would be brought to bear on curriculum and instruction. In the spirit of multiculturalism, classroom teachers and music specialists can become politically active and can work together to bring about changes in "business as usual" thinking, not only within, but outside the classroom as well.

Notes

1. In its early days, the *Music Educators Journal* was first called the *Music Supervisors' Bulletin* and later, the *Music Supervisors' Journal*. I arrived at the number six by counting the pre-1967 articles cited under the subject heading "Multicultural Education" in Arneson (1987).

2. This conceptual goal was taken from a series by Meske, Andress, Pautz, and Willman (1988, p. xxviii).

3. See Anderson & Campbell (1989, p. ix) for a discussion on this scarcity.

4. See Arneson (1987) for other titles in addition to Taylor (1983).

5. For a synopsis of the symposium, see Anderson (1991, pp. 29–33). *Teaching Music with a Multicultural Approach* is a videotape series based on the symposium itself. For more information about the tapes, contact MENC Publication Sales, 1902 Association Drive, Reston, VA 22091.

6. See two recent articles as evidence supporting the argument that *multicultural* is assumed to mean *ethnic*: Anderson (1991, pp. 29–33); and Swanson (1991, p. 39).

7. According to information provided by the Music Educators National Conference, in 1983 the student-to-music-specialist ratio was 496.2 to 1. A survey taken in 1987 of 41 states revealed a ratio of 497 to 1.

8. In this school, the terms *deaf* and *hard of hearing* are preferred over *hearing impaired*; the latter is perceived to connote deficiency rather than difference.

9. For an unconventional and intriguing view on giftedness, including musical talent, see Bloom (1985).

10. For a contemporary discussion of polymusicality, see Anderson & Campbell (1989, p. 4).

11. For example, Florey v. Sioux Falls School District 49-5 was upheld in the 8th U.S. Circuit Court of Appeals. The case stemmed from the singing of *Silent Night* in a Christmas concert, and the decision reaffirmed the legality of singing sacred music in public schools. For more discussion of this issue, see National Executive Board, "Religious music in the schools" (1984, 28–30).

References

Abeles, H. F., & Porter, S. Y. (1978). The sex-stereotyping of musical instruments. *Journal of Research in Music Education, 26*(2), 65–75.

Anderson, W. M. (1991). Toward a multicultural future. *Music Educators Journal, 77*(9), 29–33.

Anderson, W. M., & Campbell, P. S. (Eds.). (1989). *Multicultural perspectives in music education.* Reston, VA: Music Educators National Conference.

Arneson, A. J. (1987). *The music educators journal: Cumulative index 1914–1987: Including the music supervisors' bulletin and the music supervisors' journal.* Stevens Point, WI: Index House.

Beck, A. L. (1933). Are we making the most of our gifts from other lands? *Music Educators Journal, 19*(5), 20.

Bessom, M. E. (Ed.). (1972a). Music in world cultures. *Music Educators Journal, 59*(2).

Bessom, M. E. (1972b). Overtones. *Music Educators Journal, 59*(2), 5–6.

Bloom, B. S. (Ed.). (1985). *Developing talent in young people.* New York: Ballantine Books.

Coffman, D. D. (1987). Vocal music and the classroom teacher, 1885 to 1905. *Journal of Research in Music Education, 35*(2), 92–102.

Duffield, P. E. (1947). Global music: An audio-visual approach to the 'one world' concept. *Music Educators Journal, 33*(6), 21, 68–69.

Gerber, T., & Hughes, W. O. (Eds.). (1988). *Music in the high school: Current approaches to secondary general music instruction.* Reston, VA: Music Educators National Conference.

Griswold, P. A., & Chroback, D. A. (1981). Sex-role associations of music instruments and occupations by gender and major. *Journal of Research in Music Education, 29*(1), 57–62.

Koza, J. E. (1991, April). *The boys in the band: Sexism and the construction of gender in middle school music textbook illustrations.* Paper presented at the annual meeting of the American Educational Research Association, Chicago, IL.

Meske, E. B., Andress, B., Pautz, M. P., & Willman, F. (1988). *Holt music* (Teacher's ed., grade 8.). New York: Holt, Rinehart and Winston.

Moses, H. E. (1945). A good-neighbor policy for appreciation classes. *Music Educators Journal, 32*(2), 22–23.

Music in American Society: The Tanglewood Symposium. (1967). Washington D.C.: Music Educators National Conference.

Otterstein, A. W. (1938). Music in the activity program. *Music Educators Journal, 24*(4), 25–27.

National Executive Board, Music Educators National Conference. (1984). Religious music in the schools. *Music Educators Journal, 71*(3), 28–30.

Seeger, C. (1972). World music in American schools: A challenge to be met. *Music Educators Journal, 59*(2), 107–111.

Sleeter, C. E., & Grant, C. A. (1988). *Making choices for multicultural education: Five approaches to race, class, and gender.* Englewood Cliffs, NJ: Merrill/Prentice Hall.

Swanson, P. (1991). Who will take up the charge. *The Wisconsin School Musician, 61*(5), 39.

Taylor, R. G. (Ed.). (1983). The multicultural imperative. *Music Educators Journal, 69*(9).

Chapter 14

◆ ◆ ◆ ◆

Curriculum and Instruction in Primary School Physical Education: A Critique and Visionary Perspective for Reform in Teacher Education

Jepkorir Rose Chepyator-Thomson

State University of New York at Brockport

Introduction

Physical education, also called *kinesiology,* is a professional field of study that includes knowledge about motor development and human movement (with its cultural and social connections) as well as teaching methodology and learning behavior. Physical education emphasizes physical, cognitive, interpersonal, and emotional changes in people at all levels and ages of learning. The development of the whole child is the major focus of physical education in elementary and middle school grades. In essence, physical education "is education of, by, and through human movement; it contributes to the total growth and development of the child primarily through selected experiences and physical activities" (Dauer & Pangrazi, 1975, p. 2). Specifically, the aim of physical education is to develop the child's affective, cognitive, communicative, and psychomotor skills (Ragan & Shepard, 1977; Kirchner, 1978). "Learning how to learn and dealing with meaningful content" are also facets of physical education (Logsdon et al., 1977, p. 12).

The goal of physical education and education in the United States has been:

> . . . the greatest possible development of each individual for responsible democratic citizenship.
>
> Above all, physical education is an essential part of the school effort, . . . reflects the nature and needs of a democratic society in which there is respect for the interests and capacities of the individuals, . . . is organized into an unbroken flow of experiences beginning with early childhood, . . . is well-balanced and affords varied experiences that will contribute to desirable outcomes for all ages, . . . is based on rigorous criteria for content selection. (Dauer & Pangrazi, 1975, pp. 94–95)

Anchored by kinesiological and physiological studies of human movement, physical education has a disciplinary-based knowledge. It entails children's understanding of physical activities, their instrumental use of these activities, and the development of culturally valued physical attributes that allow them to participate successfully and joyfully in physical activities (Arnold, 1988, p. 4).

Physical skills and ways they are applied to games and activities are grounded in one's culture. As such, a culturally valued physical skill is a movement that fits a particular culture in society: for example, the jumping activity of the Kalenjin group in Kenya, East Africa, or the lacrosse activity of the American Indians in North America. The jumping activity of the Kalenjin group is intended to develop strength and rhythmic movements associated with various ceremonies in the culture and is a means to demonstrate manhood among the Maasai. The lacrosse activity of the North American Indians is meant to demonstrate manhood, settle disputes between the various ethnic groups, and promote healing (Brown, 1992).

Although physical education is of greatest importance to children's development in elementary and middle school grades, its implementation has not been critically examined for its appropriateness for a diverse population of students. Physical education curricula have changed dramatically since the beginning of the 20th century in that more schools offer more programs with a greater variety of activities. But there is still a dominant cultural perspective that undergirds the conceptual configurations of physical education and program operations. The dominant perspective has been limited to a specific population, mainly U.S. citizens of European descent.

The literature has not adequately addressed American Indians or African Americans in terms of conceptual frameworks or activity variations. Neither has the literature focused adequately on diversity as reflected by the U.S. population. Few culturally based movement skills of American Indian cultures are taught in elementary and middle school grades. Indeed, the role of culturally based movement skills in traditional cultures in the United States has been largely ignored in the primary school. Scant attention has been paid to the influence of social, cultural, and political factors on the type of physical activities developed for physical education class.

In this chapter, I examine the extent to which European cultures have influenced the development of physical education programs, and the paradigms that have guided the conduct of physical education in the schools. I also suggest ways of reforming physical education in teacher education such that theoretical perspectives and instructional goals developed by teachers cater to students' diversity culturally and socially.

Historical Development of Physical Education in the United States: The Eurocentric Focus

Cultural Influences

The framing of the mind of a person in the United States community has largely been shaped by the knowledge derived from European cultures. This Eurocentric focus has influenced the development of physical education, and in turn, the type of activities taught in physical education classes. Before 1900, Germany and Sweden played a major role in the development of physical education.

German Influence   German immigrants introduced Turnverein gymnastic organizations into the United States (Zeigler, 1988), which installed German gymnastics as a major form of physical education into many United States schools (Van Dalen & Bennett, 1971). Friedrich Jahn, the developer of the Turnverein organizations, believed the groups raised the levels of physical fitness and responsive discipline of the German youth and helped rehabilitate the spirit and the virtues that formed the core of the German culture (Barney, 1975).

The organizations spread knowledge about gymnastic exercises by educating the United States public on the benefits of the German system of exercise as well as influencing legislation in local and state governments (Barney, 1975). The Turners believed physical training to be an important part of children's education and that gymnastic activities promoted growth, development, and moral and mental training of the individual (Zeigler, 1988). The preparation of teachers according to the German system was established in 1866 in New York City. By the end of the 19th century, teachers graduating from the German teacher preparatory school were teaching gymnastics in the public schools.

Swedish Influence   Another major European influence on the development of physical education in the United States came from the Swedes. The Swedish form of gymnastics was developed by Per Henrik Ling and his son Hjamar. It was introduced to the United States by Norwegian Dr. Hartwig Nissen in 1883 when he visited the country as a vice-consul for Norway and Sweden. The gymnastics form was popularized by Swedish aristocrat Baron Nils Posse (Zeigler, 1988).

Posse, a graduate of Royal Central Institute of Gymnastics of Stockholm, and Mary Hemingway, a Boston philanthropist, founded the Boston Normal School of Gymnastics in 1889 with the mission of preparing teachers to teach the Swedish system of gymnastics in public schools and colleges (Zeigler, 1988). This program was guided by theories of medical and corrective gymnastics (Rice, Hutchinson, & Lee, 1969) and formed the basis for the development of physical education in many New England states and other areas with non-German populations (Zeigler, 1988). Through light calisthenic exercises, the Swedish system was seen as improving the health of school children (Rice et al., 1969) and it focused on the development of flexibility and grace of movement (Zeigler, 1988).

Danish and French Influence   Accompanying the German and Swedish influences on the development of physical education programs in the latter half of the 19th century and the first quarter of the 20th century were the Danes, who played a role in the development of physical education in the country. Danish gymnastics were originally designed for Folk Arts Schools in rural areas in Denmark and were believed to develop flexibility and general body conditioning (Zeigler, 1988). The French also had their share of influence. The Delcarte culture of the French brought rhythmic and aesthetic focus into physical education. The movements executed were of a calisthenic type and characterized by repetitive graceful movements (Van Dalen, Mitchell, & Bennett, 1953).

British Influence   The sports and games of the British have become a part of people's cultures in many countries that were part of the British empire. Wherever the British went—Australia, India, the United States—their leisure activities went with them (Rice et al., 1969, p. 95). Although many sports activities such as cricket and archery originated from Britain, many others originated from the neighboring European countries; but the English and Scots "naturalized" these sports activities (Rice et al., 1969, p. 95). Other European naturalized sports activities included golf from Holland, bowling from the Netherlands and Germany, and tennis from France. The British refined these sports activities and passed them to their colonies.

The Eurocentric focus in physical education in the United States was discussed formally at the Boston Conference of 1899. The conference brought together representatives from several European regions to discuss the direction of physical education in the United States (Zeigler, 1988). Dudley Sargent, a dominant figure in the field of physical education at the time, stated that the United States needed the following:

> The strength-giving qualities of the German gymnasium, the active and energetic properties of the English sports, the grace and suppleness acquired from the French calisthenics, and the beautiful poise and mechanical precision of the Swedish free movements, all regulated, systematized, and adapted to our peculiar needs and constitution. (Zeigler, 1988, p. 198)

It is apparent in Sargent's view that the concept of diversity in physical education was discussed in terms of European ethnic groups. Physical education in the United States assumed a Eurocentric focus at its inception not only in terms of content knowledge but also in terms of structure and philosophy.

Besides the cultural influences that have been identified, sociopolitical influences on the development of physical education occurred in times of crisis. Physical education was stressed in times of war; the overall physical fitness of citizens was given top priority — then and now (Zeigler, 1988). In wartime, the objective of physical education was to develop physical fitness. The emphasis was placed on strength, endurance, stamina, coordination, and the physical skills that were of direct benefit to the individuals joining the military service (Van Dalen et al., 1953). During the Depression in the 1930s, many people lost their jobs, and physical education was emphasized as a cure for boredom and inactivity (Zeigler, 1988).

Programs and Curricula in Primary School Physical Education

As I have noted, between 1850 and 1925, the few physical education programs sanctioned in the country (Ragan & Shepard, 1977) were of European origin. During World War II, physical education programs began to stress sports and games that were popular at the time; these sports and games continue to be emphasized in schools today (Ragan & Shepard, 1977).

Traditionally, school physical education curricula have featured sports and games, physical fitness, and movement education. Although the physical education program in elementary school has focused on new games and ethnic, folk, and creative dances (Jewett & Bain, 1985), curricular models have emphasized activity programs with a movement education focus. According to Locke (1969), movement education has centered on educational dance, basic movement, movement exploration, educational movement gymnastics, and developmental movement. Movement education has been a prescription "for the kind of gross motor skills taught to school children and for how such instruction [would be] accomplished" (Locke, 1969, p. 203). According to Ennis and Chepyator-Thomson (1991), the dominant curricular approach has had a cognitive or an analytical orientation and the language concepts used have reflected the theory developed by Rudolf Laban, a German citizen.

In terms of middle school, researchers such as Jewett and Bain (1985) have pointed out that the curricula have historically stressed survival swimming, sport skills, dance, project adventure, fitness activities, and new games—all expressed under the rubric of lifelong physical activities and designed to maintain health and productive lifestyles perceived to bring about increased productivity in the U.S. economy. The physical education curricula have focused on (1) the understanding of movement through the refinement of personal skills, (2) social understanding of people from other cultures through experiences in movement activities of many cultures, and (3) the invention of new games (Jewett & Bain, 1985).

Little attention has been focused on either nondominant groups or women in U.S. physical education programs. Historically, the programs have separated boys and girls, and boys have had more activities available to them. Girls usually could study gymnastics, calisthenics, and dance, while the activities for boys have continued to emphasize team sports (Geadelmann, Bischoff, Hoferek, & McKnight, 1989). Besides unequal activity offerings, boys generally have had access to superior instruction and facilities. Through the Education Act of 1972–Title IX, there has been an attempt to equalize physical education programs in terms of instruction and facilities. The act prohibits discrimination on the basis of sex in federally funded programs.

In summary, examination of the historical development of U.S. physical education programs has revealed that culture, politics, and social factors have played a major role in program offerings and structures. The Germans, the Swedes, the French, and the British have had a major influence on the physical education programs in elementary and middle school grades. In the following section, the different ways in which paradigms function in physical education are discussed in light of culture, politics, and the economy.

Paradigms in Physical Education

The concept of paradigms in education has been used in varying ways and it is important to note that "paradigms are not theories" (Gage, 1963, p. 95) but rather are ways to contemplate possible formulations of reality. In the context of paradigms, education has allowed people to think in different ways about the subject matter—and the outcomes have been several competing perspectives.

Researchers and teachers of physical education have conceptualized the subject in different ways:

- A fitness perspective (Kirchner, 1978; Taggart, 1985)
- A developmental physical education perspective (Hoffman, Young, & Klesius, 1985)
- A movement education perspective (Jewett & Bain, 1985)
- A humanistic physical education perspective (Hellison, 1985)

Each of these paradigms or perspectives has at different times in the 20th century guided thinking about physical education.

Physical Fitness

Physical fitness was the major emphasis in the elementary school curriculum in the 1960s and '70s (Kirchner, 1978). Its focus has been to enhance the physical fitness of children—the "ability of each person [to function depending] upon physical, mental, emotional, and social components of fitness" (Kirchner, 1978, p. 40). These include the development of strength, endurance, power, flexibility, agility, and speed in children. From this perspective, achieving a high level of physical fitness has been defined as demonstrating one's optimum physical and mental well-being (Kirchner, 1978).

A fitness-based curriculum that requires specified activity intensities and intervals is composed of health-related fitness and performance-related fitness (Hellison & Templin, 1991). Health-related fitness is concerned with cardiovascular function, body composition, and musculo-skeletal factors (Siedentop, Mand, & Taggart, 1986). Specifically, health-related fitness consists of muscular strength and endurance, aerobic capacity and other types of conditioning as well as weight control.

Performance-related fitness sometimes is referred to as motor fitness. It is concerned with broad categories of physical performance that go beyond health-related fitness concerns (Siedentop, Mand, & Taggart, 1986); it is made up of skill components necessary to perform organized sports and other physical activities that require strength, power, anaerobic capacity, and agility.

The significance of physical fitness for good health and clear thinking—sound body, sound mind (Ragan & Shepard, 1977)—developed in 1926 when United States military draftees were found to be "physically unfit for service" (p. 387). This stirred people to demand fitness and exercise programs for all United States citizens. Fitness did not become important in schools until the

1950s, however, when a large study indicated that children were less fit than European children (Ragan & Shepard, 1977; Dauer & Pangrazi, 1989). In 1956, President Eisenhower established the President's Council on Youth Fitness (Ragan & Shepard, 1977) and the school physical education curriculum began to center on fitness.

Today, fitness training for kindergarten and primary school children is the centerpiece for most physical education programs. The fitness programs emphasize health-related fitness and they are realized through participation in varying aerobic activities like jogging and jump rope. Educators who see fitness as a goal of physical education view becoming fit as an "an individual matter," and depending on one's level of fitness, a kind of "physical and mental well-being" is ascertained. However, this way of conceptualizing individuality fails to take into account social, political, and economical factors that play a large part of students' lives. The individual focus does not "empower students to make choices based on personal needs and values as well as knowledge" (Hellison & Templin, 1991, p. 16).

Essentially, fitness, important as it is for schooling, is rarely viewed as problematic. Indeed, there are drawbacks in schools' realization of the fitness paradigm in children's schooling. First, physical fitness is not seen as a social phenomenon implicated in political and economic factors. The segmentation of society into identifiable economically based neighborhoods such as a suburb, an inner city, or a welfare housing unit poses problems for students. The socioeconomic status of children is tied to their ability to participate in what are usually competition-based programs of fitness.

Students from well-off socioeconomic backgrounds have access to sports clubs or individual instruction in sports like tennis, swimming, and golf. Furthermore, parents of these students are able to involve their children in after-school physical activities because they usually have more flexible schedules, which allow them to take part in recreational activities with their children (Dixon, 1984).

Second, most physical education programs do not meet the physical fitness levels required for children to improve their cardio-respiratory functioning. Taggart (1985) has estimated that cardio-respiratory strengthening requires fitness activities to be scheduled for 15–30 minutes three to four times a week. As currently operationalized, physical education programs generally help students who already have some level of fitness—those who have access to physical activities in sports clubs or individual instruction as well as those whose parents have cars to take them to various community youth programs. Homeless children, children living in inner-city housing and others far from recreational areas such as parks, municipal pools, and spaces to play do not have the same opportunities for after-school or in-school physical fitness programs. Griffin (1985) discusses the severity of problems in operating a physical education program in one inner-city school:

> The lack of outdoor activity space prompted the physical education staff to persuade the principal to schedule physical education once a week for a double period

rather than the regularly scheduled 45 minute class twice a week. The change gave the classes time to walk across the street and use the athletic fields in the city park. Since this was a *15 minute walk each way,* using the park would have been impossible during the 45 minute class. (p. 158)

In this case, additional problems occurred at the athletic fields: first, the staff discovered that they could not use the fields because of re-seeding operations; and second, only small groups of students could be taught in these playing fields as they were not designed for large physical education classes (Griffin, 1985). In out-of-school situations, children in this predicament, like children everywhere, may develop equipment and facilities of their own choosing as a group or as individuals and create new games and play activities or modify games to their particular social and cultural environments (Chepyator-Thomson, 1990) to make life more livable.

African American children's ways of playing basketball attest to this concept of creativity; they have, as explained by Sachs and Abraham (1979), modified basketball to accommodate their social and cultural milieu by using "moves" to outmaneuver an opponent to the basket. For African Americans, basketball has helped the development of self-concept and the achievement of status in the community (Sachs & Abraham, 1979).

In summary, a fitness paradigm in the public school system requires adequate time allotted to the subject, adequate staffing, and the availability of adequate facilities and equipment for the conduct of physical education programs (Ragan & Shepard, 1977). However, far too many schools fail to fill children's needs in ways that permit an effective enactment of the fitness paradigm. Teachers have to be made aware of the social and political factors that influence the development and implementation of fitness activities in the public schools.

Developmentally Based Physical Education

The development of the child is the major focus of developmentally based physical education programs (Hoffman, Young, & Klesius, 1985). The developmentally based approach addresses the why, how, and what of movement and aims at helping children use ways of moving that are appropriate to their stage of cognitive, psychomotor, and affective development (Hoffman, Young, & Klesius, 1985). A child's psychomotor development, for example, may be reflected in her/his social and emotional development:

> If a child is not capable of coping with his/[her] physical environment with regard to societal expectations, he/[she] becomes less of a person in the eyes of society, thus social and emotional characteristics are affected. If a person lags in social and emotional aspects of total development, there may be lessened tendency to engage in physical endeavours and cooperative play with his/[her] peers. (Auxter, 1973, p. 39)

Developmentally based physical education uses an activity-based curriculum. In elementary school, the emphasis is on developing games skills, educational gymnastics skills, and dance movement skills (Siedentop, Herkowitz, & Rink, 1984; Siedentop, Mand, & Taggart, 1986). In middle school, the emphasis is on team and individual sports, fitness, recreational activities, and swimming (Siedentop, Mand, & Taggart, 1986). Children participate in a wide variety of activities in short two-to-three-week units (Hellison & Templin, 1991), featuring sports like volleyball or soccer.

Developmentally based physical education helps children progress from simple to advanced patterns of movement. Class activities are arranged in such a way that there is a relationship between each, and the curriculum takes into account the developmental ability of the children by ordering the essential activities of a class from simple to complex (Auxter, 1973). For example, the gymnasium might be divided into four sections. In section one, children throw balls at designated targets using elementary skills, while in section four, the children practice throwing activity using advanced skills. The teacher's plans for developmental experiences help children acquire qualitative changes in their social, physical and emotional types of development.

The developmentally based perspective has a major drawback: Teachers sometimes have a tendency to divide children into groups based on ability both in the classroom and the gymnasium. Such groupings can result in less-skilled children becoming tracked in physical education classes for "less-developed" learners. One way to avoid this is to use cooperative learning methods, such as having a good soccer player teach a group of children a particular soccer skill. In play situations, a teacher would introduce a "handicap" for excellent players.

Another drawback is that the kind of equipment used could determine placement in the different levels of activity participation. Familiarity with equipment such as hoops, balls, and pins plays a big role in students' acquisition of content knowledge. Students' exposure to such equipment could be based in part on the socioeconomic standing of the school or the community and also could be based on the parents' ability to provide particular experiences in their children's development.

Another disadvantage to the developmentally based physical education program is found in the Eurocentric focus in the type of games played, gymnastic and sports programs developed, and in the dances taught at the elementary and middle school levels. There has not been much deviation from European cultural groups' traditional physical activities in the curriculum and instruction programs used in public school physical education.

Movement Education

Movement education began in England as a counterpoint to structured fitness programs. In the United States, movement education became the dominant paradigm in elementary schools, particularly in the 1960s and '70s (Nichols, 1986). The goals of movement education are (1) to help children become physically fit and skillful movers in varying environmental situations, (2) to teach children to comprehend movement concepts, (3) to facilitate self-discipline and self-reliance in children so they can work on ideas either individually or in groups of two or more, and (4) to provide opportunities for creative expression (Kirchner, Cunningham, & Warrell, 1978).

As a child-centered curriculum, movement education emphasizes individual problem-solving and promotes children's abilities to adapt to their own physical and emotional potentials. It encourages a variety of activities and ways of applying the elements of space, force, time, and flow which are essential to this paradigm (Kirchner et al., 1978). Games, gymnastics, and dance activities are used to build children's abilities. The instructional patterns of movement education permit teachers to learn more about each child in a non-competitive and self-expressive manner when they are performing physical activities, to use a conversational speaking voice when addressing the students, and to guide the students individually in educational activities of the class (Kruger & Kruger, 1982). In movement education, teachers provide children with opportunities to learn at their own level of readiness; they enhance children's creativity and independent thinking by teaching in a way that encourages children's "inventiveness, initiative, and imagination" (Ragan & Shepard, 1977, p. 392). Further, movement education is designed to emphasize children's individual responsibility and self-discipline by allowing children to "assume responsibility for their own physical actions," and also to promote the perceptual-motor development of children by helping them to "develop their awareness and control of their bodies" (Ragan & Shepard, 1977, p. 392).

On the surface, the goals and instructional plans of movement education appear worthy, but the games, gymnastics, and dance activities taught by "movement" educators are grounded in Western European cultures. The elements of the movement education paradigm—space, time, flow, and force—are founded on European types of movement; for example, there is a correspondence between children's movements resulting from uses of space, flow, time, and force with movement repertoires expressed in ballet. For the movement education paradigm to reflect African movements, as evidenced in Les Ballet Africains (a dance group from West Africa that toured the United States in 1991), educators and prospective teachers must be schooled in varying cultural perspectives. Les Ballet Africains brings out the rhythms of life in West Africa; life situations are symbolized with strong rhythmic movements that are mainly characterized by the use of fine-motor rather than gross-motor muscles.

Humanistic Physical Education

The focus of a humanistic physical education paradigm is on a student's personal liberation and self-actualization (McNeil, 1985). Its major goals are the development of individuals' attitudes and feelings in relation to the subject matter. Educators with a humanistic orientation believe that "knowledge is personal and subjective and results from a person's interpretation of the world" (McNeil, 1985, p. 5). Thus, students learn the subject matter in the context of their individual capabilities.

Humanistic physical education is a student-centered curriculum that offers children a choice of activities and emphasizes process learning in an "atmosphere of understanding, compassion, encouragement, and trust" (Wiles & Bondi, 1984, p. 363). Teachers emphasize students' individuality and ask for their input into how and what they teach. Students' personal excellence in the educational performances of the class is stressed and their differing learning outcomes are allowed; the teachers acknowledge student individualities.

Hellison's (1985) concepts of self-control, self-responsibility and caring are employed in teachers' instructional plans; these concepts are used hierarchically in instruction as students move from being irresponsible to being self-responsible. With these instructional orientations, children in elementary and middle school are provided with varying movement experiences in which they acquire disciplinary-based and personally-based knowledge. The movement experiences are provided through play, physical fitness, aerobics, and general conditioning activities as well as through games, sports, and dance activities.

Humanistic physical education can be problematic in that it leaves out the conditional connections to the school curriculum that include cultural, social, political, and economic factors: School curriculum is not a neutral enterprise but interacts with society—in this respect, the curriculum is intimately connected to (1) cultural preferences of the dominant culture, (2) the social conditions of the communities in which schooling takes place, (3) the political orientations of the communities, and (4) the economic reality existing in the country or in the immediate communities.

For example, physical education for lower elementary school students was eliminated in a city school district in northwestern New York while the suburban area school districts retained their physical education programs. Because children's interpretation of their world is tied to the four factors stated in the previous paragraph, teachers must carefully develop curriculum and instruction. This is crucial for physical education programs because, in most situations, content development and its implementation have had little to do with children's cultural or social realities.

In summary, several paradigms have guided the philosophical orientation of physical education in elementary and middle schools. The elementary school curriculum is designed to allow children to develop an understanding of fundamental movement concepts and patterns, to perform the movement patterns adequately and efficiently, and to respond cognitively to new circumstances. The aim of the curriculum is to have the children master elementary forms of movement and cognition in preparation for middle school physical education.

The middle school physical education curriculum focuses on advanced, more specific forms of movement and cognition. The children are taught a variety of sport skills such as dual, individual, and team sports activities. The children acquire an appreciation of many skills and activities and learn to make intelligent choices in activity participation and other related life configurations.

A Visionary Perspective for Curricular Reform in Physical Education

A visionary perspective entails conceptualizing new possibilities for physical education. The development of new curricula in physical education should reflect not only diversification but also the changing social, cultural, and political conditions that continually alter the surroundings and goals of schools and their students. Curricular reform in physical education should accommodate the multicultural population of learners and address the issues of equity and justice as these are realized in school curricula.

Essentially, education with a multicultural perspective requires professionals to develop school programs that aid students' understanding of themselves and others, and also help them understand and appreciate the diverse ethnic and racial groups in the United States. Programs of curriculum and instruction ought to be developed in a way that they "produce awareness, acceptance, and affirmation of cultural diversity" (Grant & Sleeter, 1989, p. 53). Providing teachers and youngsters with accurate and sufficient knowledge about their own and other cultures in educational institutions is crucial for eradicating "myths and stereotypes" about people of color and other groups in the country (Sachs & Poole, 1989).

Multicultural education "is the recognition and the appreciation of diversity within the teaching content of every discipline and in the context of the whole life of the school" (Department of Education, California, p. 1). Sizemore (1990)—among others—has said "the standard [United States] school curriculum simply does not present the complete facts of history, literature, art, music, drama, science, or other aspects of [United States'] diverse cultures" (p. 82). Sizemore further pointed out that a curriculum with a pluralistic perspective takes into consideration "all the groups in society and their need for freedom, equality, work, and peace" (p. 83). Developing curriculum with a multicultural perspective provides "all pupils with a more relevant and appropriate educational experience" (Troyna & Smith, 1983, p. 9). In the following section, the development of paradigm variations in the school physical education curriculum is focused on with an emphasis on multicultural play, games, sports, and movement activities.

Paradigms

The four paradigms in curriculum discussed earlier have been accepted as viable ways to think about physical education in the United States. Two additional formulations are suggested here: social reconstruction-based and culture-based paradigms. These two paradigms, like the others, would permeate the curricula and the instructional plans developed in physical education. In these new conceptions of physical education, social issues and cultural content should be infused into the physical education curriculum.

Social Reconstruction Paradigm   In the social reconstruction paradigm, physical education addresses the unequal representation of people's cultural formulations of reality in educational institutions. Eisner (1991) calls representation a "codified" reality (p. 127) and the kind that the educational institutions have put in place is of a Eurocentric type. In physical education, a codified reality can be seen in structured movement forms—games, sports (such as basketball), and folk and social dance emphasized in children's classes.

The language, codes, and values embedded in the curriculum are of the dominant Eurocentric culture. Examples include the following:

- **Competition-based curriculum and instruction in physical education.** Essentially, the curriculum and the types of instruction that tend to be used in an activity-based program center on competition. Students are divided into formal teams at the beginning of a unit. The teacher acts as a coach, overseeing the tournaments. At the end of the unit, a team emerges as the winner of the tournament.
- **Dance-based movement forms.** The language and codes are derived from European dances. Examples include folk and square dance and ballroom dance. In part, such curricula continue to permeate schools because students in teacher education are trained in content development and in ways of teaching that follow the social, normative, and economic assumptions of the culture in which they are found. (Walters, 1989)

Curriculum and instruction derived from a social reconstruction perspective render the "collective experiences and interests of a wide range of groups" a meaningful status in the United States schools (Banks, 1991, p. 138). With a social reconstructionist perspective, physical education students learn to analyze how sports have developed in United States schools; they learn how many other cultural groups have been ignored in physical education. Specifically, children learn to play activities and games of other cultural groups in the United States. In addition, they learn the meanings associated with the play activities and games. The social reconstructionist perspective harbors ideals necessary for reforming "society towards a greater equity in race, class, gender, and handicap" (Grant & Sleeter, 1989, p. 54).

Varying movement possibilities and different types of equipment are needed to actualize a social reconstructionist physical education curriculum. The elements of dance, gymnastics, and games across cultures require physical educators to develop curricula and use instructional styles and strategies that meet the needs of all children. This is especially important because the United

States physical education curriculum has alienated children from outside the dominant culture. This alienation has taken several forms:

- The games and sports they play at home are not part of the school physical education curriculum.
- The concepts-based physical education curriculum does not use concepts outside the mainstream's cultural frameworks.
- The teaching methods and strategies such as indirect teaching and an individually based instructional strategy leave many children out of the teaching and learning situations.

Culture-Based Paradigm   If play activities and games are considered "integral to our culture" and help "enhance the health and vitality of the culture" (Hellison & Templin, 1991, p. 99), then they should be multicultural because the United States society is composed of many different racial and ethnic cultures. The knowledge selected for sharing with children should be culturally based.

Culture shapes the way students view themselves and molds their relations to various pedagogy and learning (Giroux & Simon, 1988). In this context, it is paramount to pursue the teaching of students from varying perspectives and to consider content development that takes into account the many cultures of the United States. The lack of representation of different ethnic ideals in curriculum and instruction has been noted by Hargreaves (1986), who points out a lack of opportunity for ethnic dance in the schools.

To include every child in the curriculum, the knowledge selected in its development should reflect the values and life experiences of all students, particularly from the perspective of race, gender, and class. Multicultural knowledge should be taught to students in all schools even though some schools may have a homogeneous student population (Travers & Rebore, 1987). Such knowledge ought to be derived from diverse ethnic sources so that the games played are multicultural (Chepyator-Thomson, 1990). The sources for different cultural information can include periodicals, authentic textbooks, and personal communication with people from groups outside the mainstream.

Educators can enhance their knowledge of the nonrepresented groups by subscribing to ethnic magazines and journals to acquaint themselves with these groups' social and cultural affiliations. This form of seeking knowledge is important because "curriculum along multicultural lines . . . is seen as crucial . . . in providing all pupils with a more relevant and appropriate educational experience" (Troyna & Smith, 1983, p. 9). Essentially, educators should ascertain that multicultural literature used in curriculum development includes minority group experiences and perspectives.

Another source of information about students' culture and interests is the students themselves. Drawing on students' conceptions of reality—that is, how games are organized and played in their environment—as sources for curriculum development, validates the students' lives and enhances teachers' understanding of their backgrounds. The development of a curriculum of this nature can promote a pride in children of nondominant groups and a respect for their culture in the dominant group's children.

For example, providing all students with relevant education means defining course content such that American Indian values and customs and their contribution to play forms in the United States are included. "American Indians have something different that was bestowed upon [them] by the grace of God, such as [their] songs, tribal dances, arts and crafts, [their] religion, and games and stories" (Wesley, 1961, p. 7). One way of designing a curriculum from an American Indian perspective is to invite parents to be part of the curricular development team (National Indian Brotherhood, 1984).

Frey and Allen's (1989) study of Alaskan and American Indian groups' games has provided a beginning for development of a multicultural curriculum in physical education. The groups' traditional games were used in the construction of elementary school physical education curricula in the Anchorage school district. The games were modified for safety considerations and the developmental levels of the children. The games have provided "an enjoyable and efficient way to develop multicultural awareness in students and teachers" (Frey & Allen, 1989, p. 21). The Alaskan and American Indian groups value cooperation and self-competition and emphasize "group cohesion, pain tolerance, and respect for environment as important as muscular strength, cardiorespiratory endurance, and speed" (p. 22). The traditional games of the groups reflect these values. The Alaskan and Indian groups' games require "great physical strength, agility, balance, endurance, and concentration" (Frey & Allen, 1989, p. 22). The paradigms of physical fitness and developmentally based, humanistic physical education can be identified and are valued in such a curriculum.

Although there could be a support for the authors' study of the Alaskan and American Indian groups' games, there could be a disagreement on the way they have presented the games in relation to the development of the physical education curriculum

First, the idea that "importing traditional, yet unknown, physical activities from different cultures is an exciting way to add creativity and imagination to the physical education curriculum, without having to be creative or imaginative in the traditional sense" is problematic. Frey and Allen's (1989) statements seem to rest on the assumption that children do not have to be as creative or imaginative to play and dance these games as when they might traditionally be asked to be "creative." What should be brought to the forefront is the fact that the traditional dance steps taught in United States elementary schools have been derived from European cultures and the children are asked to move "creatively" within this cultural framework. Children from other cultures can also move "creatively" within the Alaskan and American Indian groups' cultural frameworks.

Second, Alaskan and American Indian games have historically been present within these specific cultures; they were not "unknown," they were excluded from United States schools.

Third, Frey and Allen (1989) indicate that Alaskan and American Indian groups have "hundreds of games," but only "those activities that have been favourably received by the students and teachers, with teaching hints as appropriate," were presented (p. 22). Although the authors may have thought the students' and teachers' preferences were the best way to determine the games to be included in the curriculum, thematic identification of games would have been more appropriate. The curriculum developers and teachers would have been forced to identify, from the Alaskan and American Indian groups' perspectives, the themes that characterize the games.

In summary, the paradigm possibilities for reforming the physical education curriculum have been discussed with a multicultural orientation. Physical education teachers need to develop a multicultural curriculum by researching the literature for play activities and games that are characteristic of diverse groups in the United States society. Such a curriculum and its implementation must include all students in our educational institutions.

In developing a multicultural curriculum, teachers are cautioned that books, texts, or periodical articles on minority groups (population-wise) such as African Americans or American Indians may be inadequate. Therefore, teachers are encouraged to use a variety of sources in developing multicultural play activities and games for teaching physical education in schools.

Implications for Reform in Teacher Education: Curriculum Development and Implementation

Curriculum Development

Trent (1990) has argued for the inclusion of "scholarship on race and ethnicity as a core part of the preparation of the nation's teachers" (p. 360) and provides three compelling reasons for this:

1. The student body is becoming more diverse.
2. The economic future of the nation depends on meeting the educational needs of this diverse population.
3. The teaching force is becoming more female and more White.

Trent (1990) mentions a national survey indicating that teachers' competency with people of color is limited because of their "inadequate undergraduate exposure to course content familiarizing them with the experiences of minorities and limited cross-race contact or multicultural experiences in or out of school. . . " (p. 366). In the institutions of higher education, curriculum enhancement may include the creation of a multidisciplinary course focusing on developing future teachers' comprehensive knowledge of cultural differences and issues of cultural understanding.

Another way to reform the physical education curriculum is to have educators identify play activities and games of their own cultural backgrounds and compare them with those of other cultures for similarities and differences. This will help educators select classroom content that is multicultural; they would conceptualize a curriculum that reflects the diverse clientele in public school systems and teach prospective teachers accordingly.

Becoming familiar with diverse ethnic populations is also important in reforming the physical education curriculum. Higher education professionals should come to know diverse ethnic populations and try to provide prospective teachers with experiences associated with a diverse student body.

For example, attending performances by African American dance groups such as Les Ballet Africains, American Indian dance performers, or Hispanic American dance performers can help teachers view and begin to understand the cultures of diverse peoples. Knowledge gained from these experiences could be used to design relevant curriculum and answer an often-asked question: "What knowledge is of most worth in curriculum development?"

Teacher Preparation-Pedagogy

As might be expected, teachers' pedagogical practices are closely related to their individual experiences in education (Guskey, 1986). Indeed, teachers tend to teach students in the same way as they were taught. With this understanding, it is critical to take into consideration that "teachers' ideological beliefs are related, directly or indirectly, to their instructional planning and decision making" in physical education classroom settings (Rich, 1990, p. 82).

Teachers' Values and Beliefs   One's sense of self is grounded in one's values and beliefs. The values and beliefs that teachers and prospective teachers hold about themselves frame their subject matter knowledge and the practical applications of this knowledge. Teachers have personal values about physical activity (Hellison & Templin, 1991, p. 44) and these values influence not only teacher-student interactions but also teachers' instruction. Hellison and Templin (1991) have argued that we want teachers to "get in touch with their motives and values and then examine them to determine whether they hold up under scrutiny and particularly whether they are relevant for [students]" (p. 44).

Essentially, teachers and prospective teachers in physical education ought to clarify their beliefs through the development of their personal philosophies and review them periodically as they gain experience and knowledge about the subject matter (Schurr, 1980). Teachers also need to remember that children come with their own cultural frames that might conflict with the teachers' frames. Given a multicultural orientation vision in physical education, the content of instruction in teacher education ought to acknowledge student experiential and cultural frame differences. Programs should focus on "the knowledge and experience necessary to enable teachers to envision and implement a model of excellence to which all students are entitled" (Trent, 1990, p. 364).

Teachers need to maintain an environment in which all students see themselves in positive ways in games and play activities. This involves structuring activities creatively and teaching these to students in ways that enhance their learning, particularly in motor skill development. Essentially, teachers need to promote the academic achievement of all students by responding to their individual needs—regardless of race, gender, socioeconomic group or language background. Teachers need to maintain high and consistent expectations for all students and diversify their teaching techniques.

References

Arnold, P. (1988). *Education, movement, and curriculum*. New York: The Falmer Press.

Auxter, D. (1973). A philosophy of developmental physical education. In R. A. Cobb and P. M. Lepley (Eds.), *Contemporary philosophies of physical education and athletics* (p. 59). Englewood Cliffs, NJ: Merrill/Prentice Hall.

Banks, J. A. (1991, Spring). Multicultural literacy and curriculum reform. *Educational Horizons, 69*(3), 135–140.

Barney, R. B. (1975). German turners in America: Their role in nineteenth century expression and physical education legislation. In E. F. Zeigler (Ed.), *The history of physical education and sport in the United States and Canada* (pp. 111–120). Stipes Publishing Company.

Brown, J. (1992). Personal communication.

Chepyator-Thomson, J. R. (1990). Traditional games of Keiyo children: A comparison of pre- and post-independent periods in Kenya. *Interchange, 21*(2), 15–25.

Craft, M. (Ed.). (1984). *Education and cultural pluralism*. London: The Falmer Press.

Dauer, V. P., & Pangrazi, R. P. (1975). *Dynamic physical education for elementary school children*. Minneapolis, MN: Burgess.

Dauer, V. P., & Pangrazi, R. P. (1989). *Dynamic physical education for elementary school children*. Englewood Cliffs, NJ: Merrill/Prentice Hall.

Department of Education, California. (1977). *Bureau of intergroup relations*. Sacramento, CA: Bureau of Publications.

Dixon, M. (1984, September/October). Participation in physical activity: Option or privilege? *CAHPER Journal, 51*(1), 13–17.

Eisner, E. W. (1991, Spring). Rethinking literacy. *Educational Horizons, 69*(3), 120–128.

Ennis, C. D., & Chepyator-Thomson, J. R. (1991). Learning characteristics of field-dependent children within an analytical concept-based curriculum. *Journal of Teaching in Physical Education, 10*(2), 170–187.

Frey, R. D., & Allen, M. (1989). Alaskan native games—a cross-cultural addition to the physical education curriculum. *Journal of Physical Education, Recreation and Dance, 60*(9), 21–24.

Gage, N. L. (Ed.). (1963). *Handbook of research on teaching.* Chicago: Rand McNally.

Geadelmann, P. L., Bischoff, J., Hoferek, M., & McKnight, D. B. (1989). Sex equity in physical education and athletics. In S. M. Klein (Ed.), *Handbook for achieving sex equity through education* (pp. 319–337). Baltimore: John Hopkins University Press.

Giroux, H. A., & Simon, R. C. (1988). Schooling, popular culture, and a pedagogy of possibility. *Journal of Education, 170*(1), 9–26.

Grant, C., & Sleeter, C. E. (1989). Race, class, gender, exceptionality, and educational reform. In J. A. Banks and C. A. Banks (Eds.), *Multicultural education: Issues and perspectives* (pp. 46–65). Boston: Allyn and Bacon.

Griffin, P. S. (1985). Teaching in an urban, multiracial physical education program. *Quest, 37,* 154–165.

Guskey, T. (1986). Staff development and the process of teacher change. *Educational Researcher, 15*(5), 5–12.

Hannan, B. (1982). The multicultural school or schools in search of their culture. In G. Dow (Ed.), *Teacher learning* (pp. 79–110). London: Routledge & Kegan Paul.

Hellison, D. R. (1985). *Goals and strategies for teaching physical education.* Champaign, IL: Human Kinetics.

Hellison, D. R., & Templin, T. J. (1991). *A reflective approach to teaching physical education.* Champaign, IL: Human Kinetics.

Hoffman, H. A., Young, J., & Klesius, S. E. (1985). *Meaningful movement for children: A developmental theme approach to physical education.* Dubuque, IA: Kendall/Hunt.

Jewett, A. E., & Bain, L. L. (1985). *The curriculum process in physical education.* Dubuque, IA: Wm. C. Brown.

Kirchner, G. (1978). *Physical education for elementary school children.* Dubuque, IA: Wm. C. Brown.

Kirchner, G., Cunningham, J., & Warrell, E. (1978). *Introduction to movement education.* Dubuque, IA: Wm. C. Brown.

Kruger, H., & Kruger, J. M. (1982). *Movement education in physical education.* Dubuque, IA: Wm. C. Brown.

Locke, L. F. (1969). Movement education: A description and critique. In R. C. Brown, Jr., and B. J. Cratty (Eds.), *New perspectives of man in action* (pp. 200–226). Englewood Cliffs, NJ: Prentice-Hall.

Logsdon, B. J., Barrett, K. R., Ammons, M., Broer, M. R., Halverson, L. E., McGee, R., & Roberton, M. A. (1977). *Physical education for children: A focus on the teaching process.* Philadelphia: Lea & Febiger.

McNeil, J. D. (1985). *Curriculum: A comprehensive introduction.* Boston: Allyn & Bacon.

Murray, M. (1991). Media impact on women in sport and sport leadership. *Journal of Physical Education, Recreation & Dance, 62*(3), 45–47.

National Indian Brotherhood. (1984). Indian control of education. In J. R. Mallea and J. C. Young (Eds.), *Cultural diversity and Canadian education: Issues and innovation* (pp. 131–149). Ottawa: Carleton Press.

Nichols, B. (1986). *Moving and learning: The elementary school physical education experience.* St. Louis: Times Mirror/Mosby.

Ngugi wa Thiongo. (1986). *Homecoming*. London: Heinemann.

Parmee, E. A. (1968). *Formal education and culture change*. Tucson, AZ: The University of Arizona Press.

Ragan, W. B., & Shepard, G. D. (1977). *Modern elementary curriculum*. New York: Holt, Rinehart and Winston.

Rice, E. A., Hutchinson, J. L., & Lee, M. (1969). *A brief history of physical education*. New York: The Ronald Press Company.

Rich, Y. (1990). Ideological impediments to instructional innovation: The case of cooperative learning. *Teaching & Teacher Education, 6*(1), 81–91.

Sachs, M., & Abraham, A. (1979, February). Playground basketball: A qualitative field examination. *Journal of Sports Behaviour, 2*(1), 27–36.

Sachs, J. M., & Poole, M. E. (1989). Multicultural education policies in Australia and Britain: Social transformation or status quo? *Education and Society, 71*(1), 9–19.

Schoem, D., & Stevenson, M. (1990). Teaching ethnic identity and intergroup relations: The case of Black-Jewish dialogue. *Teachers College Record, 91*(4), 579–594.

Schurr, E. L. (1980). *Movement experiences for children: A humanistic approach to elementary school physical education*. Englewood Cliffs, NJ: Prentice-Hall.

Siedentop, D., Mand, C., & Taggart, A. (1986). *Physical education: Teaching and curriculum strategies for grades 5–12*. Mountain View, CA: Mayfield.

Siedentop, D., Herkowitz, J., & Rink, J. (1984). *Elementary physical education*. Englewood Cliffs, NJ: Prentice-Hall.

Sizemore, B. A. (1990). The politics of curriculum, race, and class. *Journal of Negro Education, 59*(1), 77–85.

Taggart, A. (1985). Fitness-direct instruction. *Journal of Teaching in Physical Education, 4*(2), 143–150.

Travers, P., & Rebore, R. (1987). *Foundations of education: Becoming a teacher*. Englewood Cliffs, NJ: Prentice-Hall.

Trent, W. (1990). Race and ethnicity in the teacher education curriculum. *Teachers College Record, 91*(3), 361–369.

Troyna, B., & Smith, D. T. (Eds.). (1983). *Racism, school and the labour market*. Leicester, England: AB Printers Ltd.

Van Dalen, D. B., Mitchell, E. D., & Bennett, B. C. (1953). *A world history of physical education*. Englewood Cliffs, NJ: Prentice-Hall.

Van Dalen, D. B., & Bennett, B. C. (1971). *A world history of physical education* (2nd ed.). Englewood Cliffs, NJ: Prentice-Hall.

Walters, K. S. (1989). Critical thinking in teacher education: Towards a demythologization. *Journal of Teacher Education. 40*(3), 14–19.

Wesley, C. (1961). Indian education. *Journal of Indian Education, 1*(1), 4–7.

Wiles, J., & Bondi, J. C. (1984). *Curriculum development*. London: Charles E. Merrill.

Zeigler, E. F. (1988). *History of physical education and sport*. Champaign, IL: Stipes Publishing Company.

Chapter 15

◆ ◆ ◆ ◆

Integrating Diversity and Multiculturalism in Health Education

Veronica M. Acosta-Deprez

Auburn University

Introduction

Health is a fundamental concern that transcends all cultures and peoples. It is every human being's desire to feel well and live long. Health affects one's way of looking at the world, the ability to laugh or cry, and the capacity to live and learn. The National Education Association Commission made health the top priority in its list of Seven Cardinal Principles of Education (1976) when they recognized its crucial influence on learning.

Because of its individual applicability, education about health should include information that students can integrate and relate to their own lives. Health education involves opportunities and " . . . learning experiences designed to assist individuals, groups, or communities . . . in control of their own health as they define it" (American Public Health Association, 1987). Health education is, essentially, something that needs to be tailored to the culture, if not the individual.

A multicultural approach to health education will benefit both teachers and students. The integration of cross-cultural concepts into health education will make teaching easier and more effective, and will reinforce learning as well as make it more interesting for students.

This chapter examines the relationship of culture and health and provides a rationale for integrating multicultural concepts into health education. When the teacher's health culture differs from that of the student, conflicts may result. The next section describes some situations in which these conflicts may arise. Approaches to multicultural health education also will be explored, including some perspectives and teaching guidelines.

The Need for Multicultural Health Education

Cultural beliefs and practices affect one's health. Each culture embodies a set of beliefs and practices that influence health-seeking, health maintenance, and patterns of coping with illness (MacDonald, 1988). *Culture* is defined by Wurzel (1988) as the information a group uses to create the meaning necessary for its members to survive as a group. In interacting with their environment, a group establishes rules or guidelines that include preferred ways of perceiving, judging, and organizing ideas, situations, and events. Culture represents these rules or guidelines (Maehr, 1974).

Cultural, religious, and ethnic beliefs and values must be integrated into health education programs to increase the likelihood that these programs will be effective. When students can understand and apply what is being taught in their own lives, they are more likely to learn and become interested in it. When what is taught is consistent with students' cultural beliefs and practices, students will more likely adapt healthful recommendations made by their teachers.

Cultural beliefs and practices influence children's perceptions regarding four health belief (Greene & Simons-Morton, 1984) categories: (1) the seriousness of a disease, (2) their susceptibility to the disease, (3) the benefits and costs, and (4) barriers to taking preventive action. Children from different cultural and ethnic groups have different orientations to health and illness and, therefore, vary in their perceptions about their vulnerability to health problems (Stone & Crouch, 1979). When Anglo, Hispanic, and American Indian students were asked to rank the 14 health problems they perceived as "most likely to occur," the answers varied among the three groups. Anglo students ranked upset stomach, headache, and colds at the top of the list, in that order. Hispanic students ranked headache, upset stomach, and colds; while American Indian students ranked sore throat, headache, and colds to be the problems most likely to occur.

If teachers are aware of students' perceptions regarding their health and health problems, they will be more able to cultivate disease prevention strategies that are consistent with students' beliefs. Additionally, such awareness will enable teachers to set up school health services that respond to their students' needs.

Another reason for using a multicultural approach is that health education presents a venue through which the health status of many disadvantaged population groups may be improved. Through health education, important information on prevention that targets the needs of certain population groups may be disseminated. Three of these groups are described here as examples: people with low incomes, certain race or ethnic minority groups, and people with disabilities.

People with Low Incomes

There is a great disparity between the health of the poor and those with higher incomes (Department of Health and Human Services, 1992, p. 29). Across the age spectrum, there are twice as many deaths below the poverty level than above it (Amler & Dull, 1987). The risk of death from heart disease is more than 25 percent higher for low-income people than for the overall population (National Heart, Lung, & Blood Institute, National Cholesterol Education Program, 1990). Poverty has also been associated with infant mortality, and the the likelihood of poor pregnancy outcomes such as low birth weight, prematurity, birth defects and infant death (Institute of Medicine, 1985). Poverty also is linked with high chronic disease incidence, increased vulnerability to risk factors linked to injury and disease such as obesity and high blood pressure, and tobacco use (Office on Smoking and Health, 1987; Feigelman & Gorman, 1989). Significant developmental limitations such as lack of growth and mental retardation have also been linked to poverty (National Health Interview Survey, 1988).

Racial or Ethnic Groups

Some racial or ethnic groups have suffered disparities in health status compared with the majority population. Many environmental as well as socioeconomic elements push particular racial and ethnic groups to become vulnerable to health problems and diseases (Heckler, 1985a, 1985b). Poverty, for example, increases the rate of infant mortality among African Americans and Hispanics. Living in urban or highly industrialized areas rather than in rural or less-industrialized areas places numerous racial and ethnic groups at a high risk for acquiring stress-related ailments. High-fat, high-sodium, high-sugar foods, as well as dietary patterns that characterize southern American diets, may also increase the incidence of malnutrition among racial or ethnic groups living in the South.

Several studies have suggested a high prevalence of medical and social-related problems in specific racial or ethnic groups (Furstenberg, 1987; Hopkins, 1987). Most of these problems were attributed to socioeconomic conditions although "when socioeconomic effects are set aside, disparities experienced by these population groups will still be observed" (Department of Health and Human Services, 1992, p. 32). This means that differences in health status may not solely be linked to poverty, nor environmental factors or educational attainment, but to the existence of a combination of factors which place groups in high-risk disease categories.

Besides environmental and socioeconomic factors, some members of racial or ethnic groups have also endured discrimination and inadequate treatment by the current health-care system. Some racial or ethnic groups experience conditions that can only be traced to their genetic and physical makeup. Examples of these conditions are thalassemia and sickle-cell anemia, blood disorders that are more prevalent among people of Mediterranean and African descent. Because of the rarity of these conditions, many health-care professionals may not have had the training to deal with them; thus, people who have the conditions may be misdiagnosed, or receive inadequate or inappropriate treatment.

People with Disabilities

The number of people with chronic disabilities varies from 34 million to 43 million (Department of Health and Human Services, 1992). People with disabilities are represented in all racial, ethnic, age, and gender groups. *Disability* may be defined in terms of functional limitation; it may be categorized as mental/emotional or physical; motor or sensory. Physical disabilities may include an inability to walk resulting from a congenital birth defect or an injury or leg amputation stemming from an accident. Mental disabilities may include mild to severe degrees of retardation. Emotional disabilities may result from negative environmental and societal conditions such as child abuse, alcohol or drug abuse, and sexual abuse. Negative family or cultural attitudes may increase health risks of some people with disabilities.

People with disabilities are more susceptible to secondary conditions that may occur in relation to the main cause of disability. "People with disabilities are at higher risk of future problems that can only increase the limitations that they experience" (Department of Health and Human Services, 1992, p. 39). Secondary health problems due to lack of adequate rehabilitation, personal assistance, and maintenance therapies, inconsistencies and inequities in existing programs, and lack of insurance are more likely to occur among people with disabilities.

It is the responsibility of teachers to address as many needs as possible and help all students achieve the highest level of wellness. To serve the needs of all Americans, the cultural diversity and richness of this country needs to be acknowledged and incorporated into the present curriculum. "A society as rich in cultural diversity as the United States does students disservice when its educational curriculum is primarily monolithic" (Airhihenbuwa & Pineiro, 1988). A multicultural society in which the desire to "melt" everyone into some stereotypical American image will, at best, serve only a minority elite.

While there is no single solution to the health problems of all students, teachers can help students think constructively about their health and behaviors. The next section describes prevailing personal as well as professional ethnocentrism among teachers, and potential conflicts that may arise when the teacher's culture clashes with that of the student.

Ethnocentrism and Potential Cultural Conflicts

Teachers often exhibit a degree of personal or professional "ethnocentrism"—a universal pride in one's ethnic or cultural group—which prevents them from presenting unbiased and unprejudiced cultural and ethnic viewpoints. Teachers must guard against this because many health topics are morally laden and controversial in nature and cannot be fully explored if teacher bias and prejudice predominate.

Health teachers need to understand that the profession within which they function adheres to one of many cultures of health (Spector, 1985). This health culture, grounded in the tenets of scientific medicine, attributes the cause of disease to such agents as bacteria, viruses, and chemicals; and uses disease terms such as pneumonia, influenza, or AIDS to identify the illness. Only those certified by their particular "science-based" profession are sanctioned to intervene and treat diseases and illnesses. Through their teaching and work, health teachers transmit their culture of health to students. Other ways of healing than those that have been "scientifically proven," other types of healers than those who have been certified within the laws of their profession, or other types of health knowledge are not usually recognized or accepted. As such, a sense of cultural ethnocentrism is displayed in the health education profession.

Some students have similar health cultures with that of the teacher. Others have different cultures. Those adhering to other health cultures may use terms such as *spirit possession, spells,* and *soul loss* to designate disease cause. They may attribute disease to another person and not to a pathogen or microorganism. They may sanction *spiritists, faith healers,* or *psychic surgeons* to intervene in the treatment of disease. When cultural conflicts occur, instructions or recommendations from the teacher may be irrelevant and ineffective.

Religious teachings and ethnic beliefs may often conflict with numerous health education tenets. Galli, Greenberg, and Tobin (1987) examined the religious teachings of Judaism and found that many of its precepts were incongruent with what is taught in schools and particularly in health education. Topics in the content areas of human sexuality, nutrition, drug education, and death and dying were explored.

Under Jewish Divine Law, for example, it is a man's obligation to "be fruitful and multiply" (*Genesis 1:28*). It is every man's responsibility to father at least a son and a daughter. Family planning and contraceptive education topics pose contradictions to this law. Several other sex education topics are in conflict with Jewish tenets as well. These include prohibition of male sterilization, vasectomy, induced abortion (except when the mother's life is in danger), artificial insemination (may be done only with the husband's sperm), and homosexuality. In health education, these topics are commonly discussed, dealt with, and provided as viable health options.

Nutrition education is another example where potential conflicts may occur. Jewish law prohibits the ingestion of blood in meats and therefore requires that meat be salted and koshered. Further, milk should not be consumed with meat; meat and dairy products should be cooked in separate containers, served in separate plates, and eaten with separate utensils. In health education, teachers inform students about lowering the intake of salt because of its connection to high blood pressure and other cardiovascular diseases. No attention is paid to particular food combinations, the use of eating utensils, or the serving of food.

Jewish laws and secular laws are similar in many drug education topics, although some rabbis use tobacco because they believe this is one of God's gifts (Jacobs, 1973). Several topics concerning death and dying, which are commonly discussed and presented as options by health educators, are prohibited under Jewish law. These topics include euthanasia, suicide, the Living Will, and organ transplants.

Some beliefs and values among Hispanics, Indochinese, and Christian Science students also can conflict with health education information. For example, some Hispanics believe in the "machismo" phenomenon, which emphasizes the fathering role of males—the more children one fathers, the more "manly" he becomes (Galli, Greenberg, & Tobin 1987; Russell, 1983). A health teacher who discusses contraceptive and family planning education concepts with Hispanic students may find their teachings contradict with the "machismo" belief.

Among some Indochinese, coining disease areas of the skin by scraping the skin to the point of bruising is done as a traditional healing practice of "cao gio." Health educators who may not be familiar with such a practice may construe the bruises as marks of child abuse and report this as such to the authorities. This may put health educators in embarrassing and potentially damaging situations.

Many families adhering to the precepts of Christian Science do not believe in the use of medical drugs or treatments such as immunizations, therapeutic procedures, and hospitalization. Yet, these elements and procedures are usually discussed, recommended and accepted as common practice in health education classrooms.

To implement multicultural health education is to encourage the exploration of alternative ideas of health and illness with students and provide them with opportunities to explore, critique, and analyze the dominant fundamental assumptions underlying the field of health education. In the following section, a definition of health education that is multicultural and social reconstructionist is provided and some perceptions and guidelines on how to integrate multicultural concepts into health education are explored.

Health Education That Is Multicultural and Social Reconstructionist

A multicultural health education involves developing and cultivating learning opportunities that are sensitive to the cultural values, attitudes and beliefs of particular groups. These learning opportunities should be designed and developed with the active involvement of the members of the target group taking into account the group's definition of health, and communicated in ways that are consistent with their level of understanding. Multicultural and social reconstructionist health education extends beyond education to include approaches that teach students to become critical thinkers and cultivate social action skills that enable them to actively participate in and control their own health and destiny (Grant & Sleeter, 1989).

Teachers may think it difficult and even impossible to know everything about a culture, let alone know several cultures. The heterogenous nature of racial and ethnic groups makes it difficult to compare their health attitudes and behaviors even within their own groups (Pahnos, 1992). Diverse attitudes and behaviors can be found among and within cultures and their individual members. How can teachers fulfill their tremendous teaching tasks and responsibilities, while simultaneously incorporating cultural, ethnic, religious, and social differences, concerns and issues? The following section provides some perspectives and suggestions or guidelines to help health teachers integrate multicultural and social reconstructionist principles into their teaching.

Teaching Perspectives and Guidelines

The challenge of incorporating multicultural health education is long overdue. If teachers are to respond to the health problems and needs of various cultural, ethnic, and religious groups, the best programs will promote health through the education of all these groups. In the following paragraphs, perceptions and guidelines are provided for teachers in the following areas: (1) reexamination of their educational philosophies; (2) integration of global and international education; (3) implementation of various teaching approaches, methods, and strategies; (4) recognition of students as our best resource; (5) involvement of parents and other family members in planning health education programs; (6) selection of instructional materials relevant to the target group; and (7) participation in planning and development of health materials and programs.

Teachers should reexamine and renew their educational philosophies.   The success of multicultural health education begins with the reexamination and renewal of teachers' educational philosophies (Pahnos, 1992). Teachers need to reflect on their own teachings; the ideology upon which their profession is based; their biases, prejudices, and ethnocentric conceptions about health; their roles and responsibilities as health educators; and their commitment to helping students achieve higher levels of health and wellness. Because cultural awareness and sensitivity are essential to successful teaching, multicultural health education should not only be added to the curriculum but also integrated into all other areas of teaching (Pahnos, 1992).

Teachers should exhibit a more open view about health as well as about their students and must accept the differences that exist in their culturally diverse classrooms. To do this, teachers may need to develop and practice personal characteristics and qualities that reflect this acceptance. These might include showing respect for students; being tolerant of different views and behaviors; avoiding statements that express bias, prejudice or judgment; and displaying sincerity, understanding, sensitivity, and compassion for all students. Teachers need to develop positive verbal as well as nonverbal communication skills such as being able to clarify and listen intently to students' views, show interest in their students' activities, provide words of encouragement, and accept a wide variety of responses as appropriate.

Teach multicultural education in the context of global or international education.   Kalantzis and Cope (1992) offer a perspective about multiculturalism as the key issue of our epoch. They describe the dichotomy between particularism and universalism, multicultural education, and global education. They suggest the propagation of a "new epistemology"—a combination of both: "When we study particular groups, we should use insights gained to try to reframe our understanding of the global" (p. B5). Many health topics are best approached from a transcultural standpoint rather than through a culture-by-culture (ethnicity-by-ethnicity) analysis. For example, we might critically analyze the relationships among poverty, illness, and health, or processes of coping with the AIDS disease as outgrowths of global—not just cultural—change.

Airhihenbuwa and Pineiro (1988) suggested that because health is "a global state with no boundaries," it is important to provide students with "knowledge and appreciation for multiethnicity and the relationship between health and cultural diversity" (p. 241). As such, the authors agree that a K–12 health curriculum should incorporate minority health concepts as well as those related to international health. The authors suggest seven issues that should be covered by such a curriculum: (1) learning about the different ethnic groups in the United States; (2) decision-making in minority populations; (3) minority role models; (4) learning from a minority member (contributions of minority health professionals); (5) facing myths and realities regarding ethnic minorities; (6) learning about nonhealth problems that can affect health status, such as unemployment, poverty, poor housing, and racial discrimination; and (7) practicing health by planning activities aimed at improving ethnic minority health status and establishing links among ethnic minorities and other nations or regions around the world.

Health teachers should not become overly enthusiastic about emphasizing differences in cultures and peoples. It is equally important to address the macro-culture—the similarities of health problems and dilemmas in all people. Pahnos (1992) concludes:

> Health educators must not be overzealous in their multicultural missions. In stressing the importance of separate cultures and ethnic groups, the unity of being one nation must not be lost. Students need to understand that through individual differences, we gel and collectively contribute to the nation's health practices and advances. Therefore, while we appreciate and respect individual needs and differences, a need remains to reunite and be one regarding important health and environmental concerns. (p. 26)

Use a variety of teaching approaches, methods, and strategies. Just as students differ in their ways of thinking, so too do they vary in their styles of learning (Kolb, 1984). Because of this diversity of learning styles, teachers should use several teaching approaches, methods, and strategies in teaching about health. Galli, Greenberg, and Tobin (1987) offer some suggestions on how to present health information that is relevant to students' religious and cultural beliefs. These suggestions include the following:

1. Bring a panel of religious leaders to class to explain the tenets of their religions pertaining to health education topics.

2. Assign projects and papers on various cultural viewpoints towards the topics, emphasizing the value of diversity.

3. Ask students to rank order such options as physical health, spiritual health, and societal health; ask them to value freedom to choose, moral imperative, and secular law, and to discuss their choices.

4. Present films in which characters wrestle with conflict between fitting into modern society and maintaining their cultural uniqueness, such as the film *The Chosen*. As an alternative, assign students to read books that portray a similar conflict.

5. Invite to class parents of students who grew up in other countries, and ask them to describe different ways people in their country of birth view health-related topics.

6. Encourage students to write the embassy of different countries inquiring about different practices and viewpoints related to health topics studied in class. In particular, have them write to countries with differing major religions.

7. Have students investigate school practices such as cafeteria meals and food preparation to determine how responsive these practices are to different people. Then students can suggest adjustments in these practices to better accommodate all students. These activities should be feasible and presented in a constructive rather than confrontational manner. (p. 179)

King (1982) developed a college course titled Multicultural Health Beliefs that proved to be successful, fun, and enlightening for students. With modification, this course could also be used for other grade levels. The purpose of the course was to increase students' knowledge about Hispanic, American Indian, and African American health beliefs. The course included trips to cultural areas in the southwestern United States, guest lectures on various health topics from members of the three ethnic groups, and writing opinion papers regarding the benefits and problems of experience related to the course.

Trips were made to Juarez, Mexico; Taos, New Mexico, the home of the Taos Pueblo Indian tribe; to Crownpoint, New Mexico, on the Navajo reservation land; and to San Felipe Pueblo, New Mexico, where a ceremony combining traditional American Indian and Catholic faith rituals was taking place. Guest lecturers included the director of alcoholism information of the Indian Health Service at Albuquerque, a physician in charge of a diabetes project involving American Indian populations, a student who had recently arrived from Thailand and discussed her culture and specific health beliefs, and a Cuban working to create a bicultural environment within Headstart for Hispanic populations.

The preceding example demonstrates that the success of a multicultural health education initiative depends on the teacher's creativity in using the instructional resources available within and outside the community. Through the activities in the course, students discovered how they were different as well as similar to people of other groups. The promotion of these discoveries among students also depends on the emotional atmosphere that teachers create when they plan endeavors that are relevant and interesting to students.

Recognize students as the best teaching resource while using other various resources.   Teachers need relevant multicultural resources to be effective. In attempting to find teaching resources, however, many teachers tend to look outside their immediate surroundings first before realizing the wealth of knowledge their students bring into the classroom. With the abundance of information that students have about health, they may be one of the best resources in teaching many health topics.

According to Poris (1989), diversity in student populations should not be seen as a threat, nor as a problem, but rather as an untapped resource. To capitalize on the wealth of cultures, traditions, and community identifications present among students, health educators can "bring a health topic to life" (Poris, 1989). Poris described some successful activities in the areas of drug education, sexuality education, and other basic health issues, that were implemented in multi-ethnic college classrooms (although with some modification, these may be utilized at other levels). Some of these activities include providing students with opportunities to compare and contrast health-related practices and customs in their home countries with that of the United States; putting together term projects related to drug issues with an application to the student's view of his/her own real world; and having students share, within small group structures, some myths and misinformation about human sexuality that they encountered while they were growing up. Poris concluded that, besides textbooks, there is a wealth of information that students can learn from each other, that student interest and participation is increased if the subject areas relate to the students' ethnic backgrounds, and that capitalizing on students as resources will permit fewer teacher-dominated lessons and greater opportunities for teachers to learn about their students' ethnic and cultural backgrounds, thus broadening their knowledge.

Involve parents and other members of the family in the education of their children. Parents have directly and indirectly influenced the knowledge, beliefs, values, and behaviors of children. They have the capacity to influence their children in many ways—as "models for appropriate behavior, as gatekeepers for both opportunities and barriers, and as major sources of reinforcement in most of their children's lives" (Perry et al., 1988).

The benefits of parental involvement in their children's education have been widely explored in the area of human sexuality. Fisher (1985, 1988a, 1988b) found that general family communication as well as parent-child discussion about sex seem to be important factors that affect sexuality. It was reported that parent-child communication about sex tends to delay sexual activity and encourages children to become more responsible in their approach to sexuality (Fisher, 1986). A number of studies have also suggested that while discussing sexuality, parents can transmit personal, sexual values (e.g. sexual abstinence, the use of condoms and other contraceptives) to their children (Elias & Gebhard, 1973; Fox & Inazu, 1980a, 1980b; Furstenberg, 1976; Inazu & Fox, 1980; Lewis, 1973; Spanier, 1976). Silverstein and Buck (1986) reported that a high degree of parent communication regarding sex education can foster exploration of issues among students.

The extent of the influence that parents and other family members have on their children varies among ethnic groups. In dealing with sensitive health topics, for example, some Hispanics seem more willing to counsel family members about touchy matters and to accept that advice, especially from older members, than non-Hispanics (Foulk, Lafferty, & Ryan, 1991). In other cultures, mothers are more likely than fathers to discuss sensitive topics with their children (Fox & Inazu, 1980b). In still other cultures, fathers exert more authority.

Health teachers may benefit from securing the perceptions of family members that are considered to be the most respected and have the largest influence on children's attitudes and behaviors. It is more likely that these parents will reinforce what is learned in school at home. It is also more likely that it is these parents who will either contradict or support the teaching of various health education content areas in school.

Many health topics are morally laden and controversial. For these topics to be discussed freely in school, parental consent is often necessary. Thus, it may be advantageous for schools to survey parents on the kinds of health education topics they will approve and the age level they think these topics may be appropriately taught. In this regard, schools may implement a program that is consistent with views of parents.

Several attitudinal questionnaires are available on various health topics targeted to parents and students. Many of these questionnaires can be used by teachers to assess the views of parents on different kinds of health information. Silverstein and Buck (1986), Fisher (1988a, 1988b) and Acosta (1992) have developed questionnaires on sex and AIDS education topics which can be used by teachers in assessing parental attitudes towards these topics.

Select instructional materials relevant to the needs of target groups.   Many instructional materials portray biased, stereotypical, and prejudiced notions about health. And many schools use these materials, testing students on the information. Sometimes, the information provided may conflict with students' personal beliefs, values, and experiences. The following example describes how information from a health textbook is biased in favor of the U.S. depiction of health.

The U.S. notion of ideal health is influenced, to a large extent, by the media. The ideal healthy female, for example, is portrayed as tall, very thin, and model-like. Such an ideal is beyond the reach of most healthy females. It becomes misleading for many females who do not fit this image to believe that this example is the only model that typifies health.

In one health textbook, the picture of a robust, muscular, White male lifting weights in what appears to be an expensive health club is portrayed as the ideal healthy man. As with the woman's image, the message conveyed by this picture can be very misleading. It may provide the generalization that a healthy male's body should be similar to that of the one in the picture; or that to be healthy means to subscribe to and rigidly follow the choice of exercises set in the picture; or, to an even larger extreme, believe that "proper" exercise may only be accomplished in a luxurious gym. While gymnasiums and health clubs are relatively common in the United States, recent immigrants and people living in impoverished areas and in rural localities may not have access to health clubs or even want to join them. For various personal, economic, or social reasons, they are likely to reject the gymnasium or health club milieu.

To implement multicultural health education is to debunk the widespread myths and misconceptions about health that linger within the U.S. cultural health ideal. Teachers must encourage the exploration and reflection of other health "ideals" and encourage discussion of the numerous societal and environmental factors that influence it. In addition, teachers must carefully choose their materials, and steer away from those that exhibit bias and partiality. Sometimes, even excellent books and materials may be biased or misleading in some parts. If these books are used, teachers may need to clarify and discuss these parts, or even present alternatives to the biased information.

Participate in the planning and development of culturally relevant materials. An abundance of innovative and creative resource materials exists for health education planning. However, many of these are targeted to the White population and do not meet the needs of other ethnic and racial groups (Orlandi, 1986). Additionally, while a wealth of health education materials have been translated into different languages, much of the information these materials contain is not culturally appropriate for the intended audiences. Nor is the information presented in ways that the targeted group can best understand and use.

Educational interventions focused on reducing high-risk behaviors often do not include the needs of various high-risk populations and groups (Thomas, Guilliam, & Iwrey, 1989). The increasing number of Blacks, Hispanics, and women who become victims of AIDS, for example, indicates the need for focused educational strategies and resources.

To assure that health education content is relevant to diverse population groups, health educators, especially those that are members of target groups, must participate in the design, development, and planning of these materials and not leave the decisions to nonhealth educators or nontarget group members.

Commitment to Multiculturalism

The effectiveness of health education programs depends on the extent to which teachers can increase students' knowledge about health, enhance favorable attitudes, and promote healthful behaviors. Because students' knowledge, attitudes, and behaviors are associated with their cultural, religious, and ethnic beliefs and practices, the integration of a multicultural and social reconstructionist approach to teaching becomes an essential part of health education.

Multicultural health education programs are more likely to be successful when teachers search for suggestions and guidelines that facilitate personal and professional enhancement. Some of these guidelines include a reexamination and renewal of their educational philosophies; the development and maintenance of traits characteristic of tolerance, openness, and acceptance to all students; the use of a variety of instructional methods, strategies, and approaches that are relevant to their students' needs and interests; the involvement of students as teaching resources and participants in their own learning; and taking part in the careful selection and development of culturally relevant instructional materials.

Although certain guidelines have been suggested in this chapter, the key is for teachers to recognize that what they may be instilling in the minds of students may not be what is always "right" or "good" for all of their students. Teachers, through health education, have the responsibility of promoting the health of all their students. The success of health education programs depends, to a large extent, on teachers' personal and professional commitment towards multiculturalism.

References

Acosta, V. (1992). Parents' perceptions regarding the appropriateness of AIDS education topics for their eighth grade school children. *Journal of Health Education, 22*(1), 45–50.

Airhihenbuwa, C., & Pineiro, O. (1988). Cross-cultural health education: A pedagogical challenge. *Journal of School Health, 58*(6), 240–242.

American Public Health Association. (1987). Technical report: Criteria for the development of health promotion and education programs. *American Journal of Public Health,* Washington, DC: Author.

Amler, R. W., & Dull, H. B. (1987). *Closing the gap: The burden of unnecessary illness.* New York: Oxford University Press.

Department of Health and Human Services. (1992). *Healthy people 2000 summary report.* Boston: Jones and Bartlett Publishers, Inc.

Elias, J., & Gebhard, P. (1973). Sexuality and sexual learning in childhood. In A. M. Juhasz (Ed.), *Sexual Development and Behavior,* Homewood, IL: Dorsey Press.

Feigelman, W., and Gorman, B. (1989, July-September). Toward explaining the higher incidence of cigarette smoking among Black Americans. *Journal of Psychoactive Drugs, 21*(3), 299–305.

Fisher, T. (1985). An exploratory study of parent-child communications about sex and the sexual attitudes of early, middle and late adolescents. *Journal of Genetic Psychology, 147*(4), 543–557.

Fisher, T. (1986). Parent-child communication about sex and young adolescents' sexual knowledge and attitudes. *Adolescence, 21*(83), 517–527.

Fisher, T. (1988a). *Parental sexual attitudes, family sexual communications, and adolescent sexual behavior.* Paper presented at the 96th annual convention of the American Psychological Association, Atlanta, GA.

Fisher, T. (1988b). The relationship between parent-child communication about sexuality and college students' sexual behavior and attitudes as a function of parental proximity. *The Journal of Sex Research, 24,* 305–311.

Fisher, T., & Hall, R. (1988). A scale for the comparison of the sexual attitudes of adolescents and their parents. *The Journal of Sex Research, 24,* 90–100.

Foulk, D., Lafferty, J., & Ryan, R. (1991). Developing culturally sensitive materials for AIDS education specifically targeted to migrant farmworkers. *Journal of Health Education, 22*(5), 283–286.

Fox, G. L., & Inazu, J. K. (1980a). Patterns and outcomes of mother-daughter communication about sexuality. *Journal of School Issues, 36,* 7–29.

Fox, G. L., & Inazu, J. K. (1980b). Mother-daughter communication about sex. *Family Relations, 29,* 347–352.

Furstenberg, F., Jr. (1976). *Unplanned parenthood: The social consequences of teenage childbearing.* New York: The Free Press.

Furstenberg, F., Jr. (1987). The AIDS epidemic among Blacks and Hispanics, *Milbank Quarterly, 65,* supp. 2, 460–465.

Galli, N., Greenberg, J., & Tobin, F. (1987). Health education and sensitivity to cultural, religious, and ethnic beliefs. *Journal of School Health, 57*(5), 177–180.

Grant, C., & Sleeter, C. (1989). Race, class, gender, exceptionality, and educational reform. In J. Banks and C. Banks. (Eds.), *Multicultural Education: Issues and Perspectives.* (pp. 46–64). Boston: Allyn and Bacon.

Greene, W., & Simons-Morton, B. (1984). *Introduction to health education.* Prospect Heights, IL: Waveland Press, Inc.

Heckler, M. (1985a). *Report of the secretary's task force on Black and minority health, volume II: Crosscutting issues in minority health.* Washington, DC: Department of Health and Human Services.

Heckler, M. (1985b). *Report of the secretary's task force on Black and minority health: executive summary.* Washington, DC: Department of Health and Human Services.

Hopkins, D. R. (1987, November–December). AIDS in minority populations in the United States. *PHR, 102,* 677.

Inazu, J. K., & Fox, G. L. (1980). Maternal influence on the sexual behavior of teenage daughters. *Journal of Family Issues, 1,* 81–102.

Institute of Medicine. (1985). *Preventing low birth weight,* Washington, DC: National Academy Press.

Jacobs, L. (1973). *What does Judaism say about . . . ?* New York: Quadrangle Press.

Kalantzis, M., & Cope, W. (1992, November 4). Multiculturalism may prove to be the key issue in our epoch. *Chronicle of Higher Education,* B3–B5.

King, L. (1982, September-October). Multicultural health beliefs in action. *Health Education,* 24–25.

Kolb, D. (1984). *Experiential learning.* Englewood Cliffs, NJ: Prentice Hall.

Lewis, R. A. (1973). Parents and peers: Socialization agents in the coital behavior of young adults. *Journal of Sex Research, 9,* 156–170.

MacDonald, J. (1988, June). Multicultural health education: An emerging reality in Canada. *Hygie, 7*(2), 12–16.

Maehr, M. L. (1974). *Sociocultural origins of achievement.* Monterey, CA: Brooks/Cole.

National Health Interview Survey. (1988). National Center for Health Statistics, Centers for Disease Control, Public Health Service, U.S. Department of Health and Human Services, Hyattsville, MD.

National Heart, Lung, & Blood Institute, National Cholesterol Education Program. (1990). *Report of the expert panel on population strategies for blood cholesterol reduction.* Washington, DC: U.S. Department of Health and Human Services.

Office on Smoking and Health. (1987). Unpublished data from the 1987 National Health Interview Survey.

Orlandi, M. A. (1986). Community-based substance abuse prevention: A multicultural perspective. *Journal of School Health, 56*(9), 394–401.

Pahnos, M. (1992). The continuing challenge of multicultural health education. *Journal of School Health, 62*(1), 24–26.

Perry, C., Luepker, R., Murray, D., Kurth, C., Mullis, R., Crockett, S., & Jacobs, D. (1988). Parent involvement with children's health promotion: The Minnesota home team. *American Journal of Public Health, 78*(9), 1156–1160.

Poris, B. (1989, December). Student multi-ethnicity: The untapped health education resource. *Health Education, 21*(2), 20–22.

Russell, R. D. (1983). Old ideas still valuable: A review of cultural case studies. *Journal of School Health, 53*(2), 136–139.

Seven Cardinal Principles Revisited. (1976). *Today's Education, 65*(3), 67–72.

Silverstein, C., & Buck, G. (1986). Parental preferences regarding sex education topics for sixth graders. *Adolescence, 21*(84), 971–980.

Spanier, G. B. (1976). Formal and informal sex education as determinants of premarital sexual behavior. *Archives of Sexual Behavior, 5,* 39–67.

Spector, R. (1985). *Cultural diversity in health and illness* (2nd ed.). Norwalk, CT: Appleton-Century-Crofts.

Stone, E., & Crouch, A. (1979, June). Children's perceptions of vulnerability to health problems from a cross-cultural perspective. *Journal of School Health,* 347–350.

Thomas, S., Guilliam, A., & Iwrey, C. (1989). The relationship between knowledge about AIDS and risk behaviors among Black college students. *Journal of American College of Health, 38*(2), 61–66.

Wurzel, J. (1988). (Ed.). *Toward multiculturalism.* Yarmouth, ME: Intercultural Press, Inc.

Chapter 16

◆ ◆ ◆ ◆

Multiculturalism and Educational Theatre

Mark Riherd

and

Nancy Swortzell

New York University

Introduction

While most extensively developed in the 20th century, the uses of drama and theatre as methods of teaching and learning have influenced education from the Greeks to the present (Swortzell, 1990). In ancient rituals and later religious ceremonies and secular entertainments, particular civilizations demonstrated again and again the effectiveness of this dynamic and enjoyable method of education. The current century has witnessed worldwide expansion of the field that often calls itself *educational theatre,* a term that includes two separate but interdependent forms: Drama in education (DIE) and theatre in education (TIE). DIE explores a wide spectrum of activities (domestic, social, legal, political, health-oriented, and environmental) as participants are guided by a leader through structured improvisations. By playing different roles, students elicit responses from each other while they spontaneously enact their own. It is a process that allows them to be simultaneously a participant and observer of the dramatic action. "Reflection" upon such activity and subsequent decision-making are stressed for both the individual and the group. Because DIE emphasizes classroom "improvisation," "role play" and simulation, it is often called *process* drama, whereas TIE involves *product,* a performance in a school auditorium, theatre or classroom by a company or team of actors.

Theater in Education (TIE)

TIE—distinguished by basic elements of play writing such as conflict, focus, tension, contrast, and symbolism—concentrates on traditional areas of learning and contemporary social issues. TIE programs can include every aspect of the curriculum from the humanities through the sciences. The usual program offers teachers pre- and post-performance activities prepared by the TIE team. The team suggests ways to prepare students for the performance and outlines additional activities to extend the focus of programs after the team has departed.

TIE programs, for the most part, are devised by team members, although a few companies have engaged resident or visiting playwrights to create scripts. The usual devising process entails a period of research and organization of information followed by team improvisations that explore the dramatic context of the topic.

Then members collaborate to focus and refine the materials in rehearsals and early performances. The topical nature often requires frequent changes in text and performance throughout the life of the program. During the final stages of devising, teams begin to structure the workshops that will precede or follow performances.

Before touring programs, members also write drama resource books for teachers that introduce and reinforce themes of the program through suggested dramatic activities. These booklets present ideas for independent student research and also explain basic methods of drama for inexperienced instructors.

Both DIE and TIE are motivated by the conviction that it is the responsibility of the field to bring about positive change in human behavior and social institutions. Through practical involvement followed by individual or group reflection, students often revise their ideas, actions, and perhaps in time, even their institutions. As both participants and spectators, they are placed in the center of the action where they empathize with the characters and issues at hand, reflect upon them, and subsequently make decisions that can permanently alter their attitudes and opinions.

In the early 1960s, Gordon Vallins, the director of Coventry's Belgrade Theatre in England, drafted a working method and structure to serve as a model for other British teams for the next decade. His aim was "to use theatre to tell everyone else about each other's problems" (Redington, 1983, p. 43). Vallins' initial programs used myths, legends, and local history as topics, adapting them so the themes stressed how children could help someone else. Soon, however, the Coventry team turned to specifically multicultural themes in full-day presentations such as *The Mysterious Wanderers* (prejudice against immigrant "Gypsies"), *How the Rain Came to Hweng Chow* (environment in China), and *The Emergent Africa Game* (political action in Africa). Above all, Vallins implored TIE team members to create programs to overcome superficial thinking and develop a greater understanding of the contemporary world.

The child-centered work in Coventry was not concerned merely with filling minds with information but took a direct stance against prejudice and injustice (Redington, 1983). One of its strongest multicultural projects, *Rare Earth,* was a TIE program in three parts with participatory workshops (Wyatt & Steed, 1976). In devising the plays, the team members wished to emphasize the difference between attitudes toward the world held by Westerners today and that of less-industrialized peoples.

The first play, sardonically titled *The Only Good Indian is a Dead Indian,* was a poetic dance drama that suggests that in destroying their environment, people destroy themselves. The second play, *Drink the Mercury,* presented in the style of Kabuki theatre, dealt with pollution in Minamatra, Japan. The third play, *The Ramsbottoms,* was a satiric farce that depicted a typical British family of four and focused on international greed for natural resources.

Each play was performed on a separate day, followed by workshops devised and led by members of the class (Wyatt & Steed, 1976). Schools devoted three full days so that material about survival could be experienced firsthand through theatre and drama workshops. Because of the three-day sequence, the program allowed participants time to absorb and develop ideas through the structure of theatre performance and drama workshops. In fact, at the conclusion of the TIE program, many Coventry teachers incorporated drama activities in their classes for several weeks to further explore environmental awareness and protection.

Other important TIE programs also calling for change in issues of race, gender and disability are described here, followed by a model incorporating dramatic activities to be employed in the classroom.

Race

The intense desire to combat racial prejudice motivated the Belgrade TIE team in 1976 to devise a controversial program, *Pow Wow,* which depicts the treatment of an American Indian by a White American traveling showman. Mr. Tex tells the audience he holds Black Elk captive because he is a savage who has killed White men. But later, Black Elk gains the confidence of the children by describing the philosophy of his people and the color of their daily lives. Audience attitudes are tested when they are asked to support one man or the other and team members select one of two concluding scenes based on the decision of the audience (Redington, 1983).

Raj, written by Paul Swift and performed in 1982 by the Leeds TIE team, is another multicultural program aimed at understanding and overcoming racial prejudice. One actor said he believed " . . . the main connection point was the friendship between characters . . . I think the play raised the possibility that something could be different, something might not have to be. . . . But certainly what it was doing for all is challenging the establishment view" (Multicultural Images, 1982, p. 15). Another team member reported that Asian children participated from the moment the program began as if they were saying, "Thank God, this is relevant to me, at last" (Multicultural Images, 1982, p. 7).

David Holman combined race, religion and politics as issues in *No Passeran,* produced by the Coventry team in 1977. Without directly presenting a Hitler or Franco, the play concentrated on the prevailing practice of creating scapegoats within European Fascist ideology. Emotionally powerful and socially reconstructionist in attitude, *No Passeran* was approved for inclusion in the local Coventry history curriculum and also has been widely performed in Australia, Canada, and the Untied States (Holman, 1980).

Racial problems in the Middle East conflict emerged at the heart of the Electric Theatre's 1989 program, *Homeland*, and appeared again in the Greenwich Young People's 1990 program *Circles of Fire.* This script, which examined the characters' responses to living under the apartheid system in South Africa, uses this line of "questioning": What is it that makes one person decide changes are necessary in society while another person is opposed to those changes? Why does one decide to become *actively* involved in trying to effect these changes? How can one bring about these changes? (Circles of Fire, 1990).

In the United States, The Federal Theatre Project (1936 to 1939) also questioned the social *status quo* through its "learning plays," and in living newspapers and pageants that demanded tolerance and racial understanding (Swortzell, 1986). Much later, in the '70s, the Creative Arts Team (CAT), the professional educational theatre company of the Gallatin division of New York

University, focused on racism in plays about the struggle of Rosa Parks, the career of boxer Joe Louis, and life in South Africa. As a response to an outbreak of racial violence in New York City that culminated in the Howard Beach incident, CAT produced *The Divider*, which has been performed in the United States, Canada and Scotland.

Gender

Gender study and, in particular, the roles of women in society, has been an ongoing concern of dramatists from Aristophanes' *Lysistrata* to recent works such as *The Heidi Chronicles*. Sexism became a major concern of TIE companies in the 1970s, spearheaded by the Bolton Octagon TIE's *Sweetie Pie*. Advocating women's liberation, the play espoused four goals for women: (1) equal educational opportunity, (2) equal pay, (3) 24-hour nurseries, and (4) free contraception and abortion on demand (*Sweetie Pie*, 1975, p. 15).

Two decades later, some of the attitudes presented in *Sweetie Pie* may seem dated, but certainly the factions supporting and opposing abortion issues still stimulate conflict today. The play paved the way for such other works as *Mates* in 1984 and *No Going Back* in 1990, both devised by the Greenwich Young People's Theatre and both asking young people to make decisions to change attitudes toward stereotypical gender roles and responses.

Disability

Before this century, dramatists often depicted physical and psychological disabilities as studies in deformity and evil. Even Euripides and Shakespeare portrayed people with disabilities for purposes other than sympathetic insight, positive identification or for human compassion. Contemporary practitioners, however, hope to achieve these goals by making audiences aware of how it feels to be physically or emotionally impaired. *Snap Out of It,* a two-part British program devised by the Leeds TIE team, emerged from information provided by the British National Association for Mental Health and from doctors, psychiatrists and hospital personnel.

Structured to involve audiences in real-life situations, the play created considerable concern for its characters (Chapman & Wilkes, 1975, p. 50). The first half offers a series of satiric sketches that parody a popular television "quiz" format: "by the end of the first part, all material of the 'fun' . . . and the ridicule . . . is entirely replaced by tape-recorded statistics" and the program moves into areas of disturbing commentary (Chapman & Wilkes, 1975, p. 50). This half involves direct participation through which audiences experience the bewilderment, isolation, and confusion of the mentally ill. Powerful emotional feelings raised during the workshop revealed the general ignorance among students about mental illness. The creators described this program as "neither a documentary nor a piece of ordinary 'theatre,' it was an attempt to employ the skills of the actor to augment our understanding of ourselves and our fellow man" (Chapman & Wilkes, 1975, p. 19).

While *Snap Out of It* was directed toward adults, other companies worked on similar themes for a younger audience. The Pit Prop Theatre developed a participation program that presented the problems, frustrations and misunderstandings suffered by a teen-ager with cerebral palsy. By experiencing the social indignities suffered by the physically impaired, playgoers discovered their own prejudices about the disabled. Similar concerns have generated productions by the GRIPS Theatre in West Berlin, a company that acknowledges its philosophical debt to Bertolt Brecht's *lehrstucke* (learning plays) in its teaching manuals, books, and recordings.

In the United States, *Special Class* (Kral, 1981) calls for a cast of youngsters with and without disabilities drawn from special education classrooms, including youngsters in wheelchairs, the blind, hearing-impaired and mentally retarded. As both playwright and director, Kral reflected his belief that "just because an instrument is shaped a little different, doesn't mean it can't play a beautiful tune." Coleman Jennings' script *The Early Life of Louis Braille* effectively dramatizes the struggle of a blind child (Jennings & Jennings, 1990).

Summary of TIE

Almost two decades before educators intensified their focus on multicultural theories and practices, TIE teams were basing their daily work with young people on the same concerns. Without a specific declaration of a multicultural philosophy, and even though no single team combined the issues of race, class, and gender into one play, teams insisted that programs bring their participants an experience related to the "real world" by asking questions about how this world can be changed for the benefit of all. The development of TIE has run parallel to the growth in drama (process) activity both in theory and practice, especially in English-speaking countries.

Drama in Education (DIE)

DIE is generally considered made up of informal dramatic activities in schools that are based in role play, improvisation, simulation, and theatre games. They also are aimed at developing the student's imagination, awareness of self and others, aesthetic sense, and life skills. The terms *creative drama, developmental drama,* and *drama-in-education* are basically interchangeable. In an effort to refine definitions, the process has come to mean a group activity of improvisational action guided by a leader who involves participants in role playing and spontaneously enacted situations. Because drama workshops function on the premise that participants possess equal but different talents and contributions, all ideas are listened to, put into action and considered without respect to race, creed, or gender. Frequently, several solutions to problems are enacted and conclusions or actions left open-ended.

A brief historical survey of the major theorist-practitioners reveals that although drama has been put to various uses in the past 50 years, it is always child-centered in attitude and from the beginning has had its roots in the progressive educational movement.

Harriet Finlay-Johnson was among the first in England to use drama as an effective means of teaching (Finlay-Johnson, 1911). She was followed by Henry Caldwell Cook whose effect on educational theory eventually came to be praised for his stimulating use of play, role, and ritual, particularly in exploring Greek myths and Shakespeare's plays.

In geography and history classes, students imagined new countries and carried out new systems of government; in science, they visited regional sites and collected and categorized natural elements. Most of Cook's "exercises" stressed that through drama his pupils "be taught to understand as clearly as possible the conditions of this present world in which they live" (Cook, 1917, p. 344).

But it was not until the mid-1960s, after 25 years of studying children at play, that Slade (1969) wrote *Child Drama*. Slade was the first to stress informal drama as an art form in its own right. He believed that in the process of improvising a play, children work out their emotional inhibitions and come to better understand themselves and their world. His major criterion for evaluating participation was the child's degree of involvement, spontaneity and sincerity. Way, who had worked closely with Slade at the Rea Street Drama Centre in Birmingham, extended Slade's ideas in *Development though Drama* (Way, 1967), which in the 1960s and '70s became the basis for most drama teaching in English-speaking countries. Way presented a program of systematized observation aimed at developing awareness. His credo rejected the authoritarian stance of traditional education and emphasized "doing drama" to highlight the "uniqueness of the individual" and to foster self-expression.

In the United States, Ward (1957) launched a similar art and educational movement. Moreover, her work spanned both the fields of creative drama and children's theatre. *Playmaking with Children* (Ward, 1957) stresses the values children gain from improvising a "good story." *Theatre for Children* (Ward, 1958) establishes professional guidelines for play writing and production. Ward was one of the first American teachers and directors to call for a scientific evaluation of child audiences.

McCaslin, independent of Ward, also developed an interest in child drama and theatre, which led her to chronicle the history of the movement. McCaslin's international reputation was established by numerous publications, including *Theatre for Children in the United States: A History* (1978), *Children and Drama* (1981), *Theatre for Young Audiences* (1978), *Creative Drama in the Classroom* (1990), as well as many books for young readers.

Two recent international giants of the drama-in-education world, Dorothy Heathcote and Gavin Bolton, earned their reputations through practical workshops and prolific writing. For the past 25 years, they have revised their methods to train teachers to use drama as education. Heathcote has proposed a total revision of college curricula based on the use of drama as the teaching medium. She begins with the creation of a working climate in which value judgments do not apply, but "where honesty of individual contributions is valued and respect is shown to individual ideas and methods of contribution" (Johnson & O'Neill, 1985, p. 38).

Cultural context areas for her proposed curriculum include subjects such as war, law, health, education, worship and family. She also explores the sociology of groups, myths, legends, racial tribes, and minorities, modes of communication and anthropological studies (Johnson & O'Neill, 1985). Her drama practices with autistic, blind, and brain-damaged children display a dual focus that allows the less capable child to experience the world and the capable child to comprehend the daily struggle of those less fortunate (Wagner, 1976, pp. 210–217).

For the past two decades, Heathcote and Bolton have worked together in public schools, institutes, and universities in Canada, England, and the United States. Both have shared in the creation of drama guidelines that offer teachers tested methods for conducting workshops (Bolton, 1979, 1984, 1986).

Influenced by Bolton's work, O'Neill (1988) offers teachers tangible methods of using drama in all areas of specialization: Her "structures" adjust to any desired age level, or racial or socioeconomic background. One drama lesson, titled "Imagined Worlds," allowed participants to "live through" a role and a situation they would never know, such as life in England immediately after World War II or in a large city of the future plagued by AIDS. Active involvement increases the immediacy of response because by "doing it now," students can offer possible solutions to contemporary problems (O'Neill, 1984).

The assumption that all participants are equal but different in contribution dominates the philosophy of drama-in-education. Drama involves participants in the circumstances of every situation through its use of role play, which allows participants to step directly into another's shoes. In group improvisations students experience situations of race, religion, gender, and disability; their reflections on actions bring with them new ideas that again may be tested by doing. This insistence upon "doing," "redoing," "rethinking," and "remaking," which is basic for all scientific inquiry, also governs drama as an art form.

An Educational Theatre Model

Of the two forms of educational theatre discussed in this chapter, drama in education is the more accessible and readily employable by elementary and middle school teachers. Unlike theatre in education, which requires a theatre presentation and workshops implemented by team members, DIE is designed and guided by the classroom teacher alone. The Center Plot, the model curriculum design used in this text, focuses on the subject of prejudice in multicultural education. The program, intended to be carried out in six sessions, incorporates strategies known as "critical thinking through drama," a practice that develops students' decision-making skills. (For more details about this and other drama strategies discussed in the model, please see the glossary at the end of this chapter.)

The curriculum design for The Center Plot is only an outline or plan and, as such, provides opportunities for teachers to infuse their own ideas as well as those of their students. As long as these themes and events are related to the issue of prejudice, they do not need to be the same as those included in the model. Because the length of sessions and the number of students participating will vary with each classroom, teachers should not be disappointed if they are unable to implement all six workshops or complete each strategy outlined for any one lesson. The model simply offers insights into the varied ways that DIE practices can be incorporated into the curriculum. At every step, the intention is to encourage students through an experiential mode of learning to examine their own attitudes toward people who are different from themselves and, thereby, to better understand multiculturalism. Sessions One through Three are based on a DIE curriculum design devised by the Creative Arts Team at New York University.

The Center Plot

Session One To begin the session, the teacher assumes the role of the Representative of the Ruler of a mythical country. In an authoritative demeanor, she welcomes the students to her country and hopes that, because they have been here for several days, they are rested from their long, exhausting journey. The Representative sympathizes about their past oppressed life and suggests that, because conditions will be better here, they should plan a celebration of their new freedom. Stepping out of role, the teacher questions the students about what is happening in the drama, making certain they understand that they are portraying the inhabitants of a new land and that she is also playing a role.

The teacher, once again becoming the Representative, says they should learn more about each other. The students now enact the new Citizens of the land and are asked to state their names and describe the goals they hope to achieve here. The Citizens walk quietly around the classroom, concentrating on their characters and their new lives. When the Representative claps her hands, the Citizens turn to someone nearby and, introducing themselves, describe their hopes. This procedure is repeated several times.

Out of role, the teacher divides the students into small groups and explains that these units represent their new families. They select family names and occupations, which are written on the board, and they decide upon their individual roles within the families.

The Representative says she would like to take a photograph of each family for the Country Records. Each family creates a "tableau" that expresses how the members hope to be remembered by future generations. Each family shares its tableau as the Representative "snaps" the picture.

The families are asked to create an activity to be performed for the Celebration, such as song, dance, poem, or scene, that expresses their feelings about living in a new country. The Celebration begins and the families present their activities.

The Representative reflects that they all seem to be happy, but she recognizes that their lives have not always been so, as they have come to this country to escape prejudices in their homeland. She encourages the Citizens to talk about these prejudices, examples of which are written on the board ("board work"). The Representative asks each family to select one prejudice and, using several examples, to prepare a short improvisation depicting the prejudice that occurred in their former lives.

The Representative asks them which prejudices influenced their decision to leave home. She explains that tomorrow they must begin to build a society based on a constitution with laws appropriate to their new situation. She teaches them the country's pledge of allegiance which she has written before the class begins.

Follow up: The students are asked to think of a name for their new location and two to three constitutional laws necessary for everyone's happiness and equality.

Session Two   The teacher asks the students to recall the events in Session One; then they decide on a name for their town (referred to herein as New Harmony). The students recite the pledge and assume their roles as Citizens of New Harmony. The teacher, now in role as the Representative, informs the Citizens that they have a difficult but exciting task ahead of them: the building of a new society. She asks them to join their family groups and then produces a large map of New Harmony, divided into plots of land around a center area.

The families are told to select a plot and determine a business to operate there. Each family plans and shares a short improvisation, emphasizing the importance of its business to the community; a member of the group writes the family's name and business on the map. The Citizens are informed that the center plot, as the most convenient and valuable piece of land, should be used for a special purpose, which they will determine later.

The Representative produces a large piece of paper with "CONSTITU-TION" written at the top and tells the Citizens they must list the laws that will allow everyone in New Harmony to live together. After a discussion about the rules they consider essential, each family is asked to create one law based on a prejudice inflicted upon them in their old country. The Citizens write their new laws on the constitution sheet, and the Representative reads them aloud. Each family reads the constitution aloud together and, after agreeing to live by these new rules, each family representative signs the constitution.

The Citizens determine the purpose of the center plot of land, being reminded that it is to be used by everyone in the community for something special, such as a public garden, a statue, a shrine, or a public building. The Citizens offer their suggestions and make a decision. The Representative reiterates the importance of the free society they have created. She suggests that each family stand and repeat the pledge in gratitude, a "ritual" that is continued until a high level of excitement is achieved.

Suddenly the Representative becomes distraught and quiets the students, because she has important news: Another group of people has entered New Harmony and she has heard they appear to be very different from the Citizens.

Out of role, the teacher questions the students as to what might happen in New Harmony if the information about the Strangers is true. Then, each student creates and repeats to a classmate a negative statement about the Strangers which begins, "I heard that the Strangers . . ." The activity continues with the students taking the information and exchanging it with each other, making certain that each begins, "I heard that the Strangers. . . ."

The teacher explains that some of the students will continue to be the Citizens of New Harmony in the next session, and a few will become the Strangers.

Follow up: Each student, as a Citizen, writes a letter to the Strangers, describing the importance of the society they have established in New Harmony.

Session Three   The teacher selects a small number of students from each of the family groups who will become the Strangers later in this session. At one end of the room, the teacher forms two groups of students, one a large group and the other a small group. They stand in two lines, facing each other, about 5 feet apart. One person from the larger group stands in front of the smaller group and leads members of the larger group toward the smaller group, expressing a powerful movement and sound. Reacting, the smaller group retreats at the same pace. This activity is repeated several times, with different people from the dominant group continually forcing the subordinate one to retreat. Still in their separate groups, the students discuss the meaning of this activity.

After the smaller group is informed that in this session they will become the Strangers, the two groups are delegated to different areas of the room. The Citizens are told by the teacher to select several members to inform the Strangers about life in New Harmony (the family groups, the plots of land, the pledge, the constitution). Then, the teacher informs the Strangers that their lifestyle is the opposite of the Citizens of New Harmony: (1) They live communally, not in family groups, because they believe that each person is unique, (2) they do not believe in pledges or constitutions but in the right of individuals to live as they choose as long as no one else is harmed, and (3) they are peaceful and have no desire to cause trouble.

To understand their characters, the students portraying the Strangers face each other in pairs; in turn, they practice informing each other about one aspect of their lives and why it is important to them. Simultaneously, the Citizens perform the same task, telling each other about life in New Harmony.

The Representative asks the Strangers to identify a unique skill, such as basketmaking, farming, baking, or recording history, that they perform for the society, while the Citizens are encouraged to reflect on the importance of their businesses to the success of New Harmony. Then the Strangers, working individually, "pantomime" the task at which they are expert. The teacher, after determining that the Citizens are prepared to meet the Strangers, asks them to pantomime packing for the journey. "Narration" (by the teacher): "The Citizens set out upon their journey, traveling through the forest and along the river. At midday, they came upon the Strangers at work."

The Citizens, encouraged if necessary by the Representative, challenge the Strangers about not working as a group and explain their constitution and the necessity of living by its laws. They insist that the Strangers sign the constitution as well as learn and recite their pledge. The Strangers explain, politely but firmly, that, based on the principles of their own society, they cannot perform any of these tasks. The Citizens decree that if the Strangers refuse to live by their laws, they must leave New Harmony.

In small groups, the Citizens and the Strangers plan and share improvisations:

> **The Citizens:** A scene depicting their lives if the Strangers remain and refuse to live according to the laws established by the Citizens.
>
> **The Strangers:** A scene depicting their lives if they remain in New Harmony and are forced to live according to the laws established by the Citizens.

After the scenes have been presented and the students see the opposing views, the Citizens and the Strangers are told to go to different areas of the room and sit.

Narration (to be spoken by the teacher in her own words): "From that day onward, the Citizens of New Harmony and the Strangers lived separate and mistrusting lives with neither group speaking to the other. When anything bad happened to the Citizens of New Harmony, they blamed the Strangers; likewise, when anything bad happened to the Strangers, they blamed the Citizens of New Harmony. And as the days passed into weeks and the weeks into months, and the months, finally, into years, mistrust changed to hatred. One day, the Citizens of New Harmony and the Strangers faced each other and without speaking to or even looking at each other, built a wall around the center plot, separating themselves permanently from each other."

The Strangers are asked to stand and, without speaking, to create a group tableau, entering the picture one at a time, depicting how they feel about the current situation. When all are in place, the teacher asks them to say one sentence to express their feelings. When touched by the teacher, the Strangers deliver their lines. The Strangers sit and the activity is repeated by the Citizens of New Harmony.

Session Four   The teacher asks two students (Student 1 and Student 2) to come to the center of the group and shake hands; the students "freeze," and the class identifies what they see, responding with as many different images as possible.

The teacher tells Student 1 to return to the group, while Student 2 remains in position. Another student (Student 3) joins Student 2 and creates a different image, related to the theme of "People in Conflict." Student 2 leaves and another student joins Student 3 to create yet another image. This activity continues with students depicting people in various conflict situations.

In pairs, the students continue this activity working simultaneously, creating images emphasizing the theme of "People in Prejudice Situations," sharing as many different images as possible in a brief period of time. The students then join in, one at a time, to devise a group tableau titled "Prejudice."

On the board, the teacher writes the word *prejudice* and the students offer their definitions, which are also recorded. Then she leads the students in a discussion of prejudice, referring to their written comments. The students are asked to think of an incident of prejudice they have recently seen or read about. In their groups, they create a tableau, depicting the scene at the height of conflict. They decide on a line of dialogue that they would speak to another character in the tableau. When the characters are touched by the teacher, the dialogue is spoken. Each tableau is shared in the same manner.

Based on their tableaux, the students plan improvisations for which the conflicts remain unresolved. After being presented, one of these scenes is selected for exploration in the next session.

Session Five   The conflict scene from Session Four is replayed. The teacher explains that the students will help resolve the conflict, but that to do so, they will need more information about the characters and the situation; their task is to gather that information.

The characters are "hotseated" by the students who ask questions in rapid succession to gather general information about the characters: "Where were you born?" "How old are you?" "Do you work?" "What are your hobbies?" The characters respond instantaneously, and hotseating continues for the purposes of revealing vital information about the characters and conflict(s) depicted in the scene.

One of the characters is selected to be questioned further. One student from the class stands behind that character and acts as her/his Inner Self ("doubling"). Questioning continues with the character verbalizing what s/he wants people to hear, while the Inner Self speaks what the character is actually thinking.

The teacher leads the class in a discussion about the causes of prejudice and explains that to help resolve the characters' conflicts, they must first discover the origins of the prejudices demonstrated. In small groups, students elect one of the characters and create a "flashback" scene, depicting a situation from the past which contributed to the character's current prejudices. (The characters should not be played by the students who created them.) These scenes are shared with the group.

Session Six   Before the original scene is replayed, the students portraying the characters are encouraged to be aware of any new information they may have gained about themselves and how that might affect the way they will play the scene.

The teacher tells the students they are now prepared to help resolve the conflict(s) and asks them what choices the characters have that might help them. After numerous ideas are listed on the board, the students identify one choice they believe would produce positive results and take roles to play that situation. The class assesses the results.

Other positive choices are explored through improvisation with different students taking on the roles and acting out several positive alternatives. Each improvised scene is discussed, emphasizing both positive and negative aspects. After several choices have been enacted, the students decide which would most effectively reduce prejudice. In small groups, the students create an improvisation depicting either a positive or negative result of one of the choices. These scenes are shared and analyzed by the class.

Groups from Session Four are formed again and recreate their original tableaux, depicting characters in a prejudice situation. The students then project what the behavior of these characters would be in three years if they lived by the results of their positive choices. They create new tableaux to show this. The students then move slowly and deliberately, improvising dialogue, from the Conflict Tableau to the Resolution Tableau.

Implications of The Center Plot for Multicultural Education

The expected goal of this model is to alter students' prejudicial behavior. However idealistic and unlikely it might be that this goal can be achieved in just six drama sessions, the model nevertheless allows students to learn about another group and experience a change of attitude about them, culminating in a new mode of behavior.

The DIE strategies provided in Sessions One through Three subject students to actual prejudicial behavior as both victims and oppressors. The Citizens establish their new society with laws designed to protect them from discrimination but their commitment to these laws soon becomes so consuming that they inflict upon others the same oppressions they previously sought to escape. The primary challenge for the teacher in sessions One and Two is to carefully construct opportunities for the participants to build a belief in the tenets of New Harmony.

As the Representative of the Ruler of an unspecified country, the teacher can be in an authoritative position when necessary. Also, by participating as a central character, the teacher provides students the opportunity to challenge and even contradict that position—a condition they rarely, if ever, enjoy in real life. The teacher in role, on occasion, dictates events in the drama that can be discussed out of role with the students: Was the decision fair? Did it favor some characters more than others? Did the Representative exhibit prejudice toward certain individuals? Could this have been avoided? If not, how could it have been dealt with?

Early in Session One, the teacher in role stresses that the participants previously had lived under oppressive conditions. When she asks them to discover from each other what they hope to gain by living in a new land, she lays the foundation for the conflicts to come that are related to the issue of prejudice.

The formation of family groups allows the students to instigate the development of their own society. The selection of family names and occupations provides students with specific identities and helps them develop a sense of pride. While posing for family portraits reinforces and solidifies familial units, the Celebration is intended to establish a sense of contentment and unity among the Citizens. Only when a sense of family unit has been achieved does the teacher move the drama forward by reminding them that they have not always been content. Under the cautious guidance of the teacher, the Citizens select and depict past prejudices inflicted upon them.

In Session Two, the focus moves from the family to the development of the community and the construction of a new social order. The introduction of the map of New Harmony permits the students to see themselves in relationship to the large community. The students then create their own laws, based on the prejudices they incurred previously. These laws should be carefully constructed by the entire community with the understanding that all as Citizens of New Harmony must agree to live by them. The ritual reading and signing of the constitution solidifies and reinforces the seriousness of the situation.

The decision regarding the purpose of the center plot of land is left entirely to the students, with the reminder by the teacher that the space is special and should be used for something special. By empowering the students with this control, the teacher will discover which aspects of society are most important to the students. Then, by announcing that a group of people have arrived, she asks the students to elaborate on those rumors. At this point in the drama, it is vital that the students (1) have a belief in the events of the drama and that the meaning behind this belief is "important" to them, (2) that they have a commitment to their individual family units, and (3) to the community as a whole.

In Session Three, prejudice is seen in action. The Strangers live by rules diametrically opposed to those of the Citizens. The Strangers, a small group of people, should not be presented as attempting to change the lives of the Citizens. Instead, they are a peaceful people who want only to live as they have chosen. The conflict arises when the Citizens insist that the Strangers either abide by the laws of New Harmony or leave, demonstrating the infliction of their prejudices upon the Strangers. The workshop concludes with each group suspicious and fearful of the other.

The students in sessions One through Three have experienced or "lived through" situations exploring prejudice. But in Four through Six, they are allowed to critique this issue, stand outside the drama, and analyze their own thoughts, preconceptions, presuppositions, and actions as well as those of the characters being examined. The teacher, in discussions, should refer to the situations experienced by the Citizens of New Harmony and endeavor to see that the following goals are obtained:

1. Participants should consider a variety of choices, as well as predict possible consequences of each and weigh the pros and cons or options before making a decision.

2. Participants should analyze their own attitudes and feelings toward a particular issue, as well as provide new insight into their own preconceptions.

3. Participants should step back and view a situation from another point of view, as well as encourage educated decisions, rather than ones based primarily on self-centeredness.

4. Participants should examine long-range goals that affect others as well as themselves instead of settling for immediate self-centered gratification.

5. Participants should recognize their own potential in producing change in their lives as well as in the lives of others and society.

6. Participants should learn to prioritize choices; to settle, if necessary, and at least temporarily, for a lesser solution to establish a plan for a more satisfactory one.

7. Participants should learn to accept the consequences of their actions.

8. Participants should be able to conceptualize the spiraling nature of decision-making; to understand that examination of choices leads to examination of possible consequences which, in turn, leads to decision-making. Students should begin to comprehend that decision-making is an ongoing process that requires skills for implementation that need constant honing and practice.

Summary of DIE

The theories and practices of drama and theatre in education are catalysts for changing prejudicial attitudes and for ameliorating conflicts by promoting understanding and respect for those who are different from oneself. The model included here illuminates the drama process as it examines sources and conditions of prejudice. Drama workshops offer students the freedom to investigate the world in which they live. They invite and stimulate open, flexible, and imaginative thinking so that avenues of change become apparent to the individual and to the group alike. Through a variety of dramatic activities, students explore specific issues of race, gender, ability, and disability and, rather than hearing a teacher talk about them, they actually "experience" them in performance and reflection.

The scope of multicultural learning presents vast opportunities for the use of drama and theatre techniques in the classroom. For example, the enactment of so simple and traditional a story as *Cinderella* can foster an understanding of such enduring problems as sibling rivalry, oppression, and abuse. Different versions of *Cinderella* as the fairy tale is known in other cultures can offer fascinating comparisons that range from those of ancient Egypt, China, and Russia to American Indians (Swortzell, 1992). The German version of the story even gives us a Cinderella figure who, in fact, is a boy. For older children, this same tale can be explored in its more complex variations as in the story of Cain and Abel and in the tragedy of Shakespeare's *King Lear.*

Timeless global folk and fairy tales are ideal for story dramatization, just as interesting holidays are for the revelations of their similarities and dissimilarities. In performing this age-old material, just as in dramatizing events and issues from current newspapers, different points of view soon become evident and new ideas emerge about the world as it exists today, ideas that are "alive" because they involve, enrich and empower the students who discover them by "enacting" them.

The model provided in this chapter is not intended to be copied literally but rather to suggest some possibilities available through DIE. The initial challenge confronting the teacher eager to incorporate drama into the curriculum is knowing how to begin. The following suggestions are not meant to be prescriptive, but they do provide a way to begin. As teachers have successful experiences, they will be encouraged to use other dramatic activities and strategies, culminating in the use of DIE for multicultural education as an integral element of the curriculum.

To successfully incorporate drama into their classroom, teachers make a note of the following guidelines:

1. Be thoroughly familiar with the content of the session. It is often beneficial to begin by implementing a single activity requiring no more than 10–15 minutes of class time.
2. Establish an attainable learning objective for the students.
3. Consider the dynamics of the students, including their ability to work in small groups and the amount of guidance they will require.
4. Provide enough space and time to work.
5. Realize there may be more movement and noise than usual.

6. Stimulate the students' thinking by compelling them to develop their ideas while remaining focused on the activity.

7. Recognize and acknowledge honest efforts from the students.

8. Encourage the students to develop their assessment skills by guiding their analysis of the drama and by allowing them to offer suggestions for future sessions.

9. Incorporate into the drama other areas of the curriculum, including songs, instrumental music, visual art, puppetry, dance, stories, and poems representative of various cultures.

Glossary

The following strategies have been selected for identification because they are included in The Center Plot model, and are representative of the techniques often used in drama in education workshops, incorporating "critical thinking through drama" techniques.

Board work   Responses from students during "brainstorming," which are recorded on the chalkboard; they provide concrete evidence of the students' reactions and a visible reference to be used later in the session.

Critical thinking through drama   A methodology incorporating various techniques employed in drama in education and theatre in education as well as other forms of educational theatre, including drama therapy and psychodrama, for the development of students' decision-making skills. The content examines a specific social issue relevant to the participants, such as pregnancy, drugs and alcohol, peer pressure, AIDS, abuse, prejudice, and racism.

A paradigm might begin with the creation of scenes centered on a specific issue of conflict agreed upon by the teacher and the students but intentionally left unresolved. The students then select one situation to explore and resolve, a technique referred to as processing. By employing a series of strategies, including improvisation, role play, hotseating, doubling, flashback, and "flashforward," all interspersed with frequent discussion, the students consider choices open to the characters and examine the possible consequences of these decisions in solving the conflict.

Doubling   A variation of "hotseating" in which a student becomes the "inner self" of the character being questioned. Doubling provides insight into and knowledge about the characters as well as the opportunity to weigh the differences between what characters say and what they think. (See Hotseating.)

Exercise   An activity designed to develop specific skills required for a drama session. While often implemented at the beginning of a workshop as warm-up or preparation, exercises are invaluable throughout the session, especially when the session becomes more complex. Exercises allow students opportunity to step out of the drama and reflect upon what is happening.

Flashback   A scene or "tableau" created by the students depicting a situation from the past, which provides insight into the character's present circumstances, actions, and relationships.

Flashforward   A scene or "tableau" created by the students, most often toward the end of a session, depicting the characters in a situation occurring in the future; this allows the opportunity to consider a realistic or idealistic resolution.

Follow up   Activities assigned by the teacher and completed by the students before the next workshop which provide continuity between the sessions and allow the teacher to incorporate other areas of the curriculum such as writing, art, music, and map making.

Hotseating   Questioning of characters by the student audience to increase understanding of both motive and circumstance; this technique moves the drama forward and assists in resolving the conflict.

Improvisation   The spontaneous acting out of a situation, which may be (1) unplanned by the participants, (2) planned and often rehearsed in pairs or small groups, or (3) implemented in large groups, guided by the teacher who is frequently in role. Improvisations are unpredictable, belonging to a specific moment of experience and, while not intended for performance before audiences, are shared with other members of the class.

Narration   A narrative description of "what happens next," implemented, usually spontaneously, by the teacher; provides linkage between scenes as well as information important to the participants which has not been provided in the drama.

Pantomime   The nonverbal acting out of an action or situation, in which gesture, facial expression and movement, rather than speech, are relied upon; silent acting.

Questioning   Interspersed throughout the workshop, this technique encourages the participants to confront the issues of the drama. Though most often implemented by the teacher, questioning by the students, either in or out of role, is invaluable.

Reflection   A time of contemplation initiated through statements or questions, intended to be thought about, not responded to verbally, providing a quiet and private time for the participants to internalize events and to consider the future course of the drama.

Ritual   An activity such as the passing of a sacred object, repeating a pledge, or signing a contract, initiated by the teacher—usually in role—and implemented individually by the participants; this helps build belief in and commitment to the drama.

Role play   A form of improvisation representing a group of people in a life-like event such as a party, teachers conference, or a town meeting; usually, a social situation for which students take on roles and relate to others in the group.

Tableau   Often referred to as a "frozen picture," a "still life," or a "living photograph," this strategy stops the drama at a fixed moment, allowing the participants to reflect upon what is happening and permitting the teacher to comment on the images presented: What do you think is happening here? What is that character thinking? What is the relationship among these people?

Teacher in role   The taking on of a role by the teacher, permitting participation in the drama with the students, becoming one of them, not isolated or watching. This technique allows the teacher to work from inside the drama, challenging the students, sometimes agreeing with them but often opposing them to move the drama forward.

References

Bolton, G. (1979). *Towards a theory of drama in education.* London: Longman.

Bolton, G. (1984). *Drama as education.* London: Longman.

Bolton, G. (1986). *Selected writings.* London: Longman.

Chapman, R., & Wilkes, B. (Eds.). (1975). *Snap out of it.* London: Methuen Young Drama.

Circles of fire. (1990). Unpublished manuscript. London: Greenwich Theatre-in-Education Company.

Cook, C. (1917). *The play way: An essay in educational method.* London: Heinemann.

Finlay-Johnson, H. (1911). *The dramatic method of teaching.* London: Nisbet.

Holman, D. (1980). *No passeran.* In P. Schweitzer (Ed.), *Theatre-in-education: Four secondary programmes.* London: Methuen Young Drama.

Jennings, C., & Jennings, L. (1990). *The early life of Louis Braille.* Woodstock, IL: Dramatic Publishing Company.

Johnson, L., & O'Neill, C. (Eds.). (1985). *Dorothy Heathcote: Collected writings on education and drama.* London: Hutchinson.

Kral, B. (1981). *Special class.* New Orleans: Anchorage Press.

Multicultural images: Leeds TIE team discuss their programme "Raj" with Geoff Gillham. (1982, September). London: *SCYPT Journal, 10.*

McCaslin, N. (1971). *Theatre for children in the United States: A history.* Norman, OK: University of Oklahoma Press.

McCaslin, N. (1978). *Theatre for young audiences.* New York: Longman.

McCaslin, N. (1981). (Ed.). *Children and drama* (2nd ed.). New York: Longman.

McCaslin, N. (1990). *Creative drama in the classroom* (5th ed.). New York: Longman.

O'Neill, C. (1984, Winter). Imagined world in theatre and drama. *London Drama, 6*(10).

O'Neill, C. (1988). *Drama structures: A practical handbook for teachers.* London: Hutchinson.

Redington, C. (1983). *Can theatre teach?* Oxford: Pergamon Press.

Slade, P. (1969). *Child drama.* London: University of London Press.

Sweetie Pie. (1975). London: Methuen Young Drama.

Swortzell, L. (1986). *Six plays for young people from the Federal Theatre Project.* New York: Greenwood Press.

Swortzell, L. (1990). *International guide to children's theatre and educational theatre: A historical and geographical source book.* New York: Greenwood Press.

Swortzell, L. (1992). *Cinderella: The world's favorite fairy tale.* Charlottesville, VA: New Plays, Inc.

Wagner, B. J. (1976). *Dorothy Heathcote: Drama as a learning medium.* Washington, DC: National Educational Association.

Ward, W. (1957). *Playmaking with children.* New York: Appleton-Century-Crofts.

Ward, W. (1958). *Theatre for children.* Anchorage, KY: Children's Theatre Press.

Way, B. (1967). *Development through drama.* London: Longman.

Wyatt, S., & Steed, M. (Eds.). (1976). *Rare Earth: A programme about pollution.* London: Eyre Metheun, Ltd.

Chapter 17

◆ ◆ ◆ ◆

Television and Film in the Classroom: The Presence and Absence of People of Color

Ann DeVaney

University of Wisconsin—Madison

I first met Alicia in the spring of 1990 when she spent the holidays with me. She was 5. Her mother had said she was somewhat shy and reticent, but after just one hour in my house, Alicia followed me downstairs and said privately and quite vehemently,

"I really hate my hair."

I was stunned and speechless. Whether I like it or not, I know how important hair is to the image of a young girl. I had never encountered a 5-year-old who hated her hair. My ready reserve of positive responses for children had dried up. I could only manage a weak, "Why?"

"My Mama let me grow my hair, but I hate it. I want it smooth and shiny."

I reached for a positive reinforcement. "Well, I like the way your mother fixes your hair and I like your colorful bows."

"It hurts when she fixes my hair," Alicia said. "No matter what we do. Even if we put grease on it." Her last remark was desperate.

"I really want it smooth and shiny."

Later that afternoon, I asked Alicia's mother, Carol, if she had purchased any Black dolls for her daughter.

"Yes," she answered. "But most Black dolls have uncharacteristically smooth and shiny hair.

I asked her if Alicia had seen Whoopi Goldberg on *Sesame Street* talking about her hair.

"Yes," she replied, "but one example, one image is not enough."

Then Carol told me a moving story:

I asked a friend of mine to make an authentic African American doll for Alicia. It was gorgeous, with black hair in corn rows—some tied with colorful ribbons. I wrapped it carefully in a large box and placed it under the Christmas tree. On Christmas morning Alicia was casually opening presents until she came to the big box. When she lifted the lid she gasped. It took her breath away. Her face lit up. Perplexed, she asked, 'How did I get in there? How did I get in that box?' Till this day she treats that doll differently, carefully, and with reverence.

Picturing Yourself

Have you considered how you construct your image, develop a picture of yourself? Lacan (1977) would have us believe that this construction begins at 18 months of age during what he calls a mirror stage. He says the process of differentiating ourselves from others begins when we are able to recognize our reflection in a mirror.

Although this period of development includes the society of parents and playmates, it is devoid of other societal images; it excludes the artifacts and mediated images that also contribute to the formation of a self-image. In a society that prizes individualism, it seems natural to believe that we form an image of ourselves by simply looking into a mirror, but the process is not as simple as Lacan would have us believe, and there is ample evidence to support our dependence on other images.

It can only be societal images that prompted Alicia to desire smooth hair. bell hooks recalls similar longings.

> GOOD HAIR—that's the expression. We all know it, begin to hear it when we are small children. . . . Good hair is hair that is not kinky, hair that does not feel like balls of steel wool, hair that does not take hours to comb, hair that does not need tons of grease to untangle, hair that is long. Real good hair is straight hair, hair like White folks' hair. (hooks, 1991, p. 339)

If we formed a self-image by simply looking in a mirror and differentiating ourselves from parents and playmates, why would so many African American women want "White-folks' hair?" Perhaps images of African Americans are absent from the majority of mediated images they encounter in books, films, ads, and TV.

In her 1937 novel, *Their Eyes Are Watching God,* Hurston (1990) tells a poignant story about how Jane, a 6-year-old, formed an image of herself:

> So when we looked at de picture and everybody got pointed out there wasn't nobody left except a real dark little girl with long hair standing by Eleanor. Dats where Ah was s'posed to be, but Ah couldn't recognize dat dark chile as me. So Ah ast, 'where is me? Ah don't see me.' . . . Ah looked at de picture a long time and seen it was mah dress and mah hair so Ah said:
> "Aw, aw! Ah'm colored!" (Hurston, 1990, p. 9)

Jane and her White playmates ran through all the rooms of their "big house." Certainly, there must have been a mirror in one of those rooms. Yet, she did not use the mirror to form an image of herself. And most public images in her day did not include African Americans; those that did were derogatory. She used the mirror of a private photo in which she saw her image standing next to those of her White playmates, to start forming a picture of herself.

I believe we use all available images to create pictures of ourselves. From an early age, children see images on television, in snapshots, on billboards, in magazines, and in home videos. My 3-year-old nephew has videos of himself from the time he was in utero. What influence, I ask myself, does viewing yourself in a videotape sonogram and numerous home videos have on your self-image? The images children encounter on home videos, however, are only a fraction of the faces in their lives.

All forms of art and popular culture create images by means of representation. Artists and producers use socially constructed signs and symbols to depict children or adults, Black or White, national or international people. We all use these depictions to construct our own images. Our self-image becomes a composite of reflections from real and mediated mirrors. If Black Barbie dolls have long shiny hair and syrup bottles still picture Aunt Jemima; if MTV presents young Black women dressed only as streetwalkers and Black men continue to be violent partners to White men in cop shows, African American children will continue to see themselves portrayed in stereotypical ways. It is no wonder that they often wish to relate to White images.

A classroom can be the place to teach all children to become critical consumers of these images. You can acquire and teach the skills necessary to intelligently read photos, ads, films, and television. In fact, most of us have unconsciously acquired those skills; therefore, it is the role of the classroom teacher to make apparent that which is tacit.

Reading Images

This chapter will provide you with a structural method for reading images, particularly those on television. Because this essay is limited, I will concentrate on reading representations of one stereotyped group, African Americans; however, the method is applicable to other groups as well. I hope to enable you to identify nonstereotypic representations of African Americans on television and in film. The structural method of critiquing television is borrowed from literary textual analysis.[1] Clues for the identification of credible African Americans in film and television are borrowed from critiques of Black literature in the United States.[2]

Television is a major transmitter of culture. Practices of production and reception shape our collective life in a substantial way. Standardized patterns of speech, dress, fashion, family rituals, and other group behaviors are presented in a daily parade of commercials and cable programs. We have evidence that this parade influences our purchasing and voting habits and shapes our children's behaviors, beliefs, and knowledge.

McLuhan (1964) understood the cultural effect of television when he noted that the TV screen had replaced the hearth. Many immigrants to the United States learn not only English from television, but also how to dress and behave in their new country. Broadcast television has been the major influence in the election of every president from John Kennedy to Bill Clinton. Recall how George Bush's ratings in the pre-election polls in 1988 skyrocketed when his TV ads became vicious and started attacking his opponent. Many credit his election to those ads.

Television as a Teacher

Television shapes mores, values, social habits, buying habits, and leisure time. Arguments that the medium simply reflects culture, i.e., habits, tastes, etc. of the public, are reductive, because it not only reflects, but also molds. It shapes consumption of more items than itself. To claim that television only reflects culture actually trivializes the medium and neglects to assign enough influence to it. MTV, for example, not only sells music, but clothes and hair styles as well. In addition to consumer items, MTV sells mores by modeling certain aspects of male-female interaction.

Educators, when citing amazing viewing statistics, such as the fact that children view three to four hours of television each day, often miss the point of such statistics. Viewing statistics are generally invoked when educators wish to describe reasons for students' failure at schools. But the point is that television is a powerful teacher that competes daily with the classroom teacher.

One of the major ways in which television teaches is through the presentation of human images. It is, after all, primarily a visual medium. I am interested in what faces are presented to children and how the representations help children form self-images and pictures of others. For instance, TV examples of disrespectful treatment of women and people of color abound. While it is important to understand how these images are constructed and the reason for their persistence, it is equally important to seize those scarce nonstereotypic images of women and people of color for use in the classroom.

Some cognitive theories indicate that if students are presented with mistakes and errors before they are given correct examples of the concept being taught, they will first recall the error before recalling the concept itself, or the correct application of it. So it is with images. Pictures of women dressed as streetwalkers or Chicanos presented as buffoons have an emotional effect that prompts recall faster than nonstereotypic images.

Additionally, students can relate disrespectful TV images to those they see repeatedly in other popular media. Repetition of these negative representations will certainly assist their recall. Students must, however, have the ability to read both types of images, stereotypic and nonstereotypic, and understand the messages constructed by them. In the following section, I provide a means by which students can read television images. This method of questioning the TV screen empowers viewers by enabling them to become critical consumers of all programs.

Critiquing Television

For centuries, teachers have guided students in the methods of critiquing a text. Questioning a text to discover the author's intention and the reader's interpretation is a natural classroom activity. Postmodern[3] texts, however, go beyond the written page. Students are bombarded daily with the visual texts, for example, of billboards, television, and magazines. The critiquing of those visual texts which transmit much of students' culture is a necessary curricular task. The reading of television, for instance, can become a springboard for appreciation of diverse people and ethnicities.

A television program is a visual text, which we may read in a manner similar to the way we read an essay or short story. A written text consists of words, sentences, and paragraphs while a visual text consists of frames, shots, and scenes or sequences. Just as the study of the syntax and grammar of a verbal text prepares students to read and produce printed material, so does the study of the syntax and organization of frames, shots, and sequences prepare students to read and produce television material. Students begin the study of visual texts, however, with an advantage: They have tacitly acquired many decoding skills and their study simply uncovers them.

Structure

Frame   The smallest structural unit in television is a frame. A camera is not a window on the world. People have become so used to commenting on any picture of a child by saying, "Oh, isn't that a cute baby," that the means for the construction of pictures become invisible. A baby picture is not reality, but an image mediated by the technology of photography. In this postmodern age, images are so ubiquitous they become pleasurable in themselves. It becomes easy to mistake an image for reality. Even Vice President Dan Quayle cited the image of a fictitious TV character, Murphy Brown, as a person we should not emulate.

Television news, which we want to believe, is also constructed. A televised shot of a Los Angeles riot scene is not a "slice of life." It has been constructed with intent by a director and camera person and transformed by the technology of the video camera. It probably represents the most sensational aspect of the rebellion and needs to be read by mentally juxtaposing less fiery or less violent scenes.

A frame is read not only by its content, but by what has been excluded. If we see a single televised shot of Magic Johnson advertising athletic shoes on a basketball court, we interpret his movement as if it were set within a stadium, although we may not have actually seen the stadium. This reading of visual information within the frame by mental reference to what we suppose lies outside the frame is a learned skill acquired in childhood.

You can help your students by making them aware of their image-reading skills. You can demystify this process for them by first asking them to question the frame. What lies inside and outside that electronic border? You can teach them that Michael Jackson and Michael Jordan dancing in the music video *Jam* are only electronic images on MTV. When children visited Mr. Rogers recently (Alm, 1991), they had a hard time distinguishing the real man from the image. "How did you get out [of that box?]" one boy asked Fred Rogers. Rogers explained the process of television and compared it to a photo of a real person, but as the boy left he still had to ask, "How do you get back into the box?" People want to believe that the camera is a window on the world, even when they know better.

Angle, Lighting, Distance   Other structural features beside the frame are used in the production and interpretation of a shot on television. The angle of the camera, lighting, and distance of the camera from the focal point are used by directors to construct the shot, and by viewers to read the shot. An interior shot of the Huxtable's kitchen, on *The Cosby Show*, may communicate its meaning through the use of moderately high key (bright) lighting for a cheerful and busy mood. Dr. Huxtable may be standing in the doorway and the camera shoots him from a low angle, forcing us to look up to him. The shot encourages us to admire him. A high-angle shot would make us look down on him. The camera zooms out from a tight shot of the doctor to a medium-long shot of the kitchen. We are able to admire Cliff Huxtable at close range and then see who else is in the kitchen.

The medium shot allows us to compare and contrast the people or objects within its frame. The camera may move from close-up for detail, to medium for comparison and contrast, to long shot for establishment of locale or to give an overview. It also moves from low angle where we are less powerful than the person depicted, to a level angle where we are equal to the person's image, to a high angle where we feel more powerful than the person depicted. Lighting in the shot can move through a range of low key suggesting a quiet, somber, or fearful mood to high key suggesting a cheerful or celebratory mood. Without thinking, we use these structural clues to read the image.

Motion Within a shot, the camera can move in a limited number of ways and we use each of these to layer different meanings on the shot. A camera can only zoom in or out, tilt up or down, and pan left or right. If a director moves the whole camera, she can only dolly or truck the camera, usually moving along with the moving object in the shot. Traditionally, these structural features were used in a seamless manner, so viewers would not notice them. They did not call attention to themselves. We were encouraged to believe we were watching a "slice of life."

Today's broadcast or cable television calls attention to itself by featuring the structural units we use to read TV. This is apparent on MTV and in commercials that imitate the MTV style. Innovative use of within-shot and between-shot motion makes us take notice of television; it calls attention to the clever use of techniques. After two generations of attempting to imitate reality, select television formats are calling attention to themselves. It is within these formats that we learn the nature of the medium and what it can do. It is as if a director is saying to us, "Look at what I can create," instead of, "I don't want you to know the camera is here."

Shots Frames are static. When one camera moves within a scene, it is called a shot. A shot is a series of frames. Shots are juxtaposed on television just as words are juxtaposed in a sentence. The mixing and matching of shots can deliver as many different messages as the mixing and matching of words in a sentence. There are a limited number of edits or transitions from shot to shot on TV. They are cuts, wipes, dissolves, and superimpositions. Often the last two are combined. A director can use seamless editing, which matches shot to shot and attempts to keep the camera invisible, or she can use jump cuts to jar us and call attention to the ingenuity of the camera. MTV makes excessive use of jump cuts.

Traditionally, a shot transition that suggests no passage of time or place is called a *match cut*. A *wipe* is like the curtain coming down or going up on stage and suggests the close or opening of a scene. It also suggests a passage of time and possibly place. When a TV image dissolves to black it also signals a passage of time. A *dissolve* and *superimposition* are used together for aesthetic or decorative purposes only. The speed of edits, transitions from one shot to the next, can set the tone for the scene or sequence just as tempo can set the mood in music. Staccato editing, as in the shower scene from *Psycho*, can build tension and be frightening. Long uninterrupted shots can call attention to the dialogue or other aspect of the scene that the director believes is important, or they can be used to suggest a sense of boredom.

Television as Visual Text

Like rhythm in music and syntax in language, these structural features pace the presentation of TV images and provide program continuity. Without thinking, we tacitly use these features to read the TV screen. It is similar to the linguistic process of reading a printed text. Television is a visual text that we read daily. If we read MTV in a traditional fashion, expecting matched cuts and seamless editing, we will be tossed around in the geography of the space by all the jump cuts.

In the TV text, messages are encoded visually. A *code* is a syntax pattern that can best be illustrated by reference to a verbal code. *Syntax* is the organization or arrangement of a communication. When an arrangement is consistently repeated in the production of a communication, a code develops (DeVaney, 1991). "Have a nice day," has become a code in the United States for a well-wishing goodbye. "Don't have a cow, man," is a borrowed code from television for telling someone to take it easy. "Whose been sitting in my chair?" is a code for the child listening to *The Three Bears*.

Codes develop only through repetition and we tacitly know the meaning of codes often before we can verbalize the meaning. In movie theaters, Alfred Hitchcock taught viewers to be afraid by offering a repeated visual syntax. Current film or TV watchers are frightened when a hand-held camera presents a villain's point of view (POV) shot while the camera stalks the victim in the woods or down the dark corridor of a house. The visual syntax used in the shower scene in the film *Psycho* has been repeated so often that fast-paced editing and jump cuts of body parts along with specific music have become a code for murder in a horror film.

Even when Bryant Gumbel presents the news on NBC, codes of realism are employed to make us believe in him and the news. But we are not watching Bryant Gumbel read the news, we are watching an electronic representation of him. This is one remove from reality. The camera changes him into a credible image. Camera and set codes are used to imitate reality. Among other broadcast news techniques, Gumbel is usually shot on the level, so we see him "eye to eye" and he gains our trust. It is difficult, but important, to remember that **the camera always lies**. It presents a fiction. It may record an authentic event, but that event is reshaped by the technology of television and presented as a story to us.

Your students will be empowered viewers if they understand that everything they watch on television is a text that has been constructed with intent by a director, encoded in socially constructed signs and symbols and interpreted by them as members of a community who have access to those signs and symbols. Television, therefore, can be explained in a linguistic fashion. To heighten their understanding, you may encourage their experimentation with video cameras, so they can experience the construction of a visual text just as they do the construction of an essay. This type of empowerment, however, is only the first step in the process of recognizing representations of nonstereotypic people of color, especially African Americans, on television. Such recognition includes the development of additional skills.

African Americans on Television

The 1991–92 prime time television season boasted of more situation comedies and dramatic series that starred or included African Americans than any other season to that time. On ABC, NBC, CBS, and FOX the following programs appeared: *Family Matters, True Colors, I'll Fly Away, Homefront, The Cosby Show, Fresh Prince of Bel Air,* and *Roc.* This trend has continued and can be a rich source for appropriating images of nonstereotypic African Americans for classroom presentation. You will have to search between and among these series, however, for the images you wish to include in your curriculum, because many of them tend to remain stereotyped. The popular Urkel in *Family Matters,* for example, is more of a caricature than a character; his antics are similar to a modern Step 'n' Fetchit.

Yet moments can occur in both formulaic and credible Black programs that are daring and offer us glimpses into the heart of African American social issues. *Roc* is a fairly formulaic situation comedy that sometimes takes risks. In one show, Roc's uncle informed his family that he was getting married and finally showed up with his intended, a White man. A less risky moment was presented on the *Fresh Prince of Bel Air* when the aunt brought home a White man whom she wished to marry. Such moments are ruptures in the visual text and can challenge viewers' beliefs in the unity of African Americans' values.

Although the directors of *True Colors* supplied a pat ending to one episode, it nonetheless worked against the stereotypic grain. The program was about an African American man with two teen-age sons, who is married to a White woman with one adolescent daughter. The risky episode was one in which one son, Lester, begins to expound the rhetoric of Malcolm X after reading his autobiography. Lester calls his brother a "clown in Black-face" and his sister a "bleeding heart liberal." His mother is a "White devil." Although Lester himself was usually clownish, he portrayed an authentic racial issue in the episode, and the vehicle for that portrayal is the voice of an African American leader and writer.

Identification of Responsible Images

How can we identify nonstereotypic images of African Americans on television? Some responsible representations are evident, such as the image of Whoopi Goldberg on *Sesame Street* talking about what it feels like to have black skin and curly black hair. Or, we might look for ruptures in narratives as cited above, but literary analysis offers us additional ways.

Agency

Help in identifying nonstereotypic images can come, again, from textual analysis. In novels, characters are said to be human if they incorporate *agency,* that is, if they are instrumental. If the reader feels the power of the characters because they have acted, not only reacted, they are credible. In simulating reality, producers of narratives most often display the agency of characters by allowing them to face odds from a protagonist or protagonistic force. The central character's humanity is shown by the manner in which she faces and overcomes or does not overcome those odds. In such a display, the audience may be able to see some growth in the character. Two of the central characters, Tre and Rickie, in *Boyz N the Hood* are credible because they face and overcome the odds in their childhood. Likewise, Doughboy, the troubled brother of Rickie, is credible because he does not overcome the odds. Yet, the viewer sees him thinking and struggling in a most human way to make sense of his life.

African American Literature

Another avenue open to us for the recognition of images of credible African Americans is Black literature. African American writers are the most reliable source of believable Black characters. We can study the delineation of characters in Black novels as well as investigate the themes, motifs, and styles of these books. This activity would provide us with authentic clues to the representation of African Americans on television. Gates (1988) has undertaken such an analysis and is able to describe the salient features of this literature. Surprisingly, there are rhetorical echoes of these features in current African American Hollywood films and to a lesser degree on television sitcoms and dramatic series.

Some characteristics of African American literature (Gates, 1988) that echo through films and television programs are extensive use of Black English, oppositional activity to domination within the narrative, and wide use of certain types of humor.

Black English

The rich dialect of African Americans has been preserved in Black oral and written narratives and was the vehicle used to keep the history of a culture alive when unlettered slaves told stories to their children. (Writings of these slaves and many Black free women have been collected and published. One source for these writings is in the Shaumberg Library of African American women writers of the 19th century.)

The oral preservation, however, of much of the history of the race heightens the importance of the use of Black English today, not only in novels, but also on television. In fact, the narrative nature of much of the dialogue and monologue in many novels by African Americans is essential to their plots and credibility. A recent exploration (Morrison, 1992) has been made into the way African American life and Black English influenced the structure of classical U.S. literature. To date, this influence has been denied.

While television viewers are familiar with listening to the sound of Black English employed by such comedians as Eddie Murphy, two Hollywood films display the instrumentality it has in the representation of Black teen-age boys. Black English is celebrated in all African American films, but two come to mind for their particular incorporation of the dialect for the pleasure of the audience. *Straight Out of Brooklyn* and *Boyz N the Hood* both incorporated specific Black English repartee between and among adolescent boys. It is as if a small window opens on one of the most disadvantaged groups in the United States today—adolescent Black males. Bantering, joking, and giving one another dozens (see the following "Humor" section), these boys affirm their bond with one another, against the White world, in socially horrific circumstances.

The features that Gates (1988) delineates are not discrete. Most of them are articulated in Black English and the incorporation of one is inextricably entwined with the other. Black English can be considered an overarching characteristic through which other African American narrative features are communicated.

Opposition

It should not be surprising that opposition to an oppressing social system is a theme running through Black literature. American classics such as *The Invisible Man, Native Son,* and *Go Tell it From the Mountain* are clear representations of the oppositional novel. Oppositional messages are promulgated now in many pop culture products. All the Hollywood Black films of the 1991–92 season had opposition as part of their theme. Of the 19 films produced in Hollywood by African American directors during that season, I recommend you select scenes from the following list to incorporate in your classroom.

Title	Director	Distributor
Boyz N the Hood	John Singelton	Columbia Pictures
The Five Heartbeats	Robert Townsend	20th Century Fox
Straight Out of Brooklyn	Matty Rich	Samuel Goldwyn Co.
Jungle Fever	Spike Lee	Spike Lee

Humor

Mimicry and dozens are two forms of humor articulated in African American literature, films, and TV programs. It has been suggested that humor became an essential part of Black daily life and story telling, because of a life-saving tendency to laugh in the face of adversity (Gates, 1988). Whether the development of these types of humor grew out of oppression is not the point here. Its expression in media represents an authentic cultural habit.

In a 1991 episode of *A Different World*, the women in a dorm of a Black college create a comic pageant of stereotypic images of Black women. These modern college women assume the roles of mammies, maids, and streetwalkers. Mimicking the stereotypes, the women illustrate the destructivenss of these images, but continue to probe the representations for unique qualities.

An argument arises that pits those who wish to totally deny the stereotypes and those who wish to embrace them as part of their heritage, but retain only their strong characteristics. Those who embrace these stereotypes carry the day. The message of the program is that, although media have exaggerated the representation of these Black women, the ingenuity and persistence of the original models gave courage to the Black college women.

Their situation, compared with the situation of a mammie, was completely different, yet they were able to appreciate the strength and ingenuity of these slaves and embrace them as forbearers of the Black woman's cultural heritage.[4]

This level of sophistication of Black images is rarely found on television. As evidence of the fact that we seek to find ourselves in the mirror of television, I cite the following. At my university, a large Mid-western institution, viewing rooms in both student unions were usually empty on Thursdays until *A Different World* started. Then, African American students gathered to view this program about Black college students. They did not gather to view the more highly acclaimed program, *The Cosby Show,* which aired before it.

The sophisticated scenario that appeared in *A Different World* would have been impossible to portray with African American men. Black male stereotypes were created to portray these men as socially impotent because of the threat of their perceived physical prowess. Media stereotypes of Black males are generally powerless, with one exception, and offer contemporary African American males nothing to emulate. They are usually "Uncle Toms," or "zip coons." The one exception is the representation of a brutal beast. If you think this representation is passè, a thing of the 19th century, remember the 1992 comment of the assistant secretary of mental health for the Bush Administration who said Blacks in the inner city were like "monkeys in the jungle."

What the African American college men portray and discuss on the same episode of *A Different World* is the giving of dozens. Dozens is an old form of deprecating humor in which one friend may "put down" another with a phrase that may begin, "Oh, your mother . . ." It is a jocular method of throwing barbs and is particularly masculine. In the *A Different World* episode, the college men are giving one another dozens in a dining room. One of their female classmates objects to the sexist nature of dozens. What ensues is a discussion on the origin of the activity. Although I knew the contemporary use of dozens, that episode taught me about history. The term, it was explained, arose from the selling of moderately disabled, weakened slaves, "by the dozens." A TV sitcom helped the viewers encounter and remember their national heritage.

Black images created by African Americans will persist on television and in Hollywood films, so these media will always be rich source materials for the appropriation of nonstereotypic images for the multicultural classroom.

Multicultural Curriculum

Because television competes with you as a classroom teacher, you can design a curriculum that makes space for that competition. Whatever subject you teach, you and your students can appropriate examples of nonstereotypic African Americans on television. Furthermore, the time you spend helping students realize their tacit television reading skills will empower them. They may become critical consumers of those mediated images. Placing the video technology in student hands will also teach them about the constructed nature of visual messages. It will teach them how cameras lie.

There are several ways you can teach your students to recognize responsible images of African Americans or other people of color. In addition to relying on common sense, your students may ask themselves if a character in a narrative displays agency. Also, African American literature will provide clues to help identify credible Black images. Features such as Black English, oppositional activity, mimicry, and dozens are a few hallmarks of authentic Black narration. Rhetorical echoes of Black narration appear and will continue to appear in films and on television.

Other People of Color

Educators should be aware of and include in their curricula images of groups other than African Americans, such as Hispanics, Asians, and American Indians. The structural model offered here can be applied to the analysis of representations of any person of color. If it were to be applied to a reading of Hispanic images, however, it would have to be used in its traditional critical form. In other words, it must be used to locate stereotypes.

Unfortunately, when we analyze Hispanic media images we do not have the privilege of flipping the critical model to locate credible Latina or Chicana representations. Enough emphasis has been placed on the presentation of nonstereotypic African Americans to justify a search for their credible images. Yet media representations of Hispanics, whose population figures exceed those of African Americans, are predominantly stereotypic.

A first stage of recognition must occur. Whereas students would summarily reject a Step 'n' Fetchit characterization of a Black male, they might not reject an image of a lazy Chicano. They are undereducated about Hispanic stereotypes. They might not recognize the hysterical Chicana, nor the dark, mysterious Latina as stereotypes. The structural model could be used to educate students about these stereotypes.

Another unfortunate fact about the representations of Hispanics is that educators and students need not scour popular culture artifacts to find stereotypes. Programs made for educational channels and for the classroom on videotape are fraught with stereotypes. In fact, it would be more important in this case for students to locate stereotypes in the materials prepared for them rather than on TV or in the movie theater. Construction of stereotypes, then, is not assigned to the distant Hollywood or commercial television world. Hispanic images, specifically designed for consumption by students, are often found to be patently stereotypic.

One example may crystalize the issue. In the late 1980s the respected Children's Television Workshop produced *Square One TV (SOTV)*, a mathematics program designed for after-school consumption on PBS stations by 8-to 12-year-olds. Subsequently, it was placed on videotape for use in the classroom. A 1990 study of the representation of people of color on this program uncovered the following facts:

1. *SOTV* characters with foreign accents appear regularly in each program and are always parodied.

2. Hispanic cast members are seen frequently in skits ridiculing Hispanics. They must exaggerate their accents and certain behaviors, i.e., those which make them appear sexy, mysterious, hysterical, lazy. In these skits, they are not allowed to use standard English, although they use standard English daily. (DeVaney & Elenes, 1991, p. 20)

Suffice it to say that this is an age of new racism in which program designers have relaxed their standards on equal treatment and do not think it inappropriate to poke fun at people of color.

Examples such as the *SOTV* representations abound in educational materials, but it is a mistake to believe that any instructional formula exists for multicultural studies. Even though the structural model presented here provides information about the form and codes of photographic images, educators must know enough about the culture represented before they apply the model.

In the two cases presented here, African American and Hispanic instances, I needed to understand what a stereotypic and credible image was in each culture before I began. That understanding came from a wide reading of African American literature and criticism in the first case and from my partner, a Chicana, in the second case. My knowledge of Mexican and Latin American literature and Hollywood film also helped in the second case. I describe this here to make the point that time must be spent studying the culture to be examined. A multicultural curriculum that seeks blanket lessons to study people of color will fail.

Television, Film, and Teacher Education in the United States

The study of film and television in U.S. schools of education has been and is under the purview of Instructional Technology. There is no formal space in teacher preparation programs for the study of film and television. If such study takes place, it is because of the personal interest of an education faculty member, most likely one who teaches language arts.

Such avoidance of formal media study is not tolerated in some other Western countries which require such study to be included in the curricula of elementary through secondary schools. This media curriculum is often referred to as visual or media literacy. Such literacy is eschewed in the United States for two reasons: Visual media, particularly television, are considered by American curriculum developers as vehicles that interfere with the cognitive development of students and therefore unworthy of study. Second, Instructional Technology, the only formal arena for the study of media hardware operation and selection of software, is a discipline similar to educational psychology. The epistemology of both disciplines considers the learner a single unit, a functioning brain. Learning theories that inform Instructional Technology research and, consequently, teacher education and "audio-visual" requirements are psychological in nature, either behavioral or cognitive. Teachers in training are treated as individual functioning brains who must be trained to make overheads, run slide and film projectors, and operate video and computer equipment. Their involvement with film or television programs is relegated to learning how to fill out preprinted evaluation forms.

Every educational technology, instructional technology, or audio-visual textbook printed in the United States today includes the requirements I have just mentioned—and excludes visual literacy. Many states require 3–12 instructional technology credits for teachers in training, but what is mandated is based on state department of education requirements. These requirements have been formulated by instructional technologists trained in behavioral and cognitive learning styles.

History

There are historical reasons that Instructional Technology practitioners ignore visual literacy. Instructional Technology started as a field of study after World War II. Before then, an eclectic area of audio-visual study was recognized on the periphery of serious educational studies. The only format platform for this area was the Division of Audio Visual Instruction (DAVI), part of the National Education Association. There was no formal space for the study of radio and film in the teacher education curriculum between World War I and World War II, but individual educators supported its promulgation.

DAVI was made up of educational psychologists, librarians, art teachers, English teachers, Hollywood filmmakers, radio producers, etc.—a healthy assortment of representatives with varied educational theories. Those representatives who elected to conduct audio-visual research used a potpourri of existing methods, most of which were not rigorous. (General educational research was not rigorously conducted between the two world wars.) With the onset of World War II and the induction of thousands into the armed forces, the first opportunity for rigorous audio-visual experimentation arose. These men had to be trained to operate hardware and their desire to fight needed to be honed. Film was selected as the means and operant conditioning was selected as the method of training. B. F. Skinner and other behavioralists were also drafted.

Massive experiments were conducted on learning from film and the manner in which film is affective. Two academic disciplines arose from these experiments, Instructional Technology and Communication Research, and the terrain was divided. Communication Research found a home in speech and theater departments in universities across the United States, while Instructional Technology was positioned in education departments.

That positioning is as important as what was studied in the two areas. Instructional Technology owned the war studies on film and training and continued the operant conditioning research. Their positioning in colleges of education where research was predominantly behavioral encouraged this line of inquiry. The audio-visual field, newly named Instructional Technology, had bought its formal berth in academia through the rigor of operant conditioning and continues its psychological inquiry today in cognitive science.

Communication Research, on the other hand, had designed and applied attitudinal film studies during World War II. Although the researchers' work was initially informed by behaviorism, the nature of their inquiry and their placement in academia allowed them to expand their epistemological base. As a learning theory, operant conditioning had little to offer those who studied human attitudes. Also the positioning of communication faculty in colleges of letters and science brought them into close proximity with those who studied humanities, linguistics, and sociology. Their purchase on the academic berth had to be obtained with broader notions of human learning and communication. Film studies today exist outside colleges of education in departments of communication or, in a very few cases, in media studies departments.

Visual Literacy and Structuralism

There are visual literacy curricula in some developed Western countries such as Great Britain, the Netherlands, Switzerland, and Australia—where the power of the media, especially television, is considered formidable by educators. You may wish to call the model for reading television, presented here, visual literacy, but it is not based on any visual literacy curriculum. It is based on the author's semiotic system for the reading of any television program (DeVaney & Elenes, in press) and has been labeled the grammar of television.

Labels are not important here, except when it comes to naming the structural parts of a television program. The vocabulary of this chapter provides those names and a model for the reading of television which moves systematically from small structural units to large television units. I will explain the structural theory that informs this model for the reading of television and provide a diagram of the TV structures which you know tacitly, but need to articulate to yourself and students. I encourage you to use the African American examples provided in this chapter to explain these structures to your students. I further encourage you to find examples of credible African Americans on television and use these to teach your students to read TV programs.

The model of reading television used here is based on semiotics, a specific structural method for the analysis of any communicative system. *Structuralism* is basically a belief that the form of an artifact communicates as much as the content of that artifact. *Semiotics* considers any communicative system, whether visual, verbal, written, acted, or digitized, to be essentially a language made up of signs and symbols. At the heart of semiotics is the belief that all signs and symbols are socially generated.

Semioticians would say that knowledge is primarily social, secondarily psychological. For instance, the meanings we assign to words (signs) are negotiated in daily use, agreed upon by a community of users and are sometimes renegotiated in daily use. (This is how "bad" can come to mean "good.") When meanings are agreed upon, they become codified, so the patterned syntax or organization of words (signs) may be called *codes*. Codes are central to the study of semiotics, because they lead the reader from denotative to connotative meanings.

Video structures, frame, shot, transition, and scene are also signs whose meanings have been negotiated in daily production and are agreed upon by daily viewers. When the organization of these signs becomes predictable, the TV reader is interpreting a syntax pattern or a code. As with language, the meanings of signs and codes can shift. As I explained earlier, MTV has changed the meaning of the transition known as a *cut.* Television is available for semiotic analysis, because it is made up of several communicative systems: verbal, audio, sound effects, music, and most importantly, electronic pictures. These pictures are assembled and read as a language.

The structural elements considered in this chapter are diagrammed below. Remember, they may be read in two ways, syntactically or in a denotative fashion, and paradigmatically or as codes which connote other meanings. It is not necessary that you know the words *syntactic* and *paradigmatic,* but simply the concepts behind the two labels.

"What is included in a frame is read not only by its content, but by what has been excluded. If you see a televised shot of Magic Johnson advertising athletic shoes on a basketball court, you interpret his movement as if it were set within a stadium." The structural elements of the frame supply syntactical meaning, while the imagined setting supplies paradigmatic meaning. This is akin to connotation and denotation.

"Among other broadcast news codes, Mr. Gumbel is usually shot on the level, so we can see him 'eye to eye' and he gains our trust." In this shot there are syntax patterns or codes that signify a particular meaning. The codes provide paradigmatic meaning (loosely connotative) and the organization of the shot supplies syntactic meaning (loosely denotative). The codes in this shot are drawn from the world or paradigm of broadcast news. In that world a code signifying "reality" developed in daily production practices. A believable or "real" newscaster was shot on the level; he looked straight into the camera; there was more front or "key" lighting to shorten the depth of field and bring him closer to the viewer. The only part of this code for "reality" that was original was the lighting technique; other techniques were borrowed from the world of documentary filmmaking.

Notes

1. Methods of structural textual analysis are delineated in works of Terry Eagleton, Christian Metz, James Monaco, early Roland Barthes and early Umberto Eco.

2. Critiques of African American literature can be found in works of Toni Morrison, bell hooks, Zora Neale Hurston, Henry Louis Gates, Jr., and Nellie McKay.

3. The term *postmodern* can best be explained by reference to narratives. Postmodern narratives valorize cities and technology, whereas modern narratives pit a heroic figure against technology. Modern novels explore the psyche of a heroic or antiheroic character, but postmodern novels are concerned with social interactions of people with one another and with their environment. In a

postmodern world, images from all systems of communication are as important, if not more important, than words. The form of the postmodern image communicates as much as the content. Irony and cynicism inform the style of most postmodern art. Fine and popular art are often interchangeable. Images and plots are often fractured in postmodern narratives.

4. This position is one with which I disagree. As a television analyst, I think the use of the stereotypic images does more harm than good. I can respect this position, however, as an authentic one.

References

Alm, R. (1991, November). It's reality day in the neighborhood. *Swathmore College Bulletin, 89*(3), 6–9.

DeVaney, A. (1991). A grammar of educational television. In D. Hlynka and J. C. Belland (Eds.), *Paradigms regained: The uses of illuminative, semiotic and postmodern criticisms as modes of inquiry in educational technology* (pp. 241–280). New York: Educational Technology Publications.

DeVaney, A., & Elenes, A. (in press). *Square One TV, gender, race, and ethnicity*. In R. Muffoletto (Ed.), *Educational technology and culture*. Cresskill, NJ: Hampton Press.

Gates, H. L., Jr. (1988). *The signifying monkey: A theory of Afro-American literary criticism*. New York: Oxford University Press.

hooks, b. (1991) Black is a woman's color. In H. L. Gates, Jr. (Ed.), *Bearing witness: Selections from African American autobiography in the twentieth century* (p. 339). New York: Pantheon Books.

Hurston, Z. N. (1990). *Their eyes were watching god*. New York: Harper Perennial.

Lacan, J. (1977). *Ecrits: A selection*. A. Sheridan (Trans.). New York: Norton.

McLuhan, M. (1964). *Understanding media: The extensions of man*. New York: McGraw-Hill.

Morrison, T. (1992). *Playing in the dark: Whiteness and the literary imagination*. Cambridge, MA: Harvard University Press.

◆ ◆ ◆ ◆

No person is your friend who demands your silence, or denies your right to grow.
Alice Walker

What happens to a dream deferred? Does it dry up like a raisin in the sun?
Langston Hughes

A community is democratic only when the humblest and weakest person can enjoy the highest civil, economic, and social rights that the biggest and most powerful possess.

A. Philip Randolph

A society committed to the search for truth must give protection to, and set a high value upon, the independent and original mind, however angular, however rasping, however socially unpleasant it may be; for it is upon such minds in large measure, that the effective search for truth depends.
Carl P. Haskin (New York Times, December 9, 1963)

Here everybody is now from the same village even if they come from different parts of China.
Amy Tan, The Joy Luck Club (NY: Ballantine, 1989), 300.

Part 4

◆ ◆ ◆ ◆

The Classroom and the Community

Chapter 18

◆ ◆ ◆ ◆

Field Experiences: Planting Seeds and Pulling Weeds

Marilynne Boyle-Baise

Indiana University

Christine E. Sleeter

California State University—Monterey Bay

What does it mean to experience racism? Do different racial groups experience racism the same way? What does it mean to hold a job and still live in poverty? Does housing discrimination really happen in the 1990s? How can a family consisting of a grandmother, two children, their cousin, and their neighbor be functional? What does "Indian time" really mean?

These are examples of questions that require exploration if one is to offer children an education that is multicultural and social reconstructionist. Such an education demands substantial restructuring of classroom instruction and of schooling in ways that build on strengths and aspirations of oppressed groups. This restructuring also should help all students learn and think multiculturally and examine and challenge various forms of oppression.

How do we approach such questions for ourselves, particularly with reference to groups we do not belong to? In university course work, teacher education students may encounter information about areas such as racism, classism, sexism, learning and communication styles, and cultural world views. Often this information is presented as something to memorize for a test—only to forget it later; it is not connected to any life experiences.

Duckworth (1991) tells a story from the radio show *A Hitchhiker's Guide to the Galaxy:*

> In one episode, a computer is built expressly for the purpose of answering the question, "What is the meaning of life, the universe, and everything?" When it is ready, they ask if it can answer that question. It says, yes, it can, but that it will take . . . seven million years. They say, "Well, OK, go to it." Seven million years later, whoever is around goes to learn the answer. The computer says that it does have the answer, but that it might be a little disappointing. "No, no," they say, "go ahead, what is it?" "Forty-two," the computer says. (p. 7)

Without an experiential basis in which to locate cognitive information about diversity and inequality, terms such as *institutional discrimination, oppositional identity,* or *fictive kinship system* have about as much meaning as *forty-two.*

In the teacher education program, field experiences can provide students with some experiential basis for theory presented in their course work. Learning in the field is vital to developing understandings of education that is multicultural. However, field experiences as they are normally structured are not useful for this purpose. We will critique field experiences as most teacher education students experience them, cite examples of some that are structured differently, and provide suggestions for learning from the field. We also will suggest applications of this discussion of teacher education to teaching in the elementary and middle school classroom.

The Importance of Perspective

Teachers make decisions based on what seems important and reasonable to them, assumptions which are rooted in their perspectives. Teacher perspective is defined as the following:

A construct that captures the ideas, behaviors, and context of particular teaching acts; [it is] anchored in the world of actual situations and [has] reference to particular behaviors. Therefore, a teacher perspective is a theory of action that has developed as a result of the individual's experiences and is applied in particular situations. (Ross, 1988a, p. 102)

Teachers' perspectives are rooted partially in their prior experience in school. When teacher education students enter classrooms, they enter familiar places, even if the students are unfamiliar. Familiarity with what constitutes teaching and schooling influences what they attend to and encourages them to accept and try to replicate what they see teachers doing (Britzman, 1986; Feiman-Nemser & Buchmann, 1985).

Teachers' perspectives are also rooted in their general life experiences, which provide a basis for generalizations, decisions about what is important, and styles of relating to others. Perspective acts as a filter through which teacher education students interpret course work and other experiences, as well as shaping how they approach teaching. Most preservice students take their own perspectives for granted, as natural, as the "way things are" (Armaline & Hoover, 1989). A student may not realize that his or her perspective is only one way of perceiving reality and that it may include inaccuracies, such as what children's home lives are like, how students learn, and what their community regards as worth learning.

How does teacher perspective relate directly to diversity and inequality? We will illustrate with a comparison of two groups of teachers or preservice students. McDiarmid (1990) studied a group of White, middle-class, female preservice students. Within their perspectives, good teaching was defined as covering textbook materials while keeping the classroom operating in an orderly manner. Children, especially those of color or who were poor, needed to master basic skills (as opposed to higher order thinking skills). They believed that children who performed poorly were responsible for their own failure because their home environments were inadequate or they lacked the proper attitude or ability for learning.

Similarly, Ginsburg and Newman (1985) found 12 of 14 preservice students in an urban university believed social inequality was due either to lack of effort and cultural deprivation within a free and open social system, or to individual attitudes and prejudice; only two viewed it as a result of unfair institutional structures.

In contrast, research on effective teachers for students of color illustrated a different perspective. Ladson-Billings (1990) studied eight effective teachers of African American students. She found that one of the most important factors they had in common was their culture of reference, or the cultural group on which they drew most heavily in constructing their perspectives about teaching. Seven of the eight (both African American and White) considered African American people when constituting their main culture of reference; they conscientiously turned to African American adults as their primary source of information about education of African American students.

As a result, their teaching was highly congruent with experiences and styles of their students, and built on the African American community's valuing for education. They perceived students' home and cultural background as a resource for learning rather than a cause for failure. In an ethnographic study of secondary schools, Metz (1990) found White teachers experienced great difficulty contacting many of the African American parents, but the African American teachers, who had a good conceptual map of the African American community and therefore knew how to locate the parents, did not experience this difficulty. Lack of familiarity with the African American community led the White teachers to assume their difficulties were rooted in parents' lack of concern for education.

In other words, teachers who have a strong familiarity with a racial minority group regarded students' home and neighborhood as a strong departure point for further learning; teachers without this familiarity regarded it as a hindrance to learning. One does not need to be a member of another cultural group to develop a perspective about education that genuinely includes other groups. But without working at it, one's perspective about teaching is not necessarily inclusive of any other cultural groups than one's own.

To teach within a framework of education that is multicultural and social reconstructionist requires an understanding of how institutions—including schools—perpetuate inequality, and the ability to visualize alternative institutional arrangements. One way to begin to build this understanding is to examine one's own perspectives and compare them with those of other preservice teachers to determine the ideas and beliefs that guide teaching actions.

Some of the questions that need to be raised include the following: (1) What group(s) serves as the main culture of reference for teaching? (2) What is known about the aspirations, cultural patterns, and strengths of oppressed groups? (3) In what ways should teaching relate to students' life experiences? (4) To what extent are the notions of educational equality and equity integrated into beliefs and actions? We propose that teacher education programs help preservice students reconsider and perhaps reconstruct their perspectives to support greater equality and multiculturalism. One way to examine and challenge the "web of beliefs" (McDiarmid, 1990) of preservice teachers is to carefully construct field experiences that provide a foundation on which alternative perspectives can be built.

Field Experiences in Teacher Education

Although some educators are skeptical of their value, most teachers and preservice students regard field experiences as the most important part of the teacher education program, and as a potentially powerful vehicle for connecting theories and generalizations with the "real world" of the school. Field experiences have been a part of teacher education longer than any other component, and are the most widely accepted component of teacher education. A century ago, formal teacher education consisted of practicing in the classroom, with supervision and feedback. Gradually, course work was added to precede student teaching. The longer and more complex this course work became, the more programs began to accompany at least some of the course work with early field experiences (Cruickshank & Armaline, 1986). While most states increased the number of hours required in the field, there was little alteration in the design of field experiences (Zeichner, 1981–1982). But "more" is not necessarily "better." Teacher educators should take a serious look at what is learned in the field and consider the extent to which outcomes match goals for the experience (Zeichner, 1981–1982).

Preservice students use field experiences mainly as a transition from the university to assumption of a teacher's role. Applegate and Lasley (1985), Evans (1986), and Killian and McIntyre (1988) found preservice students used field experiences to determine whether teaching was really for them, discern what good teachers did by watching them, acquire techniques to use later, practice using skills, and find out how teachers handled problems.

In addition, a considerable amount of research has found that what preservice students do in field experiences usually encourages imitation. Goodman (1985) studied field experience students, and summarized what generally happened in the field (see also Joyce, 1988; Tabachnick, Popkewitz, & Zeichner, 1980; Zeichner, 1980):

> Students had little control over either what or how content would be taught. Only a few students used techniques to encourage pupil problem-solving, self-directed learning and research, and thoughtful interpretation and expression of content. The vast majority were observed doing routine, mechanical types of teaching activities involving little creativity. However, the quantity of field experience meant that each [student teacher] said that by the end of their final practicum, they were "ready to teach." What most students meant was that they had become technically proficient: they had learned how to manage and organize the given curriculum and classroom schedule, and they had learned enough discipline techniques to feel secure in facing a classroom of twenty to thirty children. (p. 36)

In general, most preservice students perceive themselves as having learned how to teach once they have learned to take over management of routines in a cooperating teacher's classroom smoothly (Feiman-Nemser & Buchmann, 1985).

To challenge this preoccupation with copying patterns of behavior, some teacher educators encourage students to think reflectively about teaching when they are in classrooms (Beyer, 1984; Grant & Zeichner, 1984; Zeichner, 1981–1982; Zeichner & Liston, 1987). Reflective teaching is rooted in the work of Dewey (1938), who was concerned about educating students (and teachers) in a way that would help them continue to learn. To Dewey, experimentation and reflection were essential to learning and further learning; on the other hand, imitation hindered further growth and learning.

To encourage reflective teaching, Dewey described three attitudes that were prerequisites to reflective behavior:

1. Teachers need to be open-minded or willing to consider alternative possibilities or inaccuracies in accepted ways of thinking.

2. Teachers need to take responsibility for the consequences of their actions. For example, responsible teachers regard their choice of what and how to teach as important decisions about what is considered worth knowing or doing.

3. Reflective teachers need to pursue the attitudes defined above with wholeheartedness; this means open-mindedness and responsibility are integrated within normal, daily approaches to teaching and learning. (Grant & Zeichner, 1984)

Further, Dewey warned that placing teaching candidates in classrooms before they have developed the habits of reflection will result in candidates adopting the methods and recommendations of their supervising teacher (Denton, 1986).

Those who argue that field experiences should promote reflectivity disagree about exactly what this means, and consequently address it differently. (See Gore, 1987.) The approach exemplified by Cruickshank (1985) is concerned about helping preservice students learn to apply pedagogical and psychological theories to facilitate the achievement of predetermined teaching goals (such as having students learn a particular concept in the given curriculum). The assumption of this approach to reflection is that schools are structured as they should be, but that to maximize effectiveness, teachers should base as many decisions as they can on scientifically validated theories. Cruickshank developed a laboratory-type process in which students teach a carefully controlled lesson and then analyze what happened, focusing mainly on the methods used and their effect.

A different approach to reflective teaching, exemplified by Zeichner (1981–1982), is more concerned about having preservice students examine links between schooling and broader political and ethical issues. Zeichner encouraged preservice students to examine curriculum and instruction for emphasis on particular content and certain habits of learning, consider who benefitted from these curricular and instructional designs, and think about the extent to which the nature of teaching is just and fair for all students. The assumption behind his approach to reflection is that schools are not necessarily structured and run fairly for all students, and that bringing about changes that are just requires educators to question rather than take what they see for granted.

We support Dewey's ideas about reflectivity and the importance of practicing reflective behavior in preservice experiences. For purposes of learning to teach from a position of multiculturalism and social reconstructionism, field experiences need to be structured from the orientation to reflection described by Zeichner rather than the one described by Cruickshank. Our discussion in the remainder of this chapter sketches alternative field experiences that actually plant seeds of awareness about social issues, and pull the weeds of imitation.

Using the Field as a Basis for Reconstructing Teaching

To construct an education that is multicultural and social reconstructionist, one must (1) understand how oppression is institutionalized through various institutions including schools, and how people respond to it, (2) have a rich working knowledge of cultural groups other than one's own—which may entail getting past a period of initial culture shock in which negative stereotypes may be reinforced, (3) believe strongly in the desire and ability of members of oppressed groups to achieve, and recognize steps they are taking to do that, and (4) be able to translate this knowledge and belief into actions in schools that may look quite different from what one has experienced.

In reviewing the literature on field experiences in teacher education, we found only a small proportion that discussed how they could be structured to accomplish these goals. However, we also found some useful models. We will organize our description of these models into four broad categories: (1) placement in classrooms with culturally diverse student populations; (2) ethnography in communities, schools, and classrooms; (3) action research in classrooms; and (4) immersion in culturally diverse communities.

Teacher education students may wonder how such information will be helpful to them, because their field experiences usually are already structured. We suggest that preservice students apply as much of the following as possible in their field experiences, and that they supplement these as much as possible with experiences outside their programs, even if they do not receive university credit for them. In our experience, suggestions such as those discussed here have benefitted many students.

Field Experiences in Classrooms with Culturally Diverse Students

Teacher educators often recommend that preservice students have field experiences in culturally diverse schools to prepare them for the likelihood that they may teach in such schools. The assumption is that contact with children from other racial backgrounds will help develop positive attitudes, a sense of comfort, and perhaps some knowledge. A small amount of research assessed this assumption, and reported that such field experiences did indeed promote positive attitudes, although the improved attitudes may not last very long (Gipe, Duffy, & Richards, 1989; Hennington, 1981).

Based on our experience working with preservice students, however, we do not support the unqualified benefits of such an experience. Without help in processing what they see, preservice students may leave the field experience with more or stronger stereotypes than when they entered the field. For example, if one has heard that Asians are quiet or Mexican Americans are lazy, seeing a few students who fit the stereotype can confirm such beliefs.

Further, most teachers and administrators are White, middle-class professionals, and unless they have broadened their primary culture of reference, their schools and classrooms reflect almost exclusively the norms and expectations of mainstream society. One example of these norms and expectations is what is considered acceptable student behavior. For example, African American children in the classroom sometimes do not adhere to the teacher's rule about raising their hands or waiting until called on to ask or answer a question until they have been reprimanded several times. On the surface they may appear boisterous and disobedient. However, African American children may be expected to speak up in their home environments where lively discussions are normal. African American children can learn a different rule for classroom behavior, but many respond negatively to constant reprimands for a rule that may not have been explained and differs from the pattern at home.

Having said this, we encourage preservice students to locate as many field experiences as possible in schools with diverse cultural populations. Look for classrooms in which the teacher has an excellent knowledge of the strengths and interests of the students' communities. Such teachers have developed an understanding of the cultural group of the majority of the students, and probably are very comfortable with students. They are also highly successful with the students they teach. Teachers usually share with preservice students their own perspective about their students; the most helpful perspective will be one that accurately highlights students' strengths.

Field experiences in classrooms with culturally diverse students also should be combined with additional activities we describe later.

Ethnography in Communities, Schools, and Classrooms

Ethnography is not a familiar type of inquiry to many teacher educators or preservice students. Ethnographic research is a part of anthropology. Ethnographers try to understand complex settings through the eyes of the observer *and* the participants, and assume that to understand a social setting one needs to connect the observed behavior with rationales for that behavior. They collect as many kinds of information as feasible, including observations, interviews, maps, artifacts, and photographs. In addition, the ethnographer seeks to report the "truth" of a setting by including many "voices" or perspectives in the telling of the story.

Ethnographic techniques of careful observation and interviewing, and practice in discovering patterns one had not previously paid attention to, are useful for teachers. Such investigation can help teachers understand communities, schools, and classrooms, especially in culturally diverse settings, where actions and meanings are complex and people view them differently. Preservice students can learn to use processes of ethnographic research to examine the familiar world of schools and classrooms as students might see and experience them. In addition, preservice students can use ethnographic research to discover strengths and perspectives of a sociocultural group that is different from their own. Examples of both focuses for ethnographic investigations follow.

In our experience, most preservice students are largely unable to delineate dimensions of classroom life or consider what classrooms would look like from a multicultural perspective. We use this as a starting point for ethnography. For one project, we introduced six components of the classroom that preservice students were to observe and describe:

1. Aesthetic/visual environment
2. Instructional materials
3. Content of lessons
4. Social organization of the class
5. Student-student interaction
6. Student-teacher interaction

We developed questions to consider about how the classroom functioned for students from different race, class, or gender groups. For example, in regard to the aesthetic/visual environment, we asked students to draw pictures of bulletin boards, mobiles, other decorations, and learning centers. To encourage reflection from a multicultural perspective we asked them: What kinds of people seem welcome here? Does the room reflect the children and teachers' work and interests? Are there stereotypes, or are groups of people omitted?

We used class time to help students analyze their findings. We raised questions about the relationship between the site population and their observations, and asked students to consider how race, class, and gender relationships in the community at large (local, state, and national) influenced what they saw in classrooms.

We also used ethnographic methods to help preservice students investigate the curriculum taught in schools. Students collected artifacts that represented the curriculum, including textbooks, assignments, bulletin board displays, posters, and projects. These artifacts were categorized in terms of what information, skills, or attitudes were deemed "important to know" and what were relegated to the status of "nice to know."

Students also asked questions such as the following to analyze the curriculum: What information, skills, and attitudes were emphasized? To what extent was the information correct, nonstereotypic, and unbiased? To what extent was it weighted toward Euro-American male accomplishments? And, what messages were sent about race, social class, and gender through "need to know" and "nice to know" distinctions?

Gottlieb and Cornbleth (1988) and Teitelbaum and Britzman (1991) used ethnographic inquiry to examine the context of the school rather than the classroom. Preservice students were encouraged to investigate such areas as discipline procedures, racial integration, and teacher work. They were urged to speak to teachers, students, and administrators about each area. Investigations could include collection of discipline codes, neighborhood walks, school-grounds surveys, and interviews with varied members of the school population.

Data collected from such assignments can be analyzed in terms of equitable treatment of students across race, class, and gender.

Using discipline procedures as an example, the following questions could be raised: What is considered appropriate behavior? For which cultural group(s) are these expectations similar to behavioral norms in students' homes? Who is suspended most often, for what offenses? Are suspensions proportionate to the population of particular groups in the school?

Ethnographic investigations can be complex or simple, depending on available time and what one wants to accomplish. For example, some preservice students view playgrounds in inner cities as chaotic; with help in observing systematically, in a short period of time they can learn to identify organized behavior and purpose in children's activity. Speakers of "Standard English" often view other English dialects as haphazard and full of errors. With guidance, they can learn to identify grammatic and phonemic patterns they had not noticed earlier.

Ethnographic investigations can also be carried out in the community. For example, preservice students can identify community agencies that serve a particular sociocultural group (such as community centers, ethnic clubs, homeless shelters), and volunteer their time. While there, they can begin to understand why people come to the center; or they can become sensitized to the deprivations many people experience. It can also provide them with an insider's view of a self-help agency that is run by a sociocultural group the student may not have perceived as having self-help organizations.

As another example, preservice students can compare the prices of gasoline and groceries in the inner city and the suburbs. They could then investigate the type of transportation available to an inner-city resident who might want to shop in a suburban store. Students who have done this kind of investigation have been surprised to realize that the inner-city resident pays more for some items than does the suburbanite, and may need to take a long bus ride—transferring two or three times—to reach the better prices and better merchandise. The notion of institutional discrimination begins to take on substance during such investigations.

Preservice students will need help learning to interview and listen to what they hear, and to observe as carefully as possible. Much of the value of ethnography to a teacher is learning to tune in carefully to the perspectives and experiences of others, and to recognize and suspend one's own assumptions. Usually preservice students will need help interpreting their findings; the instructor should plan an active role in processing their investigations.

This is especially important when ethnography is used to learn about institutional inequality or perspectives of oppressed people. For example, Teitelbaum and Britzman (1991) reported that they cautioned students about developing generalizations from the limited data of one ethnographic study, but at the same time helped students relate their findings to social norms: "We probably play our most active role in class discussions in helping to clarify for students the relationship between the experiences they observed within the school and the social structures that exist 'outside'" (p. 181).

Action Research Activities in the Classroom

Action research is an investigation of one's own teaching practice. For example, preservice students may investigate how they initiate lessons, or the types of questions they use to guide discussion, or the extent of their consistency in carrying out managerial procedures.

The task of self-inquiry takes place through a cycle of reflection, which includes the following dimensions: plan, act, observe, and replan. Preservice students plan to study an area of their teaching, act or teach in accordance with their plan, observe or have a colleague observe their teaching, and replan or reflect about the area of study based on data collected (e.g., Gore, 1991; Noffke & Brennan, 1991; Zeichner & Liston, 1987).

Many teacher educators use action research to challenge the tendency of preservice students to imitate the teacher. They argue that the process accomplishes several purposes: First, what is taken for granted about practice is treated as problematic—opening the door for discussion. Second, students have the opportunity to take charge of their own practice and learn how to modify it if necessary (e.g., Ferguson, 1989; Hollingsworth, 1988; Noffke & Brennan, 1991; Zeichner, 1983).

Action research can promote a multicultural perspective if students study dimensions of race, class, and gender in their teaching, although action research was not usually focused in this way in the research literature we examined. This focus could easily be built into the proposal stage during which students consider what aspects of their teaching they want to study and why this has educational significance.

For example, preservice students might investigate the attention they pay to individual children. Questions for the planning stage of action research could include: What is the purpose and pattern I use for giving students attention? Who gets the most and least positive and negative attention and why? Are my actions biased in relation to race, class, or gender? The lesson could then be tape-recorded or videotaped, then analyzed for patterns in distribution of attention to students.

As another example, a preservice student could study the use of cooperative learning to promote positive cross-group interaction. During planning and analysis the following areas could be investigated: How should children be grouped and what tasks should be assigned to accomplish positive interaction among children who may differ by race, gender, social class or learning abilities?

In our experience, we found equal educational opportunity and educational equity extremely useful concepts to guide the development of action research inquiries. Reference to these concepts helps students consider race, class, and gender within investigations of classroom practice. The very task of defining these terms led to lively discussions about "access" and "outcomes" and the difference between treating students "the same" or "equally."

Following these discussions, students decided to investigate such areas as the use of rap music to teach poetry, the use of multicultural literature to broaden students' awareness of others, and the inclusion of a variety of role models (e.g., men, women, people of color, and people with disabilities) in lessons about the community. As students completed action research tasks, we asked them to reflect upon what their findings meant for providing equal opportunity or achieving educational equity for students in their classes, and to consider the implications of their findings for teaching in general.

Action research is limited for several reasons. First, preservice students usually have time to complete only one cycle of inquiry or research one question (e.g., Noffke & Brennan, 1991). These studies just begin to shed light on teaching practice and the process of studying one's own teaching. We think of it as planting seeds for further growth. This limitation can be eased somewhat by sharing inquiries in seminars. This provides a repertoire of teaching experiences and projects that speak to equity in some way.

Second, this research—like ethnography—is a case study, and in generalizing from one particular context to teaching in general, one must be cautious at the very least. For example, what can we determine about the use of multicultural literature after reading a few stories to children? What does the teaching of poetry through rap rhythms at one site tell us about teaching at other sites? These caveats do not argue for the limitation of action research itself, but rather for careful consideration of the results of the research. It is necessary to guard against reproducing practice just because it worked for one or two preservice teachers; this is the definition of *experience* that we challenge.

Immersion Experiences

The activities just discussed can help preservice students think critically about teaching, but are limited primarily to schools and classrooms. Ultimately, the best way to reconstruct one's own perspective about a wide range of topics is to spend extended time living with the people in a culturally different community.

Several things usually happen if one stays long enough. First, stereotypes about the group as a whole begin to evaporate as one gets to know individuals who differ widely from each other, many of whom contradict whatever stereotypes one came with. Second, one can see firsthand how people construct their daily living in functional and meaningful ways. At first their ways may seem different, but the longer one spends with a particular group, the more sensible their ways of doing things become.

One also gains a sense of the richness of another group's experiences, finding things that are delightful, or heartwarming, or valuable that one had not anticipated. For example, many non-Indians are immediately struck by a different conception of time on a reservation. Clock-time is often disregarded, and non-Indians are uncertain when to arrive at places or when they can expect events to happen. One's first reaction may be critical. ("They don't respect me," "They are lazy," or "No wonder nothing ever gets done around here!") But after giving one's own sense of time a chance to readjust (this may take a while), one realizes the value in structuring activities around natural rather than artificial rhythms; inner feelings become more important than the face of the clock, and one begins to pay attention to feelings one normally tunes out.

A third important feature of immersion experiences is the opportunity to listen to adults talk about circumstances they face, and how they view things. For example, in African American households it is not uncommon for dinner-table conversations to revolve around some aspect of racism that someone in the family or neighborhood has experienced (in White households, this rarely happens). If one listens nondefensively, one can learn very different perspectives about common areas of life (such as renting an apartment) that are experienced quite differently in other sociocultural groups.

Some teacher education programs have structured quite extensive immersion experiences. Campbell (1986) described a 14-year-old program that placed 250 teachers in rural areas. Preservice students lived with a rural family for eight weeks and taught in rural schools as well. The tenure and size of this program attested to positive results and program leaders said their best advertising came from students urging others to participate in the experience.

Several programs placed preservice students in either remote or urban areas where people of color constituted the majority of the population and, more often than not, poverty was pervasive (e.g., Clark, 1987; Liebert, 1988; Noordhoff & Kleinfeld, 1991). Students stayed in the placement for as little as one month, or for their entire preservice experience.

Common to these field experiences was course work about the history, culture, communication patterns, lifestyles, and political issues important to the context in which students were placed. In several programs, course work on how to collect field data was included (Noordhoff & Kleinfeld, 1991); or field projects were required and student teachers completed case studies about the community (Liebert, 1988; Noordhoff & Kleinfeld, 1991).

The results of immersion experiences reported in the literature are positive across the board. Each program enrolled more students each year and students indicated they were learning to understand and respect the lifeways of people different from themselves. Several reports were based on many years of collecting information from students' journals and evaluations (Campbell, 1986; Clark, 1987). In addition, students developed units of study that showed deep understanding of culture and ways to integrate cultural information into subject matter and teaching strategies (Liebert, 1988; Noordhoff & Kleinfeld, 1991).

One of us was certified to teach in an eight-month immersion experience, and considers it one of the most powerful experiences of her life. The main difference between such an experience and the other kinds of field experiences we have described is that one is forced to rethink many taken-for-granted ideas when confronted with a different cultural group's daily experiences. One cannot simply go home after a few hours in a site and interpret what one has seen based on familiar and comfortable ideas. One's ideas and prior beliefs are challenged and confronted, sometimes in painful ways. For White, middle-class preprofessionals, such an immersion experience may provide the first time the concept of racism or institutionalized poverty actually sinks in, and the first time strengths and perspectives of adult members of an oppressed group are truly recognized.

The drawbacks of this type of experience relate to time, organization, and personality. As Mahan reported (Clark, 1978), time in the field, often in remote areas, is required. In addition, organizing the field experiences and procuring placements take tremendous dedication from teacher educators. Also, all preservice teachers must take a long look at their ability to be flexible enough to live and work in a culture different from one's own.

Fuller and Ahler (1987) developed a substitute for a full immersion experience. They faced the problem of developing multicultural awareness on a monocultural campus (more than 90 percent of the students came from one racial group) that was geographically isolated (far from urban centers, remote reservations, or ethnic enclaves). They organized a program of cultural exchange in which preservice students became pen pals with teachers and students in three schools from geographic and sociocultural contexts different from their own.

Photographs, letters, and artifacts were exchanged and participating teachers visited the campus to share multicultural teaching experiences. While this exchange could be described as merely scratching the surface of cross-cultural sensitivity, Fuller and Ahler (1987) noted that student evaluations showed increased awareness and appreciation of the cultures studied.

Well-constructed field experiences can have powerful effects on preservice students' perspectives. For example, a White preservice student began to reconstruct her perspective about African Americans during a 50-hour field experience in a community center. She was initially frustrated by her inability to understand the young people's dialect, and assumed it was bad grammar. In her university course she was taught some grammatical rules of Black English, and encouraged to listen for patterns.

She returned to the community center and discovered that what she had perceived to be random errors were now patterns she could discern. With excitement, she went to the library and sought books about Black English for a paper for another course. A profound transformation in her perspective was taking shape. Before the field experience she had not given much thought to African American culture, assuming it to be impoverished and only moderately interesting.

In her field experience, combined with university course work, she discovered that it was not impoverished at all; the language (and other aspects of culture she would later discover) was highly patterned, interesting, and could be understood if one took the time. This was a genuine and lasting change in her perspective; she is still interested in continuing to learn about African American culture. Relatively short field experiences rarely result in such a major transformation of perspective. But even if a field experience does not completely change one's perspective, if it is well constructed, it can plant seeds that will grow.

Field Experiences in the Classroom

Most preservice students are excited and yet overwhelmed by the thought of teaching differently than they have been taught. It is difficult for them to perceive alternatives, because this requires consideration of teaching approaches that are unfamiliar, and redefinition of the essence of teaching. We found that our preservice students seem relieved to realize that they can learn along with students, through designing and completing field-experience-type learning activities. Several examples of field experiences that preservice teachers can accomplish with students follow.

The following example comes from Schniedewind and Davidson's (1983) resource guide of learning activities to promote race, class, gender, and age equity. "Who's Who In Our School?" and the extension activity "And How Do They Feel About It?" involves the examination of the division of labor at school as a way to understand the roles that racism and sexism play in work. Students identify the race, gender, and number of school personnel including teachers, custodians, secretaries, cafeteria workers, and administrators. They analyze the data by figuring the percentages of men, women, and people of color in each category and calculating these in terms of the total staff. The teacher guides a discussion of the findings and asks, for example, "In what areas did you find racial or sexual balance?" An extension of this inquiry involves interviewing staff about job opportunities, choices, and feelings about work.

Other field-experience-type activities that preservice students can develop for classroom use include collecting oral histories, taking neighborhood walks, interacting with a "sister-class" and performing community service. Oral histories are the "his-stories" and "her-stories" of people who are real to students: mothers, fathers, neighbors, friends, and acquaintances. Histories can be collected by young children and young adults, but the number of questions asked and the depth of the answers vary.

We tried "recipe histories" successfully with our preservice students (and they did the same with their students). Students asked a relative to describe a favorite family recipe, remembering who first made it and why (e.g., in one family, a flourless cake was first developed because of rationing in World War II, and in another, oxtail soup called for inexpensive meat). Students asked how the recipe became a family tradition (e.g., in several cases the recipe was passed down for generations and made only on certain occasions). We constructed this project around several research questions: What stories will be related to these recipes? In what ways will the stories be similar or different? Will the differences and similarities have anything to do with race, class, or gender? This project engendered discussion of socioeconomic issues and the nature of history, and planted seeds for further research for several students.

Taking a walk through the school neighborhood is another activity in which sights and sounds relevant to children can be noted. Students as researchers pay attention to such sights as types of homes, businesses, religious centers, and community agencies; geometric shapes in building designs, kinds of plant life and rocks; and sounds of music and language. The information collected can be used to answer questions such as: What is our neighborhood like? How does our neighborhood reflect the people who live here? What are some of the most positive things we saw in our neighborhood? What things do we think could be improved? In addition, the data provide a reference point for lesson planning relevant to the children.

Offering community service is another activity. Services may range from reading to preschool children to participating in a community self-help project. The essential component for these experiences is positive interaction with people active as "helpers" in the community. Examples of projects include taking part in a neighborhood cleanup effort, volunteering in a community agency, and "adopting" an elderly resident of a retirement home.

Yet another activity is based upon inter-school exchange. While preservice students probably would not be able to arrange this experience, we offer these examples to encourage consideration of the needs of children in monocultural schools. For these students, action must be taken beyond school walls to provide multicultural experiences. A mini-magnet could be developed around a theme that draws "sister-classes" together to study for a while. Students could visit "sister-schools" for a day-in-the-life type of exchange. Intramurals could become intermurals as sister-schools exchange sports events in which *all* children may participate. Rather than schools creating theatrical events on a school-by-school basis, a joint project could be planned.

These are just a few suggestions for extending the learning environment beyond the classroom walls. Experiences such as these can provide a rich reference of real, relevant information to use to raise questions related to the construction of our social world.

Planting Some Seeds

Providing an education that is multicultural and social reconstructionist requires a firm knowledge about how oppression works and what oppressed groups are doing to cope with and resist their oppression. One cannot just study these issues abstractly, because then they will not mean much more than the computer's answer of "forty-two."

One must ground one's awareness of oppression and diversity in experience. Field experiences can provide the opportunity to plant seeds of awareness that may continue to grow and develop. Field experiences that are well constructed can also pull the weeds of ignorance and misconception that all of us have about groups of which we are not members.

In this chapter, we hope we planted some seeds of ideas and possibilities for change, and pulled some weeds of traditional thinking about the nature of the learning environment. Teachers who take them to heart and cultivate them in practice are on the way to becoming "outstanding in the field."

References

Applegate, J. H., & Lasley, T. J. (1985). Students' expectations for early field experiences. *Texas Tech Journal of Education, 12*(1), 27–36.

Armaline, W. D., & Hoover, R. L. (1989). Field experience as a vehicle for transformation: Ideology, education, and reflective practice. *Journal of Teacher Education, 40*(2), 42–48.

Beyer, L. (1984). Field experience, ideology, and the development of critical reflectivity. *Journal of Teacher Education, 35*(3), 36–41.

Britzman, D. P. (1986). Cultural myths in the making of a teacher: Biography and social structure in teacher education. *Harvard Educational Review, 56*(4), 442–456.

Campbell, M. (1986). Preparing rural elementary teachers. *Research in Rural Education, 3*(3), 107–110.

Clark, H. (1987, July 9). Coming to understand others: J. Mahan's cultural immersion projects. *The Christian Science Monitor*, p. 27.

Cruickshank, D. R. (1985). *Models for the preparation of America's teachers*. Bloomington, IN: Phi Delta Kappa Educational Foundation.

Cruickshank, D. R., & Armaline, W. D. (1986). Field experiences in teacher education: Considerations and recommendations. *Journal of Teacher Education, 37*(3), 34–40.

Denton, J. (1986). Do early experiences in teacher education provide a meaningful context for acquiring pedagogical knowledge? *Teacher Education and Practice, 3*(1), 41–46.

Dewey, J. (1938). *Experience and education*. New York: Collier Books.

Duckworth, E. (1991). Twenty-four, forty-two, and I love you: Keeping it complex. *Harvard Educational Review, 61*(1), 1–24.

Evans, H. L. (1986). How do early field experiences influence the student teacher? *Journal of Education for Teaching, 12*(2), 35–46.

Feiman-Nemser, S., & Buchmann, M. (1985). Pitfalls of experience in teacher preparation. *Teachers College Record, 87*(1), 53–56.

Ferguson, P. (1989). A reflective approach to the methods practicum. *Journal of Teacher Education, 40*(2), 36–41.

Fuller, M. L., & Ahler, J. (1987). Multicultural education and the monocultural student: A case study. *Action in Teacher Education, 9*(3), 33–40.

Ginsburg, M. B., & Newman, K. K. (1985, March/April). Social inequalities, schooling, and teacher education. *Journal of Teacher Education*, 49–54.

Gipe, J. P., Duffy, C. A., & Richards, J. C. (1989). A comparison of two types of early field experiences. *Reading Improvement, 26*(3), 254–265.

Goodman, J. (1985). Field-based experience: A study of social control and student teachers' response to institutional constraints. *Journal of Education for Teaching, 11*(1), 26–49.

Gore, J. M. (1987). Reflecting on reflective teaching. *Journal of Teacher Education, 38*(2), 33–39.

Gore, J. M. (1991). Practicing what we preach: Action research and the supervision of student teachers. In B. R. Tabachnick & K. Zeichner (Eds.), *Issues and practices in inquiry-oriented teacher education* (pp. 186–202). London: Falmer Press.

Gottlieb, E., & Cornbleth, C. (1988). Toward reflective social studies teaching. *Teaching Education, 2*(1), 60–63.

Grant, C. A., & Zeichner, K. M. (1984). On becoming a reflective teacher. In C. A. Grant (Ed.), *Preparing for reflective teaching* (pp. 1–19). Boston: Allyn and Bacon.

Hennington, M. (1981). Effect of intensive multicultural, non-sexist instruction on secondary student teachers. *Educational Research Quarterly, 6,* 65–75.

Hollingsworth, S. (1988). Making field-based programs work: A three-level approach to reading education. *Journal of Teacher Education, 33*(4), 28–36.

Joyce, B. R. (1988). Training research and preservice teacher education: A reconsideration. *Journal of Teacher Education, 39*(5), 32–43.

Killian, J. E., & McIntyre, D. J. (1988). Grade level as a factor in participation during early field experiences. *Journal of Teacher Education, 39*(2), 36–41.

Ladson-Billings, G. (1990). Culturally relevant teaching. *The College Board Review,* No. 155, 20–25.

Liebert, D. (1988). Enhancing field experience through multicultural placements. *Teaching Education, 2*(2), 68–72.

McDiarmid, G. W. (1990). Challenging prospective teachers' beliefs during early field experience: A quixotic undertaking? *Journal of Teacher Education, 41*(3), 12–20.

Metz, M. H. (1990). How social class differences shape teachers' work. In M. W. McLaughlin, J. E. Talbert, & N. Bascia (Eds.), *The Contexts of Teaching in Secondary Schools* (pp. 40–110). New York: Teachers College Press.

Noffke, D. E., & Brennan, M. (1991). Student teachers use action research: Issues and examples. In B. R. Tabachnick & K. Zeichner (Eds.), *Issues and practices in inquiry-oriented teacher education* (pp. 186–202). London: Falmer Press.

Noordhoff, K., & Kleinfeld, J. (1991, April). Preparing teachers for multicultural classroom: A case study in rural Alaska. Paper presented at the annual meeting of American Educational Research Association, Chicago, IL.

Ross, E. W. (1988). Becoming a teacher: Development of preservice teacher perspectives. *Action in Teacher Education, 10*(2), 80–83.

Schniedewind, N., & Davidson, E. (1983). *Open minds to equality.* Boston: Allyn and Bacon.

Tabachnick, B. R., Popkewitz, T., & Zeichner, K. (1980). Teacher education and the professional perspectives of student teachers. *Interchange, 10,* 12–29.

Teitelbaum, K., & Britzman, D. P. (1991). Reading and doing ethnography: Teacher education and reflective practice. In B. R. Tabachnick & K. Zeichner (Eds.), *Issues and practices in inquiry-oriented teacher education* (pp. 186–202). London: Falmer Press.

Zeichner, K. (1980). Myths and realities: Field-based experiences in preservice teacher education. *Journal of Teacher Education, 31,* 45–55.

Zeichner, K. (1981–1982). Reflective teaching and field-based experience in teacher education. *Interchange, 12*(4), 1–22.

Zeichner, K. (1983). Alternative paradigms of teacher education. *Journal of Teacher Education, 24*(3), 3–9.

Zeichner, K., & Liston, D. (1987). Teaching student teachers to reflect. *Harvard Educational Review, 57*(1), 23–48.

Chapter 19

◆ ◆ ◆ ◆

It's Got to Be in the Plan: Reflective Teaching and Multicultural Education in the Student Teaching Semester

Maureen D. Gillette

The College of St. Rose

Introduction

Reflective teaching has been referred to as the "new zeitgeist," or fad, in North American teacher education (Zeichner & Tabachnick, 1991, p. 1). Numerous definitions of reflective teaching can be found in the education literature. The purpose of this chapter is not to detail these definitions, but to argue for a specific one that represents a multicultural, social reconstructionist approach to examining teaching. It is important for prospective teachers to learn to develop habits of inquiry and critical reflection as they refine their teaching practice during early field experiences and in the student teaching semester.

This chapter begins with a brief discussion of reflective teaching as it relates to multicultural education. Reflective teaching and multicultural education will then be examined through two vignettes, each of which describes the experiences of a prospective teacher during the student teaching semester. The manner in which each prospective teacher thought about and acted on his or her practice will be analyzed within the context of the classroom and society today.

The Reflective Teacher in a Social Reconstructionist Framework

In the previous chapter, Boyle-Baise and Sleeter noted that the roots of reflective teaching could be found in the work of Dewey (1938). Dewey defined a *reflective teacher* as one who engages in reflective action, rather than one who acts in what he called a routine manner. Routine practice is guided by unexamined tradition or imitation. Reflective action is behavior "which involves the active, persistent, and careful consideration of any belief or practice in light of the grounds that support it and the further consequences to which it leads" (Grant & Zeichner, 1984, p. 4).

Dewey (1933) described three characteristics of a reflective teacher: open-minded, responsible, and wholehearted. Each of these can be considered in light of concerns about issues of race, class, gender, language difference, differing physical and mental abilities, and sexual orientation as they manifest themselves in the classroom.

Open-mindedness is "an active desire to listen to more sides than one, to give full attention to alternate possibilities, and to recognize the possibility of error even in the beliefs that are dearest to us" (Dewey, 1933, p. 4). From a multicultural point of view, this would include such things as a willingness to see variances in students' abilities, lifestyles, and ways of problem solving as differences to be explored rather than deficiencies to be remediated or rejected without consideration.

Responsibility "involves the careful consideration of the consequences to which an action leads" (Dewey, 1933, p. 4). It is rare to find anything in teaching that is inherently neutral. Almost every decision a teacher makes and every course of action a teacher chooses have possible positive and negative consequences for students and teachers. Educators must consider the implications of their choices and actions. For example, the American Association of University Women (1991) reported research indicating that females fail to receive the same attention from their teachers that male students do, that their lessons often come from gender-biased textbooks, and that they are not encouraged to pursue careers in mathematics as are their male counterparts.

Teachers do not deliberately set out to ignore or neglect the females in their classrooms; however, part of being a responsible teacher is to systematically examine classroom policies, procedures, routines, and materials to ensure gender equity in the classroom.

Finally, *wholeheartedness* is the effort teachers put forth in becoming and remaining open-minded and responsible. Prospective teachers must take an active role in their own education by demonstrating the willingness and commitment to continually investigate and improve their teaching. This does not mean student teachers should automatically condemn or negatively criticize current classroom practices. It does mean they must approach any classroom situation with a questioning mind, turning what appear to be "normal" (or traditional) classroom practices on end and taking nothing for granted. It requires asking "why" and thinking through alternatives.

A student teacher may decide an existing practice is best; however, this decision should be reached through careful consideration of what the teacher wants to accomplish, what alternatives exist, and what the consequences of these alternatives are for the teacher and the students, now and in the future. In other words, in choosing to use a certain strategy, implement a particular curriculum, administer a certain punishment, etc., a conscious, deliberate, and informed choice has been made. The teacher does not continue a practice just because "that's the way it has always been done."

Zeichner and Tabachnick (1991) note that it would be difficult to find teachers who would say they were not reflective. Therefore, it becomes important to examine how the word *reflection* is used in practice. Often prospective teachers believe they are being reflective. They leave their field placement each day with school events weighing heavily on their minds. They spend many hours thinking about the children, their lesson plans, their interactions with the cooperating teacher, as well as myriad other factors related to teaching.

Most prospective teachers have a sincere desire to work hard at improving their teaching practice but, despite all of their thinking, some continue to implement similar management procedures and lesson plans, and have the same types of interactions with the children. They do this even if they do not consider these practices important, relevant, or effective in achieving their teaching goals (e.g., student achievement, a caring classroom environment).

Other student teachers examine their practice in a way that makes a substantial difference in their teaching and their understanding of the students. They gather data about, plan for, and implement practices they believe will help them make the educational process rewarding, personally and academically, for themselves and their students. What might make this difference?

Dewey's (1933) notion of reflective teaching is underpinned by an emphasis on self-examination that is often absent in many teacher's conceptions of reflection. It is much easier to look outside one's own practice for the cause of students' academic or social problems. It is common to hear educators placing the blame for school failure on the students (e.g., lack of motivation, laziness, learning disabilities, language differences), on family situations (e.g., single-parent homes, teen-age parents, "latch-key" children), or on larger societal problems (e.g., homelessness, drugs, violence).

While these are certainly all factors that affect a child's success in school, it is equally important for teachers to focus on their own practices in the classroom. It is possible to identify areas where they can systematically examine these practices and make changes that will maximize learning for all children by assessing the factors over which the teacher has control. These factors include designing curricula to meet the needs of a particular group of students and selecting an instructional method based on students' preferred learning styles. These assessments are more constructive than focusing on factors over which teachers have little or no control, such as the fact that a student lives in a homeless shelter.

Reflective, social reconstructionist teachers seek to understand how their actions have consequences for students both inside and outside of the classroom. They understand that schools and society play a reciprocal role in structuring inequalities and recognize the need to incorporate a concern for issues of oppression based on race, ethnicity, social class, language, physical and mental ability differences, and sexual orientation. A reflective, social reconstructionist teacher understands the importance of connecting the school and the community. This approach will be briefly compared with issues that come to the fore in other versions of reflective teaching. Then, two student teaching vignettes will illustrate some of the differences among these various approaches.

Zeichner and Tabachnick (1991) identified four varieties of reflective teaching practice that are based on Zeichner and Liston's (1990) analysis of teacher education reform traditions. The first has *academic* focus. This version "stresses reflection upon subject matter and the representation and translation of subject matter knowledge to promote student understanding" (p. 3). The second variety, a *social efficiency* model, "emphasizes the thoughtful application of particular teaching strategies that have been suggested by research on teaching" (p. 3). The third version takes a *developmental* approach, "prioritizing teaching that is sensitive to students' interest, thinking, and patterns of developmental growth" (p. 3). The fourth version, the *social reconstructionist* approach, "stresses reflection about the social and political context of schooling and the assessment of classroom actions for their ability to contribute toward greater equity, social justice, and humane conditions in schooling and society" (p. 3).

While each version of reflective teaching emerged from a particular historical tradition related to the purposes of schooling and teacher education, these are not mutually exclusive. Proponents of each acknowledge the importance of attending to issues raised in other models; however, Zeichner and Tabachnick (1991) point out that the differences among the traditions of reflection are defined in terms of "the emphasis and priority that is given to particular factors within traditions" (p. 4).

It is the degree of emphasis on a certain way of viewing reflective teaching that makes the difference. For example, those who advocate a social reconstructionist view certainly acknowledge the importance of subject matter, student understanding, research-based teaching techniques, and an emphasis on the students' interests, thinking, and development. Teachers who practice a multicultural, social reconstructionist version of reflective teaching view the substance of other versions through the lens of the larger society. Such teachers realize that without solid subject matter taught using appropriate and effective instructional techniques, as well as curricula based on the needs, interests, talents, and learning styles of the children, students will not attain the knowledge base and skills necessary to become active, participating members of society. Knowledge, skills, and personal development are not seen as individual ends but as essential components of a wider educational endeavor that helps students become active participants in improving our democratic society. A concern for issues of equity, justice, and human rights in both the teaching and the learning process serves as the backdrop for examining teaching and schooling. Zeichner and Tabachnick (1991, pp. 8–9) listed three characteristics of multicultural, social reconstructionist reflective teaching:

1. In a social reconstructionist conception of reflective teaching, the teacher's attention is focused both inwardly at their own practice . . . and outwardly at the social conditions in which these practices are situated. . . . (Kemmis, 1985)

2. A social reconstructionist conception of reflective teaching has a democratic and emancipatory impulse and the focus of the teacher's deliberations is upon substantive issues that raise instances of inequality and injustice within schooling and society for close scrutiny. Recognizing the fundamentally political character of schooling, the teacher's reflections center upon such issues as the gendered nature of schooling and of teachers' work, the relationships between race and socioeconomic group on one hand, and access to school knowledge and school achievement on the other, and the influence of external interests on the process of curriculum production. . . .

3. A social reconstructionist conception of reflective teaching includes a commitment to reflection as a communal activity. . . . It is felt that the empowerment of individuals is inadequate, and that the potential for institutional and social change is great, if teachers see their individual situations as linked to those of their colleagues. (Freedman, Jackson, & Boles, 1986)

The process of becoming a multicultural, social reconstructionist reflective teacher and sustaining this vision is not easy. It requires time, effort, and commitment. Most importantly, it requires a willingness to critically examine one's practice in light of the characteristics mentioned thus far. The following two vignettes relate the stories of two student teachers struggling with becoming reflective.

Vignette 1

"It's Not in the Lesson Plan, It's in You"

Carol,[1] a 27-year-old White female, was student teaching in an urban elementary school. She was placed in a second-grade classroom of 22 students, 9 girls and 13 boys. Five students were African American (2 girls, 3 boys), 1 was biracial (a girl), 1 was an American Indian (a girl), 1 was a Latino (a boy), and 14 were White (5 females and 9 males). The class was also socioeconomically diverse, consisting of the sons and daughters of physicians, lawyers, and local politicians as well as a number of students whose parents were unemployed or were receiving state or federal assistance.

Academically, the group was heterogeneous. Several students' reading, writing, and calculation skills were well beyond those expected of a second-grader. A large portion of the class was considered to be achieving at grade level, in that they were beginning to read, write, and calculate with ease. There was also a small group of students who had trouble identifying letter sounds and numbers and who regularly experienced difficulty completing assigned tasks.

Carol's cooperating teacher attempted to foster a humanistic environment in the classroom; however, she used a form of "assertive discipline" (Canter, 1976) that involved extrinsic rewards and public accountability (i.e., names placed on the chalkboard followed by check marks to indicate rule infractions). Although Carol was given permission to adapt classroom practices to her personal style of teaching, she attempted to maintain consistency by using her cooperating teacher's system of discipline.

As she began to assume more of the teaching duties in the classroom, she became uncomfortable with the "assertive" approach. Carol addressed her uneasy feeling with her student teaching supervisor and cooperating teacher during the seventh week of the 16-week semester. The following conversation occurred after a small group reading lesson that was observed by the supervisor:

> SUPERVISOR (toward the end of the conference):   The children were reading most of the time with the exception of Tom. . . . he didn't seem to be having his best day ever, did he?

CAROL: No.

COOPERATING TEACHER: He hasn't had a best day all week.

SUPERVISOR: What's happening with the checks? Tell me what happens with those.

CAROL: Well, we have an elaborate money system. We give them five dollars a day and then for every check they lose a dollar. And Hope is . . .

COOPERATING TEACHER: . . . on her way to her last check, and they get a time out in the office if they lose all five dollars.

CAROL: Yes, they get a time out in the office. I really notice that I'm so different, so inconsistent. Like some days I'll just barely give one or two checks and today I said to myself, "I'm just giving them checks, I'm sick of talking."

SUPERVISOR: How do you react to that if you think you're being inconsistent? How do you feel about that?

CAROL: Well, I guess I'd rather be consistent. But, if I'm inconsistent for all the kids on the same day it's not as bad. What I've really been noticing is sometimes I'll let the better kids by. I'll give them a look or something, whereas a kid who already has two or three checks, I'll give them another check. I really hate that about myself.

SUPERVISOR: When you say "better" kids, do you mean better academically or behaviorally?

CAROL: Better behaved, but a lot of times those are the better students academically.

SUPERVISOR: Is that a certain group of children? I mean, when you say that do you have names in mind?

CAROL: Yeah, I think it's those girls, Kitty and Diane and the two Lauras. And I really want to change that but I don't know why I don't.

SUPERVISOR: . . . All the names you mentioned were female.

CAROL: It just happens that those four girls are smart and pretty well behaved, but not always. They kind of get off with each other. But that group of the other four girls I give checks to regularly.

SUPERVISOR: Which group?

CAROL: It's more kind of a halo effect, you know.

SUPERVISOR: Can you think about that from a multicultural point of view? Are you comfortable talking about that, the other group?

CAROL: Yeah, it's Sherry, Val, Felicia, and Hope. I guess what bothers me is that two of those girls are Black and one is American Indian and that three out of four are from lower socioeconomic backgrounds and it happens that the other four girls are all White and upper middle class.

SUPERVISOR: And that leaves Sheila.

CAROL: Sheila is kind of in the middle academically. Behavior-wise she's great though. The only way she gets checks is for being late.

At this point, the conversation moved away from the topic of Carol's inconsistent discipline and the check mark system, and focused on Sheila. As the conference drew to a close, though, Carol returned to her confusion over her own practice:

CAROL: . . . I hate to say it but those four girls, academically and behavior-wise they're real low. Their being Black or American Indian or whatever is a contributing factor but it's not the reason. I don't think I look at them and say, "You're Black so you're going to be at the bottom" but they work together. I was bringing that up in seminar and Professor Stevens said, "You know, you have stereotypes right away." I was really confused about that. It made me think twice about it, yet I have a hard time.

Carol gave a lot of thought to her inconsistent disciplinary techniques over the course of the semester. Although she lost sleep on a couple of occasions and more than once shed some tears over this dilemma, she continued to experience difficulties, especially with the group of four girls. At the end of the semester, her concerns about fair and appropriate disciplinary techniques remained unresolved. In response to, "Tell me about your student teaching semester," Carol stated the following:

CAROL: Okay, well, a couple of things were really hard for me. . . . The discipline was really hard. That was one of the hardest things this year. I got better at it. I got better at when to let things go and when to really get on something and feel more comfortable. . . . And the kids, I think they got more mature toward the end of the year which helped me. . . .

INTERVIEWER: . . . You've talked a lot about discipline. One time I observed a conference with you and your supervisor and you were not satisfied with the check system of discipline because you saw that the non-White kids were getting checks every day. You weren't happy with your consistency. How did you ever resolve that?

CAROL: I don't think I addressed it so much. I think what I did start doing was taking the kids' side more, asking them "What's wrong? What do you want to change?" I was dealing with them on an individual level and we didn't actually use the check system as much. I think maybe at the end of the year they were maturing. I don't think we had as many discipline problems. So I guess it just kind of resolved itself. . . . I have learned that school is people, these kids, and they have their own way. You can have the best ideas in the world but they might not work out the way you planned, so you have to change. I think that's why multicultural education has to be a part of you rather than something in your lesson plan.

Carol as a Reflective Teacher

Was Carol a reflective teacher? She certainly spent many hours thinking about her discipline dilemma, but none of Carol's deliberations were systematic nor did they result in any changes in her practice. She began by implementing a disciplinary policy from a "social efficiency" approach. This caused her uncomfortable feelings when she inconsistently doled out check marks.

Indeed, Carol recognized that her actions impinged unfairly on the females of color and certain males yet she took no action to document, confirm, or negate her suspicions. She did not attempt to analyze her practices in any way. Carol then moved into a developmental approach where she reported that she tried, toward the end of the semester, to consider the students' perspectives when dealing with discipline problems.

From a multicultural point of view, Carol was not a reflective teacher. It is important to examine her dilemma and her actions on two levels, the micro (or classroom) level and the macro level, projecting the consequences of her action (or inaction) into the lives of the children outside of school and to their futures.

Carol neglected to examine the consequences of her decision to use assertive discipline procedures, despite her feelings of uneasiness. At the level of the classroom, the results of her actions can be viewed from several perspectives: the students whose names were consistently placed on the board, the students whose names were not consistently placed on the board, and the effect of her actions on the social relationships among the two groups of females and in relation to several males whose names were consistently placed on the board in the classroom.

Carol was implementing a practice that occurs in many classrooms across the United States. Children's names are placed on the board for a variety of reasons such as inappropriate behavior or missing assignments. Often a pattern develops, as in Carol's class, where the same children's names are placed on the board day after day. What consequences might this have? The children whose names are repeatedly placed on the board for behavioral reasons rarely improve their demeanor over the course of the year. Instead, they often live up to a teacher's expectations.

They begin to see themselves as "bad" or less able than their classmates because they never seem to behave according to teacher expectations or manage to complete their assignments in the allotted time. Their classmates, too, begin to ascribe these negative characteristics to their peers. At the same time, they view themselves as "good" or superior because they have successfully internalized the teacher's rules or are able to complete assigned tasks in the requisite amount of time. As Carol noted about her own practice, once this pattern is established, a teacher often continues to focus on those children who have established a reputation as "bad" or "incapable" while overlooking undesirable behaviors in those children who have established themselves as "good."

This cycle can have detrimental effects on the social relationships in the classroom. In Carol's room, the females had already segregated themselves by race and social class. The non-White females, whose names regularly appeared on the board, worked and played together. Carol correctly noted that these four girls, who came from families whose income was at the low end of the socioeconomic scale, were below grade level academically. The four White girls, whose inappropriate behaviors Carol admittedly overlooked on a regular basis, came from families in upper-level income brackets and were academically at or above grade level.

It is possible to consider the effects of these patterns on the children's lives as they progress through school and face the reality of racism, sexism, and classism outside of the classroom. Evidence indicates that once a child is labeled as behaviorally or academically different from what is considered to be normal for a grade level, this label follows a child throughout school (Oakes, 1985; Goodlad, 1981). Compounding this problem is evidence related to the relationship between a teacher's expectation and a student's academic progress. Decades ago, it was documented that children in classrooms tend to behave and perform academically according to the teacher's expectations (Rosenthal & Jacobson, 1968).

Given the situation in Carol's classroom, it is likely that the female students of color and the males whose names continuously appeared on the board will carry negative labels about themselves in their heads as they move through the grades. These labels may manifest themselves year after year if a teacher does not stop to examine what is behind the label or what factors are affecting a student's behavior and academic performance.

For the students in Carol's class, it is a grim projection. Currently, females of color are more likely to drop out of high school and college and be unemployed between the ages of 20 and 35 than White females and males. Those females of color who do not hold full-time jobs often occupy minimum-wage positions and earn lower weekly salaries than their male or White female counterparts (U.S. Bureau of the Census, 1991). It is essential that all students, but especially female students of color, are provided with positive educational experiences and early academic success if the cycle of undereducation and underemployment is to be broken.

In addition, the social relations in Carol's classroom are being cemented by academic grouping that places children of like backgrounds together for much of the school day. When a teacher groups students according to ability, often students of color are placed in the "low" group, as was the case with the girls in Carol's classroom. In a situation such as this, the children are rarely afforded the chance to work with other classmates. Opportunities to learn about and appreciate the talents and abilities, the uniqueness and similarities among class members are lost. When the peer group is limited by ability grouping or tracking, students miss the opportunity to debate issues with others who may have different opinions, or to listen to and consider multiple perspectives. In short, the degree to which students are able to become open-minded, critical thinkers is in jeopardy.

Could Carol have considered these consequences on her own, or with the assistance of her cooperating teacher and supervisor? Could she have changed her teaching patterns in response to these types of considerations? The answer is yes, if Carol had been willing to take a few risks.

The first risk would have been for her to move beyond her feelings of uneasiness and admit that, as the teacher, she played a key role in determining the behavior patterns which manifested themselves in the classroom. Carol never understood this. Rather, she concluded at the end of the semester that the behavior problems in her classroom had diminished because the students had matured. While this may have been a factor, placing the onus on the students provided Carol with an excuse for not looking further into her own actions and the effect they have on the students.

The second risk Carol needed to take was to assume the role of teacher-researcher. Once she identified the discipline dilemma, Carol could have initiated a data-gathering process to help her examine the effect of the check mark system in her classroom. For example, audiotaping or videotaping herself would have provided Carol with access to her lessons as an "outsider." She could have examined the situations in which she issued check marks. Carol also might have used a personal journal or enlisted the aid of her supervisor to assess the extent to which other factors, such as the thoroughness of her planning, affected her frustration level with the students during the lesson.

Carol sensed that the girls in her class had gathered into two social groups, one consisting of upper middle-class Whites and the other of lower-class females of color. She could have gathered data to confirm or deny this suspicion. If she confirmed it, she could have taken action to prevent this type of segregation in the classroom. For example, she could have administered a sociogram to assess the friendship patterns in her class, adding to this other data from informal observations conducted in social settings such as the lunchroom and the playground. She then could have arranged numerous cooperatively grouped learning activities where she selected the group members and arranged the learning task in a way that fostered a recognition and appreciation in all the girls for the talents and abilities of their classmates.

Carol was letting herself off the hook when she said a teacher could not plan to be a multicultural teacher, that it had to come from inside one's self. To some extent, she was correct. The characteristics of open-mindedness, responsibility, and wholeheartedness suggest that a teacher must have an awareness and an understanding of multicultural issues to address them in the classroom. But it is equally important for a teacher to *plan* for curricular and instructional practices that incorporate multicultural concerns. The second vignette provides an example of a prospective teacher who used some of the techniques noted here and planned for effective multicultural teaching in the student-teaching semester.

Vignette 2

"You Gotta Get Them Where They Are"

Tom, a 32-year-old White male, was student teaching in Mrs. Kelly's sixth-grade classroom in an urban middle school. His class was more racially, ethnically, linguistically, and socioeconomically diverse than Carol's because several elementary schools with diverse populations fed into the middle school. This brought in children who lived in one of several nearby homeless shelters as well as children who were recent immigrants from Southeast Asia.

Mrs. Kelly gave Tom freedom to design his curricular and instructional plans so that he could develop a personal teaching style. While she was concerned that he cover the material traditionally taught in the sixth grade, she was flexible and did not require him to use the textbooks and worksheets that were commonplace in her teaching.

Tom's college supervisor required that he conduct an investigation of some aspect of his teaching. Tom spent several weeks getting to know his students and their abilities. This was somewhat of a challenge for him because his cooperating teacher was paired with another teacher across the hall. As a result, he taught several groups of students daily.

Tom was most concerned with a specific class that contained 16 students who had been designated "at risk"[2] for failure by the school district. He taught this group for two periods a day, once for math and once for social studies. Because the district was experimenting with mainstreaming, a resource room teacher (a specialist in learning disabilities) was assigned to assist the students while Tom taught. After much thought, Tom decided to focus on this particular class and to examine his own teaching practices as they related to student learning styles.

Tom spent about two weeks researching the topic of learning styles before deciding to limit his investigation to auditory, visual, and kinesthetic learning. He began his self-study by collecting data related to the students' preferred learning styles. First, he distributed a questionnaire that asked the students questions such as, "I work best (check one), alone, with one other person, in a small group" and "I like the teacher to give (check one) specific directions for homework assignments, general directions, options for homework."

Next, he began a series of individual interviews to discover how students solved problems posed in math class. At the same time, he collected observational data on different occasions with the help of his supervisor and the resource room teacher. For example, he noted the names of children who asked to have directions repeated, who talked while they worked, who seemed to need quiet, and who used manipulatives to solve math problems. Tom also tape-recorded his lessons and later listened to himself and his students. He gleaned information about the students as well as his teaching, such as the amount of "wait time" he was giving during social studies discussion periods.

The initial data-gathering period lasted about three weeks. After Tom sifted through his notes and categorized the students' surveys, he discussed his data with the resource room teacher to receive her input. He made some interesting discoveries. The survey data revealed that the majority of the students preferred learning kinesthetically, that is, in a "hands-on" manner and with the help of manipulative materials. The students also preferred to work in pairs or small groups rather than alone.

Tom's observational data revealed that many of the students exhibited underdeveloped listening skills, yet the primary mode of instruction in this middle school classroom was lecture. Tom discovered that most of the students benefitted greatly from concise, written instructions. A small group of students had limited reading ability and required continued reliance on direct visual cues in conjunction with oral instructions and information. This information changed the way Tom structured the learning environment for these students. Following the data-gathering period, he had the following conversation with his college supervisor:

SUPERVISOR: So, tell me how your teaching is going so far.

TOM: The data that I collected so far has been really interesting. I found out that these particular students, all labeled "at risk," really are able to articulate how they learn best. What I realized was that almost all of them prefer to see *and* hear information and that many of them do better when they have some type of manipulatives, even in social studies.

It occurred to me that all we ever do around here is lecture to them. According to what the kids said, and my observations, that is the least effective way to get information across. Almost all of them said they like to work in pairs or small groups. Only one preferred to work alone. Almost everything we do here is done in large group lessons and there is a lot of competition—some of the kids put pressure on themselves but a lot of it comes from messages we (the teachers) send out. We're always talking about grades, the expectations that will be placed upon them in high school—succeeding, you know. I'm not really sure they understand the importance of school success later on.

SUPERVISOR: Have you thought about how you'll use all of this data you've collected?

TOM: Well, I'm really concerned about this particular group. They are already losing interest in school and I can see that some have quit trying. They've dropped out without leaving school. I think I can change the way I teach so that my lessons still teach them the stuff they need to know, yet make it interesting and fun. I'm planning on beginning some cooperative grouping activities in math and social studies. I guess

I'm really going to concentrate on math first because I see that as something they'll need immediate success in so they will not be afraid to take the courses they need should they choose to go to college.

SUPERVISOR: What will your first steps be?

TOM: Starting next week, I'm planning on having every lesson I teach use the three modalities—not only am I going to lecture to them, I'm going to provide visual aides and manipulatives. I really have to work on setting the environment so that manipulatives are seen as desirable. Some of them think they are too old to use things to help them solve math problems. I also am going to try a group process for solving problems and sharing strategies. I really need to work on the cooperative aspect rather than the competitive.

SUPERVISOR: Anything else?

TOM: Oh yeah (laughing). Let me read you some of the problems I made up to begin reviewing fractions next week. (Tom reads aloud)

1. Angelo got $12 in tips for doing chores for the senior citizens in his neighborhood. He spent ⅓ of the money getting a fade at the barber and the rest on a compact disc. How much was the fade and how much was the disc?

2. Linda, Shatiqua, and Ricki agreed to split the cost of a pizza and some soda after the basketball game. Pizza Hut had a 12-slice pizza for $12. A large Pepsi was 75 cents. Across the street at Pizza Village, there was a 9-slice pizza and pitcher of Coke for $12.50. Which was the better deal? Why? And how much did each girl pay?

I used each kid's name in a problem based on what I've learned about them and what they like to do outside of school. I figure that once they get the idea, I'll have them begin to generate some problems of their own and we'll share them in groups. I guess it could get pretty wild if they like them as well as I think they will but, hey, who says math can't be fun!

Anyway, I've got a weeklong plan where I'm balancing my lecturing about math strategies with multiple methods, like using the overhead projector, with the students working in small groups to find solutions cooperatively and share strategies. I've tried to structure the instruction and the problems according to their interests and their preferred learning styles. Wish me luck. Will you be back next week to see how this is going?

Tom began to change his instructional techniques, using cooperative strategies in mathematics to increase the students' understanding and mastery of fractions. The students reacted so enthusiastically to Tom's problems that it was difficult for him to keep up with them. The session in which students shared strategies sometimes took a whole class period, but Tom's observational notes and the students' math scores indicated that they were increasing their ability to think critically about a problem. They did not shy away from story problems and their assignments indicated they were able to apply their reasoning to problems in the textbook, a task which the cooperating teacher considered necessary to demonstrate understanding.

Tom also applied what he was learning to his social studies and science instruction. In science, he was preparing the students for a weeklong outdoor education experience. It was necessary for the students to learn many difficult concepts before the special week. They also needed to learn how to get along and appreciate the talents of their peers because the sixth grade would be spending the entire week at a campground together, an unfamiliar experience for these children of urban backgrounds.

Social studies proved especially rewarding for Tom. His experiment in math gave him the courage to develop a video magazine project in a format fashioned after *Newsweek* magazine. Students were divided into cooperative groups and assigned a general area from the magazine to research (e.g., International Affairs, National Affairs, Business, The Arts, Lifestyle). Tom prepared research packets and guided the students through the process of selecting a topic, gathering and organizing data, and making a presentation. The students developed a project that resembled a classic mix of CNN and MTV. Tom videotaped each segment and the students critiqued themselves based on criteria the teacher and the students designed together in advance.

Tom wrote the following in his journal at the end of his student teaching experience:

> With the information I gained, I had a much clearer understanding as to how I should approach providing instruction. . . . I was able to assess individual learning styles and know if there was a correlation between a student's performance on a given task and the mode of instruction. The strength of the correlation was striking to me. The improvement shown by the students when provided with manipulatives and multiple source information was dramatic when compared with their performance when given isolated written or verbal instructions. Lots of varying explanations can probably be made, taking into account my collected data and the rather crude parameters of this investigation; however, one thing is clear. . . . Students showed remarkable improvement in their ability to solve mathematical problems of a similar nature and degree of difficulty when the instruction and the learning environment was sympathetic to their desired learning style.
>
> Cooperative learning is and will be a major instructional method in my classroom. Grouping of students is traditionally random or done so as to insure appropriate (teacher desired) classroom behavior. Recognizing the value of learning style information, grouping in and of itself can become a learning enhancer for the teacher. Students can be grouped by the teacher to provide a variance of styles (in addition to abilities), allowing students to be exposed to alternative learning strategies with a successful common goal and a positive atmosphere. I was able to implement this in my math class and the results were very encouraging. I had an ongoing project where I placed students in groups of four. Within

each group, I selected individuals who demonstrated varying learning style preferences while being aware to also mix students to read technical information, extract and record necessary data, synthesize/evaluate the material and, finally, present the results. . . .

In the end, the students had worked through relatively complex problems based on data from an ecological phenology study I had prepared. It fit nicely into their science unit on mammals. Most of the questions posed to the groups were at a difficulty level beyond the individual. The group process was not only beneficial but necessary!

Tom as a Reflective Teacher

Was Tom a reflective teacher from a multicultural, social reconstructionist perspective? He may not have demonstrated all the traits listed earlier in the chapter, but as a beginning professional, he was well on his way. Tom clearly saw himself as a key to the students' academic and social success. He understood the connections between the students' success in the sixth grade and their future life opportunities. He wanted academic success for his students, the first step toward getting rid of the stigma caused by others who labeled them "at risk."

Tom accepted this responsibility by setting out to change *his* practice and *his* way of thinking about teaching to have a positive effect in the classroom. Rather than interpret the data he gathered in a way that would require the students to immediately adapt to modes of learning typically found in school (i.e., lecture), Tom concluded that it was *he* who needed to adapt his teaching style to the students. He made informed choices and sound decisions based on information he gathered about the talents, interests, and academic needs of the pupils. Tom refused to be guided solely by tradition and unexamined practice. He believed that the learning environment could and should be designed to address academic needs, to incorporate sound teaching practices, and to capitalize on students' interests.

He set out to help this group acquire the knowledge, critical thinking strategies, socialization skills, and positive attitudes necessary to be successful students. Tom used his personal knowledge of their experiences inside and outside of school to make learning relevant and fun. In these ways, he saw himself as contributing toward a more equitable and just school experience for this particular group.

Tom also attempted to involve his colleagues. He enlisted the resource teacher and his college supervisor to assist his data gathering. He consulted with school colleagues about his data and sought their advice about designing learning experiences. Tom also took charge of the supervision process, directing his supervisor to provide feedback on areas of his teaching that were of importance to him.

Tom focused his attention on his own practice, acknowledging the fact that the category "at risk" is a socially constructed label that means different things to different people. He did not let the students' diversity or an "at risk" label stand in the way of helping them to achieve success. Rather, he looked upon diversity as a positive attribute, one that he could use to build a foundation for learning. He attempted to create what Ladson-Billings (1992) has characterized as a learning community, a place where teachers and students work collaboratively and an interdependence is fostered.

Tom recognized the importance of education in shaping one's life chances and he knew that his group of racially, ethnically, and linguistically diverse students would need a solid set of academic and social skills to succeed in a school environment and a world that, in many ways, puts them at a disadvantage. Are there other things that Tom could have done in his efforts to be a reflective, social reconstructionist teacher? Of course! There is always more a teacher can do. As the students' positive attitudes and success in mathematics increased, Tom needed to move them beyond a traditional role as "consumers" of mathematical knowledge to one in which they become producers of such knowledge (Tate, 1992). In this model, the teacher "situates students in realistic problem contexts found in our multicultural society and has them analyze and solve these problems" (p. 13).

This approach requires more than addressing pizza and haircuts as topics for mathematical problem solving. Tom could have used current databases, such as demographic and employment statistics, in his teaching. For example, the students might have learned graphing skills by translating gender-based employment data (usually provided in tables) to bar, circle, and line graphs. In this way, students develop and hone important mathematical skills while learning about salary inequities and the extent to which the presentation of statistics can alter the reader's perceptions about the data. It is the teacher's role to develop and facilitate these mathematical activities and to lead discussions about their results in ways that help students make connections between mathematics and their lives. Further, the teacher must follow up such lessons by assisting the pupils in finding opportunities to use their new skills and knowledge to directly challenge existing inequities in their school, in the community, or in the larger society.

Tom did not directly address community involvement or social action. He could have done more to foster in the students a sense of themselves as politically active participants inside and outside of the classroom. He did not access the community in his attempts to connect the curriculum to the lives of the students. Yet, achievements in the student teaching semester are often limited by factors such as time, degree of autonomy, and the hard work of learning to teach. Tom built a foundation to continue his growth as a reflective, social reconstructionist teacher.

Tom concluded his teaching journal with some ideas about how he, as a teacher, could share the type of information he gleaned in his data collection with parents so they could better become partners in the educational experiences of their children. For Tom, all of this was part of "getting them where they are" so he could help take them where they wanted to go in life.

Conclusion

Grant and Zeichner (1984) have argued that becoming a reflective teacher is "both possible and desirable" (p. 17). They further suggested that this process is a necessary condition if those laboring in schools wish to contribute to revitalization and renewal of the educational system; however, they noted that prospective as well as practicing teachers have a choice: to give direction to their own professional development or to allow others to direct it for them. Given the current crises in education, a teacher has no choice. Becoming a multicultural, social reconstructionist reflective teacher is an inherent part of becoming an effective educator. Smyth (1984) quotes Jean Rudduck stating that "not to examine one's practice is irresponsible; to regard teaching as an experiment and to monitor one's performance is a responsible professional act" (p. 6). Without a multicultural, social reconstructionist type of reflectivity, teachers run the risk of indefinitely perpetuating those current school practices that turn students off to school and limit the range of possibilities in their lives.

Practicing a multicultural, social reconstructionist version of reflective teaching is essential if teachers are to play an active part in assisting all students in becoming participating citizens. Without an explicit, systematic examination of classroom practices, it becomes very difficult for a teacher to meaningfully connect his or her work in the classroom with its effect outside of school.

This is not to say that becoming a reflective teacher is easy. It requires a willingness and commitment to the time, effort, and risk-taking required to alter our actions in the classroom, especially those tied to "time-honored traditions." In Chapter 18, Boyle-Baise and Sleeter discuss several ways teachers can begin to engage in activities that encourage open-mindedness toward multicultural issues, responsibility to act on them in the classroom, and wholeheartedness in this effort. Becoming a reflective teacher includes all the things mentioned by these authors, but includes a specific focus on the place "where the action is"—the classroom.

Smyth (1989) encouraged teachers to begin becoming reflective by examining their personal biographies and their professional histories. By doing so, they can uncover the roots of taken-for-granted beliefs about the way things are "supposed to be" in teaching. This opens the door for teachers to begin "sketching out the contours of actual situations and posing problems about concrete situations" in the classroom (p. 5). Beginning teachers can focus on those things, under their own control, "which perplex, confuse, or frustrate them" (p. 5) by engaging in four forms of action with respect to their own teaching. These are described in terms of four questions that represent cyclical stages of action. Smyth (1989) uses the following as guides:

1. Describe . . . what do I do?
2. Inform . . . what does this mean?

3. Confront . . . how did I come to be like this?

4. Reconstruct . . . how might I do things differently? (p. 5)

Other questions can be added to this list to address the interplay of school and society:

5. If I do not do things differently, what will the effect be for the students, now and in the future?

6. Will this effect be different for different students?

7. How can I connect my efforts to those of others and to larger societal issues related to equity, justice, and human rights?

Embarking on the process of becoming a reflective, social reconstructionist teacher helps student teachers take control of their learning process by considering ways of reconstructing teaching that do not depend solely on "the way it has always been done" or on the methods of the cooperating teacher. Student teaching can provide an environment for the type of collegial, communal reflection described earlier as one of the three characteristics of multicultural, social reconstructionist reflective teaching.

The student teacher, the cooperating teacher, and the student-teaching supervisor can collaborate to create the type of classroom environment where multicultural, social reconstructionist reflective practice is the norm. Some may argue that this type of cooperative effort is not possible in the student teaching semester. It is true that classroom teachers, college or university programs and personnel, and student teachers themselves often set up roadblocks (e.g., policies, evaluation procedures, unwillingness to take risks) in the journey toward reflectivity; however, it does not have to be this way.

A growing body of evidence indicates that a relationship that supports reflectivity can be established among the student teacher, the cooperating teacher and the college supervisor (Gore, 1991; Noffke & Brennan, 1991; Wood, 1991). Most importantly, student teachers can, either alone or in concert with their cooperating teacher and supervisor, begin to develop habits of reflection that will ultimately make their teaching responsive to our increasingly diverse student population—a task that will benefit all of us. For unlike Carol's comment that teaching with a concern for multicultural issues cannot be "planned for," Tom's story clearly indicates that being reflective must be a part of each teacher's plan!

Notes

1. The vignettes are developed from the actual work of student teachers; however, pseudonyms are used throughout the chapter.

2. For a discussion of the problematic nature of the term *at-risk,* see Boyle-Baise and Grant (1992), Nieto (1992), or Swadener (1991).

References

American Association of University Women. (1991). *Shortchanging girls, shortchanging America*. Washington, DC: Author.

Boyle-Baise, L., & Grant, C. (1992). Multicultural teacher education: A proposal for change. In H. C. Waxman, J. Walker de Felix, J. E. Anderson, & H. Prentice Baptiste (Eds.), *Students at risk in at risk schools: Improving environments for learning* (pp. 174–193). Newbury Park, CA: Corum Press.

Canter, L. (1976). *Assertive discipline: A take charge approach for today's educator*. Santa Monica, CA: Lee Canter & Associates.

Dewey, J. (1933). *How we think*. Chicago: Henry Regnery.

Dewey, J. (1938). *Experience and education*. New York: Collier Books.

Freedman, S., Jackson, J., & Boles, K. (1986). *The effect of teaching on teachers*. Grand Forks, ND: North Dakota Study Group on Evaluation.

Goodlad, J. (1981). *A place called school*. New York: McGraw Hill.

Gore, J. (1991). Practicing what we preach: Action research and the supervision of student teachers. In K. M. Zeichner & B. R. Tabachnick (Eds.), *Issues and practices in inquiry-oriented teacher education* (pp. 253–272). London: The Falmer Press.

Grant, C. A., & Zeichner, K. M. (1984). On becoming a reflective teacher. In Grant, C. A. (Ed.), *Preparing for reflective teaching* (pp. 1–18). Boston: Allyn and Bacon.

Kemmis, S. (1985). Action research and the politics of reflection. In D. Boud, R. Keogh, & D. Walker (Eds.), *Reflection: Turning experience into learning* (pp. 139–164). London: Croom Helm.

Ladson-Billings, G. (1992). Liberatory consequences of literacy: A case of culturally relevant instruction for African American students. Paper presented at the annual meeting of the American Educational Research Association, San Francisco, CA.

Lawson, M. (1992, February 12). School's glass ceiling imperils girls, study says. *Education Week*, 1, 17.

Oakes, J. (1985). *Keeping track: How schools structure inequality*. New Haven, CT: Yale University Press.

Nieto, S. (1992). *Affirming diversity*. White Plains, NY: Longman Publishing Group.

Noffke, S. E., & Brennan, M. (1991). Student teachers use action research: Issues and examples. In B. R. Tabachnick & K. M. Zeichner (Eds.), *Issues and practices in inquiry-oriented teacher education* (pp. 186–201). London: The Falmer Press.

Rosenthal, R., & Jacobson, L. (1968). *Pygmalion in the classroom: Teacher expectation and pupils' intellectual development*. New York: Holt Rinehart & Winston.

Rudduck, J. (1984). *Teaching as an art: Teacher research and research-based teacher education*. Second Annual Lawrence Stenhouse Memorial Lecture, University of East Anglia.

Smyth, J. (1989). Developing and sustaining critical reflection in teacher education. *Journal of Teacher Education, 40*(2), 2–9.

Swadener, E. B. (1991). Children and families "at risk": Etiology, critique, and alternative paradigms. *Educational Foundations, 4,* 17–35.

Tabachnick, B. R. & Zeichner, K. M., (1991). Reflections on reflective teaching. In K. M. Zeichner & B. R. Tabachnick (Eds.), *Issues and practices in inquiry-oriented teacher education* (pp. 1–21). London: The Falmer Press.

Tate, W. (1992). Diversity, reform, and the professional knowledge of mathematics teachers: The need for multicultural clarity. Manuscript submitted for publication.

U.S. Bureau of the Census. (1991). *Statistical abstracts of the United States: 1991* (11th ed.). Washington, DC: U.S. Department of Commerce.

Wood, P. O. (1991). The cooperation teacher's role in nurturing reflective teaching. In B. R. Tabachnick & K. M. Zeichner (Eds.), *Issues and practices in inquiry-oriented teacher education* (pp. 202–210). London: The Falmer Press.

Zeichner, K. M., & Liston, D. (1990). *Traditions of reform in reflective teaching in U.S. teacher education* (Issue Paper 90–1). East Lansing, MI: National Center for Research on Teacher Education.

Contributing Authors

Veronica M. Acosta-Deprez
Veronica Acosta-Deprez is an Assistant Professor of Health Education at Auburn University, Alabama. Her professional interests in the field of health education include community health, social health, international health, multicultural health education, and AIDS and sexuality education. She has published articles related to AIDS, parental involvement in AIDS education programs, as well as teacher preparation for multicultural health education. Her primary research goals are to examine issues of class, race, and gender as these relate to multicultural health education and to continue to explore ways of educating about health from a multicultural and social reconstructionist perspective.

James A. Banks
James A. Banks is Professor of Education and Director of the Center for Multicultural Education at the University of Washington, Seattle. He has been President of the National Council for the Social Studies and has held fellowships from the National Academy of Education, the Kellogg Foundation, and the Rockefeller Foundation. Known internationally for his work in social studies and multicultural education, he was named a Distinguished Scholar/Researcher on Minority Education by the American Educational Research Association (AERA). In 1994, he received the AERA Research Review Award. He received an honorary Doctorate of Humane Letters (L.H.D.) from the Bank Street College of Education in 1993. Professor Banks has published over 100 articles in such journals as *Educational Researcher, Phi Delta Kappan, Social Education*, and *Educational Leadership*. His books include *Teaching Strategies for Ethnic Studies, Teaching Strategies for the Social Studies, An Introduction to Multicultural Education*, and (with Cherry A. McGee Banks) *Multicultural Education: Issues and Perspectives*. He is the editor (with Cherry A. McGee Banks) of the *Handbook of Research on Multicultural Education* (McMillan, 1995).

411

Marilynne Boyle-Baise

Marilynne Boyle-Baise is an assistant professor at Indiana University. Her special areas of interest are multicultural education, and social studies, and she is active in defining multicultural social studies education. Boyle-Baise has centered her research in helping in-service teachers implement multicultural education. She is the founder of a teacher-oriented advocacy group for multicultural education.

Jepkorir Rose Chepyator-Thomson

Jepkorir Rose Chepyator-Thomson is an Assistant Professor at the State University of New York at Brockport. She received her B.A., M.A., M.S., and Ph.D. from the University of Wisconsin-Madison. Her research interests center on issues of race, class, and gender in curriculum and teaching, women and sport in Kenya, and on child development and children's games in Keiyo society in Kenya. Her most recent work has been published in *Interchange*, *Social Development Issues*, and in the *Journal of Teaching in Physical Education*.

Ann DeVaney

Ann DeVaney is a professor in the Department of Curriculum and Instruction, University of Wisconsin-Madison, where she heads a graduate program in Educational Communications and Technology. Her scholarship appropriates literary models to analyze representation of women and people of color in educational and popular media and software. Her latest publication is an edited volume, *Watching Channel One: The Convergence of Students, Technology and Private Business*.

Mary Catherine Ellwein

Mary Catherine Ellwein was an associate professor of Educational Studies at the Curry School of Education at the University of Virginia until her death in 1994. Her work in assessment merges interests in qualitative research methodology, measurement, and teachers ways of knowing their students. Her dissertation, Standards of Competence: A Multi-Site Case Study of School Reform, won the outstanding dissertation award from the American Educational Research Association in 1987.

Kerry Freedman

Kerry Freedman is an Associate Professor in the Department of Curriculum and Instruction at the University of Minnesota. Her research focuses on questions concerning art and the sociology of education, particularly in the areas of the teaching and learning of aesthetic knowledge, technological influences on visual culture, and the relationship of culture to curriculum. Professor Freedman has published in art education and curriculum books and journals including *Studies in Art Education, Art Education*, and the *Journal of Curriculum Studies*. She is co-author of a book titled *Postmodern Art Education*.

Mary Lou Fuller

Mary Lou Fuller earned her doctorate in Multicultural Education from the University of New Mexico. Her research, professional presentation, consultation, and teaching include both classroom management and multicultural education. Dr. Fuller has been a classroom teacher, a school psychologist, and is currently a faculty member in the Center for Teaching and Learning at the University of North Dakota.

Geneva Gay

Geneva Gay is Professor of Education and Associate with the Center of Multicultural Education at the University of Washington-Seattle. She is the recipient of the 1990 Distinguished Scholar Award, presented by the Committee on the Role and Status of Minorities in Educational Research and Development of the American Educational Research Association, and the 1994 Multicultural Educator Award, the first to be presented by the National Association of Multicultural Education. She is nationally and internationally known for her scholarship in multicultural education, particularly as it relates to curriculum design, staff development, classroom instruction, and culture and learning. Her writings include more than 90 articles and book chapters, the co-editorship of *Expressively Black: The Cultural Basis of Ethnic Identity* (Praeger, 1987), and author of *At the Essence of Learning: Multicultural Education* (Kappa Delta Pi, 1994).

Maureen Gillette

Maureen Gillette is Assistant Professor of Teacher Education at the College of St. Rose in Albany, New York. She teaches courses in social studies methods, curriculum design and multicultural education. Her research interests address the ways in which beginning teachers conceptualize their work in terms of diversity and multicultural education.

Mary Louise Gomez

Mary Louise Gomez is an associate professor at the University of Wisconsin-Madison where she co-directs Teach for Diversity, a master's degree program (offering certification to teach in grades 1-6) grounded in concerns for social justice and equity in schooling. Professor Gomez's research focuses on how teachers' perspectives challenge, enhance, and limit our literacy teaching. Her published work includes articles in *Language Arts*, *Teaching and Teacher Education*, the *Journal of Education for Teaching*, and *Teaching Education* as well as numerous book chapters She is also the co-editor of *Complexities of Reform in Teacher Education* (forthcoming, Teachers College Press).

Carl A. Grant

Carl A. Grant is a Hoefs-Bascom Professor of Teacher Education in the Department of Curriculum and Instruction and a professor in the Department of Afro-American Studies at the University of Wisconsin-Madison. He has written or edited fifteen books or monographs in multicultural education and/or teacher education. These include *Research and Multicultural Education*, 1993; *Making Choices for Multicultural Education* (with Christine E. Sleeter), 1994; *After the School Bell Rings* (with Christine E. Sleeter), 1986; *Bringing Teaching to Life*, 1983; *Community Participation in Education*, 1979. He has also written more than 100 articles, chapters in books and reviews. Several of his writings and programs that he has directed have received awards. He is a former classroom teacher and administrator. Professor Grant was a Fulbright Scholar in England in 1982-1983 researching and studying multicultural education, and in 1990 the Association of Teacher Educators selected him as one of the 70 leaders in Teacher Education. In 1993, Professor Grant became President of the National Association for Multicultural Education (NAME). In 1994, he was named Adams Visiting Distinguished Professor at Indiana State University.

Beth Graue

Beth Graue is an assistant professor in the Department of Curriculum and Instruction at the University of Wisconsin-Madison. Her work addresses issues in early childhood education, assessment, and qualitative research methods. She is the author of *Ready for What? Constructing Meanings of Readiness for Kindergarten*.

Toni Griego-Jones

Toni Griego-Jones is Associate Dean in the School of Education at the University of Wisconsin-Milwaukee and directed the Bilingual Teacher Education Program there for six years. She is also an Associate Professor in the areas of Bilingual Education and Urban Education. Her research interests include minority parent involvement in educational reform and teachers' knowledge of the educational needs of language minority students.

Julia Eklund Koza

Julia Eklund Koza is an Associate Professor in the Department of Curriculum and Instruction and the School of Music at the University of Wisconsin-Madison; she also is a faculty affiliate in the Women's Studies Program. Professor Koza holds degrees from St. Olaf College (B.A. *magna cum laude*, 1974); the University of Iowa (M.A., 1978); and the University of Minnesota (Ph.D., 1988). Her primary performing media are piano and voice. From 1974-82 she taught junior high vocal and general music in River Falls, Wisconsin. Professor Koza's research focuses on gender issues in music instruction and on representations of gender and race in cultural artifacts. She specializes in historical studies and critical textual analyses of curricular materials. Her musicological research focuses on nineteenth-century parlor music and on the role of music in mid-nineteenth-century American life. Recent or forthcoming publications include articles in the *Musical Quarterly*, the *Journal of Research in Music Education*, *Educational Foundations*, the *Music Educators Journal*, the *Review of Education/Pedagogy/Cultural Studies*, and *The Quarterly*, and book chapters.

Jean Lythcott

Jean Lythcott is an Assistant Professor in Science Education at Teachers College, Columbia University.

Mark Riherd

Mark Riherd is the Program Director for the Creative Arts Team (CAT), the professional educational theatre campany in residence at New York University. By combining original theatre productions and participatory drama workshops, CAT motivates youth to examine pertinent social issues and curricular themes. He is also an instructor in the Program in Educational Theatre at NYU, where he teaches courses in both Drama-in-Education and Theatre-in-Education. Additionally, he conducts staff development workshops nationally and internationally in Critical Thinking Through Drama.

Christine E. Sleeter

Christine E. Sleeter is Professor of Teacher Education at the California State University-Monterey Bay. Formerly she was a high school learning disabilities teacher in Seattle. She earned her Ph.D. from the University of Wisconsin-Madison in 1981, and taught at Ripon College (in Wisconsin) and the University of Wisconsin-Parkside before assuming her current position. On the basis of her active record of publication, she was recently awarded the University of Wisconsin-Parkside annual award for Excellence in Research and Creative Activity, and the Research Award of the National Association for Multicultural Education. She has published articles about multicultural education in numerous journals. Her most recent books include *Empowerment through Multicultural Education*, *Keepers of the American Dream*, and *Making Choices for Multicultural Education* (with Carl Grant). She also edits a series of books for SUNY Press, entitled "The Social Context of Education."

Peter N. Stearns

Peter N. Stearns is Dean of the College of Humanities and Social Sciences at Carnegie Mellon University, where he regularly teaches a world history course for first-year students. His book, *Meaning over Memory: Recasting the Teaching of Culture and History* (University of North Carolina, 1993), deals with a variety of issues in humanities education. His most recent monograph is American Cool: Developing a Twentieth-Century Emotional Style (1994). Peter Stearns is also active in a number of curricular projects, including the College Board's Pacesetter World History project, and is a member of the National Board of Teaching Standards, History and Social Studies unit.

James Stewart
James Stewart is a professor in the science education area of the Department of Curriculum and Instruction at the University of Wisconsin-Madison.

Nancy Swortzell
Nancy Sortzell serves as director of the Program in Educational Theatre at New York University where she also teaches courses in acting, directing and theatre-in-education practices. In 1973 she designed and led the NYU Study Abroad Program to introduce American students to the educational theatre scene in England. The Study Abroad Program continues each year with a distinguished faculty that has included leaders in the field such as John Hodgson, Gavin Bolton and Cecily O'Neill. She holds a D.F.A. in Directing from the Yale Drama School and has directed many NYU productions for young audiences, including *Gulliver's Travels*, *The Little Humpback Horse*, and *The Hobbit*.

William F. Tate
William F. Tate is an assistant professor in the Department of Curriculum and Instruction at the University of Wisconsin-Madison. His articles "School Mathematics and African American Students: Thinking Seriously about Opportunity-to-Learn Standards" in *Educational Administration Quarterly* and "Toward a Critical Race Theory of Education" in *Teacxhers College Record* (with Gloria Ladson-Billings) reflect his interest in the political dimensions of African American education.

Index